ADVANCES IN
GLOBAL LEADERSHIP

Volume 1 • 1999

ADVANCES IN
GLOBAL LEADERSHIP

Executive Editor: WILLIAM H. MOBLEY
Personnel Decisions International

Co-Editors: M. JOCELYNE GESSNER
VAL ARNOLD
Personnel Decisions International

VOLUME 1 • 1999

JAI PRESS INC.
Stamford, Connecticut

CONTENTS

PREFACE

Welcome to the first volume of *Advances in Global Leadership*. The topic of global leadership is of interest to an increasingly broad array of individuals and organizations. Exponential advances in integration of the world's economies, global telecommunications, rapid international flows of information, capital and human resources, multinational organizations of increasingly varied structures and ownership, and derailment rates among international leaders are among the forces driving heightened interest in global leadership.

As organizations and leadership become more global, there are pressing needs for better developed conceptual models and definitions of what is meant by global leadership; better developed models, processes, and tools for developing global leaders; and a richer base of empirical evidence evaluating various definitions, conceptual models, processes, and tools for developing global leaders. Further, there is a need to integrate models and empirical evidence from multiple cultures and from non-Western authors. The published leadership literature continues to be Western-culture dominated. Yet, many of the global leadership challenges involve emerging markets and the integration of Western and non-Western cultures. There are talented individuals throughout the world working on leadership issues. These individuals need additional outlets for their work and those interested in global leadership need more exposure to authors from cultures other than their own.

The objectives of the *Advances in Global Leadership* series include:

1. Provide on at least a biennial basis a set of high-quality, invited, original papers that advance the definition, measurement, understanding, and development of global leadership.
2. Invite papers that will advance the understanding of global leadership in at least one of three ways: conceptual, empirical, and the practice of developing global leadership.
3. Draw on authors from multiple cultures, and work being done in multiple cultures, and in multiple organizational settings.

It is our intent that this series will be of value to academics conducting research and teaching on subjects related to leadership, international business, organizational behavior, international management, and related subjects; those designing and conducting executive education processes and courses dealing with developing global leadership; practitioners and consultants who are managing global leadership development processes; and individuals who are engaged in global leadership. By combining conceptual, empirical, and practitioner perspectives from multiple cultures, we hope that there will be a healthy cross-pollination of ideas and perspectives. Although every chapter may not be of value to every reader, we trust there will be a rich array of chapters that will be of value to every reader.

It is a pleasure for me to serve as Executive Editor of this series. My interest in global leadership began in the 1970s when I served as Manager of Human Resources Research and Planning for PPG Industries at a time when that firm was beginning to develop its international strategy. Later, in the 1970s, when I had returned to an academic base, I had the opportunity to serve as a Senior Fulbright Scholar in the Republic of China, and to conduct international turnover and management research and training in Asia. In the 1980s and early 1990s, as Dean of the Business School and later President of Texas A & M University, I had the opportunity to develop relationships with international business, education, and thought leaders from the private, public, and higher education sectors throughout the world. Since 1996, I have been heading the PDI Global Research Consortia (GRC), based in Hong Kong and Dallas. GRC is a near virtual organization that puts together research project teams from universities and the private sector to address international and cross-cultural organizational, leadership, and management issues identified by the multinational firms that are members of GRC or other organizations that contract with GRC. These combined experiences of the past three decades have given me a deep appreciation of the complexity and challenges of global leadership. Thus, it is a particular honor and pleasure to take on the role of Executive Editor of this series dedicated to advancing the understanding and development of global leadership.

The plan for the *Advances in Global Leadership* series is to invite guest co-editors for each volume. The co-editors for Volume 1 are Val Arnold and M. Jocelyne Gessner. Their biographical summaries are included in the section About the Editors. In addition to being highly effective communicators, these two highly talented individuals have both higher education and private sector experience that has given them unique perspectives on global leadership. Both are employed by Personnel Decisions International (PDI)—Val is PDI Senior Vice President, Executive Consulting Services; and Jocelyne is General Manager of PDI's Austin, Texas, office. Both work with multinational firms and global leadership issues on a daily basis. They are the authors of the Introduction as well as the overviews that introduce each part. Their contribution of time and substance to this volume, even with already full schedules, is deeply appreciated.

The authors contributing chapters to Volume 1 are listed in the Table of Contents and their biographical summaries are included in the section About the Contributors. Special appreciation is expressed to each of these authors for their substantive contributions. Also appreciated is their willingness to take a risk on a new series when they could have published their papers in a variety of other sources. Finally, thanks to the authors for their patience during the daunting task of meeting deadlines, even in this electronic era, while an international cast of co-authors and content and technical editors was coordinated to bring this volume to print.

Appreciation is also expressed to the three individuals who contributed to the technical editing of this volume: Michele Kay, Jan McInroy, and particularly Kim Canon who managed the completion of the project. Special thanks to Maureen Bayless, GRC Coordinator of Member Relations and Special Projects, who provided tireless communication coordination with authors, editors, and the publisher. A special note of thanks to the leadership of PDI, particularly Lowell Hellervik and Ken Hedberg, for their willingness to take innovative risk on an organization such as GRC and for providing support for this project. To the charter members of GRC (Air Products, Allied Signal, AMOCO, British Petroleum, CALTEX, Coca-Cola, Dow, Eli Lilly, Hewlett-Packard, Mobil, Motorola, PPG, and Shell International), my deepest appreciation for your support, which allows global projects such as this to be undertaken. Finally, thanks to JAI Press Publisher Herbert Johnson and Executive Editor William Cody for your confidence and support.

Even as we go to press with Volume 1, we are planning Volume 2. Already suggested for inclusion in the next volume are the topics of international joint-venture leadership and virtual or distant global leadership. Your feedback on Volume 1, as well as your suggestions for topics, authors, and format for Volume 2, are encouraged and welcomed.

William H. Mobley
Hong Kong, October 1998

INTRODUCTION

M. Jocelyne Gessner, Val Arnold, and
William H. Mobley

Leadership theories are like fingerprints: everyone has them and no two are alike. The study of leadership has been bedeviling scholars, practitioners, and leaders since humans first organized themselves. Although it is quite chic to bemoan the lack of progress in the field, we, as editors, would like to focus instead on what we have learned and are learning. To paraphrase Thomas Edison in his search for the perfect light bulb, we have not failed 5,000 times; we have merely discovered 4,999 alternative ways in which leadership functions (or does not function) across a variety of situations. And so, we widen our search to take on the challenge of global leadership.

The purpose of this book is to gather together some of the leading thinkers and practitioners in the study of global leadership, and to present the "state of the art" in ways that prove useful to a wide variety of readers. As academicians, students of management, managers, and internal and external consultants, we all find ourselves struggling to get a grasp on the realities of a highly complex and rapidly changing world. Our goal is to help you create a framework that starts to make sense of a multitude of variables and perspectives.

EXPLOSION FROM LOCAL AND REGIONAL BUSINESS TO GLOBAL

The world of business has exploded from local to global in a short period of time. What we find is *everyone* trying to cope, and to figure out how to deal with globalization most effectively. Our field is experiencing a similar chaos as we try to make sense of what is happening and begin to intervene, advise, and guide so that we all do "global" more effectively. To do this, we must step back from the theory and practices that have guided us in the past and question some of our assumptions. We must start at the beginning, and begin the process of exploration anew. To do so, we need to examine our very definitions of the words "global" and "leadership" and try to separate the mythic implications from the current business realities.

"Global" and "leadership" are perhaps two of the hottest buzz words of the 1990s. In talking about some of the things people mean by these two words, our purpose is not to define what these two words ought to mean but to raise the consciousness of how people use them differently. Without entering into an overly semantic exercise, we would like to point out a few of the ways that people use these words by suggesting some of the synonyms that are used interchangeably with often very different results. For "global," one hears also "international," "worldwide," "general," "all-encompassing," and "multinational." The variations on the theme are, at least, twofold. In one sense, the word refers to things that occur around the globe. In this way, the word means looking at things outside of one country and, often, outside of your resident country. In the other sense, we use the word "global" to convey a sense of size and scope, the idea of general versus specific, of comprehensiveness, or an attempt to encompass a larger perspective. When we take a global view of the world, then, we may be talking about not being parochial from a geographical or cultural sense. We may also be talking about how to view things in a larger, more complex way. At times, we intend the word to convey both meanings. When various authors discuss global leadership, we see variations in whether they mean less nationalistic models or more comprehensive sets of behaviors. Uncomfortably, they are often suggesting all of the above—a difficult place to begin a science.

NO AGREED UPON DEFINITION OF LEADERSHIP

To this confusion, we add the word "leadership." As a field of study, the construct of leadership has suffered greatly from definitional imprecision. As any number of authors point out, we have no agreed upon definition of leadership, much less global leadership. We struggle with whether the concept of leadership is separate from our concept of management or whether one is a subset of the other. We have heard people argue both sides of the issue. Is leadership one of the things a manager must do, or is management one of the roles a leader must play? Is leadership a set of behaviors or a set of guiding principles? Is leadership a philosophy or a blueprint? You will see a number of different assumptions implicit or explicit in the works presented in this book.

We refrain from a definitive answer, but ask you to remain sensitive to the nuances and the different conclusions one can draw depending on the original premise. As a field of study, we will need to refine our ideas and come to increased agreement. The elements of our working definition for the purposes of this book has been that leadership involves people in business settings whose job or role it is to influence the thoughts and actions of others to achieve some finite set of business goals. When we add the concept of global to the definition, we are usually in agreement that this is leadership displayed in large, multicultural contexts; that is, not just from one's native perspective. However, at this time, we are not limiting it to a specific number of other cultures. Thus, some authors will describe the challenges of working across multiple cultures simultaneously, as in someone whose job it is to manage a global enterprise (e.g., in charge of worldwide marketing for a product, or the chief executive officer [CEO] of a global company). Others will talk more specifically about being an expatriate manager trying to master the intricacies of working in a non-native culture. Both of these perspectives will legitimately be referred to as "global leadership" but the generalizability of the arguments and conclusions from one case to another needs to be carefully considered.

OUR PERSPECTIVE

Our qualifications for stepping up to this challenge derive from our collective backgrounds as scholars and practitioners in the field of leadership. The editors have worked around the world and faced challenges in selecting and developing local, regional, and global managers and leaders. The most universal experience we have had is the variations on this theme: "I don't know about you, but I'm normal. If you don't look, act, value as I do, then there must be something wrong with *you.*" We learn to see and understand our world in terms of our own experiences, and therein lies the challenge of global leadership which, by its nature, requires us to step out of what is familiar and into the brave new world of fast-paced technological changes, far-flung divisions in multinational companies, and an unparalleled wealth of diversity among our colleagues. It is the Tower of Babel come to life, and we are all rushing to figure out the riddle and make it work while moving at the speed of business. This is similar to trying to change the tires while the car is in motion.

We hail from academia and business and our interests span the gamut of global leadership issues. To better organize our thinking about how to approach the broad topic before us, we have focused on three areas, which we think will appeal to the diverse audience who may pick this book up and search for some answers. Hence, we have tried to represent some of the current thinking and activity in looking at **theoretical issues**, **quantitative studies**, and **current practice** in understanding and developing global leadership in a business context.

THE GLOBE PROJECT

We are especially proud to have one of the first publications from the GLOBE project, a comprehensive, research-focused view of leadership establishing an "empirically based theory to describe, understand, and predict the impact of cultural variables on leadership and organizational processes and the effectiveness of these processes."

The GLOBE work contrasts with Hofstede's work, some of the most broadly quoted context for writings on global leadership and intercultural issues. Hofstede's work (based on IBM) has been broadly generalized and has dominated cross-cultural psychological research as the theory used for understanding core differences in national cultures. Created from a sociological perspective, it has been used as a basis for understanding large-scale differences to minute variables. Although widely quoted and helpful in establishing an initial understanding of how to think about cultural differences, it has not necessarily been the best or most helpful model in understanding current business or employee issues. In our opinion, the framework of specific cultural values has been overextended and overgeneralized in recent years.

In contrast, you will see in the chapter by House and colleagues, which leads our research section, an attempt to create a more useable, practical theory aligned with a pragmatic and comprehensive course of research. The GLOBE project, for the first time, assumes a comprehensive, multifaceted perspective on understanding similarities and differences between cultures as they relate to business and management. Using quantitative and qualitative approaches to understand "the interrelationships between societal culture, organizational culture and practices, and organizational leadership," the GLOBE project should be one of our best sources of longitudinal, systematic, and useful theory and practical findings in the coming years.

THE STRUCTURE OF THE BOOK

The book is divided into three parts: theory, research, and practice. Each part begins with an introduction that captures the basic themes explored by the different authors, and gives a brief synopsis of the authors' perspectives. We have been fortunate to pull together an impressive group of respected researchers and practitioners to share their experiences and observations across a variety of topics concerning global leadership. In this first volume, our goal was to focus more on breadth of experience than to limit our thinking in any single direction.

We begin by looking at how scholars are thinking about global leadership. What are the issues? How should we look at leadership? What is global; what is leadership? Our authors struggle with the definitional issues, as well as the philosophical problems of universality among cultures. The question of whether our understanding of global leadership is simply a more complex version of domestic leadership (as in an additive model) or a different animal altogether is one of the dominant themes of this section.

The research section introduces several studies of global leadership. These studies tell us something about the challenges of doing research on such a broad topic, as well as providing case studies for specific cultures and contexts. One interesting aspect of this section is its relative divorce from the issues discussed in the Part I. Thus, we see a need to have answers before we are even sure of what the questions are—a common dilemma in the applied sciences.

The practice section focuses primarily on the development of global leaders. The key issues here concern defining what we are trying to develop and how to go forth most effectively. Here we see real problems that need to be solved in real time even if the theory and research are lagging.

GOING FORWARD

As you progress through the book and note the similarities and differences in what our authors are saying, we hope that you will begin to formulate your own sense of what is important to the ongoing understanding of global leadership. To help you in this endeavor, we tell you a little of how our thinking has developed as we have read the various articles and connected them to our own experiences and knowledge. We think that there are sets of characteristics and behaviors that differentiate effective global leaders from ineffective ones. We believe that one of our challenges is to figure out which of these characteristics need to be selected (i.e., necessary from the beginning) and what can be developed in the people who find themselves with the arduous responsibility of leading others in a global setting.

We believe that there is a subset of values that works well and is critical to effectiveness. We believe that leaders must learn and be aware of differences between people, and be interested in understanding and using those differences as they develop their leadership style. We think that some of the universal values concern trust and integrity, and the ability to respect the differences between people and to create an environment where people can focus on getting the work done together rather than spending time defending their right to be different. Global leaders cannot operate in a "value-free" environment and yet they cannot be too inflexible regarding values. This is the tightrope on which the global world attempts to balance on a daily basis. Global leaders need to be tolerant of differences but not of all differences (e.g., the respect of people is vital for all team members). Conflicts are inevitable, and processes of responding and resolving conflict need to be more universal. Communication skills will be increasingly critical; using language carefully and well is an ongoing challenge. Competence can be built, but we, as the architects, must work hard to create accurate blueprints to guide the future.

We shall not cease from exploration
And the end of all our exploring
Will be to arrive where we started
And know the place for the first time

—T. S. Eliot, "Little Gidding" from the *Four Quartets.*

PART I

CONCEPTUAL PERSPECTIVES

_____

INTRODUCTION TO CONCEPTUAL PERSPECTIVES

M. Jocelyne Gessner and Val Arnold

Our first section lays the groundwork for the current state of thinking about global leadership. Represented in these chapters are views that range from the epistemological to the philosophical to the political to the pragmatic. Here we see the struggle to define two terms that have almost mythic connotations: global and leadership. The combination of the two seems to bring out an almost moralistic tone in many of our authors, who view global leadership as an opportunity to tackle the challenges of creating an ideal global community characterized by tolerance and hope. Global leaders are seen by some (e.g., Clark and Matze, Dachler, Adler, Graen and Hui) as having the responsibility to create and shape a better culture, to identify and leverage the unifying human elements across cultures and situations.

To do this, most of our authors agree that global leadership must transcend what we currently conceive of as "domestic" leadership. To get from where we are now to a global conception, we must consider doing something more than just adding a few new competencies to our current recommended repertoire of leadership skills. Global leadership appears to be a more multiplicative process, changing

Advances in Global Leadership, Volume 1, pages 3-8.

both the size and scope of domestic leadership. They are relatively emphatic that we cannot take the skills that make leaders effective in their home environments and export them wholesale. Instead, we need to look for another dimension of leadership, a difficult thing to do when we are mired in our own parochialism.

The GLOBE project chapter that begins Part II would fit admirably in a section devoted to understanding the current thinking about global leadership. However, that chapter, unlike many of these, also offers a detailed program of research. In its role as boundary-spanner between theory and research, we thought you would find it interesting to first look at some of the current thinking in the field, and then see an example of taking many of the themes from this section, as well as some additional theoretical links, presented as a cogent and coherent view of what we must learn as scientists, practitioners, and leaders to get beyond our localized way of thinking.

To frame the chapters that are included in Part I, we will give you a taste of some of these themes. We start with current zeitgeist of competency modeling. Among the universal contenders for competencies and considerations of global leadership are an increased emphasis on complex interpersonal skills, the ability to understand and reconcile a multiplicity of views and people, the need to identify universal values that create a common thread across diversity, and an increased focus on collaboration as both a process and an outcome. Relationships are the currency of the global leader. The focus on relationships is partly a result of the need to unify diverse peoples and cultures, the context in which the global leader must operate. However, the emphasis on people skills is also a part of the content of the evolving global organizational culture. This snowballing movement toward organizational transformation has taken the form of learning organizations, increased partnerships, and so forth that have become the responses to dealing with the complexities created by increasing globalization.

There is also an emphasis on values as a common denominator, an appealing paradigm both in terms of its way of connecting people and the popular emphasis on principle-centered leadership. Nearly all of our authors talk about values, and it is the backbone of the seminal studies on cross-cultural comparisons among managers conducted by Hofstede, whose influence can be seen in nearly all of the thinking in this book. Furthermore, values are one of the few variables that hold promise in reasonably comparing cultures, environments, and people.

We (the editors) like to think of leadership as a continuum of managing tasks, people, and ideas. In this section, we found that most of our authors focused on the people aspect as being critical to gaining a true understanding of global leadership. A few authors (notably Adler) focus on the importance of managing ideas, with the concept of vision a noticeable watchword. Many of our theory-oriented authors paid scant attention, however, to the management of tasks. The seduction of global leadership is that it transcends the quotidian, the routine aspects of what many dismiss as "management" as opposed to the glamour of leadership. We find this trend in our theorists troubling, especially since we see and experience the challenges of managing work (i.e., accomplishing goals) across geographies as one of the land mines in doing business throughout the world. In the study and practice of leadership, it often seems that there is a chameleon-like quality, with people needing to morph between the world of ideas and strategies (leaders) and the realities of implementation and action (managers). It is, perhaps, a false dichotomy, but the underlying assumptions permeate many a discussion about the differences between what leaders and managers are expected to do in a business context. The focus on tasks reappears in Parts II and III, describing both research and practice in the arena of global leadership. A noticeable exception to this trend is the chapter by Fulkerson, who describes a model that balances tasks and people in a global context.

One other interesting way of comparing our theorists concerns the underpinnings of the person-situation-interaction continuum. The essence of this paradigm is in determining the source of leadership. Does it come from the characteristics of the person, the demands of the situation, or the interaction between the two? The old debate of whether leaders are born or made is a simplification of this issue, but the theory of leadership has shifted back and forth throughout the past century. In discussing global leadership, we see some subtle but implicit positions emerge among our theorists. The focus on competencies and skills taken by Clark and Matze, and Adler, for example, suggests more of an emphasis on the person. Hammer makes a case for the situational component, arguing that management styles evolve in adaptation to larger socioeconomic contexts. Fulkerson, Dachler, and to some extent Graen and Hui, seem to fall more into the interactionist camp, portraying global leadership as a complex interweaving of personal and situational responses.

We start with Graen and Hui's chapter on "Transcultural Global Leadership in the Twenty-first Century" as a way of framing the magnitude of the task we have set for ourselves. In exhorting the need for leaders to develop to the next level of transcultural effectiveness, they set as their goal the identification of the special developmental needs of global leaders. Using Ghoshal's model of global competitiveness as background, Graen and Hui identify new skills that will enable the global leader to create a third culture that bridges the gap between existing cultures in a diverse team. Among these skills are transcultural facilitation (an active approach to managing diversity), and creative problem solving that takes multiple perspectives into account. Academics and practitioners will find some utility in the model he creates and its implementation. In particular, the focus is on specific developmental tasks that enable one to transcend cultures and build relationships that work. The definition of global leadership, then, is the interpersonal cross-cultural relationships between leaders and followers based on mutual trust, respect, and obligation.

While Graen and Hui lay the groundwork for a model of competencies focusing on the leader, Fulkerson adds another dimension. He wants us to "focus on the proposition that a conceptual model is needed to look beyond competencies and attempt to describe the mental and behavioral processes that allow leaders to deal with the increasing complexity of global business." He challenges the competency paradigm because it is not sufficiently robust to explain the inherently intricate roles that leaders are asked to play. Instead, he proposes a systems approach in which a leadership operating system, a set of organizing principles, and a more mature understanding of environmental and contextual variables need to be addressed. He describes four filters (cultural awareness, vision, values, and decision-making style) as the basics of his leadership operating system. There are sets of questions for leaders at the end of each filter description that we think many of you will find helpful in creating your own set of guidelines to keep you future oriented and able to build on your experiences. For the more philosophical, Fulkerson raises interesting points concerning the static and idiosyncratic nature of competency models and their utility in understanding the complex and dynamic systems in which actual leaders must operate.

The next chapter, by Adler, takes a more philosophical and political slant on global leadership. Global leadership is concerned with the interaction of people and ideas among cultures, and not merely with an extension of domestic leadership. As such, global leadership needs to guide us in treating each other and the planet in a more civilized way in the twenty-first century. With this as her major thesis, Adler then suggests that many of the challenges specified in global leadership are embodied in traditionally feminine qualities such as empathy, helpfulness, caring, nurturance, interpersonal sensitivity, and so forth. Adler tries to take us beyond the traditional twentieth-century paradigms of leadership, and suggests looking at women leaders in both national politics and as business leaders.

We urge you to read this chapter carefully, not as a feminist treatise, but as a powerful exploration of new paradigms in leadership. Adler's definition of global leadership is among our favorites: "Leaders can be viewed as people whose vision, courage, and influence set ideas, people, organizations, and societies in motion toward the betterment of their organization, their community, and the world." Although the chapter certainly contains several provocative comments, the point here is not whether we agree with the author's conclusions with regard to why there are differences in men's and women's approaches to leadership, but whether her vision of what is needed for global leadership makes us think of a model that improves on our current domestic orientations. The focus on people and their interrelationships is similar to the messages presented by many of our authors in this section, but Adler is able to capture some of the nuances in what the leader represents from the perspective of one who appreciates the value of looking at things from a non-traditional perspective. A global leader, in Adler's view, is someone who represents diversity, who symbolizes people's aspirations and unites them in their humanity, who is driven by vision rather than hierarchical status, whose power is broadly based rather than traditional, and who takes a lateral path to power emphasizing the breadth of experience rather than the narrow depth of expertise.

In the next chapter, Dachler echoes the struggles we face in breaking out of our Euro-centered understanding of leadership and its practice, and emphasizes the moral imperative of the leader not to simply maintain the status quo with increased authority. He makes a strong case for the fact that global leadership is not an extension of local leadership with the addition of situational, value, economic, cultural, and societal values. He believes that the challenges of global leadership are rooted in the relational-social-societal processes (as opposed to individual attributes) that are the basis for organizational learning processes and continual transformation. Although Dachler presents the most philosophical view of all our authors, he makes certain similar points concerning the need to think of leadership as an increasingly dynamic process that transcends the individual attribute approach. He also makes a fervent plea for global leaders to focus on increasing the understanding between people and the value of relationships. Global leadership is ("must be") the mechanism that enables multiplicity rather than individuality in reconciling alternative perspectives and concerns.

Hammer, in the next chapter, switches focus from that which individual leaders bring to the table to an emphasis on the evolution of leadership styles as a reaction to the sociopolitical context of leadership. Her thesis is that national industrial relations systems shape leadership functions and behaviors as well as management policies and practices. These, in turn, incorporate societal cultural values as an influence in ways that cannot be reductionistically untangled. Her theoretical basis for this argument is the preponderance of evidence that suggests that there is a culturally specific element to leadership that cannot be ignored. She compares several national models and makes some recommendations that you will find interesting. What she adds to our understanding of global leadership, however, is the perspective that the context of national and societal values that form the basis of industrial relations has a huge impact on emerging leadership styles. She also offers some ways to consolidate culturally specific models so that we are not left with a different model for each country. Her conclusions emphasize the need to develop an exportable model that takes a longer term view than seeing employees as exploitable resources, emphasizing again the need to be relationship oriented, and a champion for differences, thus helping to ensure that all factions get a voice.

Ritchie provokes some thought in his object lesson in understanding that our initial challenge is understanding the difference between studying global leaders and actually being a global leader. Because the first rule of studying any phenomenon is realizing you must remove your own blinders, he reminds us that both scientists and managers have to understand the realities of situations, and to look for a third culture (as suggested by Graen and Hui). He cites some wonderful examples, most notably at Xerox, that demonstrate that training managers, acting more like scientists, created a better solution to a set of problems than either group acting independently. Studying global leadership requires us to be even more open to the limitations of our own perspectives and the need to question our assumptions with due diligence.

In the final chapter of Part I, Clark and Matze pick up the moral imperative theme that runs through several of the preceding chapters. They stress that global leaders have a responsibility and an opportunity to shape culture, and they postulate that at the heart of this imperative lies the need for better and more meaningful relationships. Their contribution is a construct referred to as relational competence, which aligns a system of relational processes and practices embedded within a set of core values. They describe new strategies of relating and communicating at work, with a particular focus on collaboration as a response to the increasing demands of globalization. Clark and Matze assume a definitive "people perspective." In their view, the differences between people create difficulties in globalization. Dealing with cultural differences is the essence of relating well to others. Increased interdependence and cooperation form the basis for all ways of combining businesses to meet global demands. Ultimately, people are the common unit among countries, so it makes sense to start by improving interactional skills. Although they offer a prescriptive approach, they also offer suggestions on where to start, with a focus on a set of competencies that could decrease some of the frustrations in dealing across cultures.

TRANSCULTURAL GLOBAL LEADERSHIP IN THE TWENTY-FIRST CENTURY
CHALLENGES AND IMPLICATIONS FOR DEVELOPMENT

George B. Graen and Chun Hui

ABSTRACT

In the next century, global leadership will require more than geocentric globetrotters who are content to manage foreign operations. It will demand that leaders be developed to the next level of transcultural effectiveness, at which they will learn to (1) transcend their childhood acculturation and respect very different cultures; (2) build cross-cultural partnerships of mutual trust, respect, and obligation; (3) engage in cross-cultural creative problem solving to resolve conflicts; and (4) help construct third cultures in various operations. To accomplish these goals, managers need to be transformed into "transcultural creative leaders" who can unearth the means to build cross-cultural partnerships and help to construct third cultures. This chapter outlines these challenges and more, and discusses their implications for development through the employment of a strategic framework for global competitiveness.

Advances in Global Leadership, Volume 1, pages 9-26.
Copyright © 1999 by JAI Press Inc.
All rights of reproduction in any form reserved.
ISBN: 0-7623-0505-3

The management of radical change will be one of the key global themes of twenty-first-century management. Management of the business sector will be super-charged with the relentless drive for enhanced competitiveness among existing businesses and by the rapidly expanding horizons of globalizing businesses (Phatak, 1997). Such changes have already created a revolution in organizational structures and processes, and the clarion call is to change radically into a multina-tional form or go out of business (Prahalad & Hamel, 1990). It has been argued that, in a climate of such vast changes in operating environments, managing cross-national differences is a key issue of leadership for business organizations, partic-ularly multinational corporations (Graen, Hui, Wakabayashi, & Wang, 1997).

Ghoshal (1987) presented a framework for global competitiveness that can serve as a background for our discussion of global leadership. As shown in Table 1, three categories of strategic objectives are crossed with three sources of com-petitive advantage. Strategic objectives are (1) achieving efficiency, (2) managing risks, and (3) innovation, learning, and adapting. Sources of competitive advan-tage are (1) national differences, (2) scale economies, and (3) scope economies. Achieving efficiency is concerned with the ratio of the value of its outputs to the costs of its inputs and processes. By maximizing this ratio, firms grow and create wealth. This can be achieved domestically by capitalizing on economies of scale in each activity and economies of scope across products, markets, and businesses.

Table 1. Ghoshal's Global Strategy Matrix

Strategic Objective	National Differences	Scale Economies	Scope Economies
Achieving efficiency in current operations	Benefiting from differences in factor costs— wages and cost of capital	Expanding and exploiting potential scale economies in each activity	Sharing investments and costs across products and businesses
Managing risks	Managing different kinds of risks arising from market- or policy-induced changes in comparative advantage of different countries	Balancing scale with strategic and operational flexibility	Portfolio diversification of risks and creation of options and side bets
Innovation, learning, and adapting	Learning from societal differences in organizational and managerial processes and systems	Benefiting from experience— cost reduction and innovation	Sharing learning across organizational components in different products, markets, or businesses

Source: Ghoshal, S. (1987). Global strategy: An organizing framework. *Strategic Management Journal, 8.*

It can be further accomplished by the multinational firm's achievement of savings from national differences in various factor costs in doing business.

Managing risks involves balance, diversification, and controlling damage in firms. Domestic firms attempt to balance scale issues with strategic and production flexibility and to diversify their portfolios with option positions and side deals. Multinational firms can also manage risks by capitalizing on changes in the comparative advantages of different countries.

Innovation, learning, and adapting constitute major advantages of the multinational firm in that it can learn from national differences in thought and action. It can capitalize on best practices globally and not be overwhelmed by superior external ideas. In contrast, domestic firms can benefit only from the economies of the learning curve for cost reduction and innovation and shared learning across different products, markets, or businesses. Clearly, innovation, learning, and adapting are dependent on the discovery of new and better ways of exceeding the expectations of the global markets. These are the nine cells that global leaders confront on a daily basis, and that challenge them to broaden their thoughts and actions. Global leaders need to be accepted as "insiders" within new foreign situations so that they can understand, in depth, improved methods of achieving and maintaining a competitive advantage globally (Hofstede, 1993).

The challenge of global competitiveness is to find advantageous patterns within these nine cells. This framework is useful for our discussion, because it clearly shows that domestic leadership does not include national differences; hence, it considers only six of the nine cells. This fact alone should convince a reasonable person that playing draw poker with six cards when your competitor has nine cards constitutes a competitive disadvantage. We argue that only with the development of global leaders' capability to manage cultural differences can a multinational enterprise fully enjoy its competitive advantages and meet all of its strategic objectives—that is, to fully utilize the nine cells in Ghoshal's model.

An excellent example involves Procter and Gamble's operation in coastal China (Graen, 1995). About 10 years ago the company sent global leaders to China to establish a China initiative. They carefully chose their Chinese partners and began to develop their operations. As they learned about how to operate in China, they hired a group of recent Chinese college graduates from top schools and put them through an intensive management development program using faculty members from Chinese University in Hong Kong. They treated the newcomers as insiders and developed global leadership relationships with them. The newcomers learned adeptly and have become the secret weapon of Procter and Gamble in China. These native Chinese and American managers have employed their cross-cultural leadership advantages. In contrast to the complaints made by foreign employers in China regarding the lack of risk taking or creative problem solving initiated by Chinese workers, the Procter and Gamble "whiz kids" have implemented strategies through risk taking and creative problem solving across cultures (Child, Markoczy, & Cheung, 1995).

Capitalizing on national differences in efficiencies, risks, and innovations within the matrix of economies of scale and scope is the forte of the global leader (Bartlett & Ghoshal, 1989). Effective use of these opportunities, however, requires knowledge and skill beyond that maintained by domestic leaders. It requires the development of global leadership, a goal that many multinational corporations are still trying to achieve (Bleek & Ernst, 1993). Identification of special developmental needs of global leaders and the means for their fulfillment is the subject of this chapter. We believe that this subject is extremely important, particularly since businesses are globalizing at an amazingly rapid rate. We next turn to the identification of these needs.

IDENTIFICATION OF DEVELOPMENTAL NEEDS

The most important issue of developing global leaders, as previously suggested, is learning how to manage cultural differences to enhance effectiveness, risk management, and innovation so that they complement the other six cells. By composition, multinational enterprises include members from various national and cultural backgrounds (Hofstede, 1980, 1991). Indeed, today's organizations are confronted with more diversity than ever. The world as a whole is becoming increasingly pluralistic. Many subgroups are asserting their rights as never before; and different national, cultural, and subcultural groups are demanding respect and equality. Such diversity is also reflected in the composition of the multinationals. Unfortunately, among the many cultural or subcultural groups, harmonious interaction and cooperation are far from guaranteed. Actually, it is likely that the multinationals will need to work harder to ensure that different subcultural groups can coexist. More importantly, it may not be enough for the organization to handle diversity only in a passive manner. The cost of superficial coexistence between groups with different cultural backgrounds may be great in crisis situations.

Often actions require genuine cooperation from the executing personnel in order to be effective. Thus, passive management of diversity and conflicts between cultural groups is inadequate. Instead, a new form of cultural understanding, *transcultural facilitation,* is required. New leaders will be effective to the extent that they can transcend cultures and bring the different cultural groups together. Furthermore, these so-called transcultural leaders are required to deal not only with the diversity within their organization, but also that which lies beyond its walls. As previously suggested, the actions of multinational corporations, including those conducted in foreign countries, are increasingly coming under public scrutiny. On the one hand, multinationals must find spokespeople who can answer press queries effectively, and on the other hand, they must educate the public as to what they are all about. After all, they are an integral part of the society. The multinationals that can "transcend" the differences between their cultures and the culture of the society or nation in which they operate, and gain mutual trust and respect with other constituencies in the society will be able to function more effectively. To be successful at this, they must build bridges to their employees' subcultures, and their actions must be supported by appropriate performance support systems.

To ensure that global leadership can be developed so that cross-national differences can be managed properly, we suggest four developmental requirements for global leaders: (1) cultivation of global leadership, (2) management of long-term career success, (3) enhancement of transcultural skills, and (4) resolution of organized cross-cultural complexity.

Global Leadership Experience

Gary Steel (1997) of Shell International argues that global leadership by the mature multinational enterprise depends on creating face-to-face, cross-cultural leadership at all levels within the corporation. Further, he states that most middle managers just do not understand the concept. They often equate leadership with holding a higher job title and giving orders to subordinates and do not understand the difference between compliance and commitment. In fact, they believe that anything that apparently influences another's behavior is leadership behavior. But, of course, many other sources of influence are not examples of leadership and may not achieve the same levels of risk taking and creative commitment (Dunnette, 1966). Clearly, Ghoshal's competitive advantages due to national differences cannot be fully realized without global leadership (i.e., across cultures). We define leadership in terms of incremental influence. Graen and Wakabayashi (1994) suggest that incremental influence is the influence that leaders have on followers above and beyond that of their position power. Organizational theorists and researchers have long recognized the importance of this kind of influence. For example, Drucker (1988) argues that the knowledge organization is a critical part of the new organization and that the willingness of employees to cooperate is a key to effectiveness and efficiency. Katz and Kahn (1978) use a slightly different terminology and focus on the importance of employees' spontaneous behavior for the effective functioning of an organization. Empirical research examining extra-role performance identifies employees' discretionary behavior that may relate to organizational effectiveness (cf. Organ, 1988). We suggest that leadership is defined by how leaders can exert incremental influences on followers such that they are willing to cooperate, conduct spontaneous behavior, and offer extra-role performance beyond that which can be induced by the position power of the leader. We further suggest that incremental influence is best exercised through interpersonal leadership. Let us first consider what interpersonal leadership is and is not, then explore what its challenges are in the twenty-first century, and finally consider its development implications for global leaders.

Real professional leadership influence is based on the agreement to be a cooperative follower and to go beyond one's responsibilities under specified conditions. We will elaborate on this definition as we proceed. As illustrated in Figure

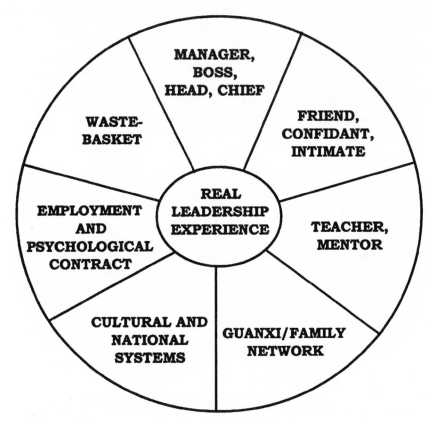

Source: Graen (1997).

Figure 1.   On-The-Job Relationships (Face-to-Face, Not Mass Media)

1, many different kinds of interpersonal on-the-job relationships have been confused with real leadership experience. Let us consider these individually, beginning with the manager, boss, head, or chief. People accept influence from their boss because it is part of their job. Bosses can be substituted without any established leadership relationship of trust, respect, and mutual obligation. People will accept the influence of strangers in these roles, but role compliance rather than commitment characterize such influence.

This confusion of leadership with management dates back to the early Ohio State and Michigan studies of effective supervision (Stogdill, 1974; Bass, 1981, 1985), investigations that attempted to discover more effective supervisory methods by focusing on supervisory behavior and unit performance. These researchers did not require that a leadership relationship exist, only that the subordinate positions report directly to the supervisory positions. The studies found that more effective supervision was concerned with both production and people and was more initiating of both structure and consideration. Later, situational contingencies were investigated (Fiedler, 1967). At some point supervision was erroneously termed leadership, but the definition of leader merely encompassed the job title and not the trust, respect, and obligation that exists between the leader and follower. Clearly, these researchers did not require any demonstration of leadership (Graen & Uhl-Bien, 1995). Unless managers actively develop real leadership across cultures, Ghoshal's advantages will be suboptimized.

Another kind of relationship frequently confused with professional leadership is that of the friend, confidant, or intimate. These are extra-job relationships, and as such they focus primarily on social and recreational activities outside of the workplace. At times, they may conflict with on-the-job professional leadership. In a series of longitudinal case studies by Elizabeth Phillips, time pressures within engineering design teams produced situations in which friendship conflicted with leadership. The results consistently demonstrated that when friendship dominated leadership, team performance suffered, but when leadership prevailed, team performance was enhanced (Phillips, Hui, & Graen, 1995; Phillips, Graen, & Hui, 1996). These studies are informative because the project deadline was the same for all 40 teams in each study, and all teams experienced a severe time crunch at the end of their projects, which forced team leaders to push themselves and their teammates to exert extra effort. Those teams with a higher friendship factor used the relationship to convince their leaders to stop pushing them so hard, and their team's product suffered. Consequently, higher friendship teams experienced inferior performance, and higher leadership teams demonstrated superior performance. Clearly, though friendship may be a functional relationship for social and recreational activities, it can prove dysfunctional for professional team performance. Cross-cultural friendships can produce many beneficial outcomes, but Ghoshal's advantage is not among them.

Teacher or mentor relationships have been confused with professional leadership, but are primarily advisory in nature and concerned with supplying knowledge and skill learning (Dreher, Dougherty, & Whitely, 1985; Kram, 1985; Whitely, Dougherty, & Dreher, 1991; Baba, Granrose, & Bird, 1995). Teachers and mentors may be leaders, but leadership is a separate relationship. Teachers and mentors are more suited to learning situations, whereas leaders are more suited to action situations. As with friendship, one can combine leadership with learning relationships; however, to achieve Ghoshal's cross-national advantages leadership must assume the higher priority position.

Guanxi and other family networks are obligation-generating systems, although they differ fundamentally from professional leadership relationships (Hui & Graen, 1998). These obligations hold only within the family network, whereas professional leadership relationships can exist between people from different family networks. Such networks may work well within family businesses, but they are no substitute for professional leadership in multinational enterprises.

Cultural and national systems that withhold social influence from outsiders have been confused with leadership (Imai, 1991). Japanese treatment of insiders ("real Japanese") and of outsiders ("Guijan") is an example. Outsiders learn very little from their Japanese hosts. These cultural networks must be circumvented before true cross-cultural leadership can capitalize on Ghoshal's national differences.

Employment contracts and psychological contracts have been confused with leadership because they address agreements that at times reach the interpersonal level. However, these contracts, both written and implied, are between people and their organizations—not between the leader and follower. One might specify an organization as a leader, but who exercises the leadership influence? This could pose a problem.

Finally, the last cell is labeled "wastebasket" (Dunnette, 1966), meaning that the influences we cannot attribute to other sources, we attribute to professional leadership. The result is not leadership but a collection of error variances that should be labeled error. Analogous to overachievers and underachievers, leadership is not measured without error.

In this chapter, global leadership is conceptualized in terms of the interpersonal cross-cultural relationship between a leader and a follower. That relationship, however, is more than influence based on formal authority, personal friendship, personal adviser relationships, familial relationships, cultural relationships, and satisfaction of organizational agreements. More specifically, global leadership is characterized by cross-cultural, professional, or work relationships involving mutual trust, respect, and obligation. Leaders who enjoy such a relationship with their followers exert an influence that goes above and beyond that of formal power. Importantly, leaders who enjoy this kind of relationship are able to induce followers to agree to go beyond their formal job requirements to make a wholesome contribution to their organization. Hence, one question is how real cross-cultural leadership can be developed to address special challenges confronting global leaders of the twenty-first century in multinational enterprises.

Long-Term Career Progress

Global leadership does not just happen to the fortunate few. It may be understood as a process that unfolds over the course of a person's career. This unfolding process can be conceptualized in terms of the management of long-term career progress. Research has shown the importance of assuming a long-term perspective to career management. The Japanese Management Progress study tracked a cohort of managers from their university years to their twenty-fifth year in a large multinational enterprise with offices throughout Southeast Asia and parts of Europe (Graen & Wakabayashi, 1994). The results showed that early behavior (during the first 3 years) on the job predicted career progress 23 years later. Also, early progress was consistently related to later progress. Once a manager was on the right track and stayed on course, the manager became a high-progress professional in terms of 360-degree evaluations, bonuses, salary, and speed of promotions. What did they do that enabled such a rosy future?

Three factors predicted career progress over this period: (1) real leadership, (2) efficacy, and (3) network. Leadership was the building of effective working relationships characterized by trust, respect, and obligation, with three or more tough supervisors during the first 3 years. Efficacy was the earning of high marks from these early supervisors for meeting difficult and ambiguous performance expectations. Finally, network was the prestige of the university contacts within the corporation. The first two factors showed their early contributions, but network's contribution surfaced later in the managers' careers. In sum, the fast-track global leaders began their careers by going beyond the minimum requirements of their jobs and building effective working relationships characterized by trust, respect, and obligation with their immediate supervisors. They also worked to clear ambiguities and to discover and fulfill the performance expectations of their supervisors. In addition, later in their careers they received career-enhancing support from their university network within the company. Moreover, Taga (1997) observed that Japanese global leaders demonstrate wider-ranging interests, better health, and increased family support than their less successful cohorts. Managing long-term career progress is certainly no easy matter, even for leader-follower dyads from the same nation or culture. The problems with managing long-term career progress compound significantly in cross-national and cross-cultural contexts. For example, cultural differences between a leader and a follower in terms of career expectations should be resolved by global leaders, who may not have sufficient time to develop cross-cultural leadership relationships with their subordinates owing to the length of their foreign job assignment. Thus, to be successful, global leaders need to understand the long-term implications of their career strategies. They need to learn how to go the extra distance and to earn respect, trust, and obligation from others, especially tough bosses, without losing the respect of their peers—and they need to learn all these things in a relatively short period of time.

Organized Complexity

The fact that cross-cultural business problems are increasingly of the organized-complexity type rather than the disorganized-complexity type poses an ongoing challenge (Graen, 1989). Disorganized complexity is characterized by problems

Table 2. Implications for Global Leadership Development

- Global leadership
- Transcultural skills
- Third cultures
- Cross-cultural creative problem solving

that can be disassembled, solved in smaller parts, and reassembled. An example of disorganized complexity is computer repair. When the monitor is broken, a technician can disconnect the damaged one, connect a new one, and the computer will operate once again. The technician does not have to study the entire computer system in order to replace the monitor. Organized complexity, on the other hand, is characterized by problems that have to be solved as a whole, in a coordinated fashion. An example is a complex computer program that must be dealt with as an interrelated whole in order to eliminate a bug. Managing across cultures involves organized rather than disorganized complexity, as it is seldom possible to disassemble a foreign culture to work within one's own culture. Thus, global leaders need to distinguish complexities in cross-national and cross-cultural management so that they may resolve such problems effectively.

Source: Graen (1997).

Figure 2.   Leadership for What?

In a multinational enterprise, for example, an effective leader must ensure that new products entering different nations are coordinated with each other, sales and supply efforts, support units, and communication and control units, so that the objectives of the programs can be achieved. As problems become increasingly organized and complex, the need for cross-functional teamwork becomes even more important. If the organized whole becomes overwhelmingly grand, then the traditional method of using individual decision makers may not prove effective. An alternative would be to incorporate insights from foremost experts into the organized complexity of a particular decision situation. Clearly, procedures in dealing with disorganized complexity will not accommodate organized complexity. We must discover relevant procedures. Perhaps multinational, cross-functional, team-based notions are required. Next, we examine the implications of these needs.

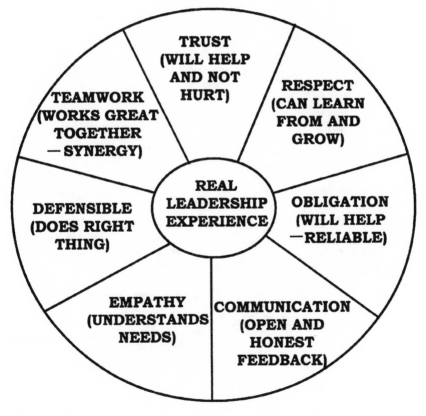

Source: Graen (1997).

Figure 3. Follower's Checklist

IMPLICATIONS FOR DEVELOPMENT
OF GLOBAL LEADERSHIP

We will now examine a critical issue, which arises after developmental needs are identified —the determination of what can be done to meet these needs (Table 2).

Global Leadership

Global leadership can be developed at all levels in the corporation to the extent that people can determine that leadership is persuading a person to become a follower under specified conditions, including what the leadership relationship means to both parties. Clearly, leadership has been associated with many different types of power that it does not merit and that should not be so named. This is much

Source: Graen (1997).

Figure 4.   Leadership Processes

more than semantics; it allows people to claim real leadership by virtue of their office without having earned it. In contrast, development of leadership knowledge and skill should include an understanding of (1) "leadership for what?," (2) follower's checklist, and (3) leadership processes (Graen & Uhl-Bien, 1995).

"Leadership for what?" is illustrated in Figure 2. According to this figure, a follower agrees to the following particular conditions: (1) persons, (2) domain, (3) location, (4) time, (5) rationale, (6) changes, and (7) risks. Leadership may appear to be open on many of these parameters, but it is only illusory and not substantive. Potential global leaders need to understand and practice the development of these real leadership experiences with their associates and not violate the implicit boundaries of the agreement.

The follower's checklist (Figure 3) describes the seven mutual components of a real leadership experience: (1) trust, (2) respect, (3) obligation, (4) communications, (5) empathy, (6) defensibility, and (7) teamwork. A potential follower requires these components before and during a real leadership experience. If they are not present, the follower will terminate the leadership experience upon discovery of that deficiency. Once this occurs, future leadership is doubtful. Global leaders need to understand and practice the development and maintenance of such

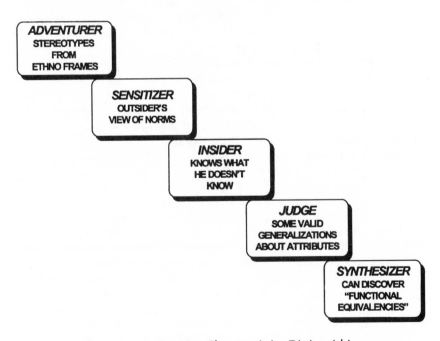

Figure 5.　Progressive Characteristics Distinguishing
Transculturals from Non-transculturals

leadership across cultures, since cross-cultural leadership seldom gets a second chance.

The leadership process (Figure 4) begins with (1) the mutual assessment of each other's potential. If the assessments are acceptable, (2) the leader makes an offer that (3) the follower accepts. Following this, the follower and leader (4) engage in role-making to develop the relationship, (5) go through a transformation to internalize it, and (6) do maintenance as necessary. Finally, they achieve (7) the highest level of leadership. Again, this process requires education and practice and is especially difficult across very different cultures. But with adequate training and practice, global leaders can develop the proper deferral of judgment and active relationship discovery they need to be successful.

Transcultural Skills

The second implication is that global leaders must develop refined transcultural skills. "Transcultural" is a term coined by Graen and associates (1997) to denote those who are able to transcend different cultures and help bring people of different cultural backgrounds together. As the composition of the organization further diversifies, the need becomes imperative for leaders to bring together groups with different backgrounds to function as a whole. We suggest that transculturals are needed to manage cross-cultural or cross-national differences within multinational enterprises. In the context of discussing the effective establishment of cross-cultural alliances, Graen and associates (1997) described five successive stages of becoming transculturals, as shown in Figure 5.

The first stage is denominated *cultural adventurer.* In this stage, one develops an adventurer's mentality toward cultures other than one's own. The second stage is that of the *cultural sensitizer.* Cultural sensitizers can attune their behaviors and attitudes to a culture other than their own. To be able to perceive a culture from that particular culture's perspective, one must learn to read and conform to the social and behavioral norms of that culture. The third stage is *discrepant culture insider.* Such insiders have been insiders in cultures that are vastly different from their own. The fourth stage is *comparative culture judge.* A leader who is a cultural adventurer, cultural sensitizer, and discrepant culture insider possesses the behavioral and affective means and the knowledge base to conduct cross-cultural negotiations. To become a true transcultural, however, he or she must also possess the cognitive means to make cross-cultural comparisons. Conducting such negotiations requires, first, the ability to conceptualize differences and similarities between cultures. A discrepant culture insider possesses the affective and behavioral prerequisite, and the knowledge base, to perceive real similarities and differences between cultures. As Dogan and Pelassy (1984, p. 133) stated, "Comparability is not an inherent characteristic of every given series of objects. It is rather a quality which is attributed by the point of view of the observer." Because different people attribute different meanings to different situations, the validity of the comparison depends on the ability of the comparative culture judges to abstract relevant and useful similarities and differences for comparison.

The fifth and final stage, *socializing synthesizers,* includes those who have been socialized into the cultures of interest, and those who can synthesize both the home culture and the second culture. Our definition of "synthesizing" has two implications. First, socializing synthesizers have the ability to identify constructs with "functional equivalence" between cultures (Dogan & Pelassy, 1984). Second, they can create or facilitate the development of third cultures that can be understood by residents in both the home culture and the second culture (Graen & Wakabayashi, 1994).

For global leaders to effectively manage the foreign office and plant differences, transcultural skills may be required. One may argue that a strong structure may overwhelm individual differences. Since multinational enterprises typically have strong structures and subordinates are required to comply with them, the transcultural approach may not be necessary. We suggest that superficial compliance will suppress differences but will not solve conflicts. To the extent that new leaders desire true cooperation and coordination from members of different cultural backgrounds, the transcultural approach surpasses the coercive approach.

Third Cultures

The third implication involves promoting new professionalism across cultures. In other words, third cultures must be built among groups of differing interests within local and foreign operations. Third cultures involve the bridging and transformation of the two cultures (Graen & Wakabayashi, 1994). In bridging cultural differences, third cultures involve a third "Xeno" component to produce a company culture that, at least, does not offend either culture and, at best, is one to which people from both cultures can commit. When bridging cultural differences, cross-cultural partners find ways to develop organizational practices and management techniques and programs that are part of the third culture (Graen & Hui, 1996).

For example, when managing in collective cultures, members of an individualistic culture may try to build collectivist components into work structure and leader-member relationships. In transforming cultures, a true third culture can be created that reflects fundamental characteristics of both business partners' cultures, plus the "Xeno" component. In other words, a third culture is a synthesized culture. To create third cultures, participants from both cultures must understand, reconcile, and transform systematic differences. Members of both cultures must find the new cultural system acceptable and must study its structure. More importantly, this new system contains elements of both cultures, plus new elements, assembled into a tailored system.

In the case of multinational enterprises, third cultures involve the bridging of the home office and foreign office cultures, which can facilitate the proper handling of seemingly incongruent sets of values and practices. Leaders who can accomplish the development of third cultures are a valuable corporate resource in the global arena. We believe that the ability to develop third cultures can be enhanced through developmental experiences in multinational situations.

Cross-cultural Creative Problem Solving

An important part of global leaders' training in third culture building is the development of creative problem-solving skills. Some may even argue that these skills are relevant to all leaders. It should be noted, however, that according to some actual management practices, creative problem solving is not required of all managers. For example, some bosses want only consenting and like-minded subordinates. Training in creative problem solving is highly related to successful third culture building. Cross-cultural creative problem solving is closely related to third culture building. In essence, third culture is a conceptual tool that focuses on the importance of bringing differences together. Creative problem solving is the actual work that must be accomplished in order to bridge the differences.

Creative problem solving has three stages: problem finding, solution making, and solution implementing (Graen, 1989). Within each stage, three processes take place: idea generation, idea evaluation, and idea selection. To identify problems requires a patient pursuit, as not all problems are immediately apparent. Instead, most problems are hidden. In the course of finding problems, one must also develop a tolerance for ambiguities. Intolerance could lead one to devise quick opinions of underlying problems without an examination of all available alternatives. Also, in the course of finding problems, one must be trained to defer judgment until all alternatives have been examined. Once problems have been identified, the solution-finding stage kicks in. Solutions should be based on a firm understanding of the underlying problem. Finding solutions involves the generation of possible solutions and the selection of the optimal solution. When implementing solutions, one must understand the importance of monitoring and adaptation. Regardless of how well organized the solutions are, one needs to recognize that contingencies exist that are beyond one's control. To the extent that one can monitor the implementation process and adapt to situational requirements, effective problem solving can be achieved.

Multicultural creative problem solving in a group context necessitates more than just the three stages discussed earlier (Ancona & Caldwell, 1992). Because multiple people will be involved in each of the three stages, negotiation and mediation skills are required. Furthermore, because people have different opinions, orientations, and interests, it is only natural for each to pursue his or her particular interests in a group problem-solving situation. However, negotiation and mediation in the context of group creative problem solving do not have the same objective as most negotiations—maximization of individual gains. Instead, negotiation and mediation in creative problem solving deal with an open-minded, interactive process marked by mutual trust and respect. In this kind of interaction, both sides are willing to express their opinions and interests in a non-imposing or non-threatening manner, to listen to other people's opinions with an open mind, to provide constructive feedback, and to strive to find mutual interests.

CONCLUSION

We are proposing here a number of challenges to global leadership development systems for the twenty-first century. Given these challenges, we propose an integrative approach to traditional global leadership development systems, which combines (1) a return to real cross-cultural leadership skills, (2) transcultural competence development, (3) third-culture–building capability, and (4) cross-cultural creative problem-solving efficacy. These four capability dimensions are viewed as interactive and, hence, must be modeled as interactive so that their outcomes are greater than the sum of their parts. We are suggesting the need to develop global leaders who can role-make real cross-cultural leadership relationships at deep transcultural levels, and who are capable of forging third cultures using cross-cultural creative problem solving. Finally, the development of global leadership knowledge and skills from these four dimensions should continue throughout the leaders' careers. Development programs that can deliver these four components will prove increasingly valuable to multinational corporations in the twenty-first century.

REFERENCES

Ancona, D. G., & Caldwell, D. (1992, July). *Speeding product development: Making teamwork work.* Cambridge, MA: Sloan School of Management.

Baba, M., Granrose, C. S., & Bird, A .C. (1995). Career planning and career development of managers in Japanese firms and U.S. subsidiaries in Japan. *Journal of Asian Business, 11,* 71-96.

Bartlett, C. A., & Ghoshal, S. (1989). *Managing across borders: The transnational solution.* Boston: Harvard Business School Press.

Bass, B. M. (1981). *Stogdill's handbook of leadership* (Rev. ed.). New York: Free Press.

Bass, B. M. (1985). *Leadership and performance beyond expectations.* New York: Free Press.

Bleek, J., & Ernst, D. (1993). *Collaborating to compete: Using strategic alliances and acquisitions in the global marketplace.* New York: Wiley.

Child, J., Markoczy, L., & Cheung, T. (1995). Managerial adaptation in Chinese and Hungarian strategic alliances with culturally distinct foreign partners. In S. Steward (Ed.), *Joint ventures in the People's Republic of China: Vol. 4. Advances in Chinese industrial studies.* Greenwich, CT: JAI Press.

Dogan, M., & Pelassy, D. (1984). *How to compare nations.* Chatham, NJ: Chatham House.

Dreher, G. F., Dougherty, T. W., & Whitely, B. (1985). Generalizability of MBA degree and socioeconomic effects on business schools graduates' salaries. *Journal of Applied Psychology, 70,* 769-773.

Drucker, P. F. (1988, January-February). The coming of the new organization. *Harvard Business Review,* 45-53.

Dunnette, M. D. (1966). Fad, fashions, and folderol in psychology. *American Psychologist, 21,* 343-352.

Fiedler, F. E. (1967). *A theory of leadership effectiveness.* New York: McGraw-Hill.

Ghoshal, S. (1987). Global strategy: An organizing framework. *Strategic Management Journal 8,* 425-440.

Graen, G. B. (1989). *Unwritten rules.* New York: Wiley.

Graen, G. B. (1995). Interview with Procter & Gamble director. Cincinnati, OH, August 7.

Graen, G. B., & Hui, C. (1996). Managing changes in globalizing business: How to manage cross-cultural business partners. *Journal of Organizational Change Management 9*(3), 62-72.

Graen, G. B., Hui, C., Wakabayashi, M., & Wang, Z. M. (1997). Cross-cultural research alliances in organizational research: Cross-cultural partnership-making in action. In C. Earley & M. Erez (Eds.), *New perspectives on international industrial/organizational psychology* (pp. 160-189). San Francisco: Jossey-Bass.

Graen, G. B., & Uhl-Bien, M. (1995). Development of leader-member exchange (LMX) theory of leadership over 25 years: Applying a multi-level, multi-domain perspective. *Leadership Quarterly 6,* 219-247.

Graen, G. B., & Wakabayashi, M. (1994). Cross-cultural leadership-making: Bridging American and Japanese diversity for team advantage. In H. C. Triandis, M. D. Dunnette, & L. M. Hough (Eds.), *Handbook of industrial and organizational psychology* (Vol. 4, pp. 415-446). New York: Consulting Psychologist Press.

Hofstede, G. (1980). *Culture's consequences: International differences in work-related values.* Beverly Hills, CA: Sage.

Hofstede, G. (1991). *Cultures and organizations.* London: McGraw-Hill.

Hofstede, G. (1993). Cultural constraints in management theories. *Academy of Management Executive 7*(1), 81-94.

Hui, C., & Graen, G. B. (1998). Guanxi and professional leadership in contemporary Sino-American joint ventures in Mainland China. *Leadership Quarterly.*

Imai, M. (1991). *Kaizen: The key to Japan's competitive success.* New York: McGraw-Hill.

Katz, D., & Kahn, R. L. (1978). *The social psychology of organizations* (2nd ed.). New York: Wiley.

Kram, K. E. (1985). *Mentoring at work: Developmental relationships in organizational life.* Glenview, IL: Scott.

Organ, D. W. (1988). *Organizational citizenship behavior: The "good soldier" syndrome.* Lexington, MA: Lexington Books.

Phatak, A. V. (1997). *International management* Cincinnati: Southwestern.

Phillips, E., Graen, G., & Hui, C. (1996). *Leadership and friendship as relational moderators of engineering team performance over a project life cycle: A replication and extension.* (Working Paper). Cincinnati: University of Cincinnati.

Phillips, E., Hui, C., & Graen, G. (1995). *Relational moderators underlying engineering team performance over the project life cycle* (Working Paper). Cincinnati: University of Cincinnati.

Prahalad, C. K., & Hamel, G. (1990, May-June). The core competence of the corporation. *Harvard Business Review,* 79-91.

Steel, G. (1997, August). *Global leadership in a mature multinational enterprise symposium on global leadership in the 21st century.* Paper presented at the meeting of the Academy of Management, Boston, MA.

Stogdill, R. M. (1974). *Handbook of leadership: A survey of the literature.* New York: Free Press.

Taga, T. (1997, June). *Careers of Japanese executives.* Paper presented at the meeting of the Association of Japanese Business Studies, Washington, DC.

Whitely, W., Dougherty, T. W., & Dreher, G. F. (1991). Relationship of career mentoring and socioeconomic origin to managers' and professionals' early career progress. *Academy of Management Journal 34,* 331-351.

GLOBAL LEADERSHIP COMPETENCIES FOR THE TWENTY-FIRST CENTURY
MORE OF THE SAME OR A NEW PARADIGM FOR WHAT LEADERS REALLY DO?

John R. Fulkerson

ABSTRACT

This chapter challenges the practitioners of executive development to move beyond the definition and cataloging of competencies and to develop an improved understanding of the full range of environmental and business forces that shape executive actions. The model presented in this chapter challenges development practitioners to examine and better understand how a given business environment interacts with individual competencies and forms, what Fulkerson defines as an individual executive's operating system. This individual operating system is a platform or set of highly individualized organizing principles from which an executive takes the actions that drive the hard side of a business (products or services) and develops the organization required to successfully execute a given business plan. Fulkerson argues that executive development practitioners must understand business demands and circum-

Advances in Global Leadership, Volume 1, pages 27-48.
Copyright © 1999 by JAI Press Inc.
ISBN: 0-7623-0505-3

stances and how executives organize their decisions and actions if development interventions are to be fully effective.

INTRODUCTION

Based on more than 25 years' experience in working with leaders, the majority of that time spent working with international leaders, presented here are a series of observations about what makes leaders globally effective. In particular, the central themes explored are how leaders think, make sense of the data and circumstances with which they are faced, and then take action. The points of view presented are intended for both aspiring and current leaders who seek increased effectiveness, and the social scientist practitioner who seeks to help to drive leadership development and is open to the possibility that new paradigms may be required to explore and explain what leaders really do.

It is reasonable to assume that of all the topics likely to capture the imagination of the global business community and the social scientist, it is the art and science of leadership that claims the most attention. It is also safe to assume that more has been written on the topic of leadership than any other single business topic. Despite all of this, it is also reasonable to assume that the consistent and accurate prediction of leadership success remains an elusive, though worthy, goal. Most efforts to describe and predict leadership begin with a listing of the competencies that successful leaders must bring to their work. However, recent literature on or about leadership is based more on observations and anecdotes relative to what leaders experience, learn, and do than on specific competencies possessed by leaders. These descriptions focus on the broader concept of what leaders do, rather than on the specific competencies that form the basis of their ability to lead. Two examples of works that develop a broader concept of leadership are those by Tichy (1997) and McCall (1998).

Tichy (1997) speaks of the importance of leadership to the health or success of an enterprise and notes that his observations and discussions with leaders point to a broader, more integrative view of what constitutes leadership than that of strictly defined competencies. Tichy's descriptions of leadership are integrative, combining leaders' actions into conceptual categories that are much broader than those usually described by competencies. His work refers to such concepts as the need for a leader to have a teachable point of view, to bring ideas to the table, to make decisions based on values, to have the personal courage to see an idea through to fruition, and to possess the sustainable energy required to get things done in complex, change-resistant, and dynamic organizations. Such broad descriptions are viewed by many leaders as more immediately translated into action, and therefore more useful than competencies.

McCall's (1998) work focuses on experiences that enable leaders to develop the wisdom and judgment required by a complex and globally competitive business environment. McCall, in particular, takes a developmental perspective and identifies the types of experiential learnings required to drive global leadership development. Both Tichy and McCall look closely at what leaders do, in various sets of circumstances, to help their respective enterprises succeed. This chapter focuses on the proposition that a conceptual model is needed that looks beyond competencies. The model will attempt to describe the mental and behavioral processes that allow leaders to deal with the increasing complexity of global business. The model presented in this chapter is intended to question whether there is a more useful paradigm than competencies for describing and developing global leadership. Further, the model is intended to raise questions and establish principles that a globally effective leader can use to help assure perpetual personal development, and to drive more appropriate business decisions and actions.

Spencer and Spencer (1993) define a competency as an "underlying characteristic of an individual that is causally related to criterion-referenced effective and/ or superior performance in a job or situation" (chap. 2, p. 9). This scientifically rigorous definition leads to the conclusion that leadership competencies can indeed be discerned and used to predict effective or superior leadership performance. While it may be true that some competencies will predict some aspects of, or be causally related to, successful leadership performance, the central theme of this chapter is that global leadership is so inherently complicated that competencies alone are not believed sufficiently robust to explain what global leaders do. In other words, although underlying individual characteristics or competencies certainly predict some of the variance found in leadership, they do not take into sufficient account the realities and complexities faced by global leaders. It could be argued that competencies are invariably a foundation or starting point for the prediction of leadership success; however, it may also be argued that competencies may be too reductionistic or micro-descriptive to catalog the full and integrative range of the actions and experiences of leaders.

Spencer and Spencer (1993) identify five types of competencies: motives, traits, self-concept, knowledge, and skills. Each type of competency, in turn, refers to the wants that drive behavior (motives); the physical characteristics or consistent responses to situations (traits); a person's attitudes, values, or self-image (self-concept); information that a person possesses (knowledge); and finally, the ability to do something (skills). Competencies then define and describe the core characteristics and behaviors that may be observed in a given leader and may be measured to predict certain aspects of leadership success. Leaders, however, do not think like scientists and are not likely to think in terms of competencies when describing their responsibilities. Leaders are more likely to think in terms of actions and outcomes.

The issue to be addressed in this chapter is not whether the five types of competencies are necessary and sufficient to predict leadership behaviors but, rather, whether the global leadership competencies demanded by the twenty-first century might more properly be viewed as systems or processes leading to actions and outcomes. Just as organizations and their actions are viewed as systems of integrated and connected parts that must work together to produce a given result, so, too, may global leadership be described in the same manner. DeGeus (1997) essentially describes both organizations and leadership as the melding of systems that assure continuous learning and thus long-term survival of an enterprise. This suggests that if we isolate what a leader brings to a given business situation (competencies) and then understand how those competencies interact with business reality, we will be in a better position to determine the mental or behavioral actions taken by the leader in his or her effort to add value to the business. If we can begin to understand and describe how these mental or behavioral actions are integrated, then we have taken the first step in the development of what will be termed here a *leadership operating system*. For example, a business leader operating in China must call upon his or her individual competencies and must match those competencies to situations in constant flux with new circumstances constantly emerging from the business operation. In the process of negotiating a new licensing agreement for the manufacture of cell phone components, an individual leader may discover that certain fundamental assumptions regarding component specifications were misunderstood, due to cultural differences, in the meanings attached to particular phrases in the manufacturer's specifications (e.g., "finished" may not mean the same thing as "assembled").

In turn, the discovery of confused terms may require a renegotiation of the terms and conditions of delivery for the product in question. A single competency, or a combination of competencies, may effectively describe what a leader "brings to the table," but may fail to describe how that leader accesses the right competencies, at the right time, in order to make the decisions and take the actions needed to make the manufacturing agreement work for both parties. This access question is the starting point for the development of a paradigm for understanding, describing, and predicting what global leaders do. The key issue to be discussed in this chapter is whether or not there exists a system or process, which will be defined, for purposes of this chapter, as a leadership operating system. An operating system describes how a leader accesses the right data and then organizes the data to take appropriate action. A leadership operating system is, therefore, defined as a combination of systematic data review, mental processes, and behavioral actions that produce or drive results.

We are reasonably well equipped to describe and catalog the information going into a leadership operating system, but we know little about the mechanisms that integrate this data. Perhaps it is time to determine if it is more useful to seek an understanding of how all the various data sources available to a leader are processed and made actionable. This new way of thinking, or paradigm, could lead to the development of a more user-friendly language for describing and developing global leadership. A leadership operating system sits conceptually between, and integrates, individual competencies and a given business proposition. It might be viewed as a flight plan that requires continuous evaluation of, and feedback from,

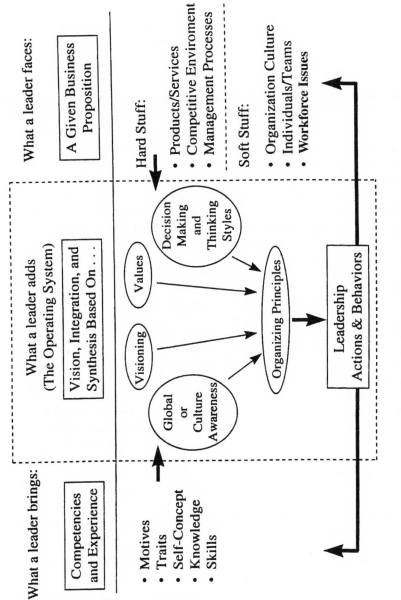

Figure 1. Global Leadership As An Operating System

31

ongoing flight data, but remains firmly focused on the destination or objective. A diagram depicting global leadership as an operating system is shown in Figure 1.

In much the same way that the act of catching a ball can be described as a combination of vision, coordination and judgment, specific leadership competencies only partially describe what is happening to a leader at a given moment and in a given business situation. The complexity of the act of catching a ball or acting as a leader requires integration and synthesis of many discrete data points. Defining a leadership operating system requires a search for the set of organizing principles that guide how a leader handles the complexity of the global business environment. These organizing principles, once identified, help to answer the simple but difficult question of, "As a leader, how do I deal with the complexities of a global business?" It is argued here that the description and discovery of the principles or conceptual frames of reference used to decide a course of action may be more useful than individual competencies.

The view presented here is that the most important act of leadership is to prepare an organization for future success. By definition, the future never really comes and is always a theory based on what a leader believes will happen, which in turn is based on his or her experience combined with knowledge, judgment, or vision. The act of leadership, then, occurs in the present but in anticipation of what the given leader believes will happen or hold true in the future. Every leader is, in a sense, trapped by the present, but constantly looking forward and attempting to arrange events and circumstances to achieve a favorable future outcome. Although this characterization of leadership may seem somewhat abstract, the capacity to predict or influence the future lies at the heart of leadership. When a leadership operating system is discussed, we will see that it is not singular competencies, but rather the method in which the complex interaction of individual competencies and business circumstances is managed that determines success. This interaction and synthesis of data can be described as taking place in a leadership operating system. Each and every individual leader can be characterized as having a unique operating system. The challenge is to determine the structure and organizing principles that guide and direct these leadership operating systems. This chapter first describes some possible components of a leadership operating system and then offers some organizing principles and questions that might be useful to the development of global leaders.

THE LEADERSHIP OPERATING SYSTEM: DATA SOURCES

The diagram of a leadership operating system shown in Figure 1 may appear complex at first glance, but it is actually based on three simple components:

1. What a leader brings to address a business issue (personal competencies)
2. What a leader faces or confronts (the reality of business proposition)

3. What a leader does to add value (competencies and business reality integrated to produce a business result)

Competencies, in the sense of the traditional definition, are viewed as input or conditions in a leadership operating system. Competencies help define what a leader can bring to a current business situation but do not address what a leader actually does in that situation when confronted with a specific business issue. On the opposite side of the leadership operating system model are the conditions a leader faces in given business situations. For the majority of social scientists, there is limited interest or focus on the business proposition by virtue of training or experience. Business proposition data are perceived as more properly the purview of business schools rather than tof social scientists. There is, however, an increasing awareness that business propositions must be integrated with competencies if leadership outcomes are to be more accurately predicted. To fully predict leadership success, it is necessary to understand individual competencies and how those competencies interact with a given business proposition. For the purpose of definition, a *business proposition* is composed of two parts: hard stuff and soft stuff. The hard stuff deals with what the business is and does, while the soft stuff addresses how people get the hard stuff done. More specifically, hard stuff is primarily composed of the products and services offered by a business. Any leader must, above all else, know a business "cold," meaning he or she must understand how that business makes money and leverages its competitive advantages. Hard stuff also refers to data derived from the competitive environment in which the business operates. The final piece of hard stuff data is the specific business management processes that allow the business to function. These include the processes that drive and direct such diverse actions as strategic and financial planning, marketing, manufacturing, management processes for achieving alignment, and human resource planning.

The soft stuff is composed of data related to the human and organizational capabilities that enable the execution of the hard business proposition. The soft stuff highlights the increasing awareness that no business proposition will succeed without an aligned, organized, motivated, and skilled workforce. Rucci, Kirn, and Quinn (1997) cite an excellent example of the relationship between business success and the need to understand organization capability in the Sears turnaround story. One of the lessons to be learned from the Sears turnaround is that the hard stuff simply will not happen unless leadership understands and communicates, on a human level, what the organization and its people must also understand and do. Data that are described as soft stuff are based more on organizational and individual capabilities, and generally originate with the organization's structure and culture. *Culture* here is defined as the various sets of understandings that guide an organization's formal or informal practices with regard to how things get done.

Armed with an understanding of basic competencies and faced with a wide variety of business propositions, a global leader must then make sense of nearly everything in the business environment in order to make the decisions and take the actions required to sustain the business. The challenge for a leadership operating system is to determine whether we can better understand the holistic and integrated actions leaders must take. If we are able to comprehend how a leader puts together or makes sense of what he or she brings to or is faced with in a given situation, we may position ourselves to select and develop global leaders more effectively. If there is a new paradigm that goes beyond competencies, it is here that its definition can begin.

COMPONENTS OF THE LEADERSHIP OPERATING SYSTEM

The Ghost in the Machine

The challenges for the development of a new global leadership paradigm include the search for the components of the leadership operating system and comprehension of how the components fit and work together. It is much easier to describe the components that have been observed in global leaders than to describe how the components fit and work together. For this discussion, first the components are described, and then an attempt is made to describe the organizing principles for the components observed in global leaders. Although it is impossible to directly observe these organizing principles, by asking the right questions we may "activate" a particular component and develop a better understanding of how a global leader's preferences and predisposition to making sense out of complex business situations are formed. In this sense, we are attempting to describe the "ghost in the machine," which allows leaders to do what they do. An improved understanding of how leaders organize their respective business realities should enhance our prediction and leadership development skills. The assumption is that the very act of asking a question focuses attention on that component of an operating system and makes that component a conscious part of the decision-making and action system. As a practical matter, if a leader simply asks the right question, then an act of added value occurs. By asking a question, the focus of attention is directed to a particular business issue (hard or soft).

For the purposes of this discussion, a leadership operating system is composed of four filters through which leaders reconfigure data and one set of organizing principles by which they consciously choose a course of action. The four filters include the leader's level of global or cultural awareness, skill at crafting a vision, deeply held values, and thinking or decision-making style. The leader or practitioner who wishes to begin to develop an understanding of the ghost in the machine needs to ask seven questions for each part of the model shown in Figure 1:

1. Competencies: Do I know myself?
2. Business Proposition: Do I know my business cold?

3. Cultural or Global Awareness: Do I fully understand the implications of cultural differences in the current business proposition?
4. Vision: Do I have a clear sense of where I want to take this business?
5. Values: Am I able to operate on, but modify when necessary, my cherished values and beliefs?
6. Thinking and Decision Making: What is the process of data review that I use to make decisions?
7. Organizing Principles: How do I organize and prioritize my efforts and actions?

Questions one and two have been addressed in the preceding discussion. Questions two through seven will now be explored in the search for new global leadership competencies and a new leadership paradigm.

Global or Cultural Awareness

As a starting point, a global leader must understand and possess cultural awareness. This means that respective leaders must be thoroughly grounded in how different cultures operate and accomplish their business objectives. Fons Trompenaars (1994) and Geert Hofstede (1991) have provided the majority of seminal work on the description of dimensions around which cultures differ. A discussion of how these dimensions effect the cross-cultural assessment of global leadership talent may be found in Fulkerson (1998). For a leader, an understanding of how cultures differ permits an understanding of how individuals and organizations with different cultural backgrounds approach practical business situations.

The purpose of this section is not to present a treatise on cultural differences, but rather to highlight the importance and relevance of understanding cultural differences as an integral part of any leadership operating system. The examples of cultural differences presented here are based specifically on the work of Trompenaars (1994). Now more than ever, global leaders must understand how different countries, organizations, and nationalities view business propositions and then translate their respective understandings into business actions. It should be kept in mind that these are not all-or-nothing characterizations; a continuum of culturally driven behavior exists between the poles of the Trompenaars' dimensions. For a leader, however, an understanding of how these dimensions influence individual, organizational, and business behavior is critical. Following is a description of Trompenaars' (1994) dimensions and their relevance to a leadership operating system:

Universalist versus Particularist Cultures

In a universalist culture, rules are viewed as applicable to everyone. For example, a red light always means stop. The law is the law and there are few exceptions. If there is an exception, it must be explained according to a carefully crafted set of rules. In a particularist culture, there may be rules, but the rights of the individual are more important than the rights of the larger community. If an individual from a universalist and an individual from a particularist culture were both asked whether they would help a friend avoid responsibility for making a marketing mistake, their responses would probably be quite different. The universalist would be more likely to say the friend is responsible and must accept the consequences of his or her actions. The particularist would presumably be willing to do almost anything to help the friend avoid trouble. In a global leadership context, the universalist leader may believe that business practices employed in the United States will and should apply everywhere in the world. The particularist leader is more likely to believe that whatever works is appropriate for a specific country or national group. For the record, universalists tend to reside in Western countries while most particularists reside in Asian countries.

Trompenaars would identify South Koreans and Russians as more particularist and Canadians and Americans as more universalistic. The implications for global leadership are immediate. If a leader leans toward a Russian style and focuses on building informal, personal relationships instead of taking the American approach of establishing a business vision that is communicated to an empowered workforce, the business outcomes may be quite different. At one extreme, we may have great relationships but limited action; at the other end of the spectrum, there may be a great deal of action but the company may be so empowered that cohesive action is neglected.

Individualistic versus Collectivist Cultures

In an individualistic culture, the individual is assumed to be the repository of responsibility and action. In a collectivist culture, the group or team sense of community is more important than any individual action. An individualistic leader is likely to place a great deal of emphasis on personal action and individual responsibility by members of the organization. The collectivist leader, on the other hand, will place greater emphasis on team and group consensus. The individualistic leader will speak in "I" terms; the collectivist leader will speak in "we" terms. The approach taken by the effective global leader will depend on the circumstances and cultural differences that are applicable to a given set of business situations and cultures. Trompenaars would describe Canada and the United States as more individualistic cultures and Nepal, Japan, and Egypt as more collectivist.

Neutral versus Affective Cultures

In a neutral culture, self-control is prized, and individual leaders are reluctant to show much emotion. In an affective culture, spontaneous actions and feelings are highly valued. In the United Kingdom and Japan, a leader is likely to show very little emotion, whereas in Italy or France a leader would demonstrate much passion and emotion. In the United Kingdom, a leader assumes a "stiff upper lip" and much less emotion than a leader in Argentina. It is no wonder that certain leaders fail to motivate others who hail from very different cultures. A leader's operating system must sort through and select the most appropriate behaviors depending on the cultural context.

Specific versus Diffuse Cultures

In a specific culture, relationships are usually based on a specific need or required action for a specific purpose. In other words, an individual may be viewed as functionary rather than as a person. The stature of a leader in a specific culture is viewed from the perspective of actions rather than personal competencies. The specific culture leader almost never addresses personal issues; the only thing that matters is whether or not a task or business action is accomplished. In a diffuse culture, the actions of the leader simultaneously coincide with a wide range and combination of personal and business actions. In the diffuse leader, the boundaries between personal and business topics are fuzzy and mixed, if they exist at all. Trompenaars would list Sweden and Switzerland as examples of specific cultures, whereas China, Indonesia, and Thailand are examples of diffuse cultures. Specific leaders get to the point very quickly and stick to an agenda, while diffuse leaders may wander from topic to topic and have difficulty staying on an agenda. This meandering can be very exasperating to a specific leader who may, on the other hand, appear to be cold and unfeeling to a diffuse community.

Ascriptive versus Achievement Cultures

In an ascriptive culture, leadership status may depend primarily on such issues as family status or wealth. In an achievement culture, a leader is revered for hard work and personal achievement. Trompenaars views countries such as Austria and Nigeria as more ascriptive than countries such as Denmark and Iceland. An ascriptive leader may behave as if all decisions made are to be carried out without question because it is that leader's right to do as he or she wishes. An ascriptive leader may view tough questions as insubordination or even prying. Achievement leaders, on the other hand, may welcome and expect challenges from experts with different points of view.

Internal Control versus External Control Leadership

The internally controlled leader derives his or her power from internal feelings. With the internally controlled leader, conflict is natural, aggression is accepted, and the leader is in charge of making things happen. The emphasis here is on "making" things happen. The externally controlled leader places more importance on working with the forces that he or she faces, and strives to compromise, rather than master, each situation. External leaders are viewed by internal leaders as too flexible and too willing to accept the status quo. The internally controlled leader is perceived as too controlling by the externally controlled leader. As an example, in a divided Germany, East Germans were characterized as more externally driven while West Germans were classified as primarily internally driven. When the external leaders were suddenly confronted with the need to rely more on individual effort than on state edicts, the transition proved difficult.

Past, Present, and Future Cultures

The perception of time and history is often culturally specific and may lead to a misunderstanding when a particular cultural perception is not shared by a different culture. Past-focused leaders may be preoccupied with tradition and protocol. Present-focused leaders are concerned with getting things done in the here and now, and may even disregard the past. Future cultures are looking at future aspirations, prospects, and longer-term strategies. Trompenaars cites the following as examples of temporally based cultures: past—Russia and Belgium; present—Venezuela and Spain; future—the United States and Italy. Although these temporal distinctions may change over time as a result of advances in modernization and technology, individual leaders should choose carefully the best actions and language to motivate and inspire organizations that have one, or a combination of, different temporal perspectives.

Global or cultural awareness is a key component of a global leadership operating system. Global leaders must be aware of both cultural proclivities and the interaction with existing business conditions. To be an effective global leader, one must understand the following questions:

1. Do I recognize my cultural bias with regard to how things should be done?
2. Do I have an understanding of how different cultures approach key business issues?
3. To what extent am I willing and capable of modifying my behavior when made aware of cultural roadblocks?

Visioning

The second component of the global leadership operating system deals with how "visioning" guides leadership actions and behavior. If a leader has sufficient competency, awareness, understanding of the business proposition, and knowledge of how different cultures perceive and approach problems, then the leader must develop a picture of where he or she wants to take the business. Most often this future picture is seen as a statement of mission, or vision for the future. Gardner (1995) examined a generation of globally influential and diverse leaders (e.g., George C. Marshall, Margaret Thatcher, and Mahatma Gandhi) and identified, from a geopolitical perspective, six broad potential misjudgments or misunderstandings that twentieth-century leadership may underestimate. Gardner's list includes: the potential for destroying an institution or process (e.g., a simple miscalculation in how a nuclear power plant is run); simplistic communication (e.g., the dumping of complex issues such as European unity into a sound bite); the increasing absence of privacy or the public availability of information (e.g., the Internet); enterprises that transcend national boundaries (e.g., the multinational or global business); nationalistic and fundamentalist reactions to global change (e.g., we must preserve our culture and traditions); and the requirement for leaders to have increasingly greater technical expertise in order to make better decisions (e.g., the need to understand how computers speed up decision making or how advances in biotechnology will affect laws). These six global trends illustrate how complex and interconnected the world is becoming, and suggest that effective global leaders must have a broader skill set than ever before if they are to avoid simplistic and potentially organization-destroying decisions. If we take Gardner's six potential misunderstandings and frame them as issues for a global business leader, we see immediate parallels. The issues, translated into business language, are as follows:

1. Assuming that a competitor is not really a serious competitor (destruction of the enterprise by simple miscalculation)
2. Instructing the organization to try harder (simplistic communication)
3. Hoarding information, intentionally or unintentionally, and not empowering members of the organization to act on that information (poor communication skills)
4. Assuming that cultural or national boundaries do not matter (cross-culturally unaware)
5. Resisting change (our way is best and we do not need to change)
6. Avoiding new learning opportunities (we do not really need to know what is happening in that market)

Gardner's points suggest that under the surface, leadership issues are quite similar and that "it is only the context that is different." What is important is that the leadership operating system must think in future terms; it must engage in *visioning*. Visioning demands judgment, experience, and a full understanding of the business or political propositions with which one is confronted.

To quote another political analogy, from Bell (1992):

> Leadership is a sense of judgment. It is judgment as to what is relevant and how to do things. The result is either people oversimplify, as Reagan did, or you try to lean the other way, become as Dukakis [George Bush's opponent in the 1988 presidential election] did, rather technocratic. So the person who can strike the right balance between the sense of complexity and the sense of judgment is increasingly rare, and that is a problem it seems to me in every society.

According to Gardner (1995), the successful leaders described in his book actively sought to communicate a compelling vision of the future (chap. 1, p. 14). For Gardner, one of the most essential elements of leadership is the ability to communicate in simple but compelling terms not how the action is to be carried out, but instead what it will look like when it is completed. Martin Luther King Jr.'s "I Have a Dream" speech is a classic example of compelling but simple communication. To develop and communicate a business vision, a global leader must thoroughly understand the business proposition and possess the ability to share that understanding with others. This is true in either politics or business leadership. The leadership operating system builds from a global awareness that is linked to the business proposition, and then interpreted through a lens of what the future may bring or what it should or could be. The global leader must have a vision of what could be, and endeavor to inspire and communicate the importance of that vision. Kao (1996) makes the point that effective leaders must go beyond the day-to-day mechanics of running of a business and constantly seek and create new ideas and inspirations. Visioning, then, is essentially a creative process that demands much more than just a thorough understanding of the business. Visioning demands a sense of what the future could or should be. Kotter (1996) notes that all of his research illustrates that businesses that continue to grow and thrive do so because they thrive on constant and creative change toward a future end state. Kotter also notes that most change initiatives fail primarily because they do not construct a shared vision of what is required to be successful in the future. Vision, in this author's judgment, requires an understanding and awareness of future possibilities as well as avoidance and fear of the status quo.

To constantly engage the visioning component of the leader's operating system, the following questions need to be asked:

1.   No matter how well (or poorly) the business proposition is doing, what is the next thing that needs to be done?
2.   How do I constantly challenge my thinking and identify new ideas?
3.   How do I identify ways to inspire others to think differently?

Values

All leaders have predisposed values and beliefs that are based on experience, and place greater value on certain actions or beliefs than others. Values or beliefs are viewed as a leader's most deeply held and change-resistant road maps. If a leader values technology more than people, then all of the actions taken by that leader will probably focus on technological solutions to issues as opposed to motivating employees to work together as a team. Rhinesmith (1993) points out that the successful global leader for the future must find value in:

1. Being a facilitator of personal and organizational development on a global scale
2. Finding new paradigms for living and working in global organizations
3. Understanding that globalization is ultimately the business of mind-set and behavior change.

Facilitating change, finding new paradigms, and understanding the need for change are rooted in values and beliefs. In their simplest form, values and beliefs are the facts that we hold to be true and do not question. Values and beliefs also allow the global leader to develop a "shorthand" for dealing with issues. This shorthand is based on learned experiences that no longer need to be examined. Examples of values are "Our manufacturing process is too slow" or "Chinese leaders believe in doing things collectively."

Hampden-Turner and Trompenaars (1993) looked at the value systems for creating wealth in seven industrialized countries: United States, Britain, Japan, Germany, France, Sweden, and the Netherlands. They concluded that the basic values and belief systems of these nations have a consistent and strong focus on accomplishment and change, and they argue that these nations may have invented a "science" of wealth creation based on the following shared values:

1. Wealth is, or can be, created by everyone (i.e., everyone can participate in a business or society's work environment).
2. Customers are valued (i.e., when the needs of the customer are met, everyone benefits).
3. Integrity is central (i.e., truth fosters feedback and change).
4. Individuals grow only with the support of a community (i.e., we must work together as teams).
5. Status is gained through achievement (i.e., individuals all have unique talents).

Hampden-Turner and Trompenaars suggest that the seven industrialized nations have created a values "shorthand" with regard to how business, industry, and societies should be led. Because these nations share common values, they can work together more efficiently than if they did not share values. In global leadership terms, a leadership operating system must seek to communicate and share values about how things get done with its respective organizations.

To activate this part of the leadership operation system, the following questions must be asked:

1. To what extent does the organization have shared values?
2. What are the prevailing values in my organization that are inappropriate to the success of the business proposition?

3. How do I share or change the values and beliefs that are productive or counterproductive in my organization?

Thinking and Decision-making Styles

The last major component of a leadership operating system deals with how a leader thinks and makes decisions. Ohmae (1982) writes, in referring to the development of a business strategy, that "breakthrough to the best possible solution can come only from a combination of rational analysis, based on the real nature of things, and imaginative reintegration of all the different items into a new pattern, using nonlinear brainpower" (chap. 1, p. 13). Ohmae is simply stating that all the components of leadership are brought to a focal point by how the leader or collective leadership thinks and makes decisions. This, in turn, suggests that every leader is predisposed to making decisions and thinking in certain ways. The leadership operating system must then be based on how a leader perceives and experiences

Table 1. Some Apparent Realities of Decision Making in Complex Organizations

Some Things a Manager Cannot Expect to Do Much About	Some Things Individual Managers Can Do	Some Things the Organization Can Do
The fact that decision making in organizations is not a totally rational, orderly process	Exercise choices in the problems to work on, which battles to fight, and where and when to cut losses	Set values and tone to support problem solving and risk
The nature of managerial work; the juggling of problems and conflicting demands	Develop intimate knowledge of the business and good working relationships with the people in it	Design organizational structure, reward, and control systems to support action rather than bureaucracy
People are flawed; they are limited information processors, have biases and emotions, and develop vested interests	Know yourself; know your strengths, weaknesses, hot buttons, and when to ask for help	Provide assignments where decision-making skills can be developed
Fundamental forces in the business environment	Develop the diverse set of skills necessary to act in different situations	Keep business strategy focused on things about which management is knowledgeable
Basic organizational components determined largely by the business one is in		

Source: McCall, M. W., Jr., & Kaplan, R. (1985). Whatever it takes: Decision makers at work. Englewood Cliffs, NJ: Prentice-Hall.

reality, and it must be organized into mental or conceptual models that are used to make decisions regarding the future of the business. McCall and Kaplan (1985) looked at decision making in leaders and concluded that for organizations to become more effective, individual leaders will have to be better prepared to act in increasingly complex decision situations. And note that decision making is an inherently messy process. McCall and Kaplan's thoughts on decision making foreshadow some of the elements found in a leadership operating system. They address the situation and the complex nature of decision making, as well as the importance of realizing personal strengths, weaknesses, and the business proposition as key elements of making good decisions. The realities of decision making in complex organizations as defined by McCall and Kaplan are shown in Table 1.

Sternberg (1997), in work related to individuals' learning processes, has identified and characterized how individuals think and stylistically make decisions. Although this work was accomplished in an educational context, the results are useful in characterizing a highly individualistic part of the leadership operating system. For a leader, it would be helpful to understand and have insight into preferred styles of decision making or thinking. Sternberg's terms are defined as follows and include my modifications in order to relate the terms to a leadership operating system context:

Functions of Thinking or Decision Making: Past, Present, Future Focus

- Executive: Following past practices and staying with structured problem
- Judicial: Evaluating and analyzing existing issues and problems
- Legislative: Creating and coming up with new ways of doing things

Forms of Thinking or Decision Making: Simple, Complex, or Prioritized Focus

- Monarchic: Single-minded and driven to task completion
- Hierarchic: Works with priorities
- Oligarchic: Multi-task driven but not necessarily prioritized
- Anarchic: Often random in approach and wide-ranging

Levels of Thinking and Decision Making: Global or Detailed Focus

- Global: Deals with large, often abstract ideas
- Local: Deals with concrete, detailed problems and issues

Scope of Thinking or Decision Making: Task or Empowered Focus

- Internal: Introverted, task-oriented, aloof
- External: Extroverted, outgoing, people-oriented

Leanings of Thinking or Decision Making: Change or Bureaucratic Focus

- Liberal: Goes beyond existing rules and creates change
- Conservative: Adheres to existing rules and procedures

Although it is impossible to directly observe the actual decision-making process, it is possible to characterize how data is analyzed and combined by asking the right questions. For the doing and acting leader, the very act of asking a question forces an awareness of what is happening to the thinking process and thus allows modifications where appropriate. The questions that drive this awareness are as follows:

1. Am I thinking of the future (creatively) or not?
2. Do I have my priorities straight?
3. Am I too global or am I buried in the details?
4. Am I working in isolation or am I empowering my organization?
5. Am I so busy asking "how" that I forget to ask if this is even the right thing to be working on?

THE LEADERSHIP OPERATING SYSTEM AS A QUESTION: ORGANIZING PRINCIPLES

The issues and questions raised in this chapter may be pushing the edge of the envelope in trying to combine too many concepts into a unified theory or method of thinking about leadership. At the end of the day, the question of whether or not any of this information is useful must be raised, followed by the question of to whom is it useful. The intent of this chapter has been both to challenge the use of competencies as predictors of leadership success and to search for ways to think differently about the experiences and actions of global leaders. We must challenge ourselves to determine what the inner essence of leadership is and how an individual actually practices the art of leadership. It seems that from a survey of the current literature, the answers are more apt to be grounded in non-academic terms. Leaders are the product of many experiences and are often caught in complex situations beyond their control. If we ask those leaders, "How do you do it?," we are apt to hear descriptions in action and non-academic terms. Leaders do not often operate in terms of competencies and experiences, nor do they micro-analyze their personal actions and experiences according to motives or purpose. Leaders are more often grounded in the future and in action terms. They are attempting to accomplish things based on what they know which is, in turn, a product of their experience, the data available to them, and how they organize the given data. The act of leadership is based on a language of outcomes and actions, not of competencies and psychological models. If we are to build a leadership operating system, and if we expect to make it a useful teaching tool for developing leaders, we must start with the experience and language of leaders. If a leadership operating system is to be useful, its components must be relevant to the experience of the global leader. It seems, then, that there are a series of practical questions that we must ask

Table 2.   Leadership Operating System—Organizing Principles

Organizing Principles	Key Question(s)
• Strategic vision is the starting point	• What are the desired longer term business outcomes? • What are the critical actions that will allow the business to thrive?
• Prioritization gives focus	• What is the difference between urgent and important? • What must be done first?
• Organizations are systems	• What are the systems and processes needed to sustain effective action? • Is the organization bogged down in tasks or is it building systems and process?
• Change is constant	• What will the future bring and what should be done about it? • How will the organization stop doing things it should no longer do?
• Organization capability is a priority	• How does the organization assure that it has the skill (capability) needed to execute its strategy? • What is the balance between skill and empowerment?
• Constant two-way communication of vision and purpose is needed	• How does the organization build a shared understanding? • How does the organization get ideas and commitment from everyone?
• No single individual or group has the answer	• How are teamwork and synergy built? • How is broad-scale information sharing encouraged and fostered?
• Personal visibility and availability are highly symbolic: positively and negatively	• Where should leadership time be spent? • How does a leader "walk the talk" and demonstrate consistent focus on what is important?
• Learning and reinventing of self is constant	• How is self-learning sustained? • What is new or different? Today? Tomorrow?
• Personal courage is a requirement	• How is constant criticism and resistance managed? • How is an organization best motivated when success is elusive or difficult to achieve?

and, at least, begin to answer in order for an individual leader to have or develop an effective operating system. The questions include:

1. What am I good at and where have I had the appropriate or inappropriate experiences?
2. What is the state and nature of the business I am trying to lead?
3. How aware am I of the broader (global) implications of my actions?
4. What is my vision for the future and what do I really know or understand?
5. What do I value and believe?
6. How do I think more effectively about what I am trying to accomplish?
7. How do I organize my thoughts and actions?

If a leader can answer these questions with some degree of certainty, he or she will have described a leadership operating system. If a leader is aware of the gaps relative to the business needs that exist in his or her leadership operating system, then he or she will be in a better position to modify, seek out new information, or change courses of action. The question that drives the need for a change in a leadership operation system is simply whether the desired business outcome is or is not being achieved. If it is, then the model and individual leadership behaviors need little or no adjustment. If it is not, or if new competitive threats are emerging, then modification of this system is required.

The final segment of the leadership operating system, if it is to be practical, must address what the individual leader, now armed with a way to think about the art of leadership, must personally do in order to maximize opportunities for success. My experience suggests that global leaders work with definite organizing principles that integrate the various components of the leadership operating system. These organizing principles may be viewed as the wisdom born of leadership experiences. As observed by the author, effective global leaders apply the organizing principles, shown in Table 2, on a consistent basis. Through application of these organizing principles, an individual leader's operating system is translated into action or behavior. The operating principles simply allow a leader to add value and make sense of the data with which he or she is confronted.

CONCLUSION

The intent of this chapter is to challenge the traditional notion that competencies are adequate for the description, prediction, and instruction of the fine art of leadership. The argument has been that, faced with emerging globalization, leadership requires broader and more user-friendly concepts and paradigms. Recent literature on leadership has focused on what leaders do and what their experiences are. The challenge is to develop a better understanding of the mental and internal processes that leaders utilize to produce business results. DeGeus (1997) views organizations as almost biological organisms composed of systems and organizing principles. It would seem that individual leaders fit in the same conceptual scheme. Competencies are very useful when describing what leaders must bring to the business table. However, the increasing complexity of global commerce will demand a more versatile and flexible leader with new skills and combinations of competencies. If we can begin to describe how the leader functions, then we can move toward instructing the leader to function more effectively. A leadership operating system may provide a map, conceptual or otherwise, that will allow a given leader to examine and reflect more objectively and with greater rationality on his or her own experience in the art of leadership.

Bartlett and Ghoshal (1991) have looked closely at the nature of future global organizations and note that the coming or emerging organization model for what they term a "transnational organization" will be much more complex than the organizational forms we know today. Bartlett and Ghoshal (1991) note that transnational organizations also have great flexibility and that multidimensional management perspectives and capabilities permit this transnational organization to respond quickly to change. Bartlett and Ghoshal found that in the companies they studied, top management was equally concerned with the perceptions and behaviors of individual managers within the organization, and that they tried to ensure that they shared an understanding of the company's purpose and values, an identification with broader goals, and a commitment to the overall corporate agenda. Such a management mentality becomes the "global glue" that counterbalances the centrifugal forces of the transnational structure and processes.

To build commitment to global goals, Bartlett and Ghoshal argue, a matrix must be created in a manager's mind. That matrix must contain clarity, continuity, and consistency of purpose. So, too, must we create a leadership operating system that helps the global leader achieve the proper balance between learning and doing. To do that effectively, it may be necessary to move beyond competencies and discover the mental systems and processes necessary to guide the inner leadership life.

REFERENCES

Bartlett, C. A., & Ghoshal, S. (1991). *Managing across borders: The transnational solution.* Boston: Harvard Business School Press.

Bell, D. (1992, October 28). A conversation with Daniel Bell. *Harvard Gazette,* 5-6.

DeGeus, A. (1997). *The living company: Habits for survival in a turbulent business environment.* Boston: Harvard Business School Press.

Fulkerson, J. R. (1998). Assessment across cultures. In P. R. Jeanneret and R. Silzer (Eds.), *Individual psychological assessment* (pp. 330-362). San Francisco: Jossey Bass.

Gardner, H. (1995). *Leading minds: An anatomy of leadership.* New York: Basic Books.

Hampden-Turner, C., & Trompenaars, A. (1993). *Seven cultures of capitalism.* New York: Doubleday.

Hofstede, G. (1991). *Cultures and organizations.* London: McGraw-Hill.

Kao, J. (1996). *Jamming: The art and discipline of business creativity.* New York: Harper Business.

Kotter, J. (1996). *Leading change.* Boston: Harvard Business School Press.

McCall, M. W., Jr. (1998). *High flyers: Developing the next generation of leaders.* Boston: Harvard Business School Press.

McCall, M. W., Jr., & Kaplan, R. (1985). *Whatever it takes: Decision makers at work.* Englewood Cliffs, NJ: Prentice-Hall.

Ohmae, K. (1982). *The mind of the strategist.* New York: McGraw-Hill.

Rhinesmith, S. H. (1993). *A manager's guide to globalization.* Homewood, IL: Business One Irwin.

Rucci, A. J., Kirn, S. P., & Quinn, R. T. (1997, January-February). The employee-customer-profit chain at Sears. *Harvard Business Review,* 82-97.

Spencer, L. M., & Spencer, S. M. (1993). *Competence at work.* New York: Wiley.

Sternberg, R. J. (1997). *Thinking styles.* Cambridge: Cambridge University Press.

Tichy, N. M. (1997). *The leadership engine: How winning companies build leadership at every level.* New York: Harper Business.

Trompenaars, F. (1994). *Riding the wave of culture.* Burr Ridge, IL: Irwin Professional Publishing.

GLOBAL LEADERSHIP
WOMEN LEADERS

Nancy J. Adler

ABSTRACT

Women will change the nature of power; power will not change the nature of women.

—Bella Abzug, State of the World Forum, 1996.

This chapter looks at the nature of global leadership and the role that women will play at the level of the world's most senior leaders, including both women presidents and prime ministers of countries and chief executive officers (CEOs) of major global companies. The chapter argues that global leadership theory is concerned with the interaction of people and ideas among cultures; global leadership is not merely an extension of domestic or multidomestic leadership. A definition of global leadership is developed that is intended to guide us in treating each other and our planet in a more civilized way in the twenty-first century than we have in the twentieth century. The experience of senior women leaders to date and the qualities often labeled as feminine qualities meet many of the challenges specified by the global leadership model.

Advances in Global Leadership, Volume 1, pages 49-73.
ISBN: 0-7623-0505-3

GLOBAL LEADERSHIP AND THE TWENTY-FIRST CENTURY

In his speech accepting the Philadelphia Liberty Medal, Vaclav Havel (1994, p. A27), President of the Czech Republic, eloquently explained that:

> There are good reasons for suggesting that the modern age has ended. Many things indicate that we are going through a transitional period, when it seems that something is on the way out and something else is painfully being born. It is as if something were crumbling, decaying and exhausting itself, while something else, still indistinct, were arising from the rubble.

Havel's appreciation of the transition that the world is now experiencing is certainly important to each of us as human beings. None of us can claim that the twentieth century is exiting on an impressive note, on a note imbued with wisdom. As we ask ourselves which of the twentieth century's legacies we wish to pass on to the children of the twenty-first century, we are humbled into shameful silence. Yes, we have advanced science and technology, but at the price of a world torn asunder by a polluted environment, by cities infested with social chaos and physical decay, by an increasingly skewed income distribution that condemns large portions of the population to poverty (including people living in the world's most affluent societies), and by rampant physical violence continuing to kill people in titulary limited wars and seemingly random acts of violence. No, we do not exit the twentieth century with pride. Unless we can learn to treat each other and our planet in a more civilized way, is it not blasphemy to continue to consider ourselves a civilization (Rechtschaffen, 1996)?[1]

The dynamics of the twenty-first century will not look like those of the twentieth century; to survive as a civilization, twenty-first century society must not look like the twentieth century. For a positive transition to take place, the world needs a new type of leadership. Where will society find wise leaders to guide it toward a civilization that differs so markedly from that of the twentieth century? While many people continue to review men's historic patterns of success in search of models for twenty-first century global leadership, few have even begun to appreciate the equivalent patterns of historic and potential contributions of women leaders (Adler, 1996). My personal search for leaders who are outside of traditional twentieth-century paradigms has led me to review the voice that the world's women leaders are bringing to society. This chapter looks at the nature of global leadership and the role that women will play at the most senior levels of world leadership.

LEADERSHIP: A LONG HISTORY

The definition of the verb "to lead" comes from the Latin *agere,* meaning to set into motion (Jennings, 1960). The word's origin derives from the Anglo-Saxon *laedere,* meaning people on a journey (Bolman & Deal, 1991). Today's meaning of the word "leader," therefore, has the sense of someone who sets ideas, people, organizations, and societies in motion; someone who takes the worlds of ideas, people, organizations, and societies on a journey. To lead such a journey requires vision, courage, and influence.

According to U.S. Senator Barbara Mikulski, leadership involves "creating a state of mind in others" (Cantor & Bearnay, 1992, p. 59). Leaders, therefore, are "individuals who significantly influence the thoughts, behaviors, and/or feelings of others" (Gardner, 1995, p. 6). Beyond strictly focusing on the role of the leader, leadership should also be thought of as interactive, as "an influence relationship among leaders and followers who intend real changes...[reflecting] their mutual purposes" (Rost, 1991, p. 102). In addition, according to Bolman and Deal (1995, p. 5), true leadership also includes a spiritual dimension:

> Two images dominate [concepts of leadership]: one of the heroic champion with extraordinary stature and vision, the other of the policy wonk, the skilled analyst who solves pressing problems with information, programs, and policies. Both images miss the essence of leadership. Both emphasize the hands and heads of leaders, neglecting deeper and more enduring elements of courage, spirit and hope.

Thus, leadership must be viewed as something more than role and process—something more than the extent to which a particular leader has been influential. To fully appreciate leadership, we must also ask the ends to which a leader's behavior is directed. From this process and outcome perspective, leaders can be viewed as people whose vision, courage, and influence set ideas, people, organizations, and societies in motion toward the betterment of their organization, their community, and the world.

While comprehensive, this definition of leadership cannot be considered historically agreed upon; indeed, no such agreed upon definition exists. After reviewing more than 5,000 published works on leadership, neither Stogdill (1974) in the 1970s nor Bass (1991) in the present decade succeeded in identifying a commonly agreed upon definition of leadership. As Bennis and Nanus (1985, p. 4) concluded:

> Decades of academic analysis have given us more than 350 definitions of leadership. Literally thousands of empirical investigations of leaders have been conducted in the last 75 years alone, but no clear and unequivocal understanding exists as to what distinguishes leaders from non-leaders and, perhaps more important, what distinguishes effective leaders from ineffective leaders.

Rather than adding once again to the already overabundant supply of leadership definitions, this article simply adds two dimensions to the historical definitions of leadership; the first is a global perspective and the second is the inclusion of women leaders and their experience in a field that has heretofore focused almost exclusively on men.[2]

GLOBAL LEADERS: GLOBAL LEADERSHIP

Global leadership involves the ability to inspire and influence the thinking, attitudes, and behavior of people from around the world. Thus, from a process and an outcome perspective, global leadership can be described as "a process by which members of...[the world community] are empowered to work together synergistically toward a common vision and common goals...[resulting in an] improvement in] the quality of life" on and for the planet (based on Astin & Leland, 1991, p. 8; Hollander, 1985). Global leaders are those people who most strongly influence the process of global leadership.

Whereas there are hundreds of definitions of leadership, there are no global leadership theories. Most leadership theories, although failing to state so explicitly, are domestic theories masquerading as universal theories (Boyacigiller & Adler 1991, 1996). Most commonly, they have described the behavior of leaders in one particular country, the United States (and, as will be discussed later, of one particular gender, men). This is particularly unfortunate for understanding global leadership since "Americans' extreme individualism combined with their highly participative managerial climate, may render U.S. management practices [including leadership] unique; that is, differentiated from the approaches in most areas of the world" (Dorfman, 1996, p. 299; also see Dorfman & Ronen, 1991; Dorfman & Howell, 1988; Hofstede, 1991). Recent research on leadership supports this conclusion in finding that the United States is unique in several respects among all of the Eastern and Western cultures that have been studied (Howell et al., 1994). For example, based on 221 definitions of leadership from the twentieth century, Rost (1991) concluded that leadership has most frequently been seen as rational, management oriented, male, technocratic, quantitative, cost driven, hierarchical, short term, pragmatic, and materialistic. Not surprisingly, many of these listed descriptors reflect some of the core values of American culture. For example, relative to people from most other cultures, Americans tend to have a more short-term orientation (e.g., they emphasize this quarter's results and daily reported share prices), a more materialistic orientation (e.g., 40 percent of Amencan managers still think that "the bottom line" is the criterion for corporate health, whereas in no other nation can one find even 30 percent of its managers who take this view; see Hampden-Turner, 1993), and a more quantitative orientation (e.g., emphasizing measurable contributions and results rather than relying on less easily quantified qualities such as success in relationship-building).[3]

Of those leadership studies and theories that are not U.S.-based, most still tend to be domestic, with the only difference from the American theories being that their cultural focus reflects the values and context of a country other than the United States; such as descriptions of Israeli leaders in Israel (e.g., Vardi, Shrom, and Jacobson, 1980) or Indian leaders in India (e.g., Kakar, 1971). The fundamental global leadership question is not, "Do American leadership theories apply abroad?" (Hofstede, 1980b), nor is it the comparative question of attempting to determine the extent to which behaviors of leaders in one culture replicate those of leaders in other cultures. Both questions frame leadership within a domestic context, the only distinction being that the former focuses on a single country (descriptive domestic theories) whereas the latter focuses on multiple countries (comparative multidomestic theories) (see Boyacigiller & Adler, 1991, 1996).

Global leaders, unlike domestic leaders, address people worldwide. Global leadership theory, unlike its domestic counterpart, is concerned with the interaction of people and ideas among cultures, rather than with either the efficacy of particular leadership styles within the leader's home country or with the comparison of leadership approaches among leaders from various countries—each of whose domain is limited to issues and people within their own cultural environment. A fundamental distinction is that global leadership is neither domestic nor multidomestic; it focuses on cross-cultural interaction rather than on either single-culture description or multi-country comparison. The Secretary General of the United Nations cannot change his message for each of the UN's more than 100 member states. Similarly the CEO of a global company cannot change her message for each of the countries and cultures in which her company operates. As we move toward the twenty-first century, the domain of influence of leadership is shifting from circumscribed geographies to globally encompassing geographies; from pan of the world—for example, a nation or domestic economy—to the whole world. Historically, such transnational leadership "...that goes beyond the nation-state and seeks to address all human beings" has been "...the most important, but rarest and most elusive, variety of leadership" (Gardner, 1995, p. 20). However, the essence of such transnational leadership was captured already centuries ago by Diogenes in his assertion to his fellow Athenians, "I am not an Athenian or a Greek but a citizen of the world" (as cited in Gardner, 1995, p. 51), and again much more recently by Virginia Woolf (1938), one of the twentieth century's thought leaders:

As a woman, I have no country.
As a woman, I want no country.
As a woman, the whole world is my country.

Within this emerging cross-culturally interactive context, global leaders must articulate a vision which, in and of itself, is global; that is, global leaders articulate the meaning within which others from around the world work and live. According to Britain's Anita Roddick (1991, p. 226), founder and CEO of the highly successful firm, The Body Shop:

Leaders in the business world should aspire to be true planetary citizens. They have global responsibilities since their decisions affect not just the world of business, but world problems of poverty, national security and the environment. Many, sad to say, [have] duck[ed] these responsibilities, because their vision is material rather than moral.

Roddick's view of global leaders as "true planetary citizens" echoes Bolman and Deal's (1995, p. 5) observation that strictly emphasizing the hands and the head of leaders misses the essence of leadership by neglecting the deeper and more enduring elements of courage, spirit, and hope. The vision of a global leader, by definition, must be broader than the particular organization or country that he or she leads.

Beyond having a worthy vision, global leaders must be able to communicate their vision in a compelling manner to people from around the world. According to leadership expert Howard Gardner (1995, p. 8 et seq.), "Leaders achieve their effectiveness chiefly through the stories they relate," both by communicating the stories and by embodying them. "Nearly all leaders are eloquent in voice," with many being "eloquent in writing as well" (Gardner, 1995, p. 34). As leaders, "they do not merely have a promising story; they can [also] tell it persuasively" (Gardner, 1995, p. 34).

Gardner (1995, p. 11) goes on to distinguish between leaders of a domain and leaders of a society. Leaders of a domain address an audience that "...is already sophisticated in the stories, the images, and the other embodiments of that domain. To put it simply, one is communicating with the experts"—such as when a medical doctor addresses other physicians. Leaders of a society "...must be able to address a public in terms of the commonsense and commonplace notions that an ordinary inhabitant absorbs simply by virtue of living for some years within a society" (Gardner, 1995, p. 12). According to Ireland's President, Mary Robinson (as described in Pond, 1996, p. 59):

> A woman leader often has a distinctive approach as the country's chief "storyteller, [personifying] a sense of nationhood and [telling] a story that also [helps] shape people's sense of their own identity." This is leadership by "influencing [and] inspiring" rather than by commanding.

As society goes global, the audience of a leader also goes global. What members of a global audience have in common is only that which is most fundamentally human to each individual. Global leaders, to a much greater extent than their domestic counterparts, must be able to communicate in terms of what is commonsense and commonplace for people worldwide; they, therefore, must communicate in the most fundamental terms of humanity. Global leaders do not enjoy the simplified reality that their domestic predecessors enjoyed of speaking primarily to people from one culture, one country, one organization, or one discipline.

GLOBAL LEADERS: WOMEN LEADERS

The feminization of leaders and of leadership is a significant development in our understanding and in the governance of global political, economic, and societal structures.[4] As we approach the end of the twentieth century, the number of women in the most senior global leadership positions is increasing and, at the same time, the style of global leadership is increasingly incorporating approaches most frequently labeled as feminine. It appears that "the economic exigenc[iesl of global competition...[are making] feminine characteristics admirable in both men and women" (Calas & Smircich, 1993).

This chapter focuses on women with positional power, women in the most senior leadership roles in major global companies and nations. The focus goes beyond the assumption that scholarship on women leaders must limit itself to women's historically more traditional mode of influence—that of influencing, primarily from behind the scenes, the men who hold society's most elite positions of power while the women themselves hold no positional power. See, for example, contemporary discussions of the influence on their respective presidential husbands of American first ladies, including the more than 50 books published on Hillary Rodham Clinton and the extensive literature on Eleanor Roosevelt (Goodwin, 1995). While the feminist literature has tended to champion the nonhierarchical notion of broadly dispersed leadership—that is, the empowerment of many leaders within society (see Astin & Leland, 1991, among many others)—in contrast to traditional, role-based, hierarchical, and more exclusive notions of leadership, this article attempts to bring the two notions back together. It asks what the nature of elite role leadership, as exhibited by women, will be in the organizationally flattened world of the twenty-first century.

WOMEN LEADERS: NUMBERS INCREASING

The "feminization of an occupation or a job refers to women's disproportionate entry into a customarily male occupation" (Fondas, 1997, p. 258, based on Cohn, 1985, and Reskin & Roos 1990). Thus, the feminization of global leadership would be the disproportionate entry of women into the most senior political and business leadership roles in the world. Is there reason to believe that we will see the feminization of global leadership in the twenty-first century? Yes. Although rarely recognized or reported in the media, one inescapable trend is that the number of the most senior global women political leaders—presidents and prime ministers of countries—is rapidly increasing, albeit from a negligible starting point. As shown in Figure 1, no women presidents or prime ministers came to office in the 1950s, three came to office in the 1960s, five in the 1970s, eight in the 1980s, and to date in the 1990s, 26 have already come to office. More than half of all women who have ever served as political leaders—26 of 42—have come into office since 1990. At the current rate of increase, we would expect to have more than twice as many women become president or prime minister in the 1990s as have ever served before. As shown in Table 1, countries as dissimilar as Sri Lanka, Ireland, and Rwanda have had women lead them.[5]

Do we see similar increases in the number of women leading major world businesses as we see among women presidents and prime ministers? Whereas the pattern among global business leaders is not yet clear, initial surveys suggest that there are not very many women CEOs.[6] According to the United Nations' 1995 report, *The World's Women,* there are no women running the world's largest corporations (as reported in Kelly, 1996, p. 21). Catalyst reports that only 2.4 percent of the chairmen and CEOs of Fortune 500 firms are women (Wellington, 1996). Moreover, only in 1997 did Britain gain its first woman chief executive of a Financial Times (FT-SE) 100 firm, Marjorie Scardino at Pearson Plc (Pogrebin, 1996).

Contrary to popular belief, however, women's scarcity in leading major corporations does not mean that they are absent as leaders of global companies. Unlike their male counterparts, most women chief executives have either created their own businesses or assumed the leadership of a family business. A disproportionate number of women have founded and are now leading entrepreneurial enterprises. According to the Small Business Administration, for example, women currently own one-third of all American businesses. These women-owned businesses in the United States employ more people than the entire Fortune 500 list of America's largest companies combined (Aburdene & Naisbitt, 1992). As the list of women business leaders in Table 2 attests, the reality is that women from around the world are leading major companies. Moreover, contrary to what many people believe, these global women business leaders neither come strictly from the West nor predominantly from the West (see Adler, 1997a).

There is, of course, a fallacy in assuming that because global women leaders are still so few in number that they are not important (Bunch, 1991, p. xi et seq.). In fact, as Charlotte Bunch (1991, p. xii), Director of the Center for Global Issues and

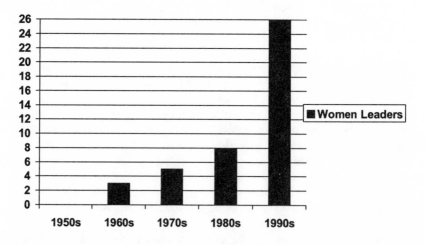

Figure 1. Increasing Numbers of Global Women Leaders

Table 1. Women Political Leaders: A Chronology

Country	Name	Office	Date
Sri Lanka	*Sirimavo Bandaranaike	Prime Minister	1960-65;1970-77, 1994-*
India	(Indira Gandhi)	Prime Minister	1966-1977, 1980-1984
Israel	(Golda Meir)	Prime Minister	1969-1975
Argentina	(María Estela [Isabel] Martínez de Perón)	President	1974-1976
Central African Rep.	Elizabeth Domitien	Prime Minister	1975-1976
Portugal	Maria de Lourdes Pintasilgo	Prime Minister	1979
Bolivia	Lidia Gveiler Tejada	Interim President	1979-1980
Great Britain	Margaret Thatcher	Prime Minister	1979-1990
Dominica	Mary Eugenia Charles	Prime Minister	1980-1995
Iceland	Vigdís Finnbógadóttir	President	1980-1996
Norway	Gro Harlem Brundtland	Prime Minister	1981;1986-89;1990-1996
Yugoslavia	Milka Planinc	Prime Minister	1982-1986
Malta	Agatha Barbara	President	1982-1987
Netherland-Antilles	Maria Liberia-Peters	Prime Minister	1984; 1989-1994
The Philippines	Corazon Aquino	President	1986-1992
Pakistan	Benazir Bhutto	Prime Minister	1988-1990; 1993-1996
Lithuania	Kazimiera-Danute Prunskiene	Prime Minister	1990-1991
Haiti	Ertha Pascal-Trouillot	President	1990-1991
Myanmar (Burma)	Aung San Suu Kyi	Opposition Leader**	1990-**
East Germany	Sabine Bergmann-Pohl	President of the Parliament	1990
Ireland	Mary Robinson	President	1990-1997
Nicaragua	Violeta Barrios de Chamorro	President	1990-1996
Bangladesh	Khaleda Zia	Prime Minister	1991-1996
France	Edith Cresson	Prime Minister	1991-1992
Poland	Hanna Suchocka	Prime Minister	1992-1993
Canada	Kim Campbell	Prime Minister	1993

(continued)

57

Table 1. (Continued)

Country	Name	Office	Date
Burundi	Sylvia Kinigi	Prime Minister	1993-1994
Rwanda	(Agatha Uwilingyimana)	Prime Minister	1993-1994
Turkey	Tansu Çiller	Prime Minister	1993-1996
Bulgaria	Reneta Indzhova	Interim Prime Minister	1994-1995
Sri Lanka	*Chandrika Bandaranaike	Executive President &	1994-*
	Kumaratunga	former Prime Minister	
Haiti	Claudette Werleigh	Prime Minister	1995-1996
Bangladesh	*Hasina Wajed	Prime Minister	1996-*
Liberia	*Ruth Perry	Chair, Ruling Council	1996-*
Ecuador	Rosalia Artega	President	1997
Bermuda	Pamela Gordon	Premier	1997-1998
Bosnian Serb Rep.	*Biljana Plavsic	President	1997-*
Ireland	*Mary McAleese	President	1997-*
New Zealand	*Jenny Shipley	Prime Minister	1997-*
Guyana	*Janet Jagan	Prime Minister, President	1997-*
Bermuda	*Jennifer Smith	Premier	1998-*
Switzerland	*Ruth Dreifuss	President	1999-*

Notes: ( ) = No longer living
* = Currently in office
** = Party won 1990 election but prevented by military from taking office; Nobel Prize laureate.

Source: Adapted and updated from Adler, (1996) © Nancy J. Adler, 1999

Table 2.   Women Leading Global Companies

Argentina	*Amalia Lacroze de Fortabat, $700 million, President of Grupo Fortabat.* Richest woman in Argentina, with nine cement companies, a rail cargo line, 18 ranches, newspaper, four radio stations, part-ownership in a satellite-communications company. *Ernestina Herrerade Noble, $l.2 billion, President and Editorial Director, Grupo Clarin.* The largest-circulation Spanish newspaper in the world.
Australia	*Imelda Roche, $237 million, President of Nutri-Metics International Holdings Pty. Ltd.* Skin cream and beauty products sold by 250,000 salespeople in 20 countries.
Brazil	*Beatriz Larragoiti, $2.9 billion, Vice President and Owner of Sul America S.A.* Insurance company with 20% of the Brazilian market.
Canada	*Maureen Kempston Darkes, $18.3 billion, President and General Manager of General Motors of Canada.*
Costa Rica	*Donatella Zigone Dini, $300 million, Chairman of Zeta Group.* Fifth largest business in Central America, conglomerate.
Egypt	*Nawal Abdel Moneim El Tatawy, $357 million, Chairman of Arate Investment Bank.*
France	*Colette Lewiner, $800 million, Chairman and CEO of SGN-Eurisys Group.* World's largest nuclear fuels reprocessing company with contracts in Japan, Jordan, Pakistan, Indonesia, and the United States. *Annette Roux, $139 million and $31.9 million, CEO of Beneteau and of Roux S.A.* Beneteau is one of world's most respected yacht builders with employees in 28 countries and exports accounting for 60% of sales. Roux is one of France's largest hardware companies. *Anne-Claire Taittinger-Bonnemaison, $100 million and $230 million, CEO of Baccarat and Vice President of ELM Leblanc.* Company represents 40% of France's handmade crystal production; 70% of sales are exports.
Hong Kong	*Joyce Ma, $112 million, CEO of Joyce Boutique Holdings, Ltd.* Designer clothes boutiques throughout Asia in China, Hong Kong, Malaysia, the Philippines, Taiwan, and Thailand, and The Joyce art gallery in Paris. *Sally Aw Sian, $237 million, Chairman of Sing Tao Holdings Limited.* Publishes one of Hong Kong's largest Chinese-language daily newspapers, *Sing Tao Daily*; also publishes overseas from Sydney to San Francisco. *Nina Wang, $l to $2 billion in assets, Chairlady of Chinachem.* Property development, primarily in Hong Kong and China.
India	*Tarjani Vakil, $1.1 billion in assets, Chairperson and Managing Director of Export-Import Bank of India.* Highest ranking female banking official in Asia; flank promotes Indian exports and helps Indian companies set up businesses abroad.
Israel	*Galia Maor, $35.6 billion, CEO of Bank Leumi le-Israel.*
Jamaica	*Gloria Delores Knight, $1.86 billion, President and Managing Director of The Jamaica Mutual Life Assurance Society.* Largest financial conglomerate in English-speaking Caribbean.

(continued)

Table 2.   (Continued)

Japan	*Mieko Morishita, $85 million, President of Morishita Jintan Co Ltd.* Leading manufacturer of breath fresheners in Japan, with soft capsule technique in demand both in Japan and abroad.
	Sawako Norma, $2 billion, President of Kodansha Ltd. Largest publishing house in Japan. One of company's international divisions publishes general trade books, including English translations of classic Japanese novels.
	Harumi Sakamoto, $1.3 billion, Senior Managing Director of The Seitu Ltd. A supermarket and shopping centre operator expanding throughout Asia; Sakamoto opened stores in Hong Kong, Indonesia, Japan, and Singapore, and plans to expand to China and Vietnam.
	Yoshiko Shinohara, $330 million, President of Tempstaff Co. Ltd. Second largest personnel agency in Japan; benefiting from demand boom for temporary services, including translation.
Malaysia	*Khatijah Ahmad, $5 billion, Chairman and Managing Director of KAF Group of Companies.* Financial services group.
The Netherlands	*Sylvia Toth, $166 million, CEO of Content Beheer.* One of the Netherland's top temporary-placement agencies; also conducts training.
Philippines	*Elena Lim, $1.14 million, President of Solid Corporation.* Diversified company makes Sony- and Aiwa-brand electronic products exported to Japan, Europe, and the Middle East; is the Philippines' largest exporter of prawns, and produces Kia Pride subcompact cars for the domestic market.
Singapore	*Jannie Say, $289 million, Managing Director of The Hour Glass Limited.* High-end retail watches, with boutiques throughout South Asia from Thailand to Australia.
South Africa	*Ai'da Ceffen, $355 million, Chairman and Managing Director of Aida Holdings Limited.* Residential commercial real estate firm.
Spain	*Merce Sala i Schnorkowski, $1.1 billion, CEO of Renfe.* Spain's national railway system, currently helping to privatize Columbian and Bolivian rail and selling trains to Germany.
Sweden	*Antonia Axson Johnson, $4.7 billion, Chairman of The Abel Johnson Group and of Axel Johnson AB.* Retailing and distribution, more than 200 companies.
Switzerland	*Elisabeth Salina Amorini, $2.28 billion, Chairman of the Board, Managing Director, and Chairman of the Group Executive Board of Societe Generale de Surveillance Holding S.A.* The world's largest inspection and quality control organization, testing imports and exports in more than 140 countries.
Taiwan	*Emilia Roxas, $5 billion, CEO of Asiaworld Internationale Group.* Multinational conglomerate.
Thailand	*Khunying Niramol Suriyasat, $200 million, Chairperson of Toshiba Thailand Co.* High technology. Started first company in 1963; established new companies in 1964, 1969, 1973, and 1976; in 1989 became director of real estate company in joint venture with Mitsui Corporation.

(continued)

Table 2. (Continued)

United Kingdom	*Ann Gloag, $520 million, Executive Director of Stagecoach Holdings PLC.* Europe's largest bus company, with 7400 additional buses running in Malawi, Hong Kong, Kenya, and New Zealand.
	Anita Roddick, $338 million, Founder and Chief Executive, The Body Shop International Plc. Body creams and lotions. with more than 1,300 stores in 45 countnes.
	Marjorie Scardino, $3.6 billion, Chief Executive of Pearson. A publishing and entertainment comglomerate, including the *Financial Times* and *The Economist.*
United States	*Sally Frame Kasaks, $658 million, CEO of Ann Taylor Inc.* Women's clothing retailer.
	Loida Nicolas Lewis, $1.8 billion, Chairman and CEO of TLC Beatrice International Holdings. Food conglomerate with operations outside of the United States.
	Linda Joy Wachner, $266 million, Chairman of The Warnaco Group, Inc. and of Authentic Fitness Corporation. Owner of both Warnaco, a lingerie maker, and Authentic Fitness Corp.
Zimbabwe	*Liz Chitiga, $400 million, General Manager and CEO of Minerals Markettag Corporation of Zimbabwe.* In foreign-currency terms, the biggest business in Zimbabwe, administers Zimbabwe's sales and exports of minerals.

Note: *Selected women who lead major global companies in countries around the world. Table states annual revenues, or, in the case of banks, assets.
Source: Based on Kelly, C. (1996). 50 World-class executives. *Worldbusiness, 2*(2), 20-31.

Women's Leadership suggests, perhaps the most important question to ask is "why so little attention has been paid to the women who have become [global] leaders and why the styles of leading more often exhibited by women are particularly useful at this critical moment in history."

THE FEMINIZATION OF GLOBAL LEADERSHIP

In addition to increasing numbers, feminization also refers to "the spread of traits or qualities that are traditionally associated with [women]…to…people [and processes] not usually described that way" (Fondas 1997, p. 258, based on Douglas, 1997; Ferguson, 1984). Hence, the feminization of global leadership—beyond strictly referring to the increasing numbers of women who are global leaders— refers to the spread of traits and qualities generally associated with women to the process of leading organizations with worldwide influence. Whereas this certainly has not been true of traditional twentieth-century leadership models, which have primarily reflected American men and their norms, it appears that twenty-first– century global leadership is increasingly being described in terms that neither reflect the masculine ideal nor the American ethos.

What is a feminine style of leadership? "Feminine is a word that refers to the characteristics of females" (Fondas, 1997, p. 260). Many authors argue "that…there are character traits, interaction styles, and patterns of reasoning, speaking, and communicating that are culturally ascribed as feminine attributes" (Fondas, 1997, p. 260). Although theorists debate whether these traits are biologically given or socially constructed, most researchers credit women "with some or all of the following qualities: empathy, helpfulness, caring, and nurturance; interpersonal sensitivity, attentiveness to and acceptance of others, responsiveness to their needs and motivations; an orientation toward the collective interest and toward integrative goals such as group cohesiveness and stability; a preference for open, egalitarian, and cooperative relationships, rather than hierarchical ones; and an interest in actualizing values and relationships of great importance to community" (Belenky, Clinchy, Goldberger, and Tarule, 1986; Chodorow, 1978; Dinnerstein, 1976; Eisler, 1987; Ferguson, 1984; Gilligan, 1982; Glennon, 1979; Grace, 1995; Hartsock, 1983; Iannello, 1992; Klein, 1972; McMillan, 1982; Miller, 1976; Scott, 1992; Spender, 1983; Tannen, 1990, 1994) (as cited in Fondas, 1997, p. 260). By contrast, as Fondas (1997, p. 260) summarizes, "traits culturally ascribed to men include an ability to be impersonal, self-interested, efficient, hierarchical, tough minded, and assertive; an interest in taking charge, control, and domination; a capacity to ignore personal, emotional considerations in order to succeed; a proclivity to rely on standardized or 'objective' codes for judgment and evaluation of others; and a heroic orientation toward task accomplishment and a continual effort to act on the world and become something new...(cf. Brod & Kaufman, 1994; Gilligan, 1982; Glennon, 1979; Grace, 1995; Kanter, 1977; Seidler, 1994)."

Studies focusing specifically on women managers—as opposed to women in general or senior-level women leaders (on whom there is as yet no body of literature)—document their "orientation toward more participative, interactional, and relational styles of leading" (Fondas, 1997, p. 259, based on Helgesen, 1990; Lipman-Blumen, 1983; Marshall, 1984; Rosener, 1990). Frequently labeled as the feminine advantage (Chodorow, 1978; Helgesen, 1990; Rosener, 1990, among others), some authors have suggested that all managers today need to incorporate a more feminine leadership style (Fondas, 1997, p. 259). As Fondas (1997, p. 259) observes, these findings, "when juxtaposed against calls for companies to improve their competitiveness by transforming themselves into learning, self-managing, empowering, and continuously improving organizations—transformations that rely upon more interactional, relational, and participative management styles lead some writers to conclude that...[women] are well-suited for managerial roles in contemporary organizations and that male [managers] need to cultivate feminine leadership traits (Aburdene & Naisbitt, 1992; Godfrey, 1996; Grant, 1988; Peters, 1989)." The current implication is that both female and male leaders also need to cultivate such feminine characteristics in their styles of leadership.

However, leadership approaches that frequently have been labeled as feminine in the North American management literature—including more cooperative, participative, interactional, and relational styles—appear to reflect male/female patterns specific to the American culture, rather than broader, universally valid patterns. Relative to American men, male managers in many other parts of the world, including those in the fastest growing economies of Asia, exhibit a more supposedly feminine style than do American men. As Cambridge management scholar Charles Hampden-Turner (1993, p. 1) notes:

America's ultra-masculine corporate value system has been losing touch progressively with the wider world. It needs a change of values, desperately, or it will continue to under-perform, continue to lose touch with the systems of foreigners, which ironically are much closer to the values in which American women are raised.... American women, who are socialized to display values antithetical yet complementary to American men, have within their culture vitally important cures for American economic decline.

It appears that some of the male/female cultural distinctions documented in the United States among domestic American women and men have been overgeneralized.

For example, as the economy shifts from the twentieth century's emphasis on mass production capitalism to the twenty-first century's emphasis on mass customization—that is, from the twentieth century's machine age emphasis on huge production runs of essentially undifferentiated products to the emerging era of products and services made in short runs and in great variety—the importance of interactional and relational styles increases. Why? Because "the future for developed economies lies in products [and services] uniquely fashioned for special persons" (Hampden-Turner, 1993, p. 6). Whereas the more typically male (from a North American perspective) universalistic approach of treating everyone the same according to codified rules worked well for mass producing products such as jeans, sodas, and hamburgers sold to a mass domestic market, a more typically feminine (from a North American perspective) particular approach works best for developing products and services—such as software—that must be tailored to the individual client and his or her particular needs. To understand particular markets and particular clients well enough to fashion suitable products and services to their needs, one must develop deep relationships. Not surprisingly, relational skills (labeled by the anthropologists as particularism and by North Americans as typically feminine) outperform the seemingly more objective approach of following the same rules with everyone (labeled as universalism by the anthropologists and as typically male by North Americans). The distinction does not appear to be strictly male/female but, rather, a difference between the approach of most American male managers and that of most other managers around the world. Results of research by Trompenaars (1993) and Hampden-Turner (1993) show that American male managers strongly prefer universalism (the less relational style), whereas executives from many very strong economies, such as Hong Kong, Japan, and South Korea, emphasize more relational values which are opposite to those of their American male colleagues (Hampden-Turner, 1993). As Hampden-Turner (1993, p. 6) summarizes, at the close of the twentieth century:

Most American male executives suddenly find themselves ill-suited to the wider world, trying
to codify the uncodifiable, flanked by a huge surplus of lawyers using cumbersome rules where
other nations enter trusting relationships with subtle communications.

According to the research, American women display a relational style of communicating that is closer to the style of most non-American managers around the world than to that of most American male managers. Given American women managers' concurrence with the relational styles of their non-American colleagues, it is not surprising that, on average, American women expatriate managers outperform their American male counterparts (Adler, 1994). It is not that the distinction between women and men identified in the American managerial literature is either incorrect or inconsequential, but only that it is incomplete. Without appreciating American male managers as outliers, it is impossible to begin to appreciate what men's and women's approaches can bring to global leadership in the twenty-first century.

GLOBAL WOMEN LEADERS: AN EMERGING PORTRAIT

Beyond knowing that their numbers are increasing and that their approaches to leadership appear to differ from those of men, what do we know about the women who are global leaders that might help us to better plan for the twenty-first century?[7]

Diversity Defines Pattern

The dominant pattern in the women leaders' backgrounds as well as in the countries and companies that select them to lead is diversity. As highlighted in Tables 1 and 2, the 37 women political leaders and their business counterparts span the globe. They come from both the world's largest and smallest countries, the richest and poorest countries, the most socially and economically advantaged and disadvantaged countries, and from every geographical region. Countries led by women represent six of the major world religions, with four women prime ministers having led predominantly Muslim countries (see Adler, 1996, 1997a).

Many people believe that female-friendly countries and companies select more women leaders. They do not. Seemingly female-friendly countries (e.g., those that give equal rights to women) do not elect a disproportionate number of women presidents and prime ministers. Similarly, companies that select women for their most senior leadership positions are not those that implement the most female-friendly policies, such as day-care centers and flextime (Wellington, 1996, as reported in Dobrzynski, 1996). For example, among the 61 Fortune 500 companies employing women as chairmen, CEOs, board members, or one of the top five earners, only three are the same companies that *Working Woman* identified as the most favorable for women employees (Dobrzynski 1996).

The fact that the countries that elect women presidents and prime ministers or have women serving as CEOs of major companies are so diverse suggests that the overall pattern is toward selecting more women as senior leaders, rather than toward a particular group of supposedly female-friendly countries and companies (such as the Scandinavian countries, companies such as Avon Products, or organizations such as Britain's National Health Service) valuing women per se. The dominant pattern is that women are increasingly being selected to serve in senior leadership positions, not that a few countries, companies, or organizations with particularly feminine cultures are choosing to select women to lead them.

People's Aspirations: Hope, Change, and Unity

Why would countries and companies, for the first time in modern history, increasingly choose to select women for senior leadership positions? It appears that people worldwide increasingly want something that women exhibit (e.g., feminine values and behavior or something that they symbolize).

Women leaders' most powerful and most attractive symbolism appears to be change. Women's assumption of the highest levels of leadership brings with it the symbolic possibility of fundamental societal and organizational change. The combination of women being outsiders at senior leadership levels previously completely controlled by men and of beating the odds to become the first woman to lead her country or company produces powerful public imagery about the possibility of broad-based societal and organizational change.

As "firsts," women assuming senior leadership positions literally bring change. When a woman is visibly chosen to become president, prime minister, or CEO when no other woman has ever held such an office and when few people thought that she would be selected, other major organizational and societal changes become believably possible. Mary Robinson's presidential acceptance speech captures the coupling of the unique event of a woman being elected Ireland's first non-male president with the possibility of national change:

> I was elected by men and women of all parties and none, by many with great moral courage who stepped out from the faded flags of Civil War and toted for a new Ireland. And above all by, the women of Ireland...who instead of rocking the cradle rocked the system, and who came out massively to make their mark on the ballot paper, and on a new Ireland. (RDS, Dublin, 9 November 1990, as reported in Finlay, 1990, p. 1)

In addition to symbolizing change, women leaders appear to symbolize unity. For example, both Nicaragua's Chamorro and the Philippines' Aquino became symbols of national unity following their husbands' murders. Chamorro even claimed "to have no ideology beyond national 'reconciliation'" (Benn, 1995). Of Chamorro's four adult children, two are prominent Sandinistas while the other two equally prominently oppose the Sandinistas, not an unusual split in war-torn Nicaragua (Saint-Germain, 1993, p. 80). Chamorro's ability to bring all the members of her family together for Sunday dinner each week achieved near legendary status in Nicaragua (Saint-Germain, 1993, p. 80). As "the grieving matriarch who can still hold the family together" (Saint-Germain, 1993, p. 80), Chamorro gives symbolic hope to the nation that it too can find peace based on a unity that brings together all Nicaraguans. That a national symbol for a woman leader is family unity is neither surprising nor coincidental.

Based on similar dynamics in the Philippines, former president Corazon Aquino, as widow of the slain opposition leader, was seen as the only person who could credibly unify the people of the Philippines following Benigno Aquino's death. Although Aquino was widely condemned in the press for naivete when she invited members of both her own and the opposition party into her cabinet, her choice was a conscious decision to attempt to reunify the deeply divided country.

Given that women leaders symbolize unity, it is perhaps not surprising that a woman business leader, Rebecca Mark, chief executive of Enron Development Corporation, and not a male executive, was the first person to successfully nego- tiate a major commercial transaction following the Middle East peace accords. Mark brought the Israelis and Jordanians together to build a natural gas power generation station.

When, as Vaclav Havel (1994, p. A27) says, the world is "going through a tran- sitional period, when something is on the way out and something else is painfully being born," it is not surprising that people worldwide are attracted to women leaders' symbolic message of bringing change, hope, and the possibility for unity.

Driven by Vision, Not by Hierarchical Status

What brings the women themselves into the most senior levels of leadership? Most women leaders are driven by a vision, mission, or cause. They are motivated by a compelling agenda that they want to achieve, not primarily by either a desire for the hierarchical status of being president, prime minister, or CEO, or a desire for power per se. Power and the presidency are means for achieving their mission, not the mission itself.

As children, none of the women leaders dreamed about becoming her country's leader, as have so many male politicians, including America's Bill Clinton and Bob Dole, and Britain's Michael Hesseltine. For example, Golda Meir's mission was to create the state of Israel and to ensure its survival as a Jewish state. Not only did she not dream of becoming prime minister, she rejected the position when it was initially offered to her. Similarly, Anita Roddick (1991, p. 126), CEO of The Body Shop, describes her contemporary vision as "corporate idealism." Her vision transcends traditional, narrowly defined economic goals; she is neither motivated to be a traditional CEO nor to focus singularly on maximizing either profits or shareholder wealth.

That women have not imagined, let alone dreamed about, leading a country or a major company is not surprising. For all of the women political leaders—except

Sri Lanka's current executive president, Chandrika Kumaratunga, who followed her prime minister mother Sirimavo Bandaranaike into office, and Bangladesh's Hasina Wajid—and most of the women corporate leaders, there have been no women predecessors and therefore no women role models. What is important for twenty-first–century leadership is that society, if it is to survive as a civilization, can no longer tolerate nor support the leadership of self-aggrandizement at the expense of the greater, now highly interrelated whole—at the expense of the world's entire population and its physical, spiritual, and natural environment.

Source of Power: Broadly Based

Who supports women in becoming senior leaders? Women leaders tend to develop and to use broadly based popular support, rather than relying primarily on traditional, hierarchical party or structural support. This is particularly apparent among the women who become political leaders who often are not seriously considered as potential candidates by their country's main political parties. They are consequently forced to gain support directly from the people, and thus foreshadow the dynamics of leadership in an organizationally flattened world.

Mary Robinson, for example, campaigned in more small communities in Ireland than any previous presidential candidate before either her party or the opposition would take her seriously. The opposition now admits that they did not seriously consider Robinson's candidacy until it was too late to stop her (Finlay, 1990). Similarly, Corazon Aquino, whose campaign and victory were labeled the People's Revolution, held more than 1,000 rallies during her campaign, while incumbent Ferdinand Marcos held only 34 (Col, 1993, p. 25). Likewise, Benazir Bhutto, who succeeded in becoming Pakistan's first woman and youngest-ever prime minister, campaigned in more communities than any politician before her. Her own party only took her seriously when more people showed up upon her return to Pakistan from exile than either they, the opposition, or the international press had ever expected (Anderson, 1993; Weisman, 1986).

In business, the disproportionate number of women who choose to become leaders of entrepreneurial businesses rather than attempting to climb the corporate ladder and break through the glass ceiling to senior leadership positions in established corporations echoes the same pattern of broadly based popular support—as opposed to traditional hierarchical support—that women political leaders enjoy, except that the entrepreneurs' support comes from the marketplace rather than from the electorate. In both cases, the base of support is outside of the traditional power structure and, therefore, more representative of new and more diverse opinions and ideas. The source of support, and therefore of power, more closely reflects the flattened network of emerging twenty-first–century organizations and society than it does the more centralized and limited power structure of most twentieth-century organizations.

Path to Power: Lateral Transfer

How do the women leaders gain power? Rather than following the traditional path up through the hierarchy of the organization, profession, or political party, most women leaders laterally transfer into high positions. For example, Gro Harlem Brundtland was a medical doctor; 6 years later she became Norway's first woman prime minister. Similarly, Charlotte Beers became both Ogilvy & Mather Worldwide's first woman chief executive as well as their first CEO brought in from outside of the firm (Sackley & Ibarra, 1995). Marjorie Scardino, Pearson's first woman chief executive, is a double outsider. As the first American CEO brought in to lead this traditional British firm, she is a cultural outsider. In addition, because the *Economist,* where Scardino previously served as managing director, is only 50 percent owned by Pearson, she is an organizational outsider. The general public was so surprised by Pearson's selection of Scardino that Pearson's stock dropped initially on the announcement of her appointment (Pogrebin, 1996).

Today's global organizations and society can only benefit from the dynamics of lateral transfers. The twenty-first century needs integration across geographies, sectors of society, and professions. It can no longer tolerate leaders with "chimney stack" careers that, in the past, have resulted in deep expertise in one area, organization, or country without any understanding of the context within which their particular organization or country operates. Transferring across organizations, sectors of society, and areas of the world allows leaders to develop alternative perspectives and an understanding of context that is almost impossible to acquire within a single setting. Due to the historic pattern of promoting men and failing to promote women to the most senior leadership positions from within organizations—most often referred to as the "glass ceiling"—women appear to have inadvertently become the prototypes of a career pattern that is needed more broadly among all twenty-first–century leaders.

Global Leadership: Global Visibility

What difference does it make that a global leader is a woman? For the women who become global leaders, it is always salient that they are women. For example, the single most frequently asked question of former British prime minister Margaret Thatcher (1995) was, "What is it like being a woman prime minister?" (to which Thatcher generally responded that she could not answer because she had not tried the alternative).

Women are new to the most senior levels of leadership. As mentioned previously, of the 37 women presidents and prime ministers, only two—in Bangladesh and Sri Lanka—followed another woman into office. All the rest of the women leaders are "firsts." Because women leaders are new, they have the advantage of global visibility. Their unique status as their countries' first woman president or prime minister attracts worldwide media attention, thereby leveraging historically domestic leadership positions into ones with global visibility and the concomitant potential for worldwide influence. For example, following the election of Mary Robinson as Ireland's first woman president:

> Newspapers and magazines in virtually every country in the world carried the story....[T]he rest of the world understood Ireland to have made a huge leap forward....Mary Robinson had joined a very small number of women....who had been elected to their country's highest office. It was, quite properly, seen as historic (Finlay, 1990, p. 149 et seq.).

Similarly, President Francois Mitterrand purposely created a worldwide media event by appointing Edith Cresson as France's first woman prime minister. Likewise, in contrast to Benazir Bhutto's male predecessor who not only complained about receiving insufficient worldwide press coverage while abroad but also fired the Pakistani embassy's public relations officer when too few journalists showed up to cover his arrival in London, Pakistan's former Prime Minister Benazir Bhutto always received extensive media coverage no matter where in the world she traveled.

Because of the worldwide media attention given to women leaders, women today are becoming global, rather than domestic, leaders as they assume roles that were primarily domestic when previously held by men. Whether by intention or consequence, the senior women leaders are at the forefront of learning how to move beyond a domestic focus to communicate on the world stage to a global audience.

Whereas many of the dynamics affecting senior women leaders are quite different from those that affect women managers (see Adler, 1997a), it should be noted that international businesswomen also receive more visibility than their male colleagues. Women expatriate managers as well as women on international business trips, for example, report being remembered more easily than their male counterparts (Adler, 1994). Compared with businessmen, global businesswomen gain access more easily to new clients, suppliers, and government officials; receive more time when meeting with international contacts; and are more frequently remembered (Adler, 1994).

THE FUTURE: GLOBAL LEADERS, WOMEN LEADERS

The confluence of twenty-first–century business, political, and societal dynamics gives leaders a chance to create the type of world that they, and we, would like to live in. It demands, as Vaclav Havel (1994, p. A27) reflected, that leaders find "the key to insure the survival of...[our] civilization,...a civilization that is global and multicultural." The increasing number of women political and business leaders brings with it a set of experiences and perspectives that differ from those of the twentieth century's primarily male leaders. The interplay of women's and men's styles of leadership will define the contours and potential success of twenty-first–

century society. The risk is in encapsulating leaders, both women and men, in approaches that worked well in the twentieth century but foretell disaster for the twenty-first century. As Dr. Frene Ginwala, Speaker of the South African National Assembly, states "...the institutions that discriminate are man-shaped and must be made people-shaped. Only then will women be able to function as equals within those institutions...." Ginwala's fundamental belief is that "women's struggle is not a struggle to transform the position of women in society but a struggle to transform society itself" (Iqtidar & Webster, 1996, p. 10). Recognizing the growing number of women leaders is the first step in creating and understanding the type of global leadership that will lead to success in the twenty-first century.

ACKNOWLEDGMENT

The author would like to thank Soraya Hassanali and Kirsten Martin for their research support and insight on this article. This article originally appeared in *Management International Review.*

NOTES

1. The opening section of this article is based on Adler's "Societal Leadership: The Wisdom of Peace" (1997b).

2. For contemporary discussions of some of the widely read leadership theories and approaches, see Bennis, 1989: Bennis & Nanus, 1985; Conger, 1989; Conger & Kanungo, 1988; Gardner, 1995: Kotter, 1988; and Rosen, 1996, among many others.

3. For descriptions of American societal and managerial culture contrasted with those of many other countries, see, among others, Hofstede, 1980a; Kluckhohn & Strodtbeck, 1961; Laurent, 1983; Trompenaars, 1993.

4. Based on Fondas (1997, p. 257) observation "that the feminization of managers and managerial work is a significant development in management thinking."

5. The Republic of San Marino, a city-state with a population of less than 25,000 people has been led since 1243 by a consul, the Co-Captain Regent, who acts as both head of government and head of state, and is elected for a period of 6 months. In modern history, four women have held the position of Co-Captain Regent, Maria Lea Pedini-Angelini (1981), Glorianna Ranocchini (1984, 1989-90), Edda Ceccoli (1991-92), and Patricia Busignani (1993). Due to the small size of the country and the frequency of changing leaders, San Marino has not been included in the statistics on global women leaders.

6. Although the results are not yet available, the author is currently involved in a major worldwide survey to identify women who head global businesses with annual revenues in excess of US$ 250 million.

7. For a more in depth discussion of the issues raised in this section, see Adler (1997a).

REFERENCES

Aburdene, P., & Naisbitt, J. (1992). *Megatrends for women.* New York: Villard Books.

Adler, N. J. (1994). Competitive frontiers: Women managing across borders. In N. J. Adler & D.N. lzraeli (Eds.), *Competitive frontiers: Women managers in a global economy* (pp. 22-44). Cambridge, MA: Blackwell.

Adler, N. J. (1996). Global women political leaders: An invisible history. An increasingly important future. *Leadership Quarterly, 7,* 133-161.

Adler. N. J. (1997). Global leaders: A dialogue with future history. *Journal of International Management, 1*(2), 21-33.

Adler, N. J. (1998). Societal leadership: The wisdom of peace. In S. Srivastava (Ed.), *Executive wisdom and organizational change* (pp. 205-221). San Francisco: Jossey-Bass.

Anderson, N. F. (1993). Benazir Bhutto and dynastic politics: Her father's daughter, her people's sister. In M.A. Genovese (Ed.), *Women as national leaders* (pp. 41-69). Newbury Park, CA: Sage.

Astin, H. S., & Leland, C. (1991). *Women of influence, women of vision.* San Francisco: Jossey-Bass.

Bass, B. (1991). *Bass & Stogdill's handbook of leadership* (3rd ed). New York: The Free Press.

Belenky, M. F., Clinchy, B.M., Goldberger, N.R., Tarule, J.M. (1986). *Women's ways of knowing: The development of self, voice, and mind.* New York: Basic Books.

Benn, M. (1995, February). Women who rule the world. *Cosmopolitan.*

Bennis, W. (1989). *Why leaders can't lead: The unconscious conspiracy continues.* San Francisco: Jossey-Bass.

Bennis, W., & Nanus, B. (1985). *Leaders: Strategies of taking charge.* New York: Harper & Row.

Bolman, L., & Deal, T. (1995). *Leading with soul.* San Francisco: Jossey-Bass.

Boyacigiller, N., & Adler, N. J. (1991). The parochial dinosaur: The organizational sciences in a global context. *Academy of Management Review, 16,* 262-290.

Boyacigiller, N., &Adler, N. J. (1996). Insiders and outsiders: Bridging the worlds of organizational behavior and international management. In B. Toyne & D. Nigh (Eds.), *International business inquiry: An emerging vision* (pp. 22-102). Columbia, SC: The University of South Carolina Press.

Brod, H., & Kaufman, M. (Eds.). *Theorizing masculinities.* Thousand Oaks, CA: Sage.

Bunch, C. (1991). Foreword. In H. S. Astin & C. Leland (Eds.), *Women of influence, women of vision* (pp. xi-xiv). San Francisco: Jossey-Bass.

Calas, M. B., & Smircich, L. (1993). Dangerous liaisons: The "feminine-in-management" meets "globalization." *Business Horizons,* 36, 71-81.

Cantor, D., & Bearnay, T. (1992). *Women in power.* New York: Houghton Mifflin.

Chodorow, N. (1978). *The reproduction of mothering.* Berkeley: University of California Press.

Cohn, S. (1985). *The process of occupational sex-typing: The feminization of clerical labor in Great Britain.* Philadelphia: Temple University Press.

Col, J. M. (1993). Managing softly in turbulent times: Corazon C. Aquino, President of the Philippines. In M. A. Genovese (Ed.), *Women as national leaders* (pp. 13-40). Newburv Park, CA: Sage.

Conger, J. A. (1989). *The charismatic leader: Behind the mystique of exceptional leadership.* San Francisco: Jossey-Bass.

Conger, J. A., & Kanungo, R. (1988). *Charismatic leadership.* San Francisco: Jossey-Bass.

Dinnerstein, D. (1976). *The mermaid and the minotaur.* New York: Harper and Row.

Dobrzyoski, J. H. (1996, November 6). Somber news for women on corporate ladder. *New York Times,* Dl.

Dorfman, R W. (1996). International and cross-cultural leadership. In B. J. Punnett & O. Shenkar (Eds.), *Handbook for international management research* (pp. 267-349). Cambridge, MA: Blackwell.

Dorfman, R W., & Howell, J. R. (1988). Dimensions of national culture and effective leadership patterns: Hofstede revisited. *Advances in international comparative management, Vol. 3* (pp. 127-150). Greenwich, CT: JAI Press.

Dorfman, R W., & Ronen, S. (1991). *The universality of leadership theories: Challenges and paradoxes.* Paper presented at the Academy of Management Annual Meeting, Miami, FL.

Douglas, A. (1977). *The feminization of American culture.* New York: Avon Books.

Eisler, R. (1987). *The chalice and the blade.* San Francisco: Harper San Francisco.

Ferguson, K. E. (1984). *The feminist case against bureaucracy.* Philadelphia: Temple University Press.

Finlay, F. (1990). *Mary Robinson: A president with a purpose.* Dublin: O'Brien Press.

Fondas, N. (1997). The origins of feminization. *Academy of Management Review,* 22, 257-282.

Gardner, H. (1995). *Leading minds: An anatomy of leadership.* New York: Basic Books.

Gilligan, C. (1982). *In a different voice: Psychological theory and women's development.* Cambridge, MA: Harvard University Press.

Glennon, L. M. (1979). *Women and dualism.* New York: Longman.

Godfrey, J. (1996). Mind of the manager. *Inc., 18*(3), 21.

Goodwin, D. K. (1995). *No ordinary time: Franklin & Eleanor Roosevelt: The home front in World War II.* New York: Simon & Schuster.

Grace, N. M. (1995). *The feminized male character in twentieth-century literature.* Lewiston, NY: Edwin Mellen Press.

Grant, J. (1988). Women as managers: What can they offer organizations? *Organizational Dynamics, 16,* 1, 56-63.

Hampden-Turner, C. (1993, December 9-10). *The structure of entrapment: Dilemmas standing in the way of women managers and strategies to resolve these.* Paper presented at the Global Business Network Meeting, New York.

Hartsock, N. C. (1983). *Money, sex, and power: Toward a feminist historical materialism.* New York: Longman.

Havel, V. (1994, July 8). The new measure of man. *New York Times,* A27.

Helgesen, S. (1990). *The female advantage: Women's ways of leadership.* New York: Doubleday.

Hofstede, G. (1980a). *Culture's consequences: International differences in work-related values.* Beverly Hills, CA: Sage.

Hofstede, G. (1980b). Motivation, leadership, and organization: Do American theories apply abroad? *Organizational Dynamics, 9,* 1, 42-63.

Hofstede, G. (1991). *Cultures and organizations: Software of the mind.* London: McGraw-Hill.

Hollander, E. R. (1985). Leadership and power. In G. Lindzey & E. Aronson (Eds.), *Handbook of social psychology.* New York: Random House.

Howell, J. R., et al. (1994). *Leadership in Western and Asian countries: Commonalities and differences in effective leadership processes and substitutes across cultures.* Center for Business Research, New Mexico State University.

Iannello, K. R. (1992). *Decisions without hierarchy: Feminist interventions in organization theory and practice.* New York: Routledge.

Iqtidar, H., & Webster, L. J. (1996). *Frene Cinwala: Speaker of the South African national assembly.* Unpublished manuscript, McGill University, Faculty of Management, Montreal.

Jennings, E. (1960). *The anatomy of leadership.* New York: Harper & Row.

Kakar, S. (1971). Authority patterns and subordinate behavior in Indian organizations. *Administrative Science Quarterly, 16,* 298-308.

Kanter, R. M. (1977). *Men and women of the corporation.* New York: Basic Books.

Kelly, C. (1996, March/April). 50 world-class executives. *Worldbusiness, 2* (2), 2-31.

Klein, V. (1972). *The feminine character: History of an ideology.* Urbana: University of Illinois Press.

Kluckhohn, F. R., & Strodtbeck, F. L. (1961). *Variations in value orientations.* Evanston, IL: Row, Peterson.

Kotter, J. (1988). *The leadership factor.* New York: Free Press.

Laurent, A. (1983). The cultural diversity of Western conceptions of management, *International Studies of Management and Organization, 13*(1/2), 75-96.

Lipman-Blumen, J. (1983). Emerging patterns of female leadership in formal organizations. In M. Homer, C.C. Nadelson, & M.T. Notman (Eds.), *The challenge of change* (pp. 61-91). New York: Plenum Press.

Marshall, J. (1984). *Women managers: Travellers in a male world.* New York: Wiley.

McMillan, C. (1982). *Reason, women and nature: Some philosophical problems with nature.* Princeton, NJ: Princeton University Press.

Miller, J. B. (1976). *Toward a new psychology of women.* Boston: Beacon Press.

Peters, T. (1989, April 11). Listen up, guys: Women fit profile of execs of future. *Seattle Post-Intelligencer,* B6.

Pogrebin, R. (1996, October 18). Pearson picks an American as executive. *New York Times,* D7.

Pond, E. (1996). Women in leadership: A letter from Stockholm. *The Washington Quarterly, 19*(4), 59.

Rechtschaffen, S. (1996). *Timeshifting.* New York: Bantam Doubleday Dell Audio.

Reskin, B. F., & Roos, R A. (1990). *Job queues, gender queues: Explaining women's inroads into male occupations.* Philadelphia: Temple University Press.

Roddick, A. (1991). *Body and soul.* New York: Crown.

Rosen, R. H. (1996). *Leading people.* New York: Viking.

Rosener, J. (1990). Ways women lead. *Harvard Business Review, 68*(6), 119-125.

Rost, J. (1991). *Leadership for the 21st century.* New York: Praeger.

Sackley, N., & Ibarra, H. (1995). Charlotte Beers at Ogilvy & Mather Worldwide, Case No. 9-495-031, Harvard Business School, Boston.

Saint-Germain, M. A. (1993). Women in power in Nicaragua: Myth and reality. In M. A. Genovese (Ed.), *Women as national leaders* (pp. 70-102). Newbury Park, CA: Sage

Scott, A. F. (1992). *Natural allies: Women's associations in American history.* Urbana: University of Illinois Press.

Seidler, V. J. (1994). *Unreasonable men: Masculinity and social theory.* London: Routledge.

Spender, D. (1983). *Women of ideas and what men have done to them from Aphra Behn to Adrienne Rich.* Boston: Routledge & Kegan Paul.

Stogdill, R. (1974). *Handbook of leadership.* New York: Free Press.

Tannen, D. (1990). *You just don't understand: Women and men in conversation.* New York: Ballantine Books.

Tannen D. (1994). *Talking from 9 to 5: How women's and men's conversational styles affect who gets heard, who gets credit, and what gets done at work.* New York: Morrow.

Thatcher, M. (1995). *Path to power.* New York: Harper Collins.

Trompenaars, F. (1993). *Riding the waves of culture: Understanding cultural diversity in business.* London: The Economist Books.

Vardi, Y., Shrom, A., & Jacobson, D. (1980). A study of leadership beliefs of Israeli managers. *Academy of Management Journal, 23,* 367-374.

Weisman, S. R. (1986, April 11). A daughter returns to Pakistan to cry for victory. *New York Times,* 12.

Wellington, S. W. (1996). *Women in corporate leadership: Progress and prospects.* New York City: Catalyst.

Woolf, V. (1938). *Three guineas.* New York: Harcourt Brace & Company.

ALTERNATIVES TO INDIVIDUAL CONCEPTIONS OF GLOBAL LEADERSHIP

DEALING WITH MULTIPLE PERSPECTIVES

H. Peter Dachler

ABSTRACT

The central argument of this chapter deals with the concern that global leadership cannot be a simple extension of traditional local leadership conceptions that seek to discover some additionally required traits and expected behaviors to accommodate the added complexity of dealing with different cultures. The theoretical focus of global leadership needs to address the complexity of context in which managers and other kinds of leaders find themselves when confronted with different cultures and new kinds of questions, ambiguities, difficulties, confusions, and other unaccustomed situations and events that are thereby implied. Traditional, individual-oriented conceptions of leadership have, for the most part, viewed global leadership as a problem of how individual leaders can adjust and accommodate to the requirements of other cultures from the experiences, understandings, habits, and so forth, that they have learned in their own cultures. Typically this has involved the processes of train-

Advances in Global Leadership, Volume 1, pages 75-98.
Copyright © 1999 by JAI Press Inc.
All rights of reproduction in any form reserved.
ISBN: 0-7623-0505-3

ing leaders in foreign languages, in understanding special features of other cultures, and in learning methods of behavior in foreign cultures that do not embarrass, hurt, or challenge people in the indigenous cultures. Often such training also involves ways in which global leaders can change indigenous understandings of organizational events and requirements that are viewed as primitive, as in need of modernization, and not in line with the business requirements of the mother company. This approach certainly has been shown to have its benefits. However, from an explanatory and practical point of view it ignores or devalues the most fundamental aspect of global leadership. The only reason why global leadership need be differentiated from local leadership is that its central meaning and function derives from dealing with the social-relational processes by which different cultural understandings of reality, of that which counts and is seen as normal, natural, rational, and ethical, are realized. (One could, of course, argue that even in local leadership situations such social-relational processes are the fundamental issues). Thus, communication, mutual understanding or misunderstanding, conflict, trust, prejudgments, and power in determining what is or is not acceptable (in other words relational processes) are at the heart of the meaning of global leadership—not individual attributes, cultural knowledge about "dos and don'ts," and prescribed behavioral patterns.

This chapter assumes the view that the dynamic complexity of context within which global leaders find themselves concerns the fundamental problem of understanding and dealing with multiple perspectives. The majority of approaches to global leadership implicitly adhere to the particularly Western idea of basic truths, of finding what is objectively factual, and, therefore, of perceiving different perspectives as leading to a competitive process of deciding what is right or wrong, true or false. This chapter outlines an alternative epistemological perspective: relational theory. An account of leadership as a social-relational process is developed that attempts to deal with multiple points of view, taking into account multiple voices, representing different but equally 'reasonable' interests, values, and logic. Suggestions are made regarding ways in which such leadership processes may be developed and put into practice. The chapter concludes with the suggestion that, depending on what kind of implicit epistemological assumptions we base our understanding of global leadership, very different consequences, some of which have far reaching ethical implications, make sense and, therefore, lead to very different realities of leadership and organizational life in multicultural contexts.

INTRODUCTION

One of the first questions that the concept of global leadership raises is whether and how it differs from what is traditionally referred to as "local" leadership and management theory. This chapter attempts to show that global leadership, if it is to have any useful meaning at all, cannot be simply an extension of local leadership perspectives with the addition of further situational, value, economic, cultural, and societal variables. Nor can the concept of global leadership warrant the idea that effective leaders demonstrate certain cross-culturally valid attributes and behaviors and that these generalized leadership patterns, if identified, can serve as a basis for defining global leadership. Global leadership, above all, involves issues that are central to the challenges faced by the globalization of our world. It is here submitted that these issues refer to some of the important determinants of whether we can realize the enormous potential of globalization, or whether the irreversible globalization process that we have set in motion will be a major factor in the demise of our world order.

This chapter takes the view that global leadership has to do with knowledge processes, with issues that ask questions about how to deal with, understand, and accept multiple perspectives (rather than seeking one correct or true logic) and multiple voices (rather than warranting one authoritative, "powerful," and most "effective" voice). In other words, global leadership addresses the urgent problem of how to understand and deal with being confronted with values, views, investments, and practices of those "not quite like us" in ways that we have never before experienced. Dominant perspectives of leadership and management theory focus on a set of individual attributes and behaviors, always ambiguously defined, and their interactions with an equally ambiguous set of situational variables as the origin of effective leadership and management (Calas & Smircich, 1988; Dachler, 1988; Dachler & Hosking, 1995). In contrast, global leadership can be understood as raising questions about listening to and taking seriously other standpoints, generating mutual understanding, avoiding misunderstandings and "meaning vacuums" that lead to fundamental conflicts, and building appreciation and tolerance as a basic requirement for realizing the potential of globalization (Cooperrider, Barrett, & Srivastva, 1995). In other words, the challenges of global leadership point to relational-social-societal processes (as contrasted to individual attributes), which provide the basis for organizational learning processes and continual transformation, for the generation of yet unknown possibilities and expansion of our understanding of the world, and for the construction of "realities" of mutual trust and growth through relational or communicative processes.

The preceding emphasis in global leadership may well be understood as somewhat idealistic and, therefore, not very "realistic" or efficient. Nevertheless, it is interesting to note the frequent and often urgent appeal for such "ideals" from many different directions. This leaves us with the perplexing question of why all of these well-intended appeals by business, economic, political, and governmental, not to mention religious and humanistic, ethical, and social institutions, have such a minute effect and are given so little credence in the everyday world. I would like to suggest that the problem lies in the process of seeking change "for the better" by increasing our efforts to continue doing what we have always done, namely to convince ourselves and others of the necessity to be more tolerant, understanding, fair, and mutually respectful. In fact, however, the structures and social processes that fundamentally contradict these appeals stay in place and are taken for granted. For example, as long as we start with the idea that individual leaders are Subjects who essentially influence, and shape their coworkers according to their interests and values, as if they were Objects in need of leading, the idea of a less competitive world with a greater understanding and development of mutuality will remain unrealistic and inefficient (Sampson, 1985). As long as we focus the problem on the historically and deep-seated questions regarding what is essential about the individual and what needs to be changed about the individual, we will inevitably end up doing "more of the same" (Watzlawick, Weakland, & Fisch, 1974) or endlessly perpetuating the status quo in a time when change and flexibility are *the* hallmarks of our world. By attributing problems to the individual's intelligence, personality, cultural norms, motivation, abilities, and so on, we ignore, misunderstand, or devalue fundamental social processes as uninteresting and "unrealistic," by which we know, feel, and understand (as well as misunderstand or inappropriately attribute meaning) in the context of the complex and many-layered webs of relations that constitute daily practice (Dachler & Hosking, 1995). If we begin with assumptions regarding leaders as entities whose nature or essence needs to be discovered, we limit ourselves to answers that are framed in terms of the effects that entitatively understood social-organizational factors have upon that nature. The picture we have constructed of the isolated, self-sufficient individual leader neatly serves the purpose of our current economic and social structure (Sampson, 1985, 1990). Such ingrained assumptions, underlying values and interests leave unexplored in the concept of global leadership what it means that above all, humans are "social animals," not isolated entities that interact with each other based on the attributes and behavioral potentials that define what is essential about their nature.

In a real sense this commonly accepted representation of leadership depoliticizes the social problems inherent in the practice of leadership by placing them at the level of the individual psyche (as is the "tradition" in psychology in general). In current leadership and management theory, politics, if it is discussed at all, takes on a rather minor role; a role usually thought of as restrictive to the success and efficiency of both individuals and organizations. And paradoxically, this happens even though it is our daily experience that politics in leadership and management is one of the core aspects of the practice and the consequences of these areas. The status quo is maintained because we find it very difficult to explicitly reflect on the way current leadership stories become plausible whereas other potentially useful but contradictory stories are felt to make little sense. It becomes difficult to realize how, in trying to make sense of the leadership narratives that we are told, we (as well as those who tell leadership stories) must rely on a vast array of implicit assumptions, values, feelings, and symbols available in society, which are reproduced and continually reconstructed during the course of narration and enactment.

As various writers (e.g., Dachler & Hosking, 1995; Gergen, 1993; Vaassen, 1996) have argued, based on Derrida's (1978) writings, the identity of any object of our consciousness lies not simply in that object itself but also in all the things it is not—in its absence as well as its presence. To say what global leadership is, is also to say what it is not. However, in any differentiation, such as leadership as an individual problem as contrasted with leadership as a social process, one view always receives a more privileged position than its "opposite." We are invited, for example, to believe that an individual definition of leadership has more "explanatory" value (is more "real") than that which the individual understanding of leadership excludes—for instance, leadership as a collective process of creating a "local reality." As we shall see, neither understanding makes sense without the other. Following the suggestion of these writers, we try to adopt an inference of supplement rather than one of contrast.

CHALLENGES AND POTENTIAL IMPLIED BY GLOBAL LEADERSHIP

Challenges to Euro-Centered Understandings of Leadership and Its Practices

A vast array of emerging technologies has introduced the world to greater interdependence and intimacy than ever before. Through the ensuing economic "pressures" for globalization of business and social life, the world confronts aims, agendas, and requirements that are very often difficult to understand outside the perspectives of a particular culture. More problematic, perhaps, is the realization that in many respects some of an indigenous culture's central assumptions and presumed views about work and economic institutions, as well as the validity in meaning of a vast array of formal and everyday actions, are called into question (Indian Institute of Management, 1996).

For instance, international Western businesses are at times confronted with the prioritization of religious practices and customs during working hours, within business organizations and in daily business practices; issues that are not central, and if at all relevant, in the daily competition for organizational survival in the Western world. In certain Asian countries management and leadership are understood to have moral and ethical bases unknown or not well understood by western companies (see Hui & Tan, this volume). Understandings of efficiency and effectiveness can differ widely in different cultures and regions. And, something nearly completely ignored by the "privileged," Euro-centered understandings of work and organization, is the degree to which these privileged understandings "pathologize" the knowledge, identity, and general understandings of indigenous cultures. In addition, of course, are the multiple differences in meaning and social appropriateness of certain concepts, words, expressions, clothing, and so on. In certain circumstances all of these factors have proven to contain great potential for misreading the meaning of a message. These are contexts in which actors-in-relation are seen as acting inappropriately, leading to conflict or at least to one party (or both) feeling embarrassment, shame, anger, or loss of face. It is not unusual to find that being shamed or made to lose face (identity) results in violence or abject withdrawal.[1]

Such issues are common in literature referencing how to deal or not to deal with indigenous cultures. And naturally, leaders and managers situated cross-culturally are caught in the middle of these paradoxes, experience difficulties in understanding, and face great ambiguity with regard to what social "realities" they might use to orient themselves as well as others in the daily and strategically oriented business process. Effective solutions to such problems, which increasingly present themselves in this globalized world, could contribute considerably toward realizing the dream of a global village. At the very least, such solutions could reduce the potentially devastating conflicts that arise among cultures with very different histories, religious and ideological orientations, cultural assumptions, and narratives relative to what is natural, normal, rational and "real."

It is understandable, from a Euro-centered perspective, to think of these issues within the individual realm and, therefore, come up with solutions that in one way or another are aimed at changing the "contents" of individuals' minds. Along these lines, global leaders are instructed how to communicate; act; dress; make decisions; impose; give in; develop their pricing, marketing, and product policies; and so on when dealing with other cultures. But although such an individually oriented approach may help reduce problems in the short run, in the long run—particularly with respect to the potential of global leadership—many crucial questions are left open, ignored, and in some sense, devalued as not relevant or not efficient. As Burr (1995, p. 101) states:

> We are invited to place value upon the lone, self-contained individual who is capable of making his or her own decisions regardless of the opinions of others, a person whose sense of morality is firmly located within his or her own mind and is not susceptible to outside influence, a person whose sense of himself or herself comes from an internally located, stable and integrated identity, and who does not have to fall back upon the regard of the group for his or her self-esteem.

By locating the intercultural understanding problem at the individual level, we acquire limited help in understanding the countless ways in which individuals and groups are embedded in a vast array of social relationships, all serving as somewhat different contexts in which a given understanding, action, or utterance takes on different meanings. The social processes, the role of language in the creation of meaning, and deep-seated notions such as leadership, power, control, and creating order in historically grown narratives within a culture out of which certain meanings of social action (but not others) become possible, are ignored. By receiving little or no attention within the presumed understanding of leadership as an individual phenomenon, all of these issues remain an unrealized potential of global leadership. Global leadership must also focus on social process questions because they serve its longer term potential by giving center stage to the issues of global transformation and mutual understanding. In a very real sense, an entitative, individualistic understanding of leadership constructs a very different perception of the reality of leadership and its organizational context than does an understanding of leadership as a social process (Dachler & Hosking, 1995).

Understanding and Accepting the Possibilities of Multiple Perspectives

Another underlying narrative to which the common understanding of leadership refers is the Cartesian distinction between mind, nature, and body. In scientific as well as commonplace understanding, Person is separated from his or her body and the surrounding nature by a knowing mind. Western consciousness understands Person as Subject who seeks to know other outside Objects according to his or her interests, pre-understandings, values, ideologies, and so forth. In that sense, he or she creates order in the "objective" world (including other people and groups) according to his or her rationale of order and predictability, and according to the understanding of his or her identity and that of the surrounding world. Individuals possess intelligence, personality, motivation, values, needs, and genetic tendencies for various traits (e.g., aggressiveness) (Lorenz, 1966) and, therefore, understand themselves and others as having intentions that are the ultimate origin of their actions and the intended consequences.

When we are confronted with other (often contradictory) meanings of actions, events, or circumstances, the central issue becomes one of determining which understanding (knowledge) best represents the nature of some ultimate standard of truth (i.e., the objective world as contrasted to subjective beliefs or fantasies). Leaders, according to our collective understanding as well as the way most leadership theories account for their stories, understand themselves to be leaders by an implicit assumption that there is a "reality" out there (e.g., subordinates who are not sufficiently motivated or who cannot be successful if he or she does not work more than 8 hours a day). They take this "reality" to be a version of events that is more valid or truthful than alternative understandings, which they cannot even consider to be "real" since they are less valid versions of that which they actually confront. Such alternative narratives or constructed realities could refer to coworkers as the leader's team colleagues, or those who assume responsibility for team tasks of their own initiative, not necessarily in the manner chosen by the leader. Alternatively, successful leaders could be viewed as those who accomplish tasks at work but view their greatest responsibility to be for their family's quality of life. Therefore, they require the time and energy necessary to help out at home with the kids and household chores. The central idea is that there is one version of events that is true, or most "reasonable," thus making all others false or less reasonable. The idea that an effective leader works more than the required number of hours is more likely to be understood as reasonable within the context of current Western assumptions, than the idea that an effective leader sets equal priorities for his or her work and familial responsibilities. There is always a search for the right, correct, and true interpretation of oneself and one's actions, and the actions and attributes of others with whom one is in relationship, as if the psychic origin of our intentions can be assessed "objectively." This is the process by which science, as well as the average person, tries to understand the one true, correct, natural, and normal "identity" of some event, circumstance, or object (Gergen, 1993; Parker, 1992; Shotter, 1993).

This essentialist understanding of the individual and his or her knowledge is one of the central limitations in realizing the potential of global leadership. If such explanations are to be useful with respect to understanding global leadership, then how is it possible to conduct business with organizations and people in very different cultures without encountering fundamental difficulties and contradictions? For reasons to be discussed later, it is impossible, or at least rather unrealistic, for Western individuals to attempt to accept indigenous perspectives as their own reality and, therefore, to have such altered understandings determine meaningful actions and what narratives provide the "logic" for those actions and assessments of events in that culture. Western, Euro-centered understandings of the world take their views as "privileged," creating a context in which indigenous perspectives often make little sense. Business organizations and international leaders and managers could not function in such a context because they would have to give up their identity and the Western definition of economics and doing business.

What is more likely to happen is that the privileged Euro-centered views and perspectives are considered the most reasonable, the most natural, and historically the most successful, "truths." It is through such constructed meaning that (1) the power of the privileged perspective is maintained; (2) indigenous understandings are minimalized as unnatural, unethical, or outdated; and (3) Western culture continues to colonize, and essentially destroy in the long run, much of the existing indigenous languages, knowledge, and values—if they have not already been reduced by Western cultural and economic imperialism to insignificance or cultural remnants. How can we find answers to such fundamental questions by focusing on the attributes leaders should have and the manner in which they should behave?

It is important to note that in the preceding arguments, Western power holders' "intentions" are not implied. Such groups are not represented as getting together with the aim of subjugating the rest of the world. In fact, such a narrative makes little sense within a social process perspective. An explanation of intentional actions by individuals alone, or in groups, is persuasive only if one refers to the individualistic, entitative narratives previously outlined. The argument developed in this chapter is such that what we understand as "Western imperialism" (either as an intentional act of powerful individuals or as a process of social construction) develops from the commonplace narratives, available in a culture at a given point in its history, which are implicitly referenced when talking (thinking) about the meaning of imperialism. It is not surprising then, that Western international organizations would not likely understand their activities as "imperialism." Note that this does not imply that "anything goes" in constructing the meaning of "imperialism" or any other "object" of understanding. Some meanings are "nonsense" by virtue of the "fact" that the narratives to which they refer (e.g., individuals, including leaders, are the result of an industrial production process in some alien society) are not commonly available within a particular culture. Moreover, a particular understanding is experienced as stable in meaning and real via the process of talking (thinking) about it when relating to others within a common language. Some tell similar stories (helping to cement a particular understanding, the "reality" of "we"), whereas others tell "different" stories that in some crucial ways question and make more ambiguous the "local" understandings (the "reality" of "we" versus "they"). In a particular community of understanding (e.g., the sales department, women in a particular organization, top management, foreigners in a plant, union members, and so on), there exist social processes through which the daily exchange of narratives about what is real and normal derive their meaning from (mostly implicit) referencing processes to commonly available assumptions and understandings in the particular context of the "group." In this way, social constructive processes develop identity and "stability" in the community of understanding, its members, and their differentiation from other understanding communities (e.g., for women, the males in an organization; for top management, the various outside stakeholders as well as managers at "lower" levels in the management hierarchy).

It is important to recognize that within such a view of knowledge development, the identity of a community of understanding (also referred to as a language community) is, despite its seeming stability, always in the process of reconstruction (justification, reaffirmation) as well as of change (deconstruction). Gergen (1995) refers to this process as "centripedal" forces. Slow but continuous change transpires as the boundaries of a language community become fuzzy with respect to the identities of other language communities. For example, the "reality" of women in an organization slowly changes in relationships or "negotiations" with men. This reality also changes through references to increasingly different narratives about the problems encountered with the "exclusivity" of the female-male distinction, which does not consider many "realities in between" (e.g., lesbians, "feminine" men, black women).

As previously discussed, the concept of what something is must also include what it is not; also, the identity of any community of understanding depends on a certain relationship with the identity of other language communities representing that which it is not. Thus, the reality of a community of understanding is not of its own "making," but instead results from the manner in which other language communities coordinate with it. Such coordination can be, on the one hand, more or less a reaffirmation of the identity of the "local group" (thus becoming part of "buying into" the reality of the "local" community of understanding). On the other hand, there are always some communities of understanding whose identities are what the "local group" is not. Central aspects of the reality (what is normal) of such a "counter-identity group" call into question, or view as unrealistic or dangerous, central aspects of the identity of the "local group." Gergen (1995) refers to such processes as "centrifugal." Such divergent understandings are, therefore, experienced as a mutual "critique" by the interacting "language communities." As Gergen (1995) attempts to illustrate, the result is a process by which the privileged language community inappropriately generalizes its understandings of what is real and true to other cultures or to other communities of understanding. In summary, what any group of understanding, including the members that view themselves as leaders, believes to be its "reality," or what they see as normal, logical, and what legitimates and gives meaning to their actions, is always a process of constructing communality, as well as deconstructing, changing and transforming the status quo.

The social processes outlined in this chapter appear to tell a story that essentially makes our experiences normal and "unavoidable." By definition, what we take to be true and valid must also be true and normal for others, if only they could understand and accept our view as the truth. This is the central challenge as well as the enormous potential of global leadership; or, in other words, an attempt to answer the question of how we can understand and effectively deal with a "reality" of multiple perspectives rather than search for one correct, true, and "obvious" answer, which leads to understanding one version as true, thus making all others basically wrong.

In many different areas of scientific, philosophical, and general literary discourse, often summarized under the label of "postmodernism" or "social constructionism" (Gergen, 1994; Sarup, 1988), it is becoming increasingly clear that a great deal of caution is necessary with respect to the prevailing idea that our observations of the world unerringly yield its nature to us. In other words, the view, so strongly embedded in our history, that conventional knowledge is based upon objective, unbiased observation of the world is being challenged. Notions of truth, of objective fact, are becoming intensely problematic, given the increasing realization that what we take to be real and normal is actually history- and culture-specific. The categories with which we apprehend the world, so neatly packaged in our language (such as leadership and followership, male and female, apples and dogs, fact and fancy) do not necessarily refer to real divisions of that world. We divide up the potential "knowledge space" in ways that make sense in our historical experience, the possibilities of our language, and currently available cultural narratives. All knowledge is derived from looking at the world from one perspective or another and serves certain interests over others. Clearly, the way we commonly think about leadership and management would make little sense (would not be "known") in a time and culture described as an agrarian or a nomadic society. And whether such notions of leadership and management make sense in many non-Western cultures is questionable.

Management and leadership make sense and are experienced as "reality," something known and factual, based on the time and the Western, industrialized world in which we currently live. All means of knowledge are historically and culturally relative. It has been impossible to find a fundamental way to warrant the prevalent idea that Western, Euro-centered ways of defining the world are necessarily better or closer to the truth than other ways. It should be clear that the view of cultural and historical relativism is itself a social construction, an alternative set of assumptions, within which one can make sense of the world. Therefore, we cannot debate whether the entitative, individualistic view of leadership or a social constructionist understanding is more or less correct, factual, and rational. But if we accept the idea of multiple realities, we can try to find agreement about accounts of leadership in the context of globalization that seem more useful, more normal and "rational" with respect to certain projects (e.g., enabling the understanding of perspectives different from our own). The crucial message is also that we cannot find a generalized way to authorize a particular understanding as the truth and the only truth. Therefore, there exists a world of multiple (and potentially equally plausible) perspectives, a world that we need to understand and accept, and in which we have to learn to live effectively.

At this point we encounter one of the central questions of this chapter. To what extent does a reference to "multiple realities" allow us to construct an understanding of the world that is more in line with an explicitly stated (and valued) project concerning globalization, and the role of global leadership with respect to that project? By discussing the potential of global leadership, we refer to a project that aims to help in constructing (understanding) a globalization process in the interest of avoiding (or at least reducing) destructive conflicts, as we have experienced throughout our history. The potential of globalization and leadership in that process lies in enhancing the quality of life defined in ways that seem meaningful within an indigenous culture, rather than one defined primarily from a Western perspective.

If, in contrast, one understands the goals of Western civilization as methods to culturally dominate the rest of the world by referring to the endless success of Western thought and understandings, including the triumph of its science and technology, then currently referenced Western narratives provide a neatly packaged legitimization of the generally accepted aim to "help" in "modernizing" the rest of the world with respect to Western interests, values, and notions about what are desirable and normal ways of living, acting, and doing business. What one constructs as normal and rational also gives meaning to the social actions in which one engages, including the legitimization of the consequences that derive from them.

We now have an important example of what was earlier described as the implicit and inappropriate generalization of a "privileged" perspective to other indigenous language communities. But this can be the case only if one takes for granted that (1) there can only be one truth, and (2) what appears to provide the stability and normality of the "realities" in Western thought must also be true for other cultures. Within such commonplace attitudes, it is difficult to consider the idea that Western definitions of success, in all its various forms, is not something "objectively" given, but instead a historically grown, Euro-culturally developed understanding. In other cultures, different realities have developed specific to those histories and cultures. The central point being made is that there is always a judgmental project implicit (often explicitly symbolized in various forms) in a certain way of constructing reality. But, contrary to seeking universal, globally realistic, and normal projects (e.g., Küng, 1997),[2] which can only be an illusion within the current arguments, the central question to be addressed is the extent to which prevalent assumptions and culturally available narratives that are being referenced are sensible or useful for the project under consideration. In that sense, the meaning of a project is always under social construction.

In light of the previous discussion, it may be possible to move toward an understanding of why the rhetoric with regard to tolerance, global understanding, and peace through learning from each other is given little meaning (not experienced as very "realistic") in the daily activities of individual leaders in business and government. The narratives that build the context in which common daily activities receive their meaning, tell very different and contradictory stories. In these stories, understandings such as being stronger and quicker will win competitions, withholding information for strategic and personal identity reasons, blaming others as "causes" for failure, and keeping relational and emotional distance in order to be seen as rational (not a "softy") and more effective, are given "reality," and legitimized as normal and natural. This kind of thinking is what restricts or even threatens the potential of that which global leadership could symbolize and accomplish.

A World with Multiple, Dominant, and Marginalized Voices

Within the context of understanding leadership as an individual phenomenon, and the aforementioned descriptions of how we normally talk about individual knowledge, understanding, and agency, two crucial processes experienced repeatedly in leadership in interindividual as well as intergroup relations, take on central meaning in understanding social relations. One is the process of blaming, of locating the cause in the attributes and actions of individuals or groups. The other is the ubiquitous value placed on the notion of competition and dominance. As previously discussed, the individualistic, essentialist understanding of Person and social interactions begins with the assumption that Person's intentions, aims, logic, and valuations of the ensuing actions are determined based on the attributes of Person in interaction with attributes of his or her situational context. In social interactions these assumptions are applied to all of the interacting individuals. From such underlying understandings a number of consequences follow.

First, is that Person sees him- or herself as Subject in the sense of experiencing him- or herself as the origin of his or her intentions and actions. Intentions and actions originate from the possession of certain knowledge, from often implicit assumptions about one's "personality" attributes, skills, emotions, values, motives, and so on. And, of course, the same kind of understanding of identity is also attributed to the others with whom one interacts. In the context of such an understanding of Person, the meaning of the interaction itself can be understood only by referencing the attributes and behaviors of the interacting partners. Whether a social relation is understood by one or both partners as a competitive, caring or trusting relationship, as one in which one individual or group is trying to use power to influence his or her opposite to do something that the opposite would not otherwise do, or as a relationship characterized by mutual growth, depends on what each of the interacting partners is understood to be and observed to be doing. Implicitly, the meaning of the interaction itself can be only a form of causal influence process initiated by the attributes and behaviors of the interacting partners. As a consequence, the process of interpreting the meaning of a relationship often results in some form of "blaming" individuals involved in the interactions, since their intentions and actions are thought to be a function of their attributes. Thus, in understanding Person as the origin of his or her actions, the "cause" for his or her behavior is sought in one or the other or both of the interacting individuals. Since the meaning of actions are always in and of themselves ambiguous, the search for causes and designation of blame or positive impact invariably constructs a process of "mutual accusation" as well as mutual defensiveness (Argyris, 1982).

As has been implied earlier, the reality of a positively assessed person derives its meaning from the reality of the characteristics and behaviors of actors that are viewed as negative. For example, in positively evaluating a person as showing commitment by towing the company line, "towing the company line" becomes a positive attribute in differentiation from a person who is, for example, "blamed" for creatively playing the devil's advocate in questioning certain aspects of the company's account of events. Thus, mutual accusation and defensiveness are also implied in the instance of a positive causal attribution to a person. When the cause of a "positive" impact in a relationship is attributed to the characteristics of an individual, his or her "hero" attributes invariably imply the characteristics of "non-heros" in the same context. Effective leaders and our understanding of the attributes that "make" them effective implicitly "blame" those who are not leaders, those who do not possess those attributes (e.g., have "wrong," ineffective attributes) and therefore need to be guided and formed. As can now be more easily understood, these dynamics very quickly lead to the search for the correct, the true, and the most reasonable or "factual" attribution to individuals. Somebody must be the perpetrator, the instigator, or the aggressor, the hero, the savior, the "transformational leader," the unimaginative one, the careless one, the one with little or less intelligence, the one with the "wrong" attitudes. All of these descriptions of individuals, commonly used in trying to explain a relationship and its "outcomes," make sense only by reference to certain determining attributes of one or both individuals (or groups). The process becomes a game without end, one that usually can be interrupted only by the use of some form of power, a topic to which the discussion will return later. To the extent that leadership is understood in such entitative, individualistic terms, the potential of global leadership is very much restricted. The project of constructing a world with a different understanding of quality of life, characterized by less contradiction and more mutual understanding and growth, is endangered. It becomes fundamentally impossible to conceive (consider realistic) the idea that in interactions there can be multiple voices, all of which can be heard, mutually respected, and understood as potentially realistic, based on the process by which they engage in discourse rather than on their attributes and intended behaviors.

Suppose we started to ask different types of questions, which, of course, make sense only in the context of a different understanding of Person and the social processes of knowing. We begin with the assumption that the identity of an individual, his or her belief that as Subject he or she is the origin of his or her intentions, feelings, and actions, can become "real" only when somebody coordinates with it, and on the basis of how that somebody coordinates with what that individual believes to be his or her "reality." For example: The chairman of the board of an international company is the last principal to come into the boardroom, which features a large, oval mahogany table. A secretary follows him, carrying his documents. He moves to take his seat at the head of the table. It is clear that from his perspective, he knows what needs to be done at this meeting. In his understanding of himself as chairman, he "knows" his intentions, which, among others, are to discuss, persuade, sell, convince, and, if necessary, force other board members to carry out the projects under discussion on the basis of what he believes to be the most efficient and effective strategy that he has developed with his staff. It is "factual" for him that, given his position and function, the most logical and most demonstrative place for him to sit is at the head of table, as has been the case for as long as he can remember. As he stops to shake hands with other board members and engages in some of the usual social niceties, a woman dressed in an elegant, flowing sari walks into the room very quietly and (seemingly) serenely and takes a seat at the head of the huge conference table. At the moment when the board members and their chairman notice what is happening, what all of them so clearly understood themselves to be doing and planning to do in the meeting as participants, is put into question.

Is this woman understood to be a representative from the World Health Organization who needs to inform the board of a terrible infectious disease that has broken out in some of their organizations across the world? An activist from a third world organization who wants to warn the board that a major strike is in the offing if certain changes are not instituted? An employee representative who wants to surprise the chairman or some board member by starting the meeting with a birthday celebration? Or a member of a feminist political action group who is intending to bring out in the open the way that women and children are exploited in some of the third world production facilities of this corporation? Whatever the reality, the "logic" of the chairman's and the board members' intentions and planned actions have in some significant ways changed. Invariably and naturally, the "reality" of this moment can be understood only through dialogue, by negotiating what is to be the common understanding between the elegant, sari-clad woman and the chairman and his board members. In this sense neither the chairman nor his board members are authors of what they see as their reality and intentions. Those individuals are always privileged or given meaning by the coordination of others.

Neither the chairman nor his board members can simply persevere with what had been their reality, and what they were fairly sure was the common understanding in the boardroom. At this time, that simply would not make any sense to anyone in the room. As the ensuing "multilogue" process takes its course, what was originally understood as the reality by all participants, including their emotions, is changing in significant ways. And within this discourse among various "voices" that speak about different (and often contradictory) understandings of what is going on, about what should be happening, about what they understand their relationship to be with the woman who "invaded" their sanctuary, the understanding of reality spoken by some of the voices becomes "privileged." They tell a story of what they interpret to be a "common" and realistic understanding, an understanding that makes sense with respect to certain mutually held assumptions available in that organization and in that particular culture. Other voices are not even heard, and still others are devalued as delivering unwarranted critique or nonsense (since their viewpoint derives its meaning as "critique" by reference to very different kinds of assumptions, interests, and values).

Rather than try to make sense of this example by searching for the participants' attributes and behaviors, we can ask how a claim to knowledge (what is the case in a given instance, what is real, logical, and so forth), including the meaning of a person's actions or the actions attributed to others, becomes "privileged" (i.e., is made "realistic" by the coordination of others and the cultural understandings that are being referenced). Similarly, it becomes possible to ask which social processes devalue or ignore other claims to knowledge.

The change in perspective suggested here is highly significant and has crucial consequences for daily action. The two types of "explanations" (in terms of individual attributes or in terms of social-relational construction processes), in the process of "telling their stories," help to construct two different kinds of realities, each establishing a different context for what is meaningful, sensible, and rational action and what is therefore inappropriate, abnormal, or irrational. In the individualistic reality, we would try to understand what attributes, reasons, power bases, and motives are held by the various actors. We would also take for granted that Person, understood as Subject who understands him- or herself as the origin of the meaning of his or her actions and intentions, also refers to that what Subject is not, namely Object. Object possesses those aspects not held by Subject. Object(ive) is what needs to be known by Subject, and changed and controlled according to Subject's interests, values, and fundamental understandings about what is to be reserved as truth. This would be the case if somebody were just observing the incident, or from the perspective of the individuals involved in these interactions. For example, the chairman will need to seek answers about the woman's identity. Is she a provocateur, dressed elegantly in an effort to get inside the boardroom, but in "fact" a person of low status, financially and otherwise? Is she a woman with a certain power base? Is she somebody of their own class, with similar interests and values? Or is she one of those "bleeding heart" women who simply cannot understand the realities of the brutal competition for organizational survival? Similarly, depending on the way the chairman relates to the people in the room, he and others will interpret what is going on by assigning certain personality attributes, social skills, diplomacy, or political acumen to the chairman or to other individuals with whom he interacts. The chairman could have the woman more or less forcibly removed from his seat or from the room, he could carry on a conversation with the woman and other board members without taking his "chair" at the head of the table, or he could show concern or willingness to change the agenda of the meeting. With each of these possibilities the principal actors would be understood as having different attributes and "reasons" for their actions.

As writers such as Gergen (1994) and others (e.g., Potter & Wetherell, 1987) have demonstrated, there is no way to warrant any particular interpretation of which attribute and which meaning of an action is "objectively" correct or true. There is always another story to which one can make reference so that a different personal characteristic can be understood as the "cause" for an intention and action. However, from a practical point of view, more important are the consequences of a particular understanding of reality in the development of useful and sensible solutions. From an entitative, individualistic perspective, the solutions, whatever they may be, will necessarily be in the realm of individual attributes and behaviors. Based on the blaming and defending process discussed earlier, individuals need to be exchanged, punished, or provided with knowledge, training, and socialization, financially rewarded or dismissed, and so forth, in order to solve the particular "construction" of the problem. Conflict needs to be resolved by determining the guilty party(ies), which then must be removed or changed for the "better," within the logic of the privileged voice. Or one will try to explain to oneself, the group, or outsiders that the actions taken are normal, understandable, ethical, and correct on the basis of certain attributes of the principal actors or the group they represent, and in light of the common project—that is, what are taken to be rationally warranted aims, interests, values, and goals attributed to the company, as if the company is also a (legally defined) individual actor.

Within the "socially constructed reality" of a social-relational perspective, very different questions are asked (questions that hardly make sense from an individualistic perspective). Correspondingly, very different "solutions" come into focus, and different actions become meaningful and can be understood as "real," normal, and logical. The focus is on what is being communicated within the various relationships. What are the different stories and assumptions to which the various actors make reference in their interactions? To what extent does the woman in the "all-powerful male" bastion of a board meeting make reference to the firmly established narrative about women's perspectives being less valued in the tough and rational practice of top decision making in business? To what extent does that make her feel insecure, defensive, or vulnerable—out of which the meaning attributed to her communications may be one of "aggressiveness"? Or to what extent does her understanding make reference to stories about an already lost cause, about the masculine perspective not being able to hear her unless she gains access to similar stories of power, as in the masculine world? To what extent can the chairman and other board members come to understand how, from their privileged perspectives so entrenched in the Western cultures, they take for granted themselves as Subject, and in order to be able to understand themselves as Subject, they see others as Objects. Object would mean something (someone) who is, relative to Subject, less active, less in control, less knowledgeable, less independently motivated and, therefore, requiring influence and change for the better for his or her own sake and for the sake of the Subject-defined order. How, in current understandings of leadership, can a leader perceive him- or herself as a leader, if there is no "counter-reality" that in some form or another indicates "non-leader"—or, in other words, perceptions that are implicitly meaningful in our language as Objects, essentially as people differentiated from the leader as "followers," or as non-leaders, who require leadership in one way or another? Otherwise, how can we understand as meaningful and even talk about the concept of leadership or management?

With respect to the earlier example of the chairman, questions about relationships as "origins" of understanding now come into focus. For example, to what extent do the chairman and his colleagues perceive the sari-clad woman as blaming them for certain deplorable states of affairs, which in their understanding make perfect sense by reason of economic narratives or technical rationality? Or to what extent can the chairman reflect on his assumptions about women in general, and the sari-clad woman in particular? Might he, for example, be able to recognize the possibility of his biased assumptions in which a sari is clothing worn by third world, usually "uneducated" (according to Western understandings of being educated), and low-status women? Or is it possible that he constructs an understanding of his relationship with her as a well-meaning patriarch who knows what is best for her, and from that knowledge attempts to "help" her (in terms of his own understandings and fundamental interests, not hers) so that he get on with "more" important business as quickly as possible? Obviously there are numerous ways that one could concoct a persuasive narrative about the reality of these relationships. The aim, however, is not to try to choose which story is the most reasonable or the most correct, since that would invariably lead to the "blaming" and defensiveness processes discussed earlier, and could in principle never be warranted on the basis of "objective" criteria. Instead, the aim is to address exactly those questions, which in current understandings are considered taboo or not very realistic. The kind of questions regarding commonplace assumptions, the referenced stories available in the given context, the different interpretations of what is happening, and the possible underlying "preconceptions," which the boardroom story attempted to illustrate, must become the focus in attempting to understand interaction processes. However, this is possible only by taking leave of the conviction that the meaning of interactions lies in talk about factual (as contrasted with emotional) things about what is objectively true (independent of the social interaction processes).

What becomes important is to understand the relational or communicative processes by which certain kinds of understandings are developed with regard to what counts and what is real. Many other equally possible understandings are difficult to see, are not considered as being relevant, and in that sense, cannot be perceived as "real." Moreover, the issue of whose viewpoint or voice is heard and whose is muted is of central concern. These long neglected issues carry enormous practical implications. They open up new possibilities of developing creative and transforming solutions. From the focus of maintaining the status quo, fundamental change is of central interest by giving attention to the ways in which understandings come about and are changed in their social "production." Also of importance is the quest for ways in which common understandings can be realized in ways that do not, from the beginning, mute certain possibilities in the context of a privileged point of view, which is taken for granted to be the correct one. It is important for organizations to overcome the "dominant logic," which preserves the status quo and silences voices for change, and for more meaningful approaches to common projects. With respect to the theme of this chapter, perhaps of primary significance is the possibility of learning to know (and therefore relate) in ways that result in mutual growth, rather than being a winner with the "best" understanding of what counts. We can become sensitive to the relational "work" that is necessary for maintaining transformative processes regarding respect for others, tolerance, and taking other opinions seriously. All appear to be necessary for organizations to help build a less conflicting world and a "mutual understanding" culture—without which they will be unable to survive in a globalized world in the long run.

THE CENTRAL MEANING OF RELATIONAL "WORK"

Thus far this chapter has tried to illustrate to what extent the potential of global leadership cannot depend on additional personal attributes of individual global leaders, or in more effective personal skills that global leaders must learn as individuals. One could even argue that global leadership makes little sense with respect to an individual manager. Why would we need the concept of global leadership if it is understood as nothing more than a manager of an internationally active organization? One interpretation of global leadership that is certainly easily available is that of another attribute, title ("I am a global leader"), and so forth, by which individual managers can attribute more importance to their point of view, and in the process, contribute to the muting of voices. As has been argued to this point, if global leadership is to have a fundamentally different meaning from what is currently understood as "local" leadership, we must start with different foundations of understanding, work with different basic assumptions, and be willing to accept as meaningful a project in which transformation toward "different" realities and possibilities is of central concern, rather than implicitly reconstructing, maintaining, and legitimizing the status quo. The discussion that follows attempts to specifically address what may be some of the "preconditions" that need to be considered in order to better realize the potential of global leadership as defined in this chapter.

In general, these preconditions refer to issues having to do with "relational work." Although relational work is talked about often, and is the topic of many research projects, books, and articles, it is here submitted that for the most part, relational work has been addressed by defining it as an individual issue. Relational work usually concerns how the interacting partners (individuals, groups, or nations) ought to act, and the wide array of personal attributes, as well as mental and psychic contents, that should be emphasized in order to achieve effective and mutually beneficial relationships. Consequently, the relational process is more or less taken for granted in the sense that a given understanding of a relationship is viewed as relatively stable based on the relative stable attributes of the interacting partners and, therefore, on the basis of relatively predictable behavior. For example, it is commonly assumed that being "head over heels in love" is a relational state that, as wonderful as it may be, will become less intense or even wear off as partners become used to each other over time (or in a way, take each other's attributes and ways of acting for granted). Romantic love is thus a kind of relationship that has somehow evolved and will, after a while, lose its original meaning, a situation about which the partners can do relatively little. On the other hand, an understanding of relationships as a social construction process of mutually known realities focuses on the enormous amount of work that is required if relationships are to have permanence in meaning, in the sense of not "wearing thin" but in a continuous development process. This means that one must proceed on the assumption that through commitment to relational work, the meaning of relationships continues to grow and becomes more extensively known with all the ensuing construction of emotions having to do with mutual trust, respect, and fundamental equality.

The Power to Enable

The preceding discussion has tried to demonstrate that in the Subject-Object understanding of relationships, power is most likely understood as "power over." Another seldom addressed definition of power is one that has been described as "power to" (Gergen, 1995). Rather than beginning with the commonplace view of being author and architect of the meaning of one's understanding of reality, and implicitly generalizing that reality to interaction partners with different or even conflicting perspectives of what counts and is real in a particular situation, one could start from a different "starting point." One could ask what the common project of a relationship is, and to what extent the implicit assumptions of the inter-acting partners, their version of the story, help or hinder such a project. Thus, rather than thinking of how, as Subject, one can structure the world of Objects with respect to one's own perspective, the goal becomes one of finding the common meanings and understandings on the basis of which sensible and meaningful actions are possible with respect to the common project. In other words, the search is for the power to define what is the case within a group, or what has been called a community of understanding, and the actions that become meaningful and acceptable in that context, as well as the actions that are not acceptable in that con-text and are experienced as irrational, unnatural, and abnormal. Given that the meaning of any state of affairs always depends on that which it is and is not, "power to" is determined not only in the eyes of individual actors (individual, group, organization), but more importantly with respect to the "opposite" and the mutual coordination processes. Therefore, "power to" implies mutual enabling, or mutually constructing of that which counts and represents what is real for all part-ners in relationship.

From Dominance to Fundamental Equality or Partnership

Although the idea of mutual enabling is often called for and addressed in books with respect to the reduction of conflicts and misunderstandings, in some sense it raises a fundamental paradox. To the extent that one starts out from the dominant narrative about individual agency, Subject-Object differentiation, and the resulting meaning of power as "power over," enabling oneself is an understanding that per-fectly fits this narrative. However, the implied differentiation from others with respect to one's own identity, as well as the fundamental reality of relationships based on competition, makes unrealistic and irrational the idea of enabling others to be in some sense "equals." How can one understand others within their logic as equally sensible, trustworthy, knowledgeable, and so forth, when one is in compe-tition with them, when one understands one's differentiation from others (who are in some sense that which one is not), and when one is confronted with claims to knowledge that obviously contradict what one holds to be true? Thus, while the idea of "we are all different but equal" is viewed as something that can be under-stood as a common project, it cannot easily become what is understood as normal and natural in the context of dominant, Western perspectives.

Let us now address what is perhaps as close as one can come to terming a meth-odology in relational constructionism. If (and that is a very big if) the common project is indeed to develop a mutual reality in which equality, fairness, mutual respect, and trust in the basic integrity of others make sense and are taken as nor-mal and natural, then one would have to (1) be able to work out the common implicit assumptions and culturally referenced narratives that legitimize and give meaning to "appropriate" social action, and (2) negotiate the extent to which the currently constructed reality hinders or helps this common project from becoming "real." Whereas on the one hand this "method" might appear too simplistic or abstract, it is worth noting the extent to which, in current understandings, it is nearly impossible to change the subject of a discussion from its "content" to the meaning of the relational processes at work. What would the "normal" reaction be, if during a meeting in which a new marketing strategy was being discussed, somebody suddenly asked a question regarding what was happening relationally during the discussion? Asked to reflect on what each participant's assumptions about him- or herself, about others, and about the kind of power, influence, implicit blaming, and defending processes might be, most likely the participants would regard the process as nonsensical, inefficient, and inappropriate. It is something that could be done in a leadership development seminar or when we are with our friends and spouses, but not when we have to address what is the most logical solution to our urgent problem among rational "men." Very likely the person asking this "stupid" question might well be blamed for disrupting the "factual" discussion and viewed as having some ulterior motive. Such reactions most likely emerge because traditional constructions make reference to a dichotomy between things factual, logical, rational, and objective (the world of hard facts) and things emotional, irrational, and subjective (the world of soft concerns, often considered feminine).

Within the aforementioned considerations, the issue of the prevailing dominance (power over) understandings of relationships, in contrast to a seemingly preferred world of partnership in the sense of a mutual understanding of "different but equal," cannot be dealt with at the individual level. Nor is it useful to attempt to make reference to discovering some underlying truth in a world independent of our language and historically culturally influenced preconceptions. The relational work required concerns the process of negotiating what kind of world "exists" (and one that we want it to be); that is, what is the actual common project. Relational work would also include "multiloguing" among participants in order to make explicit and "put on the table for discussion" the various assumptions and narratives, on the basis of which some social actions take on meaning and others are viewed as irrational and illogical. Overriding these questions is always the mutual determination of which voices (which viewpoints) are given privilege, or who the "storytellers" are, depending on how others coordinate with them, that become "privileged" to generalize their knowledge inappropriately to other language communities, and which voices are thereby muted. The idea of "different but equal" can now be understood more clearly.

"Competition" Understood in Terms of Mutual Trust and Enabling

Within the described narratives concerning differentiation, the mutuality of meaning through the interdependence of that which it is and is not, and the problem of proceeding under the assumption that a claim to knowledge is made legitimate by its degree of representation of the objective world, an understanding of relationships as a form of competition is useful. The confrontation of every reality with that which it is not, and the critique implied or the questioning of central assumptions held by a local community of understanding about what is real, including the ensuing defensive processes and attempts to generalize the local "truths" to "opposing" communities of understanding, could well be considered a form of competition. But contrary to the common perception of competition as a game with winners and losers (in the sense that losers, in the language of natural selection, are weaker and less able to survive), competition could also be viewed as a process of differentiation within a basic assumption that others are reasonable within their perspective, as Subject believes him- or herself to be within his or her perspective. In this way one could move from the endless game of mutual critique, and the search for who is right (winner) and who is wrong (loser), toward mutual transformation of a "new" and common understanding. This does not mean that we can just "make" ourselves accept others as equally reasonable, since we define "reasonable" from our own perspective. Instead, we could proceed under the assumption that what others understand to be real, even if it fundamentally contradicts our reality, is reasonable, logical, and normal within their perspectives, or within what is their reality. Within such knowing processes it becomes possible to move from viewing "opposing" perspectives as stupid, irrational, or unethical to granting others "equality" in terms of being "logical" and reasonable within their own "reality."

For example, perceptions of mental health often consider the extent to which people can be declared insane and in need of institutionalization based on whether their actions, although sensible and rational within their identity and understanding of their world, contradict fundamental narratives and assumptions within a given culture. Individual or social action becomes abnormal, perverse, and in need of remedial "treatment" to the extent that the logic of an action—that which gives meaning to the action—in some basic way contradicts and calls into question aspects of common understandings within a culture. The fact that in the history of society, individuals from less privileged groups (e.g., Gypsies, American Indians, women, homosexuals) were declared to be mentally ill and in need of (sometimes radical) treatment, illustrates such social processes. Until recently, homosexuality was officially declared a mental (or moral) illness in several Western countries (also by the Catholic Church). If one can proceed from the assumption that contradictory understandings are at least a reflection of common sense within the context of the "opposing" community of understanding, just as the local language community understands its knowledge and understanding as "common sense," a fundamental understanding of equality can be made realistic. It helps to construct a basis of mutual trust and enabling, out of which a move from mutual critique to transformation to alternative ways of understanding becomes possible. Transformed realities, however, are not predictable from the "local" perspectives of either interaction partner, as might be the case when one talks about making a compromise between conflicting viewpoints. A meaningful discourse among contradictory understandings is more likely when all participants can proceed from a basis of understanding and acceptance of equality and trust, as this chapter has attempted to redefine it. However, without the kind of relational work that has been outlined here, such a "reality" of mutually enabling competition will remain but a dream.

In outlining examples of what kind of relational work might be required for realizing the potential of global leadership, I want to emphasize that change as a result of an intervention by a person who is considered a global leader, must remain a very short-term and basically questionable undertaking. I submit that the issues raised in this chapter have enormous practical consequences in the rapidly increasing globalization of our world, and that by continuing to dogmatically maintain the status quo, we raise a fundamentally ethical question. It is time to recognize that, in assuming a particular point of view as the only reality, one contributes to the construction of a particular way of understanding the world. One privileges a particular point of view and sanctions certain types of social actions. Thereby, other voices and their alternative understandings and corresponding social actions are muted or rendered meaningless. In that sense, social actors carry the responsibility for what they help to construct or hinder. Therein lies the most fundamental challenge raised by the concept of global leadership.

NOTES

1. The seemingly impossible-to-reach peace between the Palestinian and Israeli people is a sad example of such processes.

2. In trying to accomplish such a global project, within the current view only very general "meta-theoretical" understandings, such as the dignity of life, could be viewed as realistic. However, even the issue of "dignity" has very different meanings in different historical and cultural contexts. Dignity of life in China or Iraq at this point in history certainly has a very different meaning from anything that could be considered a common understanding of dignity of life in Western civilizations. And does the increasing poverty, unemployment, and destruction of our natural surroundings in Western nations bear witness to the dignity of life? Thus, what would be the basis on which one or the other understanding of "dignity" and of "life" could be globally warranted?

REFERENCES

Argyris, C. (1982). *Reasoning, learning, and action.* San Francisco: Jossey-Bass.

Burr, V. (1995). *An introduction to social constructionism.* London: Routledge.

Calas, M. B., & Smircich, L. (1988). Reading leadership as a form of cultural analysis. In J. G. Hunt, B. R. Baliga, H. P. Dachler, & C. A. Schriesheim (Eds.), *Emerging leadership vistas* (pp. 96-121). Lexington, MA: Lexington Books.

Cooperrider, D., Barrett, F., & Srivastva, S. (1995). Social construction and appreciative inquiry: A journey in organizational theory. In D. M. Hosking, H. P. Dachler, & K. J. Gergen (Eds.), *Management and organization: Relational alternatives to individualism* (pp. 157-200). Aldershot, UK: Avebury.

Dachler, H. P. (1988). Constraints on the emergence of new vistas in leadership and management research: An epistemological overview. In J. G. Hunt, B. R. Baliga, H. P. Dachle, & C. A. Schriesheim (Eds.), *Emerging leadership vistas* (pp. 261-285). Lexington, MA: Lexington Books.

Dachler, H. P., & Hosking, D.M. (1995). The primacy of relations in socially constructing organizational realities. In D. M. Hosking, H. P. Dachler, & K. J. Gergen (Eds.), *Management and organization: Relational alternatives to individualism* (pp. 1-28). Aldershot, UK: Avebury.

Derrida, J. (1978). *Writing and difference*. Chicago: University of Chicago Press.

Gergen, K. J. (1993). *Toward transformation in social knowledge* (2nd ed.). London: Sage.

Gergen, K. J. (1994). *Realities and relationships: Soundings in social construction*. Cambridge, MA: Harvard University Press.

Gergen, K. J. (1995). Relational theory and the discourses of power. In D. M. Hosking, H. P. Dachler, & K. J. Gergen (Eds.), *Management and organization: Relational alternatives to individualism* (pp. 29-50). Aldershot, UK: Avebury.

Indian Institute of Management. (1996). *Organization development: Interventions in Indian organization* (Working Paper 1320). Ahmedabad, India: J. Parikh.

Küng, H. (1997). *Weltethos für Weltpolitik und Weltwirtschaft* [Global ethos for world politics and global economics]. Munich: Piper.

Lorenz, K. (1966). *On aggression*. New York: Harcourt, Brace & World.

Parker, I. (1992). *Discourse dynamics: Critical analysis for social and individual psychology*. London: Routledge.

Potter, J., & Wetherell, M. (1987). *Discourse and social psychology: Beyond attitudes and behavior.* London: Sage.

Sampson, E. E. (1985). The debate on individualism. *American Psychologist, 43*(1), 15-22.

Sampson, E. E. (1990). Social psychology and control. In I. Parker and J. Shotter (Eds.), *Deconstructing social psychology* (pp. 105-137). London: Routledge.

Sarup, M. (1988). *An introductory guide to post-structuralism and postmodernism*. Hemstead, UK: Harvester Wheatsheaf.

Shotter, J. (1993). *Cultural politics of every day life*. Buckingham, UK: Open University Press.

Vaassen, B. (1996). *Die narrative Gestalt(ung) der Wirklichkeit* [The narrative construction of reality]. Braunschweig, GE: Vieweg.

Watzlawick, P., Weakland, J. H., & Fisch, R. (1974). *Change: Principles of problem formation and problem resolution*. New York: Norton.

DEVELOPING GLOBAL LEADERS
A EUROPEAN PERSPECTIVE

Tove Helland Hammer

ABSTRACT

This chapter examines research on leadership models and management practices in the context of national industrial relations systems and societal cultural values in western Europe. Social security legislation, employment laws, and the position of trade unions constrain managerial action and encourage the adoption of leadership models that emphasize negotiation, compromise, and collaboration in managing divergent group interests, particularly in northern European organizations. The implications for leadership of the British, Latin, and Germanic industrial relations systems are discussed.

Management practices are shaped by two major factors: (1) the national industrial relations system, whose laws, institutions, processes, and rules regulate the relationship between management and labor, and (2) the size and ownership of organizations, which determine business strategies, governance structures, and management styles (Sisson & Marginson, 1995). Of these two, it is the industrial

Advances in Global Leadership, Volume 1, pages 99-113.
Copyright © 1999 by JAI Press Inc.
All rights of reproduction in any form reserved.
ISBN: 0-7623-0505-3

relations (or employment relations) system that differentiates one country, or cultural and geographical region, from another and therefore becomes identified with the country's or region's leadership and management when we paint with a broad brush.

In this chapter, I examine European leadership and management, using as my framework the ways in which national industrial relations systems shape leadership functions and behaviors and management policies and practices. I also make use of the research on societal cultural values, because the laws and institutions that govern employment relations in a given country or society are a reflection of the values held by its inhabitants. To place the European data in a broader perspective, however, I begin with a brief description of cross-cultural leadership research in general.

Research on cross-cultural leadership and international management has followed two broad streams. The first comprises large-scale comparative studies of attitudes, needs, values, and beliefs among managers in different countries (e.g., Bass, Burger, Doktor, & Barrett, 1979; Early, 1993; Haire, Ghiselli, & Porter, 1966; Heller & Wilpert, 1981); the second consists of case studies of management practices in individual countries (e.g., Hickson, 1993). The goal of the comparative, or *etic*, research has been to discover similarities and differences in management thinking or leadership behavior and styles across countries or cultures. The studies have often included a search for clusters of countries with similar management profiles (see, e.g., Ronen & Kraut, 1977), and I therefore refer to them as "cluster studies."

The underlying assumption in a search for commonalties is that at least one component of leadership is culture-free. The idea is that because leadership is an influence process aimed at motivating, inspiring, and enabling others to perform, there should be a set of core leadership functions that will be the same all over the world. How leaders or managers go about their tasks to fulfill these functions may naturally differ across countries and cultures.

In the more anthropological single-country studies, the emphasis has been on learning how a given country's history, economy, societal values, and norms have shaped present-day management. The assumption in this *emic* research is that leadership is culture-specific, or culturally contingent. Both the functions that leaders and managers serve, and what they do to carry out those functions will be unique to a given culture. This does not mean that leaders and managers from one culture cannot perform well in another; it means only that the processes and practices they use effectively in one culture will not necessarily work well in other cultural settings.

Cross-cultural comparison studies are not devoid of *emic* components. The clustering of countries inevitably invites a discussion of the forces that determine managers' attitudes, beliefs, and behaviors in one set of countries, but not in another (e.g., Bass et al., 1979). In a current study of leadership in 60 countries, *etic* and *emic* approaches are combined to discover leader traits and attributes that contrib-

ute to organizational effectiveness across countries, as well as leadership characteristics that are country- or culture-specific (House, Wright, & Aditya, 1997).

Early comparative research on managers' attitudes and beliefs (Bass et al.,
1979; Haire et al., 1966) and later studies of organizational governance practices
(IDE, 1981, 1993) showed remarkable similarities of responses across countries.
However, the leadership studies, at least, were conceptually simple, almost atheoretical, and methodologically weak. Reviews of more recent research have concluded that there is, in fact, no evidence for a single model of management
practices (Dorfman, 1996; House et al., 1997), an argument that supports the cultural contingency hypothesis. The culture-specificity view is also bolstered by
findings from two decades of research on cultural values illustrating that there are
substantial differences in societal values that influence people's attitudes, emotions, and behavior (e.g., Hofstede, 1980, 1991; Schwartz, 1992; Triandis, 1995).
So far there is no reason to believe that leadership and management practices are
exempt from the effects of culture.

CULTURAL VALUES AND LEADERSHIP

What are cultural values, and how would they influence leadership philosophies
and management practices? Not surprisingly, there are disagreements about the
exact nature of culture, but for the purpose of this discussion, Hofstede's (1991)
definition will serve us well. He described culture as patterns of thinking, feeling,
and acting that are programmed into the mind of each member of a group, or collectivity, through learning.

Values are strongly held beliefs about desirable end states or behaviors and can
be thought of as desirable goals that guide the selection and evaluation of behaviors and events. They differ from attitudes in that they are more general, or
abstract, and have a hierarchical order of importance (Schwartz, 1992).

To analyze leadership and management from a cultural values perspective
means to describe the values, beliefs, and norms held by leaders and followers,
management and labor, and others who influence the governance of organizations
in a society, and the behaviors that follow from these values and beliefs. When we
want to look specifically at leadership and management in the context of employment relations (as opposed to a political context, for example), we examine the
beliefs of managers and employees with regard to labor's and management's rights
and obligations in the workplace, the legitimacy and functions of interest-group
organizations such as trade unions and employers' confederations, and beliefs
about the appropriate role of the government in setting economic and industrial
policies that control how private- and public-sector organizations utilize their
resources. Of course, a country's industrial relations system is in part a reflection
of its dominant societal values (Hammer & Hartley, 1997).

The best-known and most frequently used model of cultural values was derived from Hofstede's research to discover the dimensions of national cultures. From a study of values among IBM employees in 53 countries, he identified four dimensions (Hofstede, 1980):

- *High versus low power distance*—The extent to which members of a society accept inequality in society as legitimate.
- *Individualism versus collectivism*—A description of the relationships between the individual and the group in society, either as a preference for a loosely knit social framework in which individuals take care of themselves or their immediate family, or a tightly knit social framework in which individuals can expect relatives or in-group members to take care of them in exchange for their loyalty.
- *Masculinity versus femininity*—Reference to the existence of separate or overlapping gender roles in society, where masculinity pertains to societies with distinct gender roles (men are assertive, achievement-oriented, tough, and concerned with material success, whereas women are modest, nurturing, tender, and concerned with relationships and the quality of life), and femininity pertains to societies where both men and women share the feminine role characteristics.
- *High versus low uncertainty avoidance*—The degree to which members of a society feel uncomfortable or threatened by ambiguous or unknown situations. In societies with high uncertainty avoidance, there is a stronger tendency for rules and regulations to control behavior.

A fifth dimension, *long-term versus short-term orientation to life,* was later added to the list (Hofstede, 1991).

Although the individualism versus collectivism dimension has been used most frequently to explain national variations in behaviors and attitudes (e.g., Erez, 1997; Schwartz, 1992, 1994; Triandis, 1995), power distance and uncertainty avoidance are most clearly related to differences in leadership styles and management practices (Dorfman, 1996). For this discussion of leadership and employment relations, the masculinity versus femininity dimension also proves relevant.

The reason the individualism versus collectivism dimension has less utility in this case than it would have in a comparison of leadership in Eastern and Western cultures, for example (Earley, 1993), is that in most of Europe, people have individualistic values. This is particularly the case in the United Kingdom, Ireland, all of northern Europe, and France (Hofstede, 1991).

Hofstede ranked the countries in his studies on values dimensions based on the survey responses of individual employees. He assumed that it would be valid to make inferences regarding cultural-level values from the values held by individual members of the collectivity that makes up the culture, because a person's values are produced by both the person's unique experiences and the national or social culture to which he or she belongs. It should be recognized that these data are not without problems, and the rank ordering should, therefore, not be treated as the ultimate indicator of each country's position in a values hierarchy. On the other hand, years of research on Hofstede's model, as well as empirical testing of different values models, have shown that his original category system is remarkably robust (for reviews of this research, see Dorfman, 1996; Schwartz, 1992, 1994; Triandis, 1994).

Hofstede (1980) found substantial differences between the countries of western Europe on power distance and uncertainty avoidance.[1] On power distance, or acceptance of differences in rank and status, the countries fell into two clusters. The lowest scores in the entire sample of 53 countries were found in northern and central Europe (except Belgium) and in the United Kingdom and Ireland, indicating a preference for a more equal distribution of power across organizational hierarchies, less dependence by subordinates on superiors, and an open, consultative form of leadership. In southern Europe—Spain, Portugal, Italy, France—and in Belgium,[2] power distance scores were much higher, indicating that superiors and subordinates consider one another unequal, accept autocratic leadership styles, and prefer centralized power (Hofstede, 1991).

With respect to uncertainty avoidance, or tolerance for ambiguity, the data showed that the United Kingdom, Ireland, and Scandinavia have a high tolerance for deviant and innovative ideas and behavior, open-ended discussion and decision making, and reliance on few formal rules and regulations to govern behavior. In contrast, Spain, Portugal, France, and Belgium showed high uncertainty avoidance, with the rest of northern and central Europe placing in the middle.

The masculinity versus femininity dimension has a more immediate implication for how organizational leaders manage employment relations. In cultures that score high on feminine values, there is a strong preference for harmonious relationships and distaste toward open conflict. In employment relations, management and labor prefer to solve interest-group conflicts as soon as they appear, or better still, to prevent conflict by using negotiation and compromise. In masculine cultures, displays of aggression and open conflict are expected and acceptable. Industrial disputes, such as strikes, are more likely to be seen as events to be combated than as occasions for creative dispute resolution (Hammer & Hartley, 1997).

The Nordic countries (Denmark, Norway, Sweden, and Finland) and the Netherlands scored very high on feminine values, while the United Kingdom, Ireland, the Germanic countries (Austria, Germany, Switzerland), and Italy were identified as strong masculine cultures.

GENERAL OBSERVATIONS ON EMPLOYMENT RELATIONS IN EUROPE

Next, I turn to some general observations about employment relations that shape the management of European organizations, and then offer a more differentiated picture of European leadership (for more detail on European industrial relations systems and institutions, see Brewster, 1996; Gill, 1996; Slomp, 1996; Wallerstein, Golden, & Lange, 1997).

Compared with the operations of American corporations, European firms and their managers are less autonomous. The autonomy is constrained at the national level by culture and legislation, at the corporate, or strategic, level of the firm by patterns of ownership, and at the workplace level by trade union involvement and required worker-participation programs.

National-Level Constraints

National cultural differences are reflected in social security legislation and employment laws; in requirements with regard to pay, health and safety, the working environment and hours of work, and the rights to trade union representation (this is also the case in the United States; see Wolkinson & Block, 1996); and in requirements to establish consultation and co-determination arrangements in all but the smallest companies. In addition, the European Union's Social Action Program aims to establish uniform guidelines for human resource management policies and practices that limit the ability of corporate leaders to act freely.

Corporate-Level Constraints

Private ownership is concentrated in a few hands or in small networks of substantial banks. On one hand, this gives management more freedom to plan for the long-term financial performance of the firm, avoiding the pressures for short-term profits; but, on the other hand, it allows owners closer scrutiny over, and more opportunity to intervene in, business decisions. In addition, there is high involvement by the government in directing the national economy, which has an impact on firm-level business strategies, and the state is also a major employer in its own right.

Workplace-Level Constraints

Europe is a highly unionized continent. Despite sharp drops in unionization levels in some countries during the 1980s, union density is still very high compared with the United States (where it is 11 percent in the private sector), particularly in northern Europe (ranging from 83 percent in Sweden to 23 percent in the Netherlands). The trade union movement is politically and socially important even in countries with traditionally low unionization levels, such as France (union density in France was 17 percent in 1985 [Blanchflower & Freeman, 1992], and in 1993 the estimate was under 10 percent [Sorge, 1993]). In fact, union membership figures underestimate the constraints placed on managers by employees at the workplace level for two reasons. The number of workers covered by collective bargaining agreements at the workplace is larger than the membership figures; and the industrial democracy, or co-determination, laws that dictate worker involvement in decision making, supplement, rather than supplant, the union's position at the workplace (Brewster, 1996).

PLURALIST AND UNITARIST MODELS OF LEADERSHIP

To manage within such constraints requires a leadership style, or process, that recognizes the reality of conflicting group interests and the rights of multiple stakeholders, which means that managers should subscribe to a pluralist model of organization. A *pluralist* perspective takes as given that organizations consist of a variety of groups and coalitions, some with divergent interests and some with common goals. There will always be a potential for interest-group conflict, but the conflict can give way to compromise and collaboration when it is managed carefully. Pluralism includes the view that power should be distributed throughout the organization rather than concentrated in a few hands at the top of the hierarchy. In other words, there should be a balance of power between interest groups. Leadership calls for cooperation and negotiations, and the careful balance of worker interests in job security, working conditions, and wages, with the interests of capital and management in organizational effectiveness, productivity, and profit maximization.

A *unitarist* model of organizations, on the other hand, assumes that employees and employers (or labor and management) have a common interest in maximizing productivity and firm profits. Labor-management conflict—or any other form of organizational conflict—occurs only because one party or both lose sight of the common goal and the necessity for cooperation to achieve it. Unitarism is not concerned with power differences because it assumes that common-interest partners will not exploit one another for private gain. The implication for leadership is that it facilitates a more unified authority structure in the firm.

A pluralist model of organizational life would seem to be a prerequisite for the effective management of corporations and institutions in a global economy, in which people in leadership positions are required to manage organizations across cultures and deal with increasingly diverse workforces. It should be part of management training to gain experience in leadership positions that encourage the development of the political sensitivity and social competence necessary to manage multiple group interests.

IS THERE A COMMON EUROPEAN INDUSTRIAL RELATIONS MODEL?

Europeans tend to think in terms of national models of politics, culture, and industrial relations systems. For example, most surveys of European labor relations are organized by country rather than cross-nationally (Ferner & Hyman, 1992; IDE, 1981, 1993). European industrial relations systems, however, have a basic set of features in common, which occurs in the role of the national government in economic and social life, collective bargaining arrangements, and structures designed to include employees in organizational decision making. These common elements allow us to distinguish three different models of labor relations that encompass the countries of western Europe.

The eastern European countries, which include the former German Democratic Republic, Bulgaria, the former Czechoslovakia, Hungary, Poland, and Romania, are a group of their own. I do not include them in this discussion because, as Obloj (1996) has argued, there is little to be learned about management and leadership from eastern Europe because management there was an underdeveloped practice due to its lack of relevance for organizational effectiveness during the communist regimes.

The *British* model, which also applies to Ireland, is based on very limited government intervention in the management of corporations in general, and, more specifically, the management of employment relations. British labor relations have been based on principles of voluntarism, in which the government let employers and trade unions develop their own rules and practices for managing employment relations. Both employers and unions have been deeply suspicious of any involvement with law or employment "rights" (Flanders, 1974), and British trade unions became very strong institutions in the absence of legislation. Under the Thatcher government, however, the unions lost of much of their once considerable influence at the national, organizational, and workplace levels (Hammer & Hartley, 1997). The curbs on union power, coupled with the growth of human resource management, have led to movement away from a pluralist perspective toward a unitarist model of organizational life, and to a reemergence of authoritarian styles of management (Sisson & Marginson, 1995).

Studies of management in the United Kingdom have shown that managers' use of informal meetings with union representatives to handle workplace issues has declined, while the use of direct employee-involvement programs, profit-sharing plans, and employee stock ownership schemes have increased (Poole & Scase, 1996; Tayeb, 1993). This pattern mirrors U.S. managers' preference for, and practice of, dealing with employees as individual contractors, instead of as an interest-group collectivity.

The second model is found in France, Italy, Spain, and Portugal, often referred to as *Latin Europe* because the dominant languages in these countries are Romanic. The employment picture is characterized by large public sectors, close ties between the national governments and large private firms, a great number of small businesses (particularly in Italy), and a love-hate relationship between the trade unions and the government (Slomp, 1996). The large organizations are steeply hierarchical, authority is centralized at the top, and the power distance between top and bottom is substantial.

Single-country studies of management in Latin Europe accentuate between-country differences, such as the presence of a highly educated technical elite, an emphasis on charismatic leadership, and a practice of centralized decision making in France (Sorge, 1993; Szarka, 1996), versus the importance accorded personal and familial relations in organizational governance in Italy (Edwards, 1996; Gagliardi & Turner, 1993), and a general lack of managerial professionalism in Spain and Portugal (Boisot, 1993; Inacio & Weir, 1993; Lucio, 1996). Commonalties, however, include autocratic and paternalistic leadership styles and hierarchical organizational structures reflective of high power distance values and, especially in France and Italy, combative trade unions and intense labor conflicts.

When most people think of European industrial relations, however, they have in mind the so-called *Germanic, or Nordic* model,[3] found in Scandinavia, Finland, Germany, parts of Belgium, the Netherlands, Austria, and Switzerland. Again, there are differences between these countries, but on the whole, employment relations in Germanic Europe is characterized by a strong, legally established, trade union presence both in national politics and in the workplace, and by industrial democracy laws and practices. The dominant European perspective on management, at least up until the 1990s, follows from the Germanic-Nordic industrial relations system. I will use that model to discuss those characteristics of leadership that I believe need to be developed to manage globally.

THE GERMANIC-NORDIC INDUSTRIAL RELATIONS SYSTEM

To accommodate the different interests of capital and labor, trade unions in Germanic Europe have been, for several decades, strong and well-integrated partners with employers and governments in setting social and economic policy through centralized collective bargaining. This is the traditional "tripartite," or "corporatist," model of government, which recognizes that a plurality of interests exists in society and must be accommodated. The successful integration of different group interests at the societal level produced relatively peaceful labor relations in northern Europe for many years.

During the 1960s, however, when wildcat strikes and other forms of local union militancy occurred in normally stable work environments, it became clear that worker representation on the national level was not sufficient to prevent and control labor-management conflict at the local, or workplace, level. To give the workforce another voice mechanism, these countries enacted co-determination laws that established specific structures for worker participation, such as works councils or representation on corporate boards of directors, intended to ensure that workers' interests in job security, working conditions, and wages would be balanced with the interests of capital and management.

The industrial democracy legislation had two broad goals: the integration of labor's interests into the decision making of the firm and the redistribution of power across organizational hierarchies. The overarching goal of the legislation was industrial peace (this was also the purpose behind the legislation on collective bargaining), which, in theory, should result from the convergence of worker, management, and stockholder interests that occurs when power is more widely shared between hierarchies and social classes.

The Leadership Model

The Germanic-Nordic industrial relations model requires a strong preference for harmonious and cooperative labor relations and the willingness of organizational leaders to accommodate employee interests to avoid conflict, both on a societal level and in the workplace. Managers must accept as legitimate the formal labor voice mechanisms defined in the law—trade unions and collective bargaining and the often elaborate structures established for worker participation—which means that there should be labor-management cooperation and consultation on multiple levels in the organizational hierarchy. In its purest form, organizational leadership is exercised as a management-worker partnership that allows for employee participation in the creation, as well as the implementation, of company policy.

Data from country case studies reinforce the analysis of leadership requirements implicit in the Germanic-Nordic industrial relations model. Leadership in Scandinavia is often described as egalitarian and anti-hierarchical, with an emphasis on consensus decision making and cooperative problem solving that requires the ability to explain and motivate others by persuasion (Fivelsdal & Schramm-Nielsen, 1993; Gjelsvik & Nordhaug, 1996; Joint & Grenness, 1996). In the Netherlands, successful management has been defined as being able to convince, persuade, bring people together, and forge agreements through consultation and bargaining (Mok, 1996; van Dijk & Punch, 1996). Case studies of German and Swiss management have put more emphasis on the value placed by organizations on the technical expertise of leaders and the bureaucratic rule-setting (but not rule-enforcing) role of management, than the view of leadership as an interaction process. However, the preference for collaborative and non-confrontational labor relations in these countries, as well, has resulted in management strategies that accommodate different group interests (Marr, 1996; Warner, 1996; Warner & Campbell, 1996).

The Germanic-Nordic leadership model places considerable importance on the personnel function in organizations—the management of both human resources and employment relations. The structure of capital and forms of corporate governance in northern Europe, with government controls through regulation of capital markets, long-term financing by banks, concentrated shareholdings, and an emphasis on long-term organizational performance, also encourage an emphasis on the development of a skilled workforce that is committed to staying with the firm. The German and Scandinavian training and apprenticeship programs, which are collaborative efforts between the state (through government subsidies to the employer and coordination with the educational system) and the individual employer, are a good example of a long-term management approach to the use and treatment of labor in production.

During the last decade, there has been some discussion of the future viability of a cooperative labor-management partnership model in Europe. The Scandinavian models, in particular, have shown signs of strain (Bruun, Flodgren, Halvorsen, Hyden, & Nielsen, 1992; Dølvig & Stokland, 1992). The move toward more decentralized collective bargaining seen elsewhere in Europe (Katz, 1993) has been markedly noticeable in Sweden, where the Employers' Confederation in 1990 declined to participate in the tripartite centralized collective bargaining established in 1938. Despite changes in industrial relations practices, the industrial democracy legislation that defines management's obligations to worker participation in the workplace is still intact, and there is no evidence of substantial changes in management practices.

The Costs of Negotiations, Accommodation, Compromise, and Conflict Avoidance

The Germanic-Nordic leadership model is an expensive way to do business. A high-skill, high-wage labor force actively involved in corporate governance certainly means high labor costs, and it could also mean inefficient and suboptimal corporate decision-making. For example, it has been argued that the industrial democracy legislation, with its emphasis on accommodating the different interests of capital and labor to ensure industrial peace, has made Norwegian managers place too much focus on maintaining internal harmony and too little on increasing their firm's competitive position in the external market (Reve, 1994). A similar argument is raised in a study of Dutch managers, which claims that the Netherlands' cultural tradition of tolerance, compromise, and pragmatism leads to management by constant consultation and undermines managers' willingness to take risks and be innovative (van Dijk & Punch, 1993).

On the other hand, a study of large-scale organizational changes in 220 Norwegian firms showed that the cooperative partnership model made it possible for management to make decisions about downsizing and restructuring with minimal involvement by the workforce and without causing much conflict (Hammer, Ingebrigtsen, Irgens Karlsen, & Svarva, 1994). Managers' response to market demands for rapid and radical change was not unduly hampered by unions or prescribed worker participation. The researchers attributed the findings of management-dominated, low-conflict organizational change projects to the long-term investment in labor-management collaboration at all levels of the firm. The legally mandated collaboration in Norway had over time forced both managers and labor leaders at the firm level to develop ways to work together that either prevented large conflicts, even on distributive issues, or served to contain the conflicts that arose. Based on years of experience, local union leaders and employees had learned that their interests would be accommodated to the extent possible in management's search for solutions to problems facing the firm.

I argue that the development of leaders for a global economy should incorporate the view, or perspective, on labor found in the Germanic-Nordic model; that is, to consider employees as corporate assets, to be trained and developed to produce long-term, value-added service, with legitimate rights represented in organizational decision making for the purpose of promoting labor-management cooperation and industrial peace. The opposite view of labor, as a commodity in production whose labor power should be purchased at the lowest possible price, to be used and expended as the employer's needs dictate, can be economically successful in the short run but will not do well in the long run in an economy that increasingly demands high-quality production to customer specifications, short time to market, low inventory production scheduling, and reliable delivery.

This argument does not imply the wholesale adoption of the worker participation structures defined in the European co-determination legislation or the presence of trade union representation and collective bargaining. The important component of leadership to be derived from the Germanic-Nordic model is an acceptance of the legitimacy of different group interests in organizations, a willingness to grant opposing interests a voice in organizational decision making, and the ability to manage conflict through negotiation.

In discussions about transforming the management of American organizations, it is often assumed that the leadership model emphasized in this chapter requires adherence to a specific set of cultural values. In particular, it is assumed that Europeans in general, including managers, have more collectivist values, whereas Americans are much more individualistic. Research on the effects of societal values on industrial relations, however, has shown that the values of North American and European employers are quite similar. In fact, their initial responses to the emergence of trade unionism around the turn of the century were very much the same, with both focused on destroying or containing the unions. The difference we see today, between the open hostility to unions displayed by American managers and the acceptance of and cooperation with them by European managers, resulted from the European governments' decisions, from approximately 1880 forward to accommodate labor's demands for political reasons, which, in turn, forced the employers to adapt to a political reality (Adams, 1981).

Similarly, European employers did not welcome either the prospect or the reality of co-determination (IDE, 1981), but they adapted to the requirements of the legislation in such a way that it does not seem to have diminished their ability to manage their firms. Decision-making processes have changed with the incorporation of labor interests, but the relative power of management and labor has not (IDE, 1993).

The German-Nordic leadership model should be seen primarily as a pragmatic one, in which some traditional management prerogatives are traded for workforce cooperation and commitment over the long term. The model is therefore exportable.

NOTES

1. The countries in eastern Europe, with the exception of Yugoslavia, were not included in Hofstede's study.
2. Belgium is a country with two strong cultures, one dominant among the Flemish-speaking population and the other dominant among the French-speaking Wallons.
3. I am calling the industrial relations and leadership models of northern Europe the "Germanic-Nordic" model because the industrial relations model is found in the region we call Germanic Europe, but it is usually identified in research literature as the "Nordic" model.

REFERENCES

Adams, R. (1981). Theoretical dilemmas and value analysis in comparative industrial relations. In G. Dlugos & K. Weiermaier (Eds.), *Management under differing value systems* (pp. 277-293). New York: Walter de Gruyter.

Bass, B. M., Burger, P. C., Doktor, R., & Barrett, G. V. (1979). *Assessment of managers. An international comparison.* New York: Free Press.

Blanchflower, D., & Freeman, R. (1992). Unionism in the U.S. and other advanced OECD countries. *Industrial Relations, 31*(1), 56-79.

Boisot, M. H. (1993). The revolution from outside: Spanish management and the challenge of modernization. In D. J. Hickson (Ed.), *Management in western Europe: Society, culture, and organization in twelve nations* (pp. 205-228). New York: Walter de Gruyter.

Brewster, C. (1996). Human resource management in Europe. In M. Warner (Ed.), *International encyclopedia of business and management* (pp. 1873-1882). London: Thompson Business Press.

Bruun , N., Flodgren, B., Halvorsen, M., Hyden, H., & Nielsen, R. (1992). *The Nordic labour relations model: Labour law and trade unions in the Nordic countries—today and tomorrow.* Aldershot, UK: Dartmouth.

Dølvig, J. E., & Stokland, D. (1992). Norway: The "Norwegian model" in transition. In A. Ferner & R. Hyman (Eds.), *Industrial relations in the new Europe* (pp. 143-167). Oxford: Blackwell.

Dorfman, P. (1996). International and cross-cultural leadership. In J. Punnitt & O. Shenkar (Eds.), *Handbook for international management research* (pp. 267-349). Cambridge, MA: Blackwell.

Early, P. C. (1993). East meets West meets Mideast: Further explorations of collectivistic and individualist work groups. *Academy of Management Journal, 36,* 319-348.

Edwards, V. (1996). Management in Italy. In M. Warner (Ed.), *International encyclopedia of business and management* (pp. 2918-2925). London: Thompson Business Press.

Erez, M. (1997). A culture-based model of work motivation. In M. Erez & P. C. Early (Eds.), *New perspectives on international industrial/organizational psychology* (pp. 193-242). San Francisco: New Lexington Press.

Ferner, A., & Hyman, R. (1992). *Industrial relations in the new Europe.* Oxford: Blackwell.

Fivelsdal, E., & Schramm-Nielsen, I. (1993). Egalitarianism at work: Management in Denmark. In D. J. Hickson (Ed.), *Management in western Europe: Society, culture, and organization in twelve nations* (pp. 27-46). New York: Walter de Gruyter.

Flanders, A. (1974). The tradition of voluntarism. *British Journal of Industrial Relations, 12,* 352-370.

Gagliardi, P., & Turner, B. A. (1993). Aspects of Italian management. In D. J. Hickson (Ed.), *Management in western Europe: Society, culture, and organization in twelve nations* (pp. 149-166). New York: Walter de Gruyter.

Gill, C. (1996). Industrial relations in Europe. In M. Warner (Ed.), *International encyclopedia of business and management* (pp. 1974-1984). London: Thompson Business Press.

Gjelsvik, M., & Nordhaug, O. (1996). SR-Bank: From regulated shelter to deregulated storm. In F. Chevalier & M. Segalla (Eds.), *Organizational behavior and change in Europe: Case studies* (pp. 202-237). Thousand Oaks, CA: Sage.

Haire, M., Ghiselli, E. E., & Porter, L. (1966). *Managerial thinking: An international study.* New York: Wiley.

Hammer, T. H., & Hartley, J. F. (1997). Individual-union-organization relationships in a cultural context. In M. Erez & P. C. Early (Eds.), *New perspectives on international industrial/organizational psychology* (pp. 446-492). San Francisco: New Lexington Press.

Hammer, T. H., Ingebrigtsen, B., Irgens Karlsen, J., & Svarva, A. (1994, August). *Organizational renewal: The management of large-scale organizational change in Norwegian firms.* Paper presented at the conference on Transformation in European Industrial Relations, Helsinki, Finland.

Heller, F. A., & Wilpert, B. (1981). *Competence and power in managerial decision-making: A study of senior levels of organization in eight countries.* London: Wiley.

Hickson, D. J. (Ed.). (1993). *Management in western Europe: Society, culture, and organization in twelve nations.* New York: Walter de Gruyter.

Hofstede, G. (1980). *Culture's consequences: International differences in work-related values.* Beverly Hills: Sage.

Hofstede, G. (1991). *Cultures and organizations: Software of the mind.* London: McGraw-Hill.

House, R. J., Wright, N. S., & Aditya, R. N. (1997). Cross-cultural research on organizational leadership: A critical analysis and a proposed theory. In M. Erez & P. C. Early (Eds.), *New perspectives on international industrial/organizational psychology* (pp. 535-625). San Francisco: New Lexington Press.

IDE International Research Group. (1981). *Industrial democracy in Europe.* Oxford: Clarendon Press.

IDE International Research Group. (1993). *Industrial democracy in Europe revisited.* New York: Oxford University Press.

Inacio, A. P., & Weir, D. (1993). Management in Portugal. In D. J. Hickson (Ed.), *Management in western Europe: Society, culture, and organization in twelve nations* (pp. 191-204). New York: Walter de Gruyter.

Joint, P., & Grenness, T. (1996). Management in Scandinavia. In M. Warner (Ed.), *International encyclopedia of business and management* (pp. 3021-3028). London: Thompson Business Press.

Katz, H. C. (1993). The decentralization of collective bargaining: A literature review and comparative analysis. *Industrial & Labor Relations Review, 47* (1), 3-22.

Lucio, M. M. (1996). Management in Spain. In M. Warner (Ed.), *International encyclopedia of business and management* (pp. 3056-3061). London: Thompson Business Press.

Marr, R. (1996). Management in Germany. In M. Warner (Ed.), *International encyclopedia of business and management* (pp. 2860-2867). London: Thompson Business Press.

Mok, A. L. (1996). Management in the Benelux countries. In M. Warner (Ed.), *International encyclopedia of business and management* (pp. 2666-2671). London: Thompson Business Press.

Obloj, K. (1996). Management in eastern Europe. In M. Warner (Ed.), *International encyclopedia of business and management* (pp. 2716-2722). London: Thompson Business Press.

Poole, M., & Scase, R. (1996). Management in the United Kingdom. In M. Warner (Ed.), *International encyclopedia of business and management* (pp. 3085-3097). London: Thompson Business Press.

Reve, T. (1994, April). Scandinavian management: From competitive advantage to competitive disadvantage? *Tidsskrift for Samfunnsforskning, 568-582.*

Ronen, S., & Kraut, A. I. (1977, Summer). Similarities among countries based on employee work values and attitudes. *Columbia World Journal of Business, 89-96.*

Schwartz, S. H. (1992). Universals in the content and structure of values: Theoretical advances and empirical tests in 20 countries. In M. Zanna (Ed.), *Advances in experimental social psychology* (Vol. 25, pp.1-65). Orlando: Academic Press.

Schwartz, S. H. (1994). Beyond individualism and collectivism: New cultural dimension of values. In U. Kim, H. C. Triandis, C. Kagatcibasi, S. C. Choi, & G. Yoon (Eds.), *Individualism and collectivism: Theory, method, and applications* (pp. 241-263). Thousand Oaks, CA: Sage.

Sisson, K., & Marginson, P. (1995). Management: Systems, structure, and strategy. In P. Edwards (Ed.), *Industrial relations: Theory and practice in Britain* (pp. 89-122). Oxford: Blackwell.

Slomp, H. (1996). *Between bargaining and politics: An introduction to European labor relations.* New York: Praeger.

Sorge, A. (1993). Management in France. In D. J. Hickson (Ed.), *Management in western Europe: Society, culture, and organization in twelve nations* (pp. 65-88). New York: Walter de Gruyter.

Szarka, J. (1996). Management in France. In M. Warner (Ed.), *International encyclopedia of business and management* (pp. 2851-2858). London: Thompson Business Press.

Tayeb, M. (1993). English culture and business organizations. In D. J. Hickson (Ed.), *Management in western Europe: Society, culture, and organization in twelve nations* (pp. 47-64). New York: Walter de Gruyter.

Triandis, H. C. (1994). Cross-cultural industrial and organizational psychology. In H. C. Triandis, M. D. Dunnette, & L. M. Hough (Eds.), *Handbook of industrial and organizational psychology* (Vol. 4, pp.103-172). Palo Alto: Consulting Psychologists Press.

Triandis, H. C. (1995). *Individualism and collectivism.* San Francisco: Westview Press.

van Dijk, N., & Punch, M. (1993). Open doors, closed circles: Management and organization in the Netherlands. In D. J. Hickson (Ed.), *Management in western Europe: Society, culture, and organization in twelve nations* (pp. 167-190). New York: Walter de Gruyter.

Wallerstein, M., Golden, M., & Lange, P. (1997). Unions, employer associations, and wage-setting institutions in northern and central Europe, 1950-1992. *Industrial and Labor Relations Review, 50,* 379-401.

Warner, M. (1996). Management in Switzerland. In M. Warner (Ed.), *International encyclopedia of business and management* (pp. 3062-3064). London: Thompson Business Press.

Warner, M., & Campbell, A. (1993). German Management. In D. J. Hickson (Ed.), *Management in western Europe: Society, culture, and organization in twelve nations* (pp. 89-107). New York: Walter de Gruyter.

Wolkinson, B. W., & Block, R. N. (1996). *Employment law: The workplace rights of employees and employers.* Cambridge, MA: Blackwell.

RECONCILING I/O PSYCHOLOGY AND EXECUTIVE PERSPECTIVES ON GLOBAL LEADERSHIP COMPETENCIES

Richard J. Ritchie

ABSTRACT

There is a gap in industrial and organizational psychology between what is known about leadership in organizations from research and theory development and what is done in practice. This chapter identifies some of the factors that contribute to the existence of this gap and suggests steps that can be taken be to close the gap. If this gap can be reduced or eliminated, there are potential benefits for employers, employees, and scientific psychology.

Over the past 40 years, industrial and organizational (I/O) psychologists have made major contributions to both theory and practice related to leadership in organizations (see Bass, 1990; Hughes, Ginnett, & Curphy, 1996; Locke, 1992; Ritchie, 1994,). In spite of these significant advances in our understanding of the factors that contribute to effective leadership and the methods that can be used to

Advances in Global Leadership, Volume 1, pages 115-125.
Copyright © 1999 by JAI Press Inc.
All rights of reproduction in any form reserved.
ISBN: 0-7623-0505-3

improve the quality of leadership (e.g., through selection and development), leadership as it is actually practiced in organizations often falls far short of what it needs to be for organizations to thrive, let alone survive. The many deficiencies of leadership in practice have been well documented by the humorist Scott Adams (Adams, 1997) and by more serious academic researchers (Kotter, 1995).

One of the major reasons for this situation is the gap that exists between I/O psychologists and business executives. This chapter examines some of the factors that contribute to the continuation of different perspectives between psychologists and executives on leadership issues, including the definition of global leadership competencies, identification of leadership potential, and so on. If psychologists wish to increase their impact on the lives of people in organizations, it is important for them to understand the reasons why a gap exists and to develop new approaches to building partnerships with business executives.

To begin with, it is important to understand that business leaders are likely to see things differently than I/O psychologists do. Furthermore, these differences in perspective have the potential to contribute to conflict between "us" and "them" about leadership, with regard to such issues as the proper methodologies to use to identify global leadership competencies, the proper labeling and definition of those competencies, and the use of the competencies when making personnel decisions. The following are some of the factors that can contribute to conflict between psychologists and executives:

- Lack of credibility with executives
- Lack of a common language
- Ready-fire-aim philosophy
- Superstitious beliefs
- Culturally based differences in perceptions
- Politically motivated objections

CREDIBILITY

One reason a gap exists is that many psychologists lack the credibility required to influence executives. Before you can get to the point of surfacing and reconciling differences, you have to be able to convince executives that it is worthwhile for them to spend time talking with you. Some executives may not appreciate the value an I/O psychologist can bring to the discussion. For example, Chester Bernard (1948), a former president of New Jersey Bell Telephone Company, expressed the opinion that: "Leadership has been the subject of an extraordinary amount of dogmatically stated nonsense." When one looks at the hundreds (or thousands) of books that have been written about leadership, Chester Bernard's statement is probably as true today as it was 40 years ago. You have to be able to establish your credibility as an expert who can help the firm be more successful in the marketplace.

The importance of credibility in leadership has been described by Kouzes and Posner (1993, p. 22): "We want to believe their [leaders'] word can be trusted, that they have the knowledge and skill to lead, and that they are personally excited and enthusiastic about the direction in which we are headed." Psychologists must demonstrate the same characteristics when they work with executives.

COMMUNICATION

Another source of conflict can be failure to communicate. Psychologists and executives use different vocabularies. Scientific psychology has developed very sophisticated methods for designing research studies and analyzing the data generated in those studies. Psychology has also developed its own language and style of communicating. One who looks at a recent issue of the *Journal of Applied Psychology* or the *Academy of Management Journal* is likely to find studies utilizing such methods as meta-analysis, path analysis, and multiple regression. The typical executive is not familiar with the research rationale and methods of psychologists. In addition, articles accepted for publication in research journals are written in a style that can be incomprehensible to the average person.

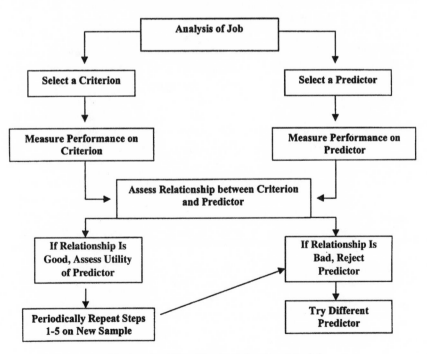

Figure 1.   The Classic Selection Model

In the course of our academic training to become I/O psychologists, we studied statistics and experimental design and were exposed to the theoretical and scientific bases for much of the work carried on in our field. Those of us who studied personnel selection were taught that there are specific procedures to follow to ensure that any selection process we developed could withstand both scientific and legal scrutiny. We learned that I/O psychology has well-developed methods for analyzing work to identify the skills, abilities, and other characteristics needed to perform that work successfully. In addition, I/O psychologists are knowledgeable about how to identify those characteristics properly while meeting legal and regulatory requirements. Figure 1 is adapted from what Paul Muchinsky (1993) described in his I/O psychology textbook as the "Classic Selection Model." It represents an approach that could be used by an I/O psychologist to identify global leadership competencies. The model provides a useful tool for psychologists in the development of a selection procedure, but it would be seen as having little value by an executive who believes in a "ready, fire, aim" philosophy.

That same executive would probably be very impatient with a psychologist who insisted that a thorough job analysis was required as the first of several steps that could lead to the implementation of a selection process. For both scientific and legal reasons, job analysis is important. As Sid Gael (1988, p. xv) stated in his *Job Analysis Handbook,* "The importance of precise and accurate job information cannot be overemphasized, considering the impact that decisions based on job information have on individual job applicants and employees and organizations." A challenge for the psychologist is to explain the rationale for the process used to identify leadership competencies in terms that are relevant to the executive. What kinds of terms are relevant to the executive? When asked about critical business challenges, executives are most likely to say improving product quality and enhancing customer service (Kouzes & Posner, 1993). The psychologist will have more success in persuading the executive when he or she can present a convincing story showing that application of sound research methods will enhance the capability of the organization to meet critical business challenges.

SUPERSTITIOUS BELIEFS

Executives often develop their own personal theories about the characteristics needed to be a successful global leader. These personal theories may be quite accurate. At other times, the characteristics that executives feel are important may seem to the I/O psychologist to be problematic. For example, sometimes a characteristic that an executive believes to be important is based on superstition (e.g., height over 6 feet tall), or may appear to be unmeasurable (e.g., lean and mean), or may be political (e.g., who nominated this candidate), or may be cultural (e.g., only relatives can be trusted in this position).

Several years ago, a local newspaper (*Morris County Daily Record,* 1993) reported the results of a survey of members of the Association of Executive Recruiters. The respondents were asked to indicate the most unusual characteristics they had been asked to look for in identifying candidates for an executive position. Responses included such criteria as:

- Over 6 feet tall
- 10 Handicap or lower in golf
- Fiddle player, knowledgeable about Scandinavian folk songs, and a storyteller
- No one wearing eyeglasses (they do not look open and trustworthy)
- One who has run a marathon and can jog and talk business simultaneously

There is a high probability that these preferred characteristics are based on superstitious beliefs. At least one of them, however, can actually be linked through job analysis to the position for which it was required. By the way, here is a hint: the position was branch manager of a bank located in a smaller community in Norway. In the community where the bank is located, the success of the bank in attracting and retaining customers can be enhanced by someone who can be the center of attention at community festivals and other events.

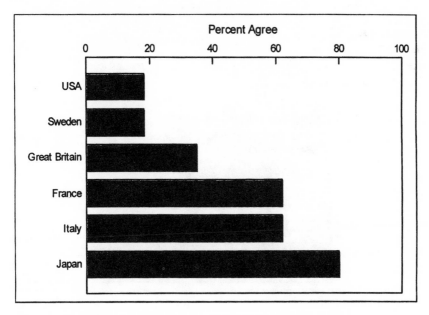

Source: Laurent (1992).

Figure 2. The Importance of Having Precise Answers

Another potential area for conflict between psychologists and business leaders is culturally based differences in perception. As Geert Hofstede (1980) observed, "Many of the differences in employee motivation, management styles, and organizational structures of companies throughout the world can be traced to differences in the collective mental programming of people of different national cultures."

People are generally not aware of the ways in which culture affects how we see and interpret the world around us. Let us look at a simple example. How would you respond to this question? Do you agree or disagree with the following statement: "It is important for a manager to have at hand precise answers to most of the questions that his subordinates may raise about their work"? Andre Laurent (1992) has gathered responses to this question from managers from a number of different countries. Figure 2 shows results from selected countries.

Let us look at another example drawn from research conducted by Fons Trompenaars (1993, p. 51). How would you respond to the following question?

There are two ways in which people can work:
   A. One way is to work as an individual, alone. In this case you are very much your own boss. Individuals decide most things themselves and how they get along is their own business. You only have to take care of yourself without expecting others to look out for you.

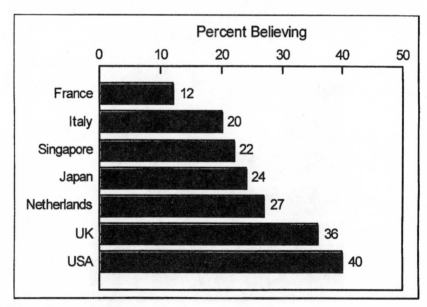

Source: Trompenaars (1993).

Figure 3. Two Ways to Work: The Percentage of Respondents Believing in Individual Decisions

    B. Another way is working in a group where everyone works together. Everyone has something to say in the decisions that are made, and everyone can count on one another.

Figure 3 contains selected data from Trompenaars' research using this question.

Suppose you are seeking to identify the competencies needed to be an effective global leader. You have collected job analysis data that include responses to these two questions. Based on your answer to the first question, how likely is it that you will eventually include "having precise answers at hand" somewhere in the recommended set of competencies? Or based on your response to the second question, what competencies would be included if individualism were stronger than collectivism or vice versa? As you can see, the perceived importance of having precise answers at hand or of working individually or collectively depends to a great extent on underlying cultural factors. Most people from the United States may respond differently to questions like these than people from Japan or other countries.

POLITICALLY MOTIVATED OBJECTIONS

A number of experts have written about the importance of politics in understanding organization behavior. For example, Steers (1988) recognized that organizations are political entities. He also noted political processes produce much of the goal-related effort in organizations. Thus, some of the reasons a gap may exist between psychologists and executives are political. For example, I had the opportunity to consult with a joint venture company in Ukraine. There were several partners in the joint venture, including two European companies, a Ukrainian company, and a U.S. company. The head of human resources was a Ukrainian who had risen through the ranks of the Ukrainian government. The value of using tests to improve selection decisions was discussed with him. He acknowledged that tests may be useful someday but offered a variety of reasons why tests were not needed today. Later, discussions with others familiar with the Ukrainian culture uncovered the fact that it was common for hiring managers to make selection decisions based on the likelihood that the new hire could be counted upon to be personally loyal to the hiring manager. If merit were used to select people, the loyalty of the new hire would be uncertain. It appears likely that the human resources head was unwilling to take that risk.

    Other examples of objections that may be politically motivated, include: I know one when I see one; this is the way we've always done it (or the variation, let's do it the way that company does it); we're different, so what was done somewhere else doesn't apply here; and protection of turf or prerogatives of position. It is important for psychologists to understand the real reasons underlying objections and to utilize appropriate tactics for overcoming those objections (see, e.g., Tichy, 1983).

CLOSING THE GAP

There are many strategies and tactics that can be utilized to reconcile the different perspectives of I/O psychologists and business executives. Successful resolution of differences can lead to both a superior end product and successful implementation of that product. Failure to resolve the differences can prevent the project from getting off the ground or, if the project does get started, guarantee that the end result will never be implemented by the organization.

Research and implementation focus on somewhat different sets of issues. The primary concerns for research are selecting and conceptualizing the problem, designing and executing the data collection, analyzing and interpreting the results, and extending the design to follow interesting leads. The primary concerns of implementation are identifying and diagnosing the problem, gaining sponsorship and resources, setting goals and developing procedures, handling interpersonal "politics," and producing results (Hakel, Sorcher, Beer, & Moses, 1982). Business executives are more likely to be interested in implementation than research. Psychologists need to be concerned about both research and implementation.

Good research *and* effective implementation can both be achieved. An example demonstrates one effective approach to reaching this goal while reducing the chance of irreconcilable differences. This approach was developed and used by Hal Tragash (1996) when he was at Xerox. At the time, Xerox had been going through a period of significant changes that were needed to adapt to its changing business environment. Some of these changes impacted the nature of the relationships between employees and the firm. In Hal's work with senior Xerox executives, it became apparent that a new social contract between Xerox and its employees had to defined and implemented. Hal has excellent research skills, and he could easily have conducted the research needed to get the job done. He could have done all the data collection, data analysis, and interpretation. He could have written an impressive report to Xerox that in all likelihood would have been quickly forgotten. Instead, Hal formed a team of high-potential managers to define the answer. After being trained by Hal in the basics of social science, the team gathered and analyzed data, interpreted the results, and drew conclusions about the meaning of the new social contract. As a result of Hal's approach, the new social contract was successfully defined, and—equally as important—the process of gaining acceptance for it was accelerated.

Virginia Boehm (1982) suggested a model for conducting research that can meet the needs of the scientific community and business executives (see Figure 4). She acknowledges that from a scientific perspective, the model is messy in terms of methodology, complexity, statistical analysis, and the conclusions that can be drawn. If her model is followed, however, it can lead to greater organizational support for conducting the research and greater acceptance of the results.

If psychologists want to play a significant role in executive selection, development, or succession planning, they need to be effective in anticipating and resolv-

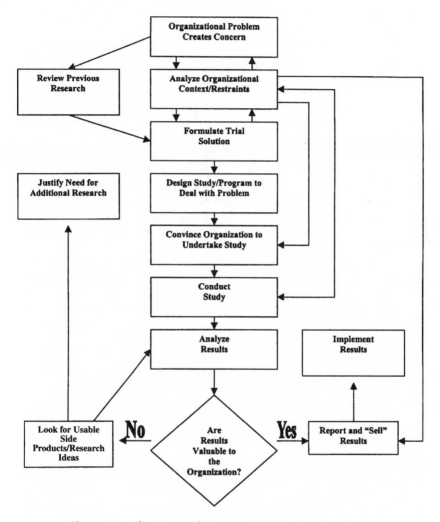

Figure 4. The Research Process Within Organizations

ing conflict between executives and themselves. This may mean successfully shifting the thinking of executives away from personal theories about desired characteristics in executives toward characteristics that are more strongly related to the success of a business. Or it may been enabling people from different cultural backgrounds to understand the perceptions of others, and to reach agreement on issues.

Based on my own experience, discussions I have had with colleagues, and other sources (Hakel et al., 1982), here is a list of tactics that can help build rapport with executives and reduce or eliminate potential sources of conflict:

- Learn to speak and understand the language of business; for example, topics such as gaining competitive advantage, enhancing customer service, and understanding financial statements.
- Identify interests of key persons and constituencies, and seek to form partnerships with them based on common interests. If sponsorship power is lacking, it will be difficult to gain access to the resources needed to complete the project, or to have the support needed to implement the results.
- Identify project objectives, and potential problems and objections that would make it difficult to achieve those objectives, up front, and begin to formulate ways to solve those problems or overcome the objections.
- Make sure everyone has the same understanding of the purpose of the work, and the outcomes to be achieved. When the parties have different expectations about results and delivery schedules, the project is likely to fail.
- Negotiate adequate resources and time schedules up front; for example, if you need access to employees for data gathering, how you will get a sufficient number in a timely manner.
- Be prepared to change direction if it becomes appropriate to do so. Changing business conditions or early study results may indicate the original objectives of a project are no longer relevant, and the choice is either to change direction or kill the project. There can also be changes in key personnel associated with the project. If an executive or manager moves on to other responsibilities, momentum and support for the work can be lost.
- Keep all parties informed of progress and the final results. It is important to communicate regularly in order to maintain interest and support for the project, and ultimately, to ensure implementation of the final product.
- Maintain a sense of urgency in driving the project to completion. Many executives are more concerned about achieving short-term business objectives than in investing in efforts that offer vague promises of future benefits.

Reconciling differences in perspectives is important from both a research and practice perspective. In his classic book, Hugo Munsterberg (1913) described a vision for industrial psychology:

> We must not forget that the increase in industrial efficiency by future psychological adaption, and by the improvement of the psychological conditions is not only on the interest of employers, but still more of the employees; their working time can be reduced, their wages increased, their level of life raised.
> The economic experimental psychology offers no more inspiring idea than the adjustment of work and psyche by which mental dissatisfaction with work, mental depression and discouragement may be replected in our social community by overflowing joy and perfect inner harmony.

Reconciling differences is the first step in advancing science and providing value to organizations and their employees.

REFERENCES

Bass, B. M. (1990). *Bass and Stogdill's handbook of leadership* (3rd ed.). New York: Free Press.

Bernard, C. A. (1948). *Organization and management.* Cambridge, MA: Harvard University Press.

Boehm, V. R. (1982). Research in the "real world: A conceptual model. In M. D. Hakel, M. Sorcher, M. Beer, & J. L. Moses (Eds.), *Making it happen: Designing research with implementation in mind.* Beverly Hills, CA: Sage.

Gael, S. (1988). *The job analysis handbook for business, industry, and government.* New York: Wiley.

Hakel, M. D., Sorcher, M., Beer, M., & Moses, J. L. (1982). *Making it happen: Designing research with implementation in mind.* Beverly Hills, CA: Sage.

Hofstede, G. (1980). Motivation, leadership, and organization: Do American theories apply abroad? *Organizational Dynamics, 18,* 42-63.

Hughes, R. L., Ginnett, R. C., & Curphy, G. J. (1996). *Leadership: Enhancing the lessons of experience.* Chicago: Irwin.

Kotter, J. P. (1995). Leading change: Why transformational efforts fail. *Harvard Business Review, 73,* 59-67.

Kouzes, J. M., & Posner, B. Z. (1993). *Credibility: How leaders gain and lose it, why people demand it.* San Francisco: Jossey-Bass.

Laurent, A. (1992). The cross-cultural puzzle of human resource management. In V. Pucik, N. M. Tichy, & C. K. Barnett (Eds.), *Globalizing management: Creating and leading the competitive organization.* New York: Wiley.

Locke, E. A. (1992). *The essence of leadership: The four keys to leading successfully.* Lexington, MA: Lexington Books.

Morris County Daily Record. (1993). Executive recruiters describe unusual search requests.

Muchinsky, P. (1993). *Psychology applied to work: An introduction to industrial and organizational psychology.* Pacific Grove, CA: Brooks/Cole.

Munsterberg, H. (1913). *Psychology and industrial efficiency.* Boston: Houghton Mifflin.

Ritchie, R. J. (1994). Using the assessment center method to predict senior management potential. *Consulting Psychology Journal, 46,* 16-23.

Steers, R. M. (1988). *Organizational behavior* (3rd ed.). Glenview, IL: Scott Foresman.

Tichy, N. M. (1983). *Managing strategic change: Technical, political, and cultural dynamics.* New York: Wiley.

Tragash, H. (1996). Personal communication.

Trompenaars, F. (1993). *Riding the waves of culture: Understanding cultural diversity in business.* London: The Economist Books.

A CORE OF GLOBAL LEADERSHIP:
RELATIONAL COMPETENCE

Barbara D. Clark and Michael G. Matze

ABSTRACT

In this chapter, we first present the whole global system that we must consider when looking at global leadership. Since business is becoming the dominant institution on our planet, as people in business (global leaders), we are now required to view ourselves as citizens of the world. Increased responsibilities and endorsement of multiple bottom lines come with this enlarged citizenship. We discuss how meeting the challenge of this global responsibility requires developing genuinely new ways of thinking, feeling, behaving, and relating with one another. The key is how we conduct relationships with each other. In response to this urgent need, we introduce the model of Relational Competence. This model is a coherent framework for learning new interdependent ways of participating in relationships both locally and cross-culturally. Improved Relational Competence helps support human learning, employee development, and performance improvement. We show how applying new strategies of relating and developing within mutually enhancing relationships at work—as in the rest of our world—can help bring congruency and possibility to a vision of a humane, sustainable, and peaceful world.

Advances in Global Leadership, Volume 1, pages 127-161.
Copyright © 1999 by JAI Press Inc.
All rights of reproduction in any form reserved.
ISBN: 0-7623-0505-3

Relation is the essence of everything that exists.

—Meister Eckhart

INTRODUCTION

In this chapter, we define and discuss the importance of global leadership. Global leadership requires expertise in conducting complex, cross-cultural, multi-perspective relationships between individuals, organizations, and networks. To accomplish this, we present the concept of Relational Competence. The model of Relational Competence is presented as a guiding framework for the selection, development, and continual activation of effective global leadership at all levels in an organization.

WHAT IS GLOBAL LEADERSHIP?

We use the term *global leader* to refer to each of us as contributors to the shaping of our future, particularly in the globalization of business organizations. Business has been the vehicle for the rapid globalization of our world and business is being called upon to provide a new kind of leadership for this transition. As people in business (global leaders), we are now required to view ourselves as citizens of the world. With this enlarged citizenship comes both rights and responsibilities. This new kind of leadership requires us to go beyond our current leadership theories. As noted by Jeff Gates (1998, p. 173) in his recent book, *The Ownership Solution: Toward a Shared Capitalism for the 21st Century Business,* "With globalization comes a fundamental shift in how we see our world, how we see our relationship to the world and how we make commitments and assign our allegiances."

Globalization requires that we no longer restrict our view of leadership to a set of individual characteristics or to a person of influence or authority in an organization. Leadership is a relational activity. By relational, we focus not exclusively on the individual, but on what happens *between* individuals and organizations; that is, what happens in the relationship. Leadership is a relational activity of facilitating people to identify, clarify, and activate appropriate action. This new kind of leadership, which we refer to as relational leadership, involves facilitating people to do the work of co-creating what they believe to be important and ethical, as well as activating appropriate action in organizations.

Global leadership is a more complicated relational activity that involves facilitating people to do this work in an exceedingly more complex process of co-creating what they believe to be important from a global, local, and cross-cultural perspective. Using a global, local, and cross-cultural perspective involves learning how to respect, understand, and appropriately relate with people from different cultures within an organization and a nation, as well as different cultures within different countries.

Global leadership requires "relational" work. Relational work involves understanding and accepting as valid, multiple perspectives and multiple voices in cocreating what the participants believe to be important and ethical. This relational work requires the global leader to develop proficiency in conducting *mutually* enhancing relationships with other leaders, governments, organizations, employees, customers, suppliers, stockholders, local citizens, and many other stakeholders with various interests and concerns.

Global leadership also involves the complex balancing of economic, social, cultural, and environmental goals—both within and among nations and organizations. In addition to the challenging complexity of balancing multidimensional goals and relationships, this new relational work requires embracing a set of values that have not traditionally been a part of business. Ohmae (1990) discusses how survival in our new economic system depends on cooperation and interdependence, not conflict and independence. If our survival depends on cooperation and interdependence, then our traditional domination and competition-based models of how human beings relate with each other are no longer functional in this interconnected world. We need to learn to operate business from a relational model of leadership that supports the reality of our interdependence and promotes cooperation. This relational model of leadership needs to emphasis the necessity of our relating and relationshipping from a base of equality, respect, mutuality, and nonjudgmental curiosity with the goal being that of the mutual enhancement of all participants.

THE IMPORTANCE OF GLOBAL LEADERSHIP

In discussing the importance of global leadership, let us first remind ourselves of the incredible rate of change, explosion of knowledge, and rapid globalization of our world. Each of us experiences the impact of these changes almost moment to moment in our daily lives. We experience change in the most routine activities such as reading the morning paper and discovering that our jokes about needing a clone have suddenly become a real possibility. Changes are occurring in activities related to economic survival such as finding that there has been another reorganization at work and our job no longer exists. The waves of fundamental change have affected all of our major institutions—government, businesses, churches, professional occupations, education, families, and communities. We also need to notice how these fundamental changes are not only being experienced on all levels in our society, but these transitions are being echoed worldwide. Every day we see examples of changes that a few decades ago we would not have thought possible. Consider such examples as the disbanding of the Soviet Union, the reuniting of Germany, the joining of the European countries into a common currency, the emergence of Asia as an economic giant, the near collapse of the Asian economy, and the enormous spiraling worldwide impact of Asia's financial crisis.

It is important for us to fully realize that never before in our history have such enormous systemic changes occurred simultaneously in so many nations (Gates, 1998). This worldwide, systemic transition of breakdown and breakthrough is leading to a new social alignment that recognizes our interdependence on each other, our complete interconnection with our environment, and the necessity of major developments occurring in the realm of human relationships. There is a basic movement in this world and it is toward "relation," not separation. In organizations, we must transform our traditional patterns of conducting relationships in order to be successful in this rapidly transforming world.

Some readers may be asking, "What does this have to do with global leadership?" Our answer is, *everything!* Global leadership plays a key role in shaping the future of global transformation, whether for good or ill. Besides having to facilitate major transitions while continuing to conduct daily business activities, global leadership is also challenged by far more than traditional economic concerns. In our present world, we face massive threats to our physical, social, economic, cultural, and spiritual environment. In their writings on global consciousness, Elgin and LeDrew (1997, p. 4) direct our awareness to the global picture:

> In 1992, over 1,600 senior scientists, including a majority of the living Nobel laureates in the sciences, signed and released a document entitled Warning to Humanity. In it, they stated powerfully the need for fresh approaches to thinking and living. They declared that "human beings and the natural world are on a collision course...that may so alter the living world that it will be unable to sustain life in the manner that we know." They concluded by giving the following, simple warning to the human family. "We, the undersigned senior members of the world's scientific community, hereby warn all humanity of what lies ahead. A great change in our stewardship of the earth and the life on it is required, if vast human misery is to be avoided and our global home on this planet is not to be irretrievably mutilated."

Learning new approaches to our stewardship of the earth and its people is both a phenomenal challenge and opportunity. We are faced with the challenge of developing global leadership that can facilitate the changes that will be required for us to create a positive sustainable future for our planet and its people. Creating a positive sustainable future means that we have to learn and implement effective relational strategies that enable us to balance economic, social, cultural, spiritual, and environmental goals while conducting capitalism in a manner that will meet our current needs without endangering or eliminating the resources necessary for future generations to meet their needs.

Business is increasingly being called upon to respond to this global crisis. Why must business and its global leadership take responsibility for preserving the planet and its people? Business is being called upon because it is rapidly becoming the dominant institution on our planet. Business is one of the most influential institutions that operate both globally and locally. With this freedom to conduct business globally through the use of global resources comes the increasing responsibilities of global citizenship. Besides having responsibility to the global quality of life, business institutions also have the necessary resources to meet the challenges we are facing. These resources include experience with responding to rapid change, more flexibility than other institutions, financial access and knowledge and, most importantly, access to the most talented and creative people on the planet.

The world, its inhabitants, and its future generations are depending upon global leadership to activate our organizations to facilitate the solutions for a positive sustainable future. However, as stated by Gates (1998, pp. 291-292), "The corporate entity is often single-mindedly mission-oriented, operating with sometimes shockingly little concern for the risks its financial-return agenda imposes on the world around it, including many stakeholders who are put at risk without any voice in the matter or the risk imposed on the voice-less environment." This traditional model of conducting business has long been practiced but is no longer tolerable considering our heightened awareness that these practices are destroying our planet, our people, and our local communities.

Fortunately, there is a growing recognition by business leadership and society of the urgent need for a new, more humane, socially and ecologically responsible business ethos (Eisler, 1993). Meeting the challenge of this global responsibility will require taking a relational approach to developing genuinely new ways of thinking, feeling, behaving, and relating with one another. As global leaders, if we want to create a positive sustainable future, we must start by identifying, acknowledging, challenging, and then changing the underlying values that implicitly endorse the rapid destruction of our planet and its inhabitants solely for financial profits. A meaningful alternative would be to implicitly and explicitly embrace the underlying values and relational actions that lead to long-term profits that are made after accounting for the human, social, and environmental issues. Relational Competence provides a relationally based system of values, beliefs, processes, and practices that are essential for global leadership in the shaping of this positive, sustainable future.

WHAT IS RELATIONAL COMPETENCE?

Relational Competence is a concept that has several different aspects. In simplest terms, it is the extent to which a person or organization can effectively and appropriately manage relationships across a diversity of settings. The central focus is on conducting the kind of relationships that foster people's development. Relational Competence organizes a variety of relational concepts and skills into an overarching coherent framework. This framework is organized using the best practices from relationship, communication, interpersonal, and emotional competencies but is also much more. Relational Competence is a way of looking at the world in which one's personal life and business life is viewed as a series of highly interconnected relationships with others. A person high in Relational Competence understands the importance of interdependence and the necessity of conducting relationships with emotional accountability. A leader high in Relational Competence considers it critical that relationships be well managed so as to provide important outcomes such as mutual growth, creative ideas, and new knowledge for everyone involved in the relationship. A leader high in Relational Competence sees that relating in such a way that all parties achieve these outcomes, provides immediate and long-term benefits to both himself or herself and to the organization.

People vary in the degree of Relational Competence they bring to each of their interactions. The quality of our Relational Competence can vary across different settings such as local business settings, cross-cultural settings, or in our home lives. In relationships, one participant alone cannot determine the quality of Relational Competence. The level of our competence emerges from the quality of the engagement between all participants within the relationship. However, our individual choices, attitudes, values, thoughts, emotions, behaviors, and ways of relating contribute substantially to the quality of outcomes in our relationships. Relational Competence has a learned component and, thus, with proper training and experiences, we can improve our Relational Competence.

All business is conducted through relationships. There are different kinds of relationships and different ways to conduct relationships. One kind of relationship unilaterally advances our own agenda and relationships are valued as a means of accomplishing one's own ends. It is quite another kind of relationship when we mutually value each participant's concerns and relationships as a means of fostering development and enhancing all participants. Relational Competence promotes the latter kind of relationship.

This definition suggests that Relational Competence requires a comprehensive integration of values, cognitions, emotions, behaviors, and communication elements. Later in the chapter we describe these elements in greater detail and explore how they are interrelated.

IMPORTANCE OF RELATIONAL COMPETENCE

There is a growing awakening in many business organizations that the quality and integrity of all relationships must become our predominant concern. As Wheatley (1994) noted, "We are coming to understand the importance of relationships and non-linear connections as the source of new knowledge. Our task is to create organizational forms that facilitate these processes." However, most business organizations have neither the underlying value system nor a coherent, theoretical framework for conducting growth-promoting human relationships. Relational Competence aims at such a unification by considering the major domains of human relations research—relationship, communication, interpersonal, and emotional competencies—from an integrated relational perspective. Relational Competence contributes to the revision of how we understand and participate in human relationships in our business organizations. This revision places mutually enhancing relationships as the central and essential aspect of creating a positive, long-term sustainable future for an organization. Relational Competence is an approach to human relationships that offers global leadership a shift in how relationships are conducted.

Do We Really Need to Change?

Our cultural and personal belief systems about how to conduct relationships with others were instilled early in our lives, reinforced in our formal education, and then performed in our work life. However, in this century, change has been so dramatic that these belief systems are not adequate to be fully effective in our complex, rapidly changing, and multicultural world. Many organizations and their people have patterns in their relationships that are based on old beliefs and assumptions. These old beliefs and assumptions include domination of others, power over others, exaggerated self-sufficiency, independence, every person for himself or herself, aggressive competition among each other, unlimited natural resources, greed, and disconnection.

Through these old beliefs and assumptions, we have created considerable human alienation and a deteriorating physical ecology. Harmon and Hormann (1993, p. 27) illustrated this when they wrote: "We are alienated from nature, of which we are a part and upon which we utterly depend. As a result, we foul our own nest and threaten the Earth's life-support systems necessary for our prospering and, in the end, for our survival. We are alienated from our work, since that has in so many cases become devoid of meaning. We are alienated from each other, since the sense of joint commitment to any transcendent goals is so weak. And, being deeply confused about our own being, we are alienated from ourselves."

How Have We Become so Disconnected from Other Living Systems?

There are several reasons why we have allowed ourselves to become disconnected from ourselves, others, and nature. In Western society we have put our human development almost exclusively in the service of our individual and organizational economic development. We have educated our intellect and accumulated our material wealth. At the same time, we have seriously diminished our connection with other people and ourselves. In our disconnection from ourselves, we greatly diminished our self-awareness through the illusion of a mind/body split; cut ourselves off from our inner knowledge by minimizing our feelings, insights, and intuition; and failed to explore our own creative impulses. We disconnect from others when we measure time spent with family, friends, and in community concerns only in terms of economic costs. As we pursue financial security, even when this interferes with family and friends, involvement with civic issues, and a sense of belonging, we begin to experience a disconnection from what gives us meaning in our lives. In his article on development from a relational perspective, Bergman (1991) states that he believes that the seeds of misery in our lives "are planted in disconnection from others, in isolation, violation, and dominance, and in relationships which are not mutually empowering." In our postindustrial era, we have placed little value on relationships based on connection, compassion, creativity, and cooperation.

Relational Competence provides a framework that enables us to transform our traditional patterns of communicating and conducting relationships. For the most part, when we do not have an alternative belief system, we stay in the old patterns of relating and conducting relationships. The tools of Relational Competence can help us enlarge the scope of our awareness of others and ourselves, create new perspectives about our relationships, and help us engage in relational work in our business relationships. Relational Competence supports the knowledge of our interdependence by increasing our connection and cooperation with one another. It provides us an alternative way of relating and participating in relationships in today's rapidly changing and multicultural world.

Using the principles of Relational Competence to transform the way we conduct our business relationships can have enormous benefits for people and their organizations. Improved relationships help support human learning, employee development, and performance improvement. When people feel connected to each other at work, they are more invested in their organization and their work projects. Relationships put the constraints or expansion into a work project. By improving relationships, many constraints are removed from the project. A higher quality of relationships enhances the speed and success of information transfer. Improving the quality of interactions between people paves the way for more efficient project completion. More and more research is showing that the quality of relationships in an organization correlated strongly with organizational productivity, reduced turnover, profit, and customer satisfaction (Hatfield, 1998).

How Did We Get Here?

During the 1980s, it started becoming increasingly clear that many of the generally accepted ways of structuring organizations and conducting management were no longer working. Most organizations were top-heavy bureaucratic structures with extensive control systems designed to produce conformity in employees (Ghoshal & Bartlett, 1997). Up to this time, most organizations had voiced a genuine concern for people and had acknowledged that people were important to the success of business. However, running the business and dealing with human being were separated into two areas, "hard side" and "soft side." The "hard side," getting the product out the door, was ranked as the most important priority. The "soft side," concern and commitment to people, was a lesser priority. It should come as no surprise that bureaucracy and the stifling of individual initiative were identified as the main problems causing the deterioration in formerly successful businesses.

How Has the Problem Been Dealt with?

Over the past two decades, many organizations have been experimenting with different structuring arrangements and management methods. Many of these approaches have lacked an overall organizing principle other than change itself. Many of these methods have turned out to be incongruent with stated organizational goals. Some of these modern management approaches have allowed organizations to sidestep the deeper issues underlying what they are doing, and they have not provided the long-term transformation needed. For example, setting up innovative groups outside a parent company while keeping an authoritative hierarchy in place does not change the overall structure of the organization. Excessive downsizing does not demonstrate concern and commitment to people nor engender commitment and creativity in the people that remain with the organization after the latest downsizing. It is not realistic to expect that, after a rapid restructuring that involves reducing hierarchy through flattening, these same employees will quickly become well-developed entrepreneurs who are eager to take initiative. Although many of us do welcome new opportunities to take initiative, most experienced people have experienced enculturation and pressure to conform to a restrictive organizational culture.

Nevertheless, over the past decade, many organizations have tried out ways to move from increasingly obsolete vertical-control systems to leadership systems built on purpose, process, and people (Bartlett & Ghoshal, 1995). Companies are making tremendous efforts to change both the formal and informal structures within their organizations. Some companies are changing the basic processes by which they operate. Organizations are changing the way they manage, changing their reward systems, and even altering the criterion for the hiring and promoting of employees. The changing structure of organizations with decentralizing, downsizing, and flattening has led to a new emphasis on an individual's participation and responsibility throughout all levels of the organization. In this new structure, the concept of managing people has shifted from the control of people to one in which the leaders are expected to create an environment conducive to creativity, flexibility, innovation, vision, inspiration, and trust. However, often people do not know what kind of environment actually supports these positive outcomes, much less know how to create it. A lot of attention has been paid to trying to make these organizational changes (Gordon, Morgan, & Ponticell, 1994; Schein, 1992; Sherriton & Stern, 1996). However, Ghoshal and Bartlett (1997, p. 38) cite examples "of how modern management approaches and rational corporate models are creating an environment in which thousands of capable individuals are being crushed and constrained by the very organizations created to harness their energy and expertise."

In this rapidly changing global economy, there is an increasing acknowledgment that people in organizations hold the largest key to the financial success. In their book, *Going Global,* Taylor and Webber (1996, p. xviii) state that "the essential factor in business is people. That may seem counterintuitive; after all, the New Economy is propelled by faster and faster technology, instant communications, borderless companies, and fluid capital. Yet people matter more than ever—and more than any other element. Put simply, the quality of a company cannot exceed the quality of people who choose to work there." In this global economy, these two priorities, "soft side" and "hard side" of business, have become increasingly interwoven. Gradually, the "soft side"—values, relationships, and people's ways of interacting—is emerging as the fundamental wellspring to generating the "hard side." In response to the awareness of the importance of people in organizations, companies are experimenting with a variety of people-centered management models.

Recognizing that a longer term and broader-based change is needed, many companies are attempting to change their organizational cultures to be more people-centered. A recent review of the literature on globalization, cross-cultural issues, leadership, and current business practices reveals there is emerging an increased attention on people-centered themes. These themes include:

- Importance of people to the organization
- Creation of organizational cultures that support people's creativity, flexibility, vision, inspiration, and trust
- Priority of building and maintaining relationships both locally and globally
- Effectiveness of team building
- Construction of learning organizations that foster partnerships
- Emphasis on community building

While people-based models are popular, few companies have integrated them as their operating philosophy. Gates (1998, p. 148) speculates that this "may be because corporate managers find it disconcerting to discover the full extent of the duties they are now expected to perform and the interpersonal skills they need to possess." As organizations are attempting to change their cultures to be more people-centered, they are discovering some barriers to implementing these changes. Whereas most people are verbalizing support of these cultural changes in theory, some people are having difficulty implementing these changes in their relational actions.

Why Are Organizations Having Trouble Implementing People-Centered Changes?

Why would we be having trouble implementing culture changes involving people's ways of interacting with each other? Organizations have certainly conducted a substantial amount of training in interpersonal skills and interpersonal communication. While interpersonal skills are vital for each of us, many of these skills have been learned in an organizational culture based on the old business paradigm. The old business paradigm supports disconnection from ourselves, each other, and the environment. Organizations are having difficulty implementing people-centered cultural changes because there has been no central organizing principle or framework for altering the outdated implicit and explicit values that support this disconnection. Thorough organizational culture change cannot be accomplished without an understanding of our own personal underlying cultural indoctrination, which is embedded in our values, beliefs, emotional expressions, language, thinking, meaning-making, behaviors, interpersonal skills, and patterning of our relationships. Unless the underlying cultural values of how we treat one another are changed, attempts to change organizational culture will not succeed.

A critical component of increasing Relational Competence involves helping people identify these implicit and explicit cultural values concerning the way we view and treat other people. Relational Competence also offers the tools to help us identify and change the cultural values that create barriers to optimal interactions and growth-promoting relationships. These tools help us illuminate the hidden processes that create change. Our new implicit and explicit values must embrace equality, respect, and connection through mutually enhancing relationships. This new *relational* framework will enable us to change the underlying cultural values that are constraining our ability to reach our optimal potential in our organizations.

Change to What?

In the model of Relational Competence, the cultural change focus cannot be exclusively on people or just be people-centered. Our focus must be on increasing our ability to build the kind of relationships with others that will support each person's development. This means we need to focus on improving the *relationships* through which people's development takes place. We need to learn how to conduct relationships that are person-enhancing and organization-enhancing. There are several steps in this process. The first step will require that we first understand and probably change the implicit and explicit values by which we view and conduct relationships.

Organizations have been making enormous changes in an attempt to adopt new approaches and change the structures by which business is conducted. However, without an underlying coherent organizing framework for changing our implicit and explicit value systems, many organizations are still trapped in old models or fall back into the old paradigm of conducting business. We have found that a person's real values about relationships have a subtle but inevitable way of being communicated, and have an effect on everything a person does. We propose that if there are not some modifications in underlying values concerning the importance of relationships, there are no essential changes in organizations.

MODEL OF RELATIONAL COMPETENCE

The model of Relational Competence is a human relations operating system and model for facilitating change. In order to be effective in this global environment, global leadership will need to facilitate organizational change on four different levels. These include change within (1) the self and how we relate with others, (2) the work group, (3) the total organization, and (4) the alliances, joint ventures, and networks with other organizations.

The model of Relational Competence is organized in the most profound sense around the understanding of the relational nature of human beings and how we develop *within* relationships during our entire life span. From this relational perspective, instead of focusing exclusively on the individual, the focus on the relationship *between* individuals is highlighted. Using a relational approach of development *within* relationships, this model integrates many previous concepts into a single coherent framework. This framework is integration of theory and practice from individual, relationship, group, and organizational research and from our experience in training Relational Competence. The importance of this single coherent framework is that it enables us to approach all of our human and organizational relationships from an overarching relational operating system. This new paradigm will help us to emphasize the importance of ongoing relatedness and connection in all of our actions. It identifies new educational strategies for learning to conduct growth-enhancing relationships. It helps us to effectively deal with cross-cultural differences, thereby preventing and reducing conflicts. Finally, this relational operating system provides us the tools for dealing appropriately with the powerful feelings generated in relationships.

The model of Relational Competence is based on three fundamental organizing principles: (1) the relational approach, (2) development within relationships, and (3) the complexity of our world view.

Relational Approach

Success in this global economy requires a relational approach, and more specifically, a focus on the quality of relating and relationship *between* individuals and organizations. Relational Competence is based on the knowledge that we as human beings are—in our essence—relational. The essential key to flourishing is the strengthening of our connections with other people and with our environment. To amplify this interconnection, it is important to move our emphasis from an exclusively individual focus to a more inclusive relational focus. In the relational approach, the major focus is on what goes on *between* people rather than their individual differences. The interpersonal approach traditionally focuses on individuals and individual behavior. Although individual differences certainly influence the quality of our relating, the major focus of change in the relational approach is to alter what goes on *between* people and *between* organizations.

When we positively change what goes on between people and between organizations, there will be a positive change in the individual. This individual positive change will then lead to positive change in the relationships and thus positive change for the organization for a whole.

The relational approach recognizes that as individuals, we change during the process of our interactions in relationships with others. An individual can best be conceptualized as an internalized system of relationships and can be referred to as a "relational self" (Clark & Matze, 1991). Our individual or "relational self" emerges out of the interactions in relationships. In relationships throughout our life span, we learn who we are through our interactions with others, we change through our interactions with others, and we depend on our interactions with others to support and maintain our relational self (Villard & Whipple, 1976). These relational interactions affect the quality of the relationships we develop with others. The relationship in turn affects the quality of the relational interactions. The relational view acknowledges that people are constantly affected by their relationships, and that growth-promoting interactions are person-building. Our current view of relationships needs to acknowledge this reflexive process (Sass, 1994).

Development *within* Relationships

Relational Competence emphasizes the exhilarating potential of development *within* relationships. This approach fosters new relational leadership through more pervasive human development at all levels of an organization. Organizations and people mutually benefit when every person is in the process of achieving his or her maximum potential through lifelong developmental learning within relationships. This development is most effectively facilitated through mutual, growth-promoting relationships.

The concepts of Relational Competence are based on the knowledge that from our conception and throughout our life span, all of our mental or psychological development takes place within relationships with others. In our Western culture, we have overemphasized the "individual." For example, we have created an illusion that healthy psychological development takes place mainly through increased independence or separation from others. However, most developmental research (Beebe & Lachmann, 1996) now shows that the "individual self" actually emerges out of our interactions *within* relationships rather than from our increasing separation and isolation from others. Some interaction patterns within relationships are more effective than others in the facilitation of mental or psychological growth. Miller (1988, p. 2) wrote: "Almost all theorists agree that people develop by interaction with other people. No one develops in isolation. In these interactions, if women or men are not acting in ways that foster others' development, they inevitably are doing the reverse, that is participating in interactions in ways that do not further other people's development." As global leaders, we need to learn the difference between interactions that are growth-promoting and interactions that are not growth-promoting. We need to develop expertise in how to foster and facilitate one another's development through mutually enhancing relational interactions.

Relational Competence provides the relationally based values and tools to unleash the potential of development within mutually enhancing relationships. Our lack of acknowledgment of our relational nature has lead to many underdeveloped competencies in the arena of relating and relationships in most areas of our lives. As has been noted by Surrey (1987, p. 5), our Western society "does not emphasize the importance of ongoing connection, and has not given enough support or educational experience to the skillful engagement of differences, conflicts, and powerful feelings in relationships. As a result, this relational pathway of development is obscured; its potential remains unacknowledged and undeveloped." Relational Competence provides a relationally based course of action (curriculum) and the educational strategy for facilitating appropriate relational work in our organizations. This curriculum helps create our expanded awareness with the practical tools for implementing this awareness into daily actions. This curriculum offers global leadership a systematic way of developing proficiency in conducting mutually enhancing relationships across multiple cultures.

Complexity of World View

Relational Competence provides a relationally based curriculum that provides a bridge to help us increase the complexity of our world view. According to Kegan (1994, p. 133), this curriculum requires "us not only to increase our fund of knowledge (a change in what we know), but to transform qualitatively the very *way* we know." This is a new role for global leaders in the context of business, and its mastery involves a very challenging curriculum of personal mastery and relationship development. This will require taking a relational approach to developing genuinely new ways of thinking, feeling, behaving, and relating with one another. The model of Relational Competence provides organizations and their global leadership a curriculum for making this transition.

The relational work of Relational Competence opens a pathway through which the development of fuller consciousness is helped. Consciousness in its normal definition usually means the conscious awareness we have as humans, that is, our being aware of being aware. For this chapter, we will use a broader definition offered by Mitchell and Williams (1996, p. 155), in which they say consciousness "implies the broad scope of mental phenomena—awareness, intentionality, problem-solving abilities, as well as its strict meaning of conscious awareness or being aware of being aware." Kegan (1994) believes we require a bridging curriculum with the goal of helping more people reach fuller consciousness. He states (1994, p. 164) that fuller consciousness "happens through transformational education, a 'leading out' from an established habit of mind." The curriculum and educational strategy of Relational Competence is designed to help a higher order of complexity of consciousness come into existence. Mutually enhancing relationships pro-

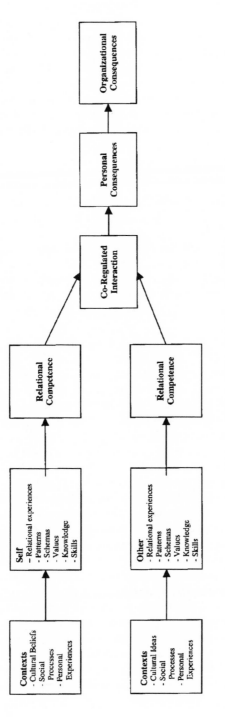

Figure 1. Model of Relational Competence

vide a context for collaboratively building the bridge to a higher order of mental complexity. Expanding the complexity of our consciousness will help global leaders to handle what Kegan refers to as the mental demands of modern life. Through the tools of Relational Competence, we can anchor new information in what is already known and create a bridge to what needs to be known in order to meet our ever increasing complexity of mental demands. The bridging curriculum of Relational Competence will take us from novice to expert as we develop proficiency in conducting complex, cross-cultural, multi-perspective, mutually enhancing relationships between individuals, organizations, and networks.

COMPONENTS OF THE MODEL OF RELATIONAL COMPETENCE

Understanding the model of Relational Competence requires information about multiple components. These components are illustrated graphically in Figure 1. The boxes in the figure are variables and will be defined later. Arrows connect the boxes. These arrows represent the causal relationships. An arrow from one box to another means the variable(s) in the first box influence the variables in the second.

Contexts: Cultural, Social, and Personal

The first set of boxes is the Contexts. The upper Context box is for the Self and the lower is for the Other. This method demonstrates that there are at least two people in any relationship and the components influencing Relational Competence are different for each person. In each Context box the figure lists Cultural Beliefs, Social Processes, and Personal Experiences.

We are all born into and live in a *cultural* context. Most of the time we are unaware of its continual influence on us. The cultural context is created by the core cultural values and beliefs that develop from shared assumptions about what is good, moral, and aesthetic. These core cultural assumptions can be seen in ideologies, philosophies, and institutions. These produce knowledge and power through historical, economic, political, legal, and social factors.

The *social* context is made up of the socio-psychological processes of custom, norms, roles, and expectations. Using the core cultural values and beliefs, our institutions generate normalized rules of behavior. For example, a culture's core cultural values and beliefs are reflected in child-rearing practices, scripts for social interactions, scripts and practices for relationships, business organizations, legal systems, language, religious systems, and the media.

Our *personal* experiences are the subjective experiences that stem from the core cultural beliefs and the social context. These experiences occur in the relationships we have in our family life, schools, churches, work settings, social settings, and other daily activities. The core cultural and social contexts are repeatedly experienced in our daily activities and gradually become firmly established in our inter-actions with others.

Each individual is constantly being influenced by these cultural, social, and per-sonal contexts. These contexts are interactional systems that create our knowledge of relationships and our mental programs for how to conduct relationships. They are not static but are in perpetual cycles of mutual influence. If we wish to under-stand how to relate better with others, we must learn how these different contexts effect not only ourselves, but also the other person. This is one of the steps in improving Relational Competence.

Self and Other

The next pair of boxes is the Self and the Other. The arrows to these two boxes indicate that the Cultural, Social, and Personal contexts have a strong and direct influence on who we are. The same is true for the Other in the relationship. From conception throughout our life span, we are bombarded with experiences. As we organize these experiences, our self develops patterns that reflect our learned modes of dealing with situations and are always in some way shaped by the situations themselves. These experiences become combined into the components of the Self and Other boxes: Relational Experiences, Patterns, Schemas, Values, and Know-ledge. From our relational experiences with others, we develop regularities in our patterns of sensations, thoughts, feelings, and actions when engaging with others. These patterns of experiences are sometimes referred to as relational schemas.

Relational Competence

The next box represents the level of Relational Competence that the Self and Other bring to the interaction. As we have discussed before, the level of Relational Competence is much more than just a set of interactional skills. It includes a set of a series of things such as values, relational processes, and relational practices, which we will discuss later in the chapter.

Co-regulated Interaction of Participants

The next box refers to the actual interaction. Both participants bring their con-texts, individual characteristics, and degree of Relational Competence to this interaction. What occurs in the interaction is regulated by the participants. Fogel (1993, p. 61) labels this process as "co-regulation" and suggests that this process "emphasizes the dynamically changing individual at the very moment of transac-tion with others: an individual whose behavior and goals are not entirely planned in advance but emerge creatively out of social discourse." This illustrates an important point. The interaction process within relationships can be a creative pro-cess and the important outcomes can emerge from this creative process.

Personal Consequences

There can be some very positive personal consequences from this co-regulated interaction if this process is carried out competently. According to Mitchell (1998), we experience our self through a matrix of relations with others that includes our self, the other, and the space in between. This space in between self and other is where interaction and action takes place. What happens in this space in between is continuously flowing back and forth, penetrating both self and other, and thereby, changing self and other at the moment of interaction. It is this process that holds the greatest possibility for development. If what goes on between self and other is growth promoting, then each person will experience himself or herself as expanded and enhanced. This sense of empowerment can then be transferred to other relationships. This can create an ever-increasing series of enhancing relationships.

Organizational Consequences of Interaction

Finally, the quality of the interaction and personal consequences has a powerful influence on organizational outcomes. It is here that problems get solved, differences are worked out, conflicts resolved, innovations arise, and foundations are set for future positive interactions. These outcomes occur if the relationshipping is competent. If it is not, the outcomes are drastically reduced.

Feedback Loops

Although not shown in the figure, there are feedback relationships in the full model whereby one variable has back-effects through some of the other variables. For example, if organizational consequences such as creative decisions or conflict resolution occur, these can change the person's values and improve the person's relational competence. This will change the way the person interacts in the future, which will then lead to further improvements in personal and organizational consequences.

Five Domains of Relational Competence Expertise

We have talked about Relational Competence in a number of ways. We now focus on the specific expertise required for Relational Competence. The five domains of expertise not only help define the concept of Relational Competence, but also point to what needs to be trained to improve it.

The five domains of expertise that form the basis of Relational Competence and the effectiveness tools that encompass this approach include:

- Relationally Based Values
- Emotional Intelligence

- Relational Work—Processes and Practices
- Relationship Development and Sustainment
- Cross-cultural Dialogue

Relationally Based Values

As human beings we are conceived, biologically wired, born, and live our whole lives within a relational matrix. All our relationships, whether at work or home, have a profound effect on our health and growth. All human beings deserve a social, emotional, spiritual, and physical workplace environment that supports optimal growth and development. This environment does not come naturally in the work setting. A business environment that supports optimal growth and development has to be developed. This environment can be facilitated through an adoption of relationally based implicit and explicit values that support the essential relational work for deep structural change.

Old business paradigm values. The old business paradigm was based on seeing human beings as machine-like instead of social beings. People were hired to fit jobs and were expected to conform to that which the job required. The emphasis on specialized tasks caused people to experience compartmentalization in their work. People became disconnected from one another in the pursuit of the bottom line. What became increasingly ignored was people's need to be a part of a community. This old business paradigm was influenced by previous theories of childhood and life span development that promoted disconnection. These older developmental theories presented a model of healthy development as one in which we needed to achieve separation from others, autonomy, independence, and repression of emotional experiences. The focus of development was on achieving identity through comparisons, competition, disconnection, and superiority.

This old paradigm promoted competition as the predominant way of relating in a business setting. In Western culture, "From the very earliest years in school through the highest levels of education, we are urged to compete, not to 'cheat' by cooperating with others, not to taste the benefits of the co-creation that can come from working in teams" (Joba, Maynard, & Ray, 1993, p. 51). These same authors point out (1993, p. 51) that we have continued to embrace competition as the way to conduct business even though "research in almost every human science field since the late 1800s has indicated that cooperation is a superior form of relationship in nature and organizations, psychologically, physiologically, and economically." This old value system contradicts the values needed to make teams, relationships, and communities work well. We have discovered that we cannot afford to continue using the same implicit and explicit cultural values that support separation, alienation, and disconnection in the face of overwhelming evidence that all living systems are profoundly interconnected and interdependent upon one another for survival.

As we learn to become more connected in relation to ourselves, others, and the environment, and gain a sense of greater purpose through work, we are likely to find it difficult to continue to believe that it is possible to conduct our business relationships from a different set of values than we use in our other relationships. We do not really have two lives, one personal life and one business life. We have one life and we spend the majority of our waking hours in our organizations. We have been encouraged to believe that it is okay and ethical to have two different sets of values, one set for conducting business relationships and another for conducting other relationships. In the old business paradigm, we justify undermining or betraying other people by the cliche that "business is business." We rationalize that throat-cutting aggression is necessary in business. In order to deal with this double life, we have to create barriers inside of ourselves. We tell ourselves that we would not behave this way in our personal life without acknowledging that we are the same person in all of our contexts. It is important for us to begin to face that what we do in our business relationships reflects our integrity and values in the same way as in all of our other relationships.

It is important for us to recognize that all of life is interrelated. We are all in a network of mutual interconnection. Whatever affects one of us directly, such as being exploited in business, affects all of us indirectly.

Our cultural conception of humankind has been greatly influenced by a hierarchical model. A hierarchical model is one in which each person is organized or classified according to rank or authority. There is not something inherently wrong with a hierarchical model itself. The problem comes when one human being is seen as more worthwhile than another human being because he or she occupies a higher level in the hierarchy. In the old business paradigm, this treating of one human being as more valuable than another is exactly what became the norm in organizations as well as society in general. This type of dysfunctional behavior leads to a "power over" way of relating rather than a "power-sharing" way of relating. As adults, many of us try to take on the position of having power over others. However, the "power over" position is seldom safe because it is never a secure position and someone else is usually vying for it. The person in the "power over" position is usually being challenged so he or she becomes threatened and defensive. This leads to a loss of his or her full freedom to act. In addition, organizations lose the potential creative contribution of the people who are in "power under" positions. On the other hand, in mutual interactions where both people are contributing and "power sharing," both people report feeling comfortable and empowered.

The historical focus on human beings as essentially separate rather than connected has led to an interactional system that is referred to as subject-object relating. Subject-object relating, with its emphasis on separateness and disconnection in development, has led to a potentially distancing form of relating. This means that the subject (us) interacts with others as if they were just objects, not feeling human beings with needs. This infers viewing others as "things" to be used for our gratification. At work, this type of subject-object relating happens when an employer relates to employees as "hired help" and has an attitude that the employee should be willing to work at all hours regardless of the employee's outside activities or commitments. The employee is treated as an object used solely to gratify what the employer wants at that moment.

We are also doing subject-object relating when we refer to people who have specialist knowledge as "knowledge capital" or "intellectual capital." While seemingly clever, this language exposes the discrepancy between the theory in use— employees are just a means (objects) to an end (capital)—and the espoused theory—people are important. Using people as objects is not only mistreatment of people but is also self-defeating for the organization. When people are treated and related to as objects, they become angry and less productive, and eventually leave the organization or sabotage the goals of an organization. This type of subject-object interaction eventually leads to overall financial loss for the company. A reduction in subject-object relating and an increase in subject-to-subject (human-to-human) relating save organizations many financial losses related to low productivity, low morale, and lack of retention.

Too much positive and creative potential is uncultivated owing to the lack of mutually growth-promoting and inspirational interactions in the workplace. In our organizations, we need a new set of implicit values that are congruent with explicit values concerning the appropriate treatment of all human beings. These values must include, but go beyond, basic human rights. The values must alter many of our implicit cultural concepts regarding other human beings and ourselves.

New business paradigm values. In the model of Relational Competence, our underlying value system is one that respects the worth, value, creativity, and the potential for growth and development of every human being. We believe that every person, family, group, and organization can only reach their potential when treated with respect, empathy, and with deep, non-judgmental interest.

The model of Relational Competence offers organizations a shift from the old business paradigm to a new business paradigm. This model supports a shift in what is valued in human and organizational relationships. When we recognize people's basic nature as social beings, we realize the necessity of allowing jobs to fit people. We can see how creativity flows from flexibility and interaction with other people. We support a cultural shift from competition to cooperation; a shift from impersonal to personal communication; a shift from disconnection to connection; a shift from using people to valuing people; a shift in the way we view relationships; and, a shift from single bottom line to multiple bottom lines.

As adult workers, we have enormous potential for creativity, generosity, love, kindness, forgiveness, empathy, appreciation, sensitivity, trust—all of humankind's finest features. We also have the potential for vengeance, hate, blame, malevolence, insensitivity to others, destruction of others and our environment— some of humankind's worst features. It is the relationship with others both at work and home and how we are perceived and treated by others that will influence the degree to which each of these capacities becomes the underlying value system that guides our lives and our treatment of others and ourselves. Just as we first develop our selves in emotionally significant relationships with others, as working adults, we continue to grow or not grow in emotionally significant relationships with others. Some interactions with others are more helpful in the developmental change process than others. Interdependence, cooperation, mutual respect, mutual empathy, mutual understanding, and co-creating a shared reality are some of the relational values and practices that global leaders and organizations will need to incorporate in order to create a positive sustainable future.

Relational Competence is based on the premise that we learn our values and ways of relating with others from our experiences in relationships early in life. If we believe that human beings are basically good, we will treat them as if they are, and thereby enable them to relate to us more sincerely. If we believe that human beings are not basically good and we treat them as such, it heightens tension and negativity and makes cooperation very difficult. Since we know ourselves to be a common humanity, treating others with a lack of respect tends to stifle our own inner being with the lessening of joy, spontaneity, and creativity. A change in our concept of human beings and the importance of their welfare will lead to changes in our behavior toward others and ourselves. We can learn new values and more appropriate ways of interacting with others. We can learn to relinquish ties to our less growth-promoting values and relational patterns, thereby allowing openness to new and richer values and more developmentally enhancing relationships.

Emotional Intelligence

The second domain of Relational Competence expertise is learning to use our intelligence to manage our emotional life in a growth-promoting way. Goleman (1995) referred to this process as developing emotional intelligence. Emotional intelligence involves the self-awareness of recognizing one's emotions from moment to moment and being able to manage these emotions in an appropriate way. Emotional intelligence also involves using empathy to recognize and be appropriately responsive to the emotions of others.

As humans we use emotions as signals to guide our decisions, actions, and interactions. We frequently are not consciously aware of how this signaling process works, because in Western culture we have not learned to fully understand our emotions. Emotions are an essential part of what gives our human lives vitality and meaning. One need only observe sportii.g events, religious rituals, religious conflicts, business meetings, and family gatherings to see the enormous outpouring of emotions in interactions in all cultures. In order to use our emotions in an intelligent manner, we must begin by returning the centrality of emotions to their rightful place in our own culture.

New emotional competencies will make a crucial difference in the corporation's success. Kelly (1993, p. 91) quotes Jim Autry as saying, "Work is a community we come into, and we live in it, we love in it, we fear in it, we have anger, we cry. We hate one another sometimes. The workplace is filled with all the passions of life. So where in the world did we ever get this notion that at work you have to be this calm, impassive, detached person?" As noted by Goleman (1998, p. 29), "more and more companies are seeing that encouraging emotional intelligence skills is a vital component of any organization's management philosophy." The business world's attempts to ignore emotions or inappropriately manage emotions have led to more financial losses, more illnesses, more misunderstandings, more lost productivity, and more loss of profitable relationships than any other one single factor in organizations. Organizational theories and practices must recognize the centrality of emotions in the hiring, retaining, motivating, discharging, and evaluating of employees. The care and handling of emotions is the essential ingredient of creating business environments that are conductive to creativity, flexibility, innovation, vision, inspiration, and trust.

If we can accept the importance and centrality of emotions in our organizations, then our next step is to learn the meaning and appropriate management of our own emotions and the appropriate responsiveness to other people's emotions. In our organizations, it is through understanding emotions and being appropriately responsive to the emotional component of interaction that true mutual growth takes place. Agreements, misunderstandings, and repair of misunderstandings are all emotionally generated and resolved. We will never get rid of emotions, nor should we continue to try. What we must learn to do is understand and manage the centrality that emotions play in the quality of our life. One aspect of emotional intelligence is responsive listening and responsive communication. These skills require the understanding and appropriate responsiveness to the emotions of others. This appropriate emotional responsiveness is essential to the development of trust, openness, increased dedication, and enhanced productivity. For example, the emotional experiences of people influence their openness to the implementation of new technology. When training a person to use new technology on the job, the successful implementation of technology will depend on the trainer's ability to appropriately respond to the emotional experience of the user. Learning and using the skills of emotionally responsive communication will also lead to more successful implementation of new technology, increased ability to manage the change process, and the increased capacity to create mutually empowering relationships in all interactions.

The principles and tools of Relational Competence can guide global leadership in the development of increased emotional competencies in local as well as cross-cultural settings. These new competencies include the ability to interact through empathic transactions (Clark, 1991) with others. Global leadership can learn how to avoid the devastating effects of shaming and non-empathic communication in the workplace as well as learn how to repair disruptions in empathic communication.

Relational Work—Processes and Practices

The third area of expertise in Relational Competence is learning how to do the essential relational work necessary for mutually growth-enhancing relationships. This relational work involves constructive and effective ways of interacting with one another. This relational work is how we will be able to change our relationships with one another in our organizations. These practices and processes enable us to change our relationships from those that inhibit growth to relationships that promote growth.

This area of expertise in Relational Competence is of substantial importance. A variety of the best practices from relationship, communication, interpersonal, and emotional competencies are organized into a coherent human relations operating system. This operating system is organized using the relational approach of focusing on what happens *between* people and organizations. The system is also organized around the principle that significant development takes place *within* relationships. All of the relational work is conducted from the new business paradigm of relationally based values. When these best practices are carried out from a coherent human relations operating system using the new business paradigm of relationally based values and a relational approach for interacting, the results are profound and long lasting. These best practices include but are not limited to appreciative inquiry, generative inquiry, conducting dialogues, empathic transactions, relational empathy, responsive listening, emotional competencies, and a variety of other growth-promoting practices. Overall, the relational work involves trust-promoting relational communication processes and practices that involve understanding and accepting as valid, multiple perspectives and multiple voices. The relational work involves a number of critical practices and processes that influence day-to-day relationships:

- Understanding and managing emotions that affect self-worth, trust, cooperation, and actions in the workplace
- Developing responsive listening techniques
- Learning to have mutually enhancing dialogues that include reflecting, validating, and empathizing
- Recognizing the various perspectives each person brings to an interaction
- Interpreting the diverse meanings we apply to statements and actions (meaning-making)
- Repairing misunderstandings before they have an impact on the productivity and objectives of the organization

Developing our local and global potential depends on human cooperation. Human cooperation is generated through relational work. Relational work can improve the quality of our interactions with others. The quality of Relational Competence depends on the kind of connection that occurs between people when they relate in ways that maximize the presence of their authentic humanness. People's explicit and implicit choices about what to disclose and what to attend to, combine to define the quality of the contact between them. Stewart (1995) discusses the importance of openness while interacting with others. He points out that "being open can mean being both receptive to others' ideas and feelings and willing to disclose. A person can be open in the sense that he or she is tolerant, broadminded, and willing to listen (open to input) and open in the sense that he or she does not hesitate to share ideas and feelings with others (open with output)."

Many interactions at work are not mutually growth enhancing. In fact, the destructive interactions and the shortage of growth-enhancing relationships provide the basis for many problems in our organizations and society. Individual differences in interacting relationally are learned early in life. However, with appropriate structured and experiential learning, these competencies can be significantly enhanced to benefit the global leader and the organization. Our ability to understand, develop, and refine the underlying processes and practices of Relational Competence brings added value to our organizations through our expanded relational capacities.

Relationship Development and Sustainment

The fourth domain of expertise in Relational Competence is how to start, develop, and sustain relationships that enhance both self and others. The most important work to be done by relational leaders is to learn how to build mutually empowering relationships. Since all business is conducted through relationships, the quality of our relationships determines the quality of our business results. Most of us have been unaware of this critical factor in business. In their book, *Dialogue,* Ellinor and Gerard (1998) point out that we seem to be culturally blind to the all-important factor of relationships because we focus almost exclusively on getting the work done instead of how we get results through working with others. They state, "Our relationships with others are often the last thing we consciously focus on. In our rush to complete our work, we may not realize the damage we do to some of the most important relationships we have."

Learning to initiate, develop, and sustain effective and mutually enhancing relationships involves relationship knowledge and a wide range of abilities that must be coordinated. According to relationship expert, Duck (1995, p. 312), "Relationshipping is actually a very complicated and prolonged process with many pitfalls and challenges. Relationships do not just happen; they have to be made—made to start, made to work, made to develop, kept in good working order and preserved from going sour." Relational work must continue throughout the life of a relationship in order to keep it alive and well.

The role of management in organizations is changing. There is now far more emphasis on the effectiveness of personal relationships in communicating complex information (Bartlett & Ghoshal, 1995). Many managers are also realizing the necessity of building networks of relationships throughout the organization through which all people can exchange information and develop ideas. From this perspective, relationships are seen as important for the transfer of information and learning. Research indicates that the quality of the relationship determines the quality and speed at which information is transferred within and across organizations.

Quality relationships are developed in the ongoing creation of a mutually empathic dialogue. In this kind of dialogue, each person is challenged to stay present and responsive to others. It is important for each participant to stay motivated to remain real, vital, purposeful, and honest in the relationship. Mutually empowering relationships are the source of a leader's power and effectiveness, not weaknesses or threats to effectiveness (Miller, 1989).

Miller (1989) has written about how the positive effect created in one relationship can be transferred to action and movement across many relationships. As we engage in more knowledge-increasing interactions, we are motivated to seek increasingly complex networks of relationships, both within our present relationships and with new connections. This process enables global leaders throughout the organization to grow more skillful in the engagement of differences, conflicts, and multiple priorities. The relational connections make it possible for mutual strengths to be activated, experienced, validated, and sustained. These interactions make it possible for global leaders and organizations to successfully navigate the complex territory of multifaceted perspectives and challenges in our growing global community.

With the increasing necessity to form strategic alliances across the wide spectrum of industries, developing and sustaining healthy relationships has become a priority for enabling these partnerships to endure. Companies forming strategic alliances have faced some of the same challenges found in personal partnerships. Lessons learned include the following: (1) the alliance really begins after the deal is signed; (2) the best people to manage the partnership are the ones who set it up; (3) partners have to sort out decision making processes, conflict resolution, and learn how to be flexible; (4) partnerships need to be managed and monitored; (5) the lack of regular communication between the point people contributes to the breakdown of the alliance; (6) without ongoing attention and focus on common goals, the partnership can wither and die; (7) alliances have a discouraging rate of failure and this is very costly; and (8) some key reasons for failure of the partnership are (a) unequal or untapped levels of competence, (b) alliance was not considered central by both partners, and (c) partners were untrained in how to make relationships work (Maynard, 1996).

Relationships in strategic alliances and networks also face the enormous challenge of adapting and melding cultures together. This cultural blending may include different global cultures as well as organizational cultures. With the prediction that the formation of strategic alliances will be rapidly increasing, it is imperative that organizations focus on ways to improve relationship development and sustainment.

Many organizations now have subsidiary locations worldwide. One challenge faced by the organization in these situations is how well a subsidiary embraces the global strategy of headquarters, particularly if this strategy does not result in the best results for the individual subsidiary. The strength of the relationship between headquarters and subsidiaries may be the crucial leverage point.

Cross-cultural Dialogue

The fifth domain of Relational Competence expertise is the Cross-cultural Dialogue. One of the most demanding challenges facing global leaders is how to effectively and appropriately develop, facilitate, and manage cross-cultural relationships. These relationships are so challenging because they involve very high levels of complexity and multiplicity. The multiplicity includes differences in people, cultures, and organizations. At the very minimum, this requires us to pay attention to culture, gender, race, ethnicity, religion, and sexual orientation. In our cross-cultural relationships, as well as in all our relationships, it is important for us to take a relational approach. The "Cross-cultural Dialogue" is a specific mechanism that helps global leaders to organize and conduct the complex challenge of multidimensional processing. It also helps increase the effectiveness of work projects in cross-cultural situations. The process of the Cross-cultural Dialogue is shown graphically in Figure 2.

Co-regulated Interaction

The first set of circles shows how the Cross-cultural Dialogue begins with the co-regulated interaction. As was illustrated earlier in the diagram of the model of Relational Competence, both participants bring all their cultural contexts, individual characteristics, and degrees of Relational Competence to this interaction. What goes on in this interaction is co-regulated by both people from their culturally learned interaction patterns. It is extremely important that we understand that even though people have the same mental processes that transform sensory input into knowledge, different cultures vary in the way they organize, transmit, and act upon information.

The first step in this co-regulated interaction is best established by making efforts to understand how others construct their reality. This requires that we develop the capacity to *respect* diversity. When we try to reduce this process to only skills training we run into the problem of people just learning to say or do what is politically correct. Although learning to be politically correct with regard to diversity is a good starting place, it is still leaves the unfavorable attributions and stereotyping seething right under the surface. In respecting diversity, we can learn that what another culture does or believes make sense to them. It is our job to understand what they do or believe from their perspective. That does not mean that we agree with their ways or would do the same thing ourselves. Our relational

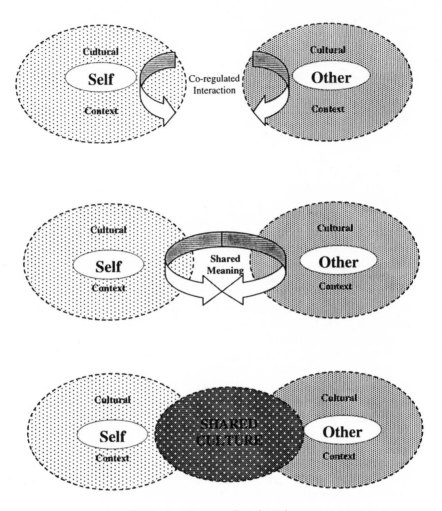

Figure 2. Cross-cultural Dialogue

work is to attempt to see it from their viewpoint, not from our viewpoints. Understanding that these behaviors are about adapting to one's particular environment or culture enables us to make more sense of a person's actions that seem very different or even bizarre to us. People's behavior makes more sense to us if we view it from a larger context rather than just disregarding the person as inferior or not worthy of respectful treatment.

In order to establish empathic communication across cultures, we must understand other cultures emotional systems. Once we have mastered the management of our own emotions and the appropriate responsiveness to the emotions of others in our own culture, we are then ready to learn how we can connect with people in other cultures in a relationally competent way. This will involve learning their culture's emotional management system. When interacting with someone from a culture different from our own, we need to begin by understanding the emotions in their culture, the meaning of those emotions in their culture, and appropriate responses to their emotions according to their culture's expectations. In joint projects, the other culture will need to develop the same information about our culture's method of emotional management. This can lead to a shared understanding of the appropriate way to make sense of the emotions and the appropriate responses to these emotions as they arise in daily business activities.

Shared Meaning

The second set of circles in Figure 2 shows how our emotionally responsive, co-regulated interaction provides a basis for building shared meanings between the communicators. By using the Cross-cultural Dialogue, we can learn to dialogue about what is really important, such as underlying values and belief systems, espoused values and belief systems, emotionally laden meaning-making, and how to create mutually satisfying alternatives for all participants. When engaging with others, it is important to watch for the properties of the dialogue, and to watch for each person's capacity to enter, share, and shape meaning in the dialogue.

We can establish a meaningful bond necessary for an ongoing successful relationship. This ongoing bond will be established through three important interdependent needs—kinship, reliance, and validation (Basch, 1995). Kinship is the assumption that through trust we will be sufficiently welcomed and valued. Through the Cross-cultural Dialogue we find that there is a possibility of being understood, that whatever our individual differences, we may be able to stand on common ground. Once kinship is established, we develop the capacity for reliance. Reliance is the freedom to utilize the other person's guidance. As mutual meaning-making progresses, we are then able to develop the capacity for validation, which is the readiness to be assured, enriched, and encouraged by another's understanding. Through the Cross-cultural Dialogue, we are able to meet the interdependent and cross-cultural needs of kinship, reliance, and validation. This in turn helps us establish new mutual meaningful alternatives through each culture's participation. This process can release the exhilarating potential that makes for extraordinary project outcomes for all people involved.

Shared Culture

The third set of circles in Figure 2 shows how a "shared culture" develops from the ongoing dialogue. In working together, neither culture has to give up its values, traditions, rituals, or the other activities that make it a unique culture. Through the Cross-cultural Dialogue, we can move beyond these differences. We have created a shared culture from which to conduct a joint work project. This shared culture can be a source of mutual power and effectiveness. Our mutual strengths can be expanded, validated, and activated into successful work projects. The strength we experience in these joint projects will be experienced as powerful and sustaining. The empowerment we experience in this shared culture can then be transferred to action across many other complex relationships.

In summary, the most complex challenge for global leaders is dealing with multiple realities and multiple perspectives in multiple cultures. The process of the Cross-cultural Dialogue, as shown in Figure 2, will enable global leaders to deal with multiple perspectives in ways that lead to the development of new mutual meanings and alternatives. By using the Cross-cultural Dialogue, we can accelerate our understanding of others. We can learn that another person's reality makes sense given a particular background of experiences. We can mutually shape the goal of understanding each other's perspective and the meaning-making process. The ongoing mutual meaning-making process increases each participant's understanding of the other and further develops the Cross-cultural Dialogue. Through this process, we have a way to effectively work cross-culturally through the activation of a mutual plan of action on shared projects.

BENEFITS OF RELATIONAL COMPETENCE

Relational Competence has profound benefits to organizations and the people who work in them. One particular place in which benefits will be great is organizations whose employees work in teams. Experience is showing that enormous power can be generated and released in effectively designed work teams (Orsburn, Moran, Musselwhite, & Zenger, 1997). Research shows that people working together with integrity, authenticity, and collective intelligence are profoundly more effective than people working together in ways based on politics, narrow self-interest, and competition among themselves (Leavitt & Lipman-Blumen, 1995). Therefore, learning to build more innovative and effective teams through relationship building needs to become a high priority in organizations. Moreover, in global organizations, virtual teams are being created, and these require an even higher level of interpersonal connections, trust, and communication to keep these teams working smoothly, spanning the geographical distance between team members (Handy, 1995).

In addition to improving team building, Relational Competence helps organizations improve their ability to provide continuous learning at every level of the company. Learning and the transfer of knowledge take place through relationships. Starting in the late 1970s with the writings of Argyris and Schoen (1996), there was a gradual acceptance of the necessity of organizational learning and by 1990, there was a near explosion of interest in learning organizations. By the mid-1990s, there was a general understanding across disciplines that the process of continuous learning is imperative. Senge's work (1990, 1994) struck a chord about the growing need for building learning organizations and his books became popular reading for progressive professionals. Although learning organizations started with the purpose of increasing competitive edges through increasing knowledge, their purpose has evolved to include fostering partnerships with others and building learning communities that go beyond boundaries within and between organizations. In organizational learning, there is increased emphasis on relational themes such as partnerships and community building through interdependency and cooperation designed for the benefit of the whole.

Another relational theme that is gaining increased attention in organizational literature is the importance of building communities at work. The experience of being part of a community is a felt sense of belonging to a larger network of shared interests and concerns. Building communities means finding a way in organizations where employees, customers, and vendors feel connected to each other and feel a part of something important. Many people are experiencing a deterioration of the former traditional shared community values that used to be shared in neighbors, families, schools, and churches. People are yearning to feel connected to others and to feel part of a community. People are turning to their workplace to try to create shared values and a sense of belonging. Some organizations are beginning to understand the importance of creating an environment that supports community building. One factor contributing to the organization's desire to build communities is the growing awareness that the company needs knowledgeable people to stay with the company more than the knowledgeable people need them (Stewart, 1997). Therefore, belonging to an organizational community may meet an employee's need to belong, increase loyalty to the organizational community, and facilitate the diffusion of an individual's specialized knowledge to other members of the community. In essence, community building leaves the organization less vulnerable to the loss of that which some organizations view as valuable people, and others view as valuable knowledge.

As is pointed out by Levey and Levey (1995, p. 109), "Quality relationships are at the heart of community." The central focus of Relational Competence is how to build quality relationships in our work settings. Therefore, Relational Competence offers organizations the essential relationally based values, practices, and tools for building positive, sustainable communities within organizations.

New research by The Gallup Organization found a strong connection between several of the issues addressed in the model of Relational Competence and the profitability of a business. Hatfield (1998-1999, p. 5) states, "Through forty years of workplace research, Gallup has isolated a critical core of issues fundamental to sustained business growth. Having leaders who manage with heart is a decisive one." He also states, "our research indicates there are definite bottom line benefits to fostering emotional intelligence, a pursuit that, in the past, has been regarded as optional or a frequently deferred expense. Employee satisfaction—boosted by such things as good quality relationships with managers and coworkers and respect for their importance, future, and connectedness—is a direct route to customer satisfaction, as well as productivity, profit, reduced turnover, and other critical outcomes."

THE CHALLENGE

Mutual growth-enhancing change is of critical importance. A growing number of people are realizing that genuine solutions to these challenges lies in the realm of raising human consciousness. It is imperative that we become conscious of the kind of global business world that we are in the process of creating. If we as global leaders want to have an impact in shaping the direction of this change, then the time for action is now. Relational Competence must become an integral part of our strategic planning process. We have strategies for getting what we want financially, for expanding markets, and for developing innovative products. With the focus becoming more on relationships and how we develop our creativity and flexibility through growth-promoting interactions, organizations need a strategy for making this possible. Keeping in mind the phenomenal importance of developing a life-sustaining relational ecology both locally and globally, organizations that develop a Relational Competence strategy give their organizations a distinct market advantage by giving people an opportunity to grow their relational capacities, along with production and profit. We must develop a Relational Competence strategy that will enable us to develop our mutual growth-enhancing relational capacities along with a deepened ethical and spiritual life to match our outer technological powers. This Relational Competence strategy needs to be designed to lead to the improvement of relationships through mutually enhancing interactions and more compassionate behavior toward one another in the work setting. This strategy needs to be about how to develop relationship capacities that have the greatest impact on individuals, organizations, and society as a whole. This strategy needs to create an organizational culture that supports Relational Competence as well as how to select, develop, and use it to continually activate and evoke ongoing change.

Kegan (1994) described how we are metaphorically "in over our heads" with the complexity of the demands of our modern day life. If we were in over our heads in 1994, we can speculate that we are even deeper in over our heads as we approach the millennium. We are facing some very important questions and we have some very serious choices to make during this time when all our systems are in transition. We need to ask ourselves about what kind of world we are in the process of creating. If we want a world of competition, conflict, and destruction, we are doing fine. If we want a world of understanding, cooperation, and prosperity for all people and our planet, we must chose alternative ways of conducting our business relationships.

What can we as global leaders do? As global leaders, we can take on the challenge to facilitate the creation of a better world and a more positive sustainable future. We can do this by making a choice to learn how to serve a higher purpose, one that will benefit all living systems, through our organizations. We can adopt new paradigms that are based on relational, ethical, and spiritual principles in business, as well as in all other areas of our lives. We can learn to facilitate the development of others and ourselves into fuller people, and unite our people in organizations in the pursuit of objectives worthy of our best efforts. Our strongest human motivations appear to be a striving for competence and connection. Most of us want a sense of connection and commitment to work that is meaningful and makes a difference in our world. Global leadership has the opportunity to facilitate this vision into being.

Global leadership has an immense responsibility in shaping the future of global transformation, whether for the greater good of all, or for our demise. What we now need is global leaders who will invest in the challenging curriculum of personal and relational development. This may mean giving up some of our traditional ways that have brought us achievement in the past. Enhanced relational capabilities are essential for us in order to deal appropriately, effectively, and competently with the vast complexity and diversity that we face in our organizations, communities, nations, and world. Through the curriculum of Relational Competence, global leadership can learn to participate in effective, multi-perspective, and mutually enhancing relationships, as well as learn how to facilitate people worldwide in the process of developing a more viable and sustainable model of conducting business. Each of us can learn to offer something more real and vital of ourselves, a more communicative form of engagement and relation. We believe that all of us have something very important and positive to contribute during this transition. It is left to each of us to choose how we will engage with others in our work lives, and that choice is not a single event but a continual process. Constructive, sustainable living requires continual choice. Who will lead? Will you?

REFERENCES

Argyris, C., & Schoen, D. A. (1996). *Organizational learning II*. Reading, MA: Addison-Wesley.

Bartlett, C.A., & Ghoshal S. (1995, May-June). Changing the role of top management: Beyond systems to people. *Harvard Business Review,* 132-142.

Basch, M. F.(1995). *Doing brief psychotherapy.* New York: Basic Books.

Beebe, B., & Lachmann, F. (1996). Mother-infant mutual influence and precursors of psychic structure. In A. Goldberg (Ed.), *Frontiers in self psychology: Progress in self psychology* (Vol. 3, pp. 3-25). Hillsdale, NJ: Analytic Press.

Bergman, S. (1991). Men's psychological development: A relational perspective. *Work in progress,* No. 48, 1-13. Wellesley, MA: Stone Center Working Paper Series.

Clark, B. (1991). Empathic transactions in the deconfusion of child ego states. *Transactional Analysis Journal,* 21, 92-98.

Clark, B., & Matze, M. (1991, October). Developmental organization of self: A relational approach. Paper presented at Institute for Integrative Psychotherapy, Kent, CT.

Duck, S. (1995). Our friends, ourselves. In J. Stewart (Ed.), *Bridges not walls* (pp. 312-315). New York: McGraw-Hill.

Eisler, R. (1993). Foundation for a new world order. In M. Ray & A. Rizler for the World Business Academy (Eds.), *The new paradigm in business: Emerging strategies for leadership and organizational change* (pp. 276-280). New York: G. P. Putnam's Sons.

Elgin, D., & LeDrew, C. (1997). Global consciousness change: Indicators of an emerging paradigm. *Millenium Project*.

Ellinor, L., & Gerard G.(1998). *Dialogue* (p. 13). New York: Wiley.

Fogel, A. (1993). *Developing through relationships* (pp. 26-42). Chicago: University of Chicago Press.

Gates, J. (1998). *The ownership solution: Toward a shared capitalism for the 21st century* (pp. 146-155). Reading, MA: Addison-Wesley.

Ghoshal, S., & Bartlett, C. A. (1997). *The individualized corporation* (pp. 59-68). New York: Harper-Collins.

Goleman, D. (1995). *Emotional intelligence*. New York: Bantam.

Goleman, D. (1998). *Working with emotional intelligence*. New York: Bantam.

Gordon, E. E., Morgan, R. R., & Ponticell, J. A. (1994). *Futurework*. Westport, CT: Praeger.

Handy, C. (1995). Trust and the virtual organization. *Harvard Business Review* (May-June): 40-50.

Harman, W., & Hormann, J. (1993). The breakdown of the old paradigm. In M. Ray & A. Rizler for the World Business Academy (Eds.), *The new paradigm of business: Emerging strategies for leadership and organizational change* (pp. 16-27). New York: G. P. Putnam's Sons.

Hatfield, D. (1998-1999, December-January). Gallup organization: New research links emotional intelligence with profitability. *The InnerEdge*, 5-8.

Joba, C., Maynard, J. B., Jr., & Ray, M. (1993). Competition, cooperation and co-creation: Insights from the world business. In M. Ray & A. Rizler for the World Business Academy (Eds.), *The new paradigm of business: Emerging strategies for leadership and organizational change* (pp. 50-56). New York: G. P. Putnam's Sons.

Kegan, R. (1994). *In over our heads: The mental demands of modern life*. Cambridge, MA: Harvard University Press.

Kelly, M. (1993). The president as poet: An intimate conversation with Jim Autry. In M. Ray & A. Rizler for the World Business Academy (Eds.), *The new paradigm of business: Emerging strategies for leadership and organizational change* (pp. 90-99). New York: G. P. Putnam's Sons.

Leavitt, H. J., & Lipman-Blumen, J. (1995, July). Hot groups. *Harvard Business Review,* 109-16.

Levey, J., & Levey, M. (1995). From chaos to community at work. In K. Gozdz (Ed.), *Community building: Renewing spirit & learning* (pp. 105-116). San Francisco: Sterling & Stone.

Maynard, R. (1996, May). Striking the right match. *Nation's Business,* 18-28.

Miller, Jean Baker. "Connections, Disconnections, and Violations"Work in Progress, No. 33, 1-9. (1988) Wellesley, MA: Stone Center Working Paper Series.

Mitchell, S.A. (1988). *Relational concepts in psychoanalysis*. Cambridge, MA: Harvard University Press.

Mitchell, E., & Williams, D. (1996). *The way of the explorer* (pp. 154-155). New York: G. P. Putnam's Sons.

Ohmae, K. (1990). *The borderless world*. New York: HarperBusiness.

Orsburn, J. D., Moran, L., Musselwhite, E. & Zenger, J. H. (1997). *Self-directed work teams: The new American challenge*. Burr Ridge, IL: Irwin.

Sass, C. (1994). On interpersonal competence. In K. Carter & M. Persnell (Eds.), *Interpretive approaches to interpersonal communication*. Albany, NY: State University of New York Press.

Schein, E. H. (1992). *Organizational culture and leadership*. San Francisco: Jossey- Bass.

Senge, P. (1990). *The fifth discipline*. New York: Doubleday.

Senge, P., Kleiner, A., Roberts, C., Ross, R. B., & Smith, B. J. (1994). *The fifth discipline fieldbook*. New York: Doubleday.

Sherriton, J., Stern, J. L.. (1996). *Corporate culture/team culture*. New York: Amacom.

Stewart, J. (1995). *Bridges not walls* (p. 32). New York: McGraw-Hill.

Stewart, T. A. (1997, March). Brain power: Who owns it…How they profit from it. *Fortune*, 105-10.

Surrey, J. (1987). Relationship and empowerment. *Work in progress,* No. 30. Wellesley, MA: Stone Center Working Paper Series.

Taylor, W. C., & Webber, A. M. (1996). *Going global* (p. xviii). New York: Penguin Group.

Villard, K., & Whipple, L. (1976). *Beginnings in relational communication* (p. 65). New York: Wiley.

Wheatley, M. J. (1994). *Leadership and the new science* (p. 67). San Francisco: Berrett-Koehler.

PART II

RESEARCH PERSPECTIVES

INTRODUCTION TO RESEARCH PERSPECTIVES

M. Jocelyne Gessner and Val Arnold

Making the transition from Part I on current thinking to Part II on some of the current research that is being done, we are proud to begin this section with a chapter by House and colleagues. The House article, describing the GLOBE project, bridges the all-too-prevalent gap between theory and research, laying out a theoretical approach to global leadership with a plan for systematic research across 64 cultures using common instruments and theory over the course of the next several years. We believe that it is safe to say there has been no attempt like it in the field of leadership, and we anxiously await each new development. It is a felicitous wedding of theory and methodology with good scientific principles and practices underlying an ambitious foray into multicultural involvement. We have included it in our research section because it does propose an explicit program of research, something that distinguishes it from the more general theoretical work in our first section.

What you will find interesting is the fundamental questions the chapter poses concerning the extent to which leadership is culturally contingent. Are some pieces truly universal (that is, transcending culture) and some more culturally spe-

Advances in Global Leadership, Volume 1, pages 165-169.
Copyright © 1999 by JAI Press Inc.
All rights of reproduction in any form reserved.
ISBN: 0-7623-0505-3

cific? This study proposes to look at both the etic and the emic (universal and specific) issues rather than to create a false dichotomy by forcing us to explore just one side or the other. Of particular interest is that this multicultural group of researchers have agreed on a definition of leadership: "the ability of an individual to influence, motivate, and enable others to contribute toward the effectiveness and success of the organizations of which they are members." Note the convergence between this definition and the one that Adler introduces in Part I of the book.

As suggested by our theorists in the previous section, the GLOBE researchers see values as a way of understanding the context in which a leader must operate. They identify "human universals" to which leaders must pay attention; these values are captured in their eight core dimensions, which reflect "important aspects of the human condition." Furthermore, like our interactionists in Part I, they believe that there is also a "task environment imperative" concerning universals of what businesses must do to ensure their survival.

The other three chapters in this section are examples of some of the research that has been conducted on cross-cultural and global leadership issues. They have more in common with each other than with the chapter by House and colleagues, per se, and are actually relatively representative of the kinds of research that has been done to date. Each chapter has its individual merits and addresses a specific concern or population of interest, and yet, collectively we again see the fragmentation and narrow focus that is typical as scientists move from theory to data collection. The scope changes from the vague and general concept of "what is a global leader" to a necessarily strictured view of what can we find out about people in this kind of job in this kind of place. Thus, we see the oft-repeated and characteristic shift in focus from discussing **leaders** to studying **managers**.

In further describing the remaining three chapters, we want to emphasize the logistical demands of conducting cross-cultural and global research. Each of these authors is to be commended for the creativity and perseverance required to collect the samples, with the concomitant difficulties of time, distance, language, culture, and cooperation. No single study could ever begin to address the complexities raised by the concept of global leadership; yet, each of these chapters contributes relevant knowledge and adds to our collective experience regarding the difficulties of translating theory into meaningful research. We are reminded of the riddle asking how one eats an elephant; the answer is "one bite at a time." What proves interesting is the search for similarities and differences in both how different authors chose their "bite of the elephant," and what questions remain not just unanswered, but unasked. We also struggle with how to separate the scientist from the science. As researchers we find it difficult not to make assumptions about human behavior and values, likely a culturally bound understanding. It will be difficult to truly be objective and empirical in determining legitimate variables when we are likely to be trapped within the bounds of our own paradigms.

The rest of this introduction is devoted to summarizing the three studies that follow, along with our sense of what may be important to tying together the conclusions of this research. To frame your exploration of these chapters, we will tell you a bit more about what we think characterizes these studies. First, you will probably notice that we have switched gears from the theory perspective of defining global leadership as "globally" as possible. In operationalizing this construct, our authors have tended to emphasize the managerial role more than the "leader" role, as well as comparing cross-cultural dimensions and target populations. With little systematic research to build on, researchers have found it hard to step as far outside the paradigms of how we study domestic leadership as they have been encouraged to by our theorists. Second, we also noticed that the practical application of conducting this research was implicitly or explicitly concerned with how to develop an expatriate manager to operate in a non-native culture. Third, in moving from "leader" to "manager," we also made a level shift, with target populations being mid-level managers and not the implied executives that the theorists hoped would have real power to shape the future and the new world order. In fact, the theorists emphasized the "people" aspects of leadership whereas the researchers keep finding the task aspect critical (Scandura, Von Glinow, and Lowe; and Hui and Tan). Is this a fundamental discrepancy between the myth of leadership and the reality of managing?

Finally, you will find our researchers struggling with how to build relevant skills in their target populations, but you will see little rhetoric about which competencies or skills one needs to be a truly global manager. The competencies suggested in Part I, such as coping with change, tolerance for ambiguity, and ability to communicate across cultures, are not discussed here. What we see instead is a focus on whether we can translate what we do know about leadership (via management jobs) into this larger context. Scientifically, this is a reasonable place to start, but it demonstrates again how often our reach (theoretically) exceeds our grasp (empirically).

Scandura, Von Glinow, and Lowe focus in their chapter on the Middle East, a virtually ignored population of managers in management literature. Their theoretical approach hinges on the Ohio State model, looking at consideration and initiating structure—the task and people theme we referenced in the theory section introduction. Their rationale was to benchmark against something familiar in order to be able to better understand the differences. They conclude that it is possible that there is a culturally bound aspect of understanding what is expected of leaders, and the relationship between leadership and organizational outcomes.

Two aspects of this study may be of particular interest to you. First, it is a good example of a cross-cultural application of a key U.S. leadership theory. Second, it is a valuable case study providing insight into Middle East culture for those of you practicing or working with nationals in the region. There are reasons to believe that widely accepted U.S. leadership styles will not translate there, which is hardly surprising to our sophisticated readers, and completely supportive of the contentions of most of our theorists in Part I. Thus, the evidence supports the idea that we cannot merely translate a leadership style from culture to culture; the unasked question is how can we better understand the systems in which the leaders and employees operate. As researchers, how can we better understand the assumptions underlying another culture when our very understanding of cause and effect (and which variables are legitimate outcome measures) are rooted in our own cultural base? Is job satisfaction a legitimately universal outcome variable across cultures?

The next chapter provides a variation on the theme of task and people orientation. Hui and Tan look at the moral component of effective leadership among Chinese managers. Interestingly they find that morality may be important in determining how much effort and productivity Chinese employees are willing to exert to complete a task. In determining the morality of a task, the Chinese look to the morality of their leader as a guide. There may even be a compensatory effect in that a moral leader may be seen as effective even when the task and relationship aspects of leadership are missing. It is even suggested that you can be perceived as low on the task part of leadership, and still be effective if you are high on morality, although typically leaders are not perceived to be high on both task orientation *and* morality/character. We can conclude that you must either be good at getting the work done, or morally upright and beyond reproach to be considered effective.

Of interest to us is the clear connection to the moral imperative approach to global leadership described by our theory authors in Part I. The emphasis on values and idea of servant leadership (e.g., Greenleaf) is a recurring theme among our authors. It appears that being ethical is clearly an important attribute of the global leader, although the nuances of what constitutes the key behaviors may be culturally specific. This conclusion seems consistent with the approach taken by the GLOBE researchers.

Our final chapter in this section is a study of cross-cultural competencies by Hazucha and colleagues. To the authors' knowledge, it is the only study of competencies accomplished in this venue. The seminal study in cross-cultural comparisons done by Hofstede concerns differences in values and, indeed, most of the additional work has focused there as well. Hazucha and colleagues use a common instrument, translated in several languages, to assess differences in competencies, which they then link to Hofstede's framework.

Of particular interest to us was their finding that the four countries they looked at were equally similar to each other in management competencies, although there were differences between countries in cultural values. This may provide support for the GLOBE project's contention that there are business universals that drive similarities that transcend culture, and fits well with our assertion in the introduction that the business and organizational environment potentially creates a common denominator for leadership expectations that is critical to understand. Hazucha and colleagues' study was done in a single multinational firm, as was Hofstede's original study with IBM. Ignoring the effect of a strong organizational culture may be misleading in drawing conclusions about global leadership.

There is also a possible connection between this study and the theoretical model proposed by Fulkerson in Part I of the book. Hazucha and colleagues begin to spell out some of the necessary competencies, but do not yet address the boundary conditions that are a part of Fulkerson's model. Some of these boundary conditions could be related to the differences in cultural values that can be seen even though the competency ratings are similar. Also, in connecting this study with the two previous studies in this section which look at task and people orientations, it might be helpful to categorize the competencies as task versus people oriented and see if this gives us insight into cultural specificities.

The unasked questions remain tantalizing. In reading this section, however, focus on what we have discovered and how it helps us to better understand how truly complex this issue is.

CULTURAL INFLUENCES ON LEADERSHIP AND ORGANIZATIONS
PROJECT GLOBE

ABSTRACT

GLOBE is both a research program and a social entity. The GLOBE social entity is a network of 170 social scientists and management scholars from 62 cultures throughout the world, working in a coordinated long-term effort to examine the interrelationships between societal culture, organizational culture and practices, and organizational leadership. The meta-goal of the Global Leadership and Organizational Effectiveness (GLOBE) Research Program is to develop an empirically based theory to describe, understand, and predict the impact of cultural variables on leadership and organizational processes and the effectiveness of these processes.

This monograph presents a description of the GLOBE research program and some initial empirical findings resulting from GLOBE research. A central question in this part of the research concerns the extent to which specific leadership attributes and behaviors are universally endorsed as contributing to effective leadership and the extent to which the endorsement of leader attributes and behaviors is culturally contingent.

Advances in Global Leadership, Volume 1, pages 171-233.

We identified six global leadership dimensions of culturally endorsed implicit theories of leadership (CLTs). Preliminary evidence indicates that these dimensions are significantly correlated with isomorphic dimensions of societal and organizational culture. These findings are consistent with the hypothesis that selected cultural differences strongly influence important ways in which people think about leaders as well as societal norms concerning the status, influence, and privileges granted to leaders.

The hypothesis that charismatic/value-based leadership would be universally endorsed is strongly supported. Team-oriented leadership is strongly correlated with charismatic/value-based leadership, and also universally endorsed. Humane and participative leadership dimensions are nearly universally endorsed. The endorsement of the remaining global leadership dimensions—self-protective and autonomous leadership—varies by culture.

We identified 21 specific leader attributes and behaviors that are universally viewed as contributing to leadership effectiveness. Eleven of the specific leader characteristics composing the global charismatic/value-based leadership dimension were among these 21 attributes. Eight specific leader characteristics were universally viewed as impediments to leader effectiveness. We also identified 35 specific leader characteristics that are viewed as contributors in some cultures and impediments in other cultures. We present these, as well as other findings, in more detail in this monograph.

A particular strength of the GLOBE research design is the combination of quantitative and qualitative data. Elimination of common method and common source variance is also a strength of the design strategy. Future directions, research strategies, and anticipated contributions are presented in anticipation of continued GLOBE efforts.

Robert J. House
University of Pennsylvania
Principal Investigator

Paul J. Hanges
University of Maryland
Principal Investigator;

S. Antonio Ruiz-Quintanilla
Cornell University
GLOBE Coordinating Team

Peter W. Dorfman
New Mexico State University
GLOBE Coordinating Team and representing Mexico

Mansour Javidan
University of Calgary
GLOBE Coordinating Team and representing Iran

Marcus Dickson
Wayne State University
Principal Investigator

Vipin Gupta
Fordham University
Senior Globe Research Associate

and

Ikhlas A. Abdalla, Arab Fund for Economic & Social Development, representing Qatar

Babajide Samuel Adetoun, Appropriate Development Associates, representing Nigeria

Ram N. Aditya, Louisiana Tech University, Senior GLOBE Research Associate

Hafid Agourram, University of Quebec—Montreal, representing Morocco

Adebowale Akande, Potchefstroom University, representing South Africa

Bolanle Elizabeth Akande, Center for Sustainable Development and Gender Issues, representing Nigeria

Staffan Akerblom, Stockholm School of Economics, representing Sweden and member of the GLOBE Coordinating Team

Carlos Altschul, Universidad de Buenos Aires, representing Argentina

Eden Alvarez-Backus, Sony Electronics, representing the Philippines

Julian Andrews, University of Alberta, representing Canada

Maria Eugenia Arias, independent consultant, representing Costa Rica

Mirian Sofyan Arif, University of Indonesia, representing Indonesia

Neal M. Ashkanasy, University of Queensland, representing Australia

Arben Asllani, Bellevue University, representing Albania

Guiseppe Audia, London Business School, representing Italy

Gyula Bakacsi, Budapest University of Economic Sciences, representing Hungary

Helena Bendova, Jihoceske Univerzit, representing the Czech Republic

David Beveridge, Western Illinois University, representing Bolivia

Rabi S. Bhagat, University of Memphis, representing the U.S.A.

Alejandro Blacutt, Universidad Catolica Bolivian, representing Bolivia

Jiming Bao, Fudan University, representing China

Domenico Bodega, University of Luigi Bocconi, representing Italy

Muzaffer Bodur, Bogazici University, representing Turkey

Simon Booth, University of Reading, representing England

Annie E. Booysen, University of South Africa, representing South Africa

Dimitrios Bourantas, Athens University of Economics and Business, representing Greece

Klas Brenk, Univerziti Ljubljana, representing Slovenia

Felix Brodbeck, University of Munich, representing Germany and

member of the GLOBE Coordinating Team

Dale Everton Carl, University of Calgary, representing Canada

Philippe Castel, Universite de Bourgogne, representing France

Chieh-Chen Chang, National Sun Yat-Sen University, representing Taiwan

Sandy Chau, Lingnam College, representing Hong Kong

Frenda Cheung, Hong Kong Polytechnic University, representing Hong Kong

Jagdeep Chhokar, Indian Institute of Management—Ahmedabad, representing India and member of the GLOBE Coordinating Team

Jimmy Chiu, City University of Hong Kong, representing Hong Kong

Peter Cosgriff, Lincoln University, representing New Zealand

Ali Dastmalchian, University of Lethbridge, representing Iran

Jose Augusto Dela Coleta, Centro Universitario do Triangulo, representing Brazil

Marilia Ferreira Dela Coleta, Universidade Federal de Uberlandia, representing Brazil

Deanne N. den Hartog, Vrije Universiteit—Amsterdam, representing the Netherlands

Marc Deneire, University of Nancy 2, representing France

Gemma Donnelly-Cox, University of Dublin—Trinity College, representing Ireland

Christopher Earley, University of Indiana, representing China

Mahmoud A. E. Elgamal, Kuwait University, representing Kuwait

Miriam Erez, Israel Institute of Technology, representing Israel

Sarah Falkus, University of Queensland, representing Australia

Mark Fearing, Lincoln University, representing New Zealand

Richard H. G. Field, University of Alberta, representing Canada

Carol Fimmen, Western Illinois University, representing Bolivia

Michael Frese, University of Giessen, representing Germany

Pingping Fu, Chinese University of Hong Kong, representing China

Mikhail V. Gratchev, Institute of World Economy and International Relations, representing Russia

Celia Gutierrez, Complutense University, representing Spain

Mohamed Abou Hhashha, Alexandria University, representing Egypt

Frans Marti Hartanto, Institut Technologi Bandung, representing Indonesia

Markus Hauser, University of Pennsylania, Senior Globe Research Associate

Ingalill Holmberg, Stockholm School of Economics, representing Sweden

Marina Holzer, Altschul Consultores, representing Argentina

Michael Hoppe, Center for Creative Leadership, representing the U.S.A.

Jon P. Howell, New Mexico State University, representing Mexico

Elena Ibrieva, University of Nebraska—Lincoln, representing Kazakhstan

John C. Ickis, INCAE, representing Costa Rica

Zakaria Ismail, Universiti Kebangsaan Malaysia, representing Malaysia

Slawomir Jarmuz, University of Opole, representing Poland

Jorge Correia Jesuino, Instituto Superior de Sciencias do Trabalho e da Empresa, representing Portugal

Li Ji, Hong Kong Baptist University, representing Singapore

Kuen-Yung Jone, Kaohsiung Medical College, representing Taiwan

Geoffrey Jones, University of Reading, representing England

Revaz Jorbenadse, Tbilisi State University, representing Georgia

Hayat Kabasakal, Bogazici University, representing Turkey

Mary Keating, University of Dublin—Trinity College, representing Ireland

Jeffrey C. Kennedy, Lincoln University, representing New Zealand

Jay S. Kim, Ohio State University, representing South Korea

Giorgi Kipiani, Georgian Academy of Sciences, representing Georgia

Matthias Kipping, University of Reading, representing England

Edvard Konrad, Universiti Ljubljana, representing Slovenia

Paul L. Koopman, Vrije Universiteit-Amsterdam, representing the Netherlands

Fuh-Yeong Kuan, Shu-Te Institute of Technology, representing Taiwan

Alexandre Kurc, University of Nancy 2, representing France

Marie-Francoise Lacassagne, Universite de Bourgogne, representing France

Sang M. Lee, University of Nebraska—Lincoln, representing Albania and Kazakhstan

Christopher Leeds, University of Nancy 2, representing France

Francisco Leguizamon, INCAE, representing Costa Rica

Martin Lindell, Swedish School of Economics and Business Administration, representing Finland

Jean Lobell, AcXEL International, representing the Philippines

Fred Luthans, University of Nebraska—Lincoln, representing Albania and Kazakhstan

Jerzy Maczynski, University of Wroclaw, representing Poland

Norma Mansor, University of Malaysia, representing Malaysia

Gillian Martin, University of Dublin—Trinity College, representing Ireland

Michael Martin, University of Nebraska—Lincoln, representing Albania

Sandra M. Martinez, New Mexico State University, representing Mexico

Cecilia McMillen, University of San Francisco de Quito, representing Costa Rica

Emiko Misumi, Institute for Group Dynamics, representing Japan

Jyuji Misumi, Institute for Group Dynamics, representing Japan

Moudi al-Homoud, Kuwait University, representing Kuwait

Nabil M. Morsi, Alexandria University, representing Egypt

Phyllisis M. Ngin, Melbourne Business School, representing Singapore

Jeremiah O'Connell, Bentley College, representing Spain

Enrique Ogliastri, Universidad de los Andes, representing Colombia and member of the GLOBE Coordinating Team

Nancy Papalexandris, Athens University of Economics and Business, representing Greece

T. K. Peng, I-Shou University, representing Taiwan

Maria Marta Preziosa, Instituto para el Desarrollo de Ejecutivos en la Argentina, representing Argentina

Jose M. Prieto, Complutense University, representing Spain

Boris Rakitsky, Institute of Perspectives and Problems of the Country, representing Russia

Gerhard Reber, Johannes Kepler University, representing Austria

Nikolai Rogovsky, International Labor Organization; representing Russia

Joydeep Roy-Bhattacharya, Independent literary author, GLOBE Project Manager (1994-1998)

Amir Rozen, Israel Institute of Technology, representing Israel

Argio Sabadin, Universiti Ljubljana, representing Slovenia

Majhoub Sahaba, Groupe EFET, representing Morocco

Colombia Salom de Bustamante, Universidad de los Andes, representing Venezuela

Carmen Santana-Melgoza, Smith College, representing Mexico

Daniel Alan Sauers, Lincoln University, representing New Zealand

Jette Schramm-Nielsen, Copenhagen Business School, representing Denmark;

Majken Schultz, Copenhagen Business School, representing Denmark

Zuqi Shi, Fudan University, representing China

Camilla Sigfrids, Swedish School of Economics and Business Administration, representing Finland

Ahamed Sleem, Alexandria University, representing Egypt

Kye-Chung Song, Chungnam National University, representing South Korea

Erna Szabo, Johannes Kepler University, representing Austria

Albert C. Teo, National University of Singapore, representing Singapore

Henk Thierry, University of Tilburg, representing the Netherlands

Jann Hidayat Tjakranegara, Institut Technologi Bandung, representing Indonesia

Sylvana Trimi, University of Nebraska—Lincoln, representing Albania

Anne S. Tsui, Hong Kong University of Science and Technology, representing China

Pavakanum Ubolwanna, Thammasat University, representing Thailand

Marius W. van Wyk, University of South Africa, representing South Africa and member of the GLOBE Coordinating Team

Marie Vondrysova, University of South Bohemia, representing the Czech Republic

Jürgen Weibler, University of Hagen, representing Switzerland

Celeste Wilderom, Tilburg University, representing the Netherlands

Rongxian Wu, Suzhou University, representing China

Rolf Wunderer, University of St. Gallen, representing Switzerland

Nik Rahiman Nik Yakob, Universiti Kebangsaan Malaysia, representing Malaysia

Yongkang Yang, Fudan University, representing China

Zuoqiu Yin, Fudan University, representing China

Michio Yoshida, Kumamoto University, representing Japan

Jian Zhou, Fudan University, representing China[1]

INTRODUCTION

To what extent is leadership culturally contingent? The Global Leadership and Organizational Behavior Effectiveness Research Program (GLOBE), as well as a substantial amount of other empirical research (House, Wright, & Aditya, 1997), has demonstrated that what is expected of leaders, what leaders may and may not do, and the status and influence bestowed on leaders vary considerably as a result of the cultural forces in the countries or regions in which the leaders function. For instance, Americans, Arabs, Asians, English, Eastern Europeans, French, Germans, Latin Americans, and Russians tend to glorify the concept of leadership and consider it reasonable to discuss leadership in the context of both the political and the organizational arenas. People of the Netherlands, Scandinavia, and Germanic Switzerland often have distinctly different views of leadership. Consider the following statements taken from interviews with managers from various countries:

- Americans appreciate two kinds of leaders. They seek empowerment from leaders who grant autonomy and delegate authority to subordinates. They also respect the bold, forceful, confident, and risk-taking leader, as personified by John Wayne.
- The Dutch place emphasis on egalitarianism and are skeptical about the value of leadership. Terms like *leader* and *manager* carry a stigma. If a father is employed as a manager, Dutch children will not admit it to their schoolmates.
- Arabs worship their leaders—*as long as they are in power!*
- Iranians seek power and strength in their leaders.
- Malaysians expect their leaders to behave in a manner that is humble, modest, and dignified.
- The French expect leaders to be "cultivated"—highly educated in the arts and in mathematics.

Does extant empirical research literature confirm the expectations that are implied in the preceding statements? Because we are just beginning to understand how the role of culture influences leadership and organizational processes, numerous research questions remain unanswered. What characteristics of a society make it more or less susceptible to leadership influence? To what extent do cultural forces influence the expectations that individuals have with respect to the role of leaders and their behavior? To what extent will leadership styles vary in accordance with culturally specific values and expectations? To what extent does culture moderate relationships between organizational processes, organizational form, and organizational effectiveness? What principles or laws of leadership and organizational processes transcend cultures?

We do not have comprehensive answers to these questions, but progress has been made in a number of areas (see House et al. [1997] for an extensive review of relevant leadership literature). This chapter describes a programmatic effort undertaken to explore the fascinating and complex effects of culture on leadership and organizational processes

THE NEED FOR CROSS-CULTURAL LEADERSHIP THEORY AND RESEARCH

Given the increased globalization of industrial organizations and increased inter-dependencies among nations, the need for better understanding of cultural influences on leadership and organizational practices has never been greater. Situations that leaders and would-be leaders must face are highly complex, constantly changing, and difficult to interpret. More than ever before, managers of international firms face fierce and rapidly changing international competition. The trend toward the global economic village is clear, and the twenty-first century may very well become known as the century of the "global world" (McFarland, Senen, & Childress, 1993). Since effective organizational leadership is critical to the success of international operations, this globalization of industrial organizations presents numerous organizational and leadership challenges. For instance, the cultural diversity of employees found in worldwide multinational organizations presents a substantial challenge with respect to the design of multinational organizations and their leadership. What practical knowledge and advice does the management literature provide to assist leaders in adapting to cultural constraints? Unfortunately, though the need for such information clearly exists, little if any help is available at this time (House & Aditya, 1997; House et al., 1997). Cross-cultural research and the development of cross-cultural theory are needed to fill this knowledge gap.

From a scientific and theoretical perspective, compelling reasons exist for considering the role of societal and organizational culture in influencing leadership and organizational processes. Because the goal of science is to develop universally valid theories, laws, and principles, there is a need for leadership and organizational theories that transcend cultures. There are inherent limitations in transferring theories across cultures. What works in one culture may not work in another culture. As Triandis (1993) suggests, leadership researchers will be able to "fine-tune" theories by investigating cultural variations as parameters of those theories. In addition, a focus on cross-cultural issues can help researchers uncover new relationships by forcing investigators to include a much broader range of variables often not considered in contemporary theories, such as the importance of religion, language, ethnic background, history, or political systems (Dorfman, 1996). Thus, cross-cultural research may also help to develop new theories of leadership and organizational processes and effectiveness, as well as to fine-tune existing theories

Table 1.   GLOBE-Participating Countries

Albania	France	Kazakhstan	(Caucasian sample)
Argentina	Georgia	Kuwait	South Africa
Australia	Germany	Malaysia	(Indigenous sample)
Austria	(former FRG)	Mexico	South Korea
Bolivia	Germany	Morocco	Spain
Brazil	(former GDR)	Namibie	Sweden
Canada	Greece	Netherlands	Switzerland
China	Guatemala	New Zealand	(French speaking)
Colombia	Hong Kong	Nigeria	Switzerland
Costa Rica	Hungary	Philippines	(German speaking)
Czech Republic	India	Poland	Taiwan
Denmark	Indonesia	Portugal	Thailand
Ecuador	Iran	Qatar	Turkey
Egypt	Ireland	Russia	United States
El Salvador	Israel	Singapore	Venezuela
England	Italy	Slovenia	Zambia
Finland	Japan	South Africa	Zimbabwe

by incorporating cultural variables as antecedents and moderators within existing theoretical frameworks.

While the research literature on cross-cultural leadership has blossomed in the last 15 years (House et al., 1997), it is often atheoretical, fraught with methodological problems, and fragmented across a wide variety of publication outlets (Dorfman, 1996). More important, far more questions than answers exist regarding the culturally contingent aspects of leadership. Project GLOBE is intended to contribute theoretical developments and empirical findings to fill this knowledge deficiency.

THE GLOBE RESEARCH PROGRAM

The idea of a global research program concerned with leadership and organization practices (form and processes) was conceived in the summer of 1991. In the spring of 1993, a grant proposal was written that followed a substantial literature review and development of a pool of 753 questionnaire items. GLOBE was funded in October 1993, and the recruiting of GLOBE Country Co-Investigators (referred to hereafter as CCIs) began.[2] In this section, we present an overview of Project GLOBE.

GLOBE is a multi-phase, multi-method project in which investigators spanning the world are examining the interrelationships between societal culture, organizational culture, and organizational leadership. One hundred seventy social scientists and management scholars from 62 cultures representing all major regions of the world are engaged in this long-term programmatic series of cross-cultural leadership studies. Table 1 lists the countries in which cultures are being studied as part of the GLOBE research.[3]

GLOBE was conceived and initially designed by the first author of this mono-graph as the Principal Investigator. He was later joined by Michael Agar, Marcus Dickson, Paul Hanges, and S. Antonio Ruiz-Quintanilla as Co-Principal Investigators. Because cross-cultural research requires knowledge of all the cultures being studied, we have developed a network of approximately 170 Country Co-Investigators (CCIs) who are social scientists or management scholars from around the world. The CCIs, together with the Principal Investigators and Research Associates, constitute the members of the GLOBE community.

The CCIs are responsible for leadership of the project in a specific culture in which they have expertise. Their activities include collecting quantitative and qualitative data, ensuring the accuracy of questionnaire translations, writing country-specific descriptions of their cultures in which they interpret the results of the quantitative data analyses in their own cultural context, and contributing insights from their unique cultural perspectives to the ongoing GLOBE research. In most cases, CCIs are natives of the cultures from which they are collecting data, and in most cases, they reside in that culture. Some of the CCIs are persons with extensive experience in more than one culture. Most cultures have a research team of between two and five CCIs working on the project. The GLOBE Coordinating Team (GCT) coordinates the activities of the project as a whole.[4] The GCT is also responsible for designing quantitative measures and qualitative methods, performing cross-cultural statistical analyses, and coordinating efforts to present results of the project to the scholarly community. To date, CCIs have made over 90 presentations at professional meetings and over 30 papers and book chapters have been written.

An initial goal of the GLOBE Project was to develop societal and organizational measures of culture and leader attributes that are appropriate to use across all cultures. We have accomplished this in the first phase of the research project. Items were analyzed by conventional psychometric procedures (e.g., item analysis, factor analysis, generalizability analysis) to establish nine dimensions of societal culture and nine isomorphic dimensions of organizational culture. In addition, as part of the first phase of the project, we were able to identify six underlying dimensions of global leadership patterns that are viewed by managers as contributors or impediments to outstanding leadership. The psychometric properties of these scales exceed conventional standards (Hanges, House, Dickson, Ruiz-Quintanilla, Dorfman & 103 coauthors, 1997, under review).

One of the major questions addressed by GLOBE research concerns the dimensions by which societal and organizational cultures can be measured. We identified nine dimensions of cultures that differentiate societies and organizations. That is, with respect to these dimensions, there is high within-culture and within-organization agreement and high between-culture and between-organization differentiation.

A second major question addressed by GLOBE concerns the extent to which specific leader attributes and behaviors are universally endorsed as contributing to effective leadership, and the extent to which attributes and behaviors are linked to cultural characteristics. We found that cultures can be differentiated on the basis of the leader behaviors and attributes that their members endorse. We also found high within-culture agreement with respect to leader attributes and behaviors that are viewed as contributors or impediments to effective leadership. These leader behaviors and attributes constitute Culturally endorsed implicit Leadership Theories (CLTs).

Of the six global leader behavior dimensions of CLTs, two of these dimensions are universally viewed as contributors to effective leadership, one is nearly universally endorsed as a contributor, and one is nearly universally perceived as an impediment to outstanding leadership. The endorsement of the remaining two dimensions varies by culture. In addition, we identified 21 specific leader attributes or behaviors that are universally viewed as contributors to leadership effectiveness and 8 that are universally viewed as impediments to leader effectiveness. Further, 35 specific leader attributes or behaviors are viewed as contributors in some cultures and impediments in other cultures. We present these, as well as other findings, in more detail on the following pages.

Project GLOBE also addresses questions relevant to how societal cultural forces influence organizational form and effectiveness. We describe the research questions, hypotheses, and research design relevant to both leadership and organizational aspects of GLOBE in some detail further on.

Project GLOBE employs both quantitative and qualitative methods to provide richly descriptive, yet scientifically valid, accounts of cultural influences on leadership and organizational processes. Quantitative aspects include measurement of societal culture, organizational culture, and leadership attributes and behaviors. Contemporaneous with the quantitative analysis, qualitative culture-specific research is being conducted in the same cultures. Qualitative culture-specific interpretations of local behaviors, norms, and practices are being developed through content analysis of data derived from interviews, focus groups, and published media.

The planned GLOBE research program consists of four phases. GLOBE Phase 1 was devoted to the development of research instruments. Phase 2 is devoted to assessment of nine dimensions of societal and organizational cultures and tests of hypotheses relevant to the relationships among these cultural dimensions and cultural-level implicit theories of leadership. Phase 2 also concerns relationships between organizational contingencies (size, technology, environment), organizational strategy, organizational form and processes, and organizational effectiveness. Phase 2 data collection has been completed. A projected third phase of the research project will investigate the impact and effectiveness of specific leader behaviors and styles on subordinates' attitudes and job performances and on leader and organizational effectiveness. Phase 3 will also be directed toward the identification of emic (culture-specific) aspects of leadership and organizational practices, as well as the longitudinal effects of leadership and organizational practices and organizational form on organizational effectiveness. A projected fourth phase will employ field and laboratory experiments to confirm, establish causality, and extend previous findings.

GLOBE Objectives

The meta-goal of GLOBE is to develop an empirically based theory to describe, understand, and predict the impact of specific cultural variables on leadership and organizational processes and the effectiveness of these processes. Specific objectives include answering the following fundamental questions:

1. Are there leader behaviors, attributes, and organizational practices that are universally accepted and effective across cultures?
2. Are there leader behaviors, attributes, and organizational practices that are accepted and effective in only some cultures?
3. How do attributes of societal and organizational cultures affect the kinds of leader behaviors and organizational practices that are accepted and effective?
4. What is the effect of violating cultural norms relevant to leadership and organizational practices?
5. What is the relative standing of each of the cultures studied on each of the nine core dimensions of culture?
6. Can the universal and culture-specific aspects of leader behaviors, attributes, and organizational practices be explained in terms of an underlying theory that accounts for systematic differences across cultures?

Construct Definitions of Leadership and Culture

Leadership has been a topic of study for social scientists for much of the twentieth century (Yukl, 1994), yet there is no consensually agreed-upon definition of leadership (Bass, 1990). A seemingly endless variety of definitions have been developed, but almost all have at their core the concept of influence—leaders influence others to help accomplish group or organizational objectives. The variety of definitions is appropriate, as the degree of specificity of the definition of leadership should be driven by the purposes of the research. Smith and Bond (1993) specifically note: "If we wish to make statements about universal or etic aspects of social behavior, they need to be phrased in highly abstract ways. Conversely, if we wish to highlight the meaning of these generalizations in specific or emic ways, then we need to refer to more precisely specified events or behaviors" (p. 58). The GLOBE goals are both etic (investigating aspects of leadership and organizational practices that are comparable across cultures) and emic (examining and describing culture-specific differences in leadership and organizational practices and their effectiveness). We recognize and expect that the evaluative and semantic interpretation of the term *leadership,* and the ways in which leadership and organizational processes are enacted, are likely to vary across cultures, but we also expect that some aspects of leadership will be universally endorsed.

In August 1994 the first GLOBE research conference was held at the University of Calgary in Canada. Fifty-four researchers from 38 countries gathered to develop a collective understanding of the project and to initiate its implementation. In this meeting considerable time was spent generating a working definition of *leadership* that reflected the diverse viewpoints held by GLOBE researchers. A consensus with respect to a universal definition of organizational leadership emerged: *the ability of an individual to influence, motivate, and enable others to contribute toward the effectiveness and success of the organizations of which they are members.* Note that this is a definition of *organizational* leadership, not leadership in general. Simonton (1994, p. 411), speaking of leadership in general, defines a leader as a "group member whose influence on group attitudes, performance, or decision making greatly exceeds that of the average member of the group." The GLOBE project concerns the phenomenon of organizational leadership, not leadership in general.

As with *leadership*, there is no consensually agreed upon definition among social scientists for the term *culture*. Generally speaking, *culture* is used by social scientists to refer to a set of parameters of collectives that differentiate the collectives from each other in meaningful ways. The focus is on the "sharedness" of cultural indicators among members of the collective. The specific criteria used to differentiate cultures usually depend on the preferences of the investigator and the issues under investigation, and tend to reflect the discipline of the investigator. For the GLOBE research program, we theoretically define *culture* as shared motives, values, beliefs, identities, and interpretations or meanings of significant events that result from common experiences of members of collectives and are transmitted across age generations. Note that these are *psychological* attributes and that this definition can be applied at both the societal and the organizational levels of analysis.

GLOBE Operational Definition of Culture

The most parsimonious operationalizations of *societal* culture consist of commonly experienced language, ideological belief systems (including religion and political belief systems), ethnic heritage, and history. Parallel to this, the most parsimonious operationalizations of *organizational* culture consist of commonly used nomenclature within an organization, shared organizational values, and organizational history. For purposes of GLOBE research, therefore, culture is operationally defined by the use of measures reflecting two kinds of cultural manifestations: (1) the commonality (agreement) among members of collectives with respect to the psychological *attributes* specified earlier; and (2) the commonality of observed and reported *practices* of entities such as families, schools, work organizations, economic and legal systems, and political institutions.

The common cultural attributes we have chosen to measure are indicators of shared modal values of collectives. These values are expressed in response to questionnaire items in the form of judgments of *What Should Be*. Emphasis on values grows out of an anthropological tradition of culture assessment (Kluckhohn & Strodtbeck, 1961). Another measure of culture, modal practices, is measured by indicators assessing *What Is*, or *What Are*, common behaviors, institutional practices, proscriptions and prescriptions. This approach to the assessment of culture grows out of a psychological/behavioral tradition, in which it is assumed that shared values are enacted in behaviors, policies, and practices. This assumption will be tested as part of Project GLOBE.

The GLOBE Conceptual Model

The theoretical base that guides the GLOBE research program is an integration of implicit leadership theory (Lord & Maher, 1991), value/belief theory of culture (Hofstede, 1980), implicit motivation theory (McClelland, 1985), and structural contingency theory of organizational form and effectiveness (Donaldson, 1993; Hickson, Hinings, McMillan, & Schwitter, 1974). The relevant and essential features of each of these theories are briefly described in the following paragraphs. The integrated theory is then described. For a more detailed description of the integrated theory, see House et al. (1997).

Implicit Leadership Theory

According to this theory individuals have implicit theories (beliefs, convictions, and assumptions) about the attributes and behaviors that distinguish leaders from others, effective leaders from ineffective ones, and moral leaders from evil ones. Implicit leadership theories influence the values that individuals place on selected leader behaviors and attributes, and their motives relevant to acceptance and enactment of leader behavior. The following propositions express the major assertions of implicit leadership theory.

1.   Leadership qualities are attributed to individuals, and those persons are accepted as leaders, on the basis of the degree of fit, or congruence, between the leader behaviors they enact and the implicit leadership theory held by the attributers.
2.   Implicit leadership theories constrain, moderate, and guide the exercise of leadership, the acceptance of leaders, the perception of leaders as influential, acceptable, and effective, and the degree to which leaders are granted status and privileges.

There is substantial experimental evidence in support of this theory (Hanges, Braverman, & Rentsch, 1991; Hanges, Lord, Day, Sipe, Smith, & Brown, 1997; Lord & Maher, 1991; Sipe & Hanges, 1997).

Value/Belief Theory

Hofstede (1980) and Triandis (1995) assert that the values and beliefs held by members of cultures influence the degree to which the behaviors of individuals, groups, and institutions within cultures are enacted, and the degree to which they are viewed as legitimate, acceptable, and effective. Hofstede's version of value/ *belief* theory includes four dimensions of cultural values and beliefs: Individualism versus Collectivism, Masculinity versus Femininity, Tolerance versus Intolerance of Uncertainty, and Power Distance (Stratification) versus Power Equalization. We have substituted two cultural dimensions labeled Gender Egalitarianism and Assertiveness for Hofstede's Masculinity dimension. As explained later, we also measured Collectivism with two, rather than one, scale. Finally, we have added three additional dimensions: Humanistic, Performance, and Future Orientation. Collectively, the nine dimensions reflect not only the dimensions of Hofstede's theory but also David McClelland's theories of national economic development (McClelland, 1961) and human motivation (McClelland, 1985). The humanism, power distance, and performance orientation of cultures, when measured with operant (behavioral) indicators, are conceptually analogous to the affiliative, power, and achievement motives in McClelland's implicit motivation theory. We believe that the nine core GLOBE dimensions reflect important aspects of the human condition.

Implicit Motivation Theory

Implicit motivation theory is the theory of non-conscious motives originally advanced by McClelland, Atkinson, Clark, and Lowell (1953). In its most general form the theory asserts that the essential nature of human motivation can be understood in terms of three implicit (non-conscious) motives: achievement, affiliation, and power (social influence). In contrast to behavioral intentions and conscious values, which are predictive of discrete task behaviors for short periods of time under constant situational forces (Ajzen & Fishbein, 1970), implicit motives are predictive of (1) motive arousal in the presence of selected stimuli, (2) spontaneous behavior in the absence of motive-arousal stimuli, and (3) long-term (as long as 20 years) individual *global behavior patterns*, such as social relationship patterns, citizenship behavior, child-rearing practices, and leadership styles. While McClelland's theory is an individual theory of non-conscious motivation, the GLOBE theory is a theory of motivation resulting from cultural forces.

Structural Contingency Theory

The central proposition of this theory is that there is a set of demands that are imposed on organizations that must be met if organizations are to survive and be effective. These demands are referred to as organizational contingencies. It is

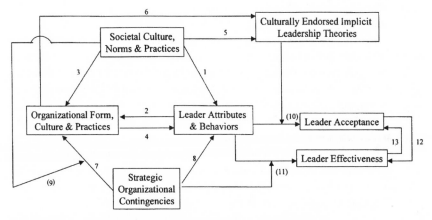

Note: Numbers in parentheses indicate an interaction among two adjoining arrows.

Figure 1. The Globe Theoretical Model

asserted that these contingencies influence organizational form and practice and that congruence between the demands of the contingencies and organizational form and practice is associated with organizational effectiveness. While this is a popular theoretical perspective, its empirical verification is mostly limited to small sample studies of organizations in industrialized countries (Child, 1981). Hickson and colleagues (1974) have asserted that the propositions of structural contingency theory are universal and culture-free. This assertion rests on the assumption that organizational contingencies impose demands on organizations that are so strong that it is imperative for all organizations to respond to them in essentially the same way in order to perform effectively and survive in competitive environments. We refer to this assertion as the *task environment imperative*. Child (1981) has presented a serious challenge to this assertion.

The Integrated Theory

A diagram of the integrated theory is presented in Figure 1.

The central theoretical proposition. The central theoretical proposition of the integrated theory is that the attributes and entities that distinguish a given culture from other cultures are predictive of the practices of organizations and leader attributes and behaviors that are most frequently enacted, acceptable, and effective in that culture. The integrated theory consists of the following propositions, which are also shown in the system diagram in Figure 1:

1. *Societal cultural values and practices affect what leaders do.* Substantial empirical evidence supports this assertion (House et al., 1997). First, founders of organizations—the organizations' original leaders—are immersed in their own societal culture, and they are most likely to enact the global leader behavior patterns that are favored in that culture. Founders influence the behavior of subordinate leaders and subsequent leaders by use of selective management selection criteria, role modeling, and socialization. Further, the dominant cultural norms endorsed by societal cultures induce global leader behavior patterns and organizational practices that are differentially expected and viewed as legitimate among cultures. Thus, the attributes and behaviors of leaders are, in part, a reflection of the organizational practices, which in turn are a reflection of societal cultures (e.g., Kopelman, Brief, & Guzzo, 1990).

2. *Leadership affects organizational form, culture, and practices.* Founders of organizations establish the initial culture of their organizations (e.g., Schein, 1992; Schneider, 1987; Schneider, Goldstein, & Smith, 1995), and founders and subsequent leaders continue to influence the organizational culture (e.g., Bass, 1985; Miller & Droge, 1986; Schein, 1992; Thompson & Luthans, 1990; Yukl, 1994).

3. *Societal cultural values and practices also affect organizational form, culture and practices.* Societal culture has a direct influence on organizational culture, as the shared meaning that results from the dominant cultural values, beliefs, assumptions, and implicit motives endorsed by culture results in common implicit leadership theories and implicit organization theories held by members of the culture (e.g., Lord and Maher, 1991; House et al., 1997).

4. *Organizational form, culture, and practices also affect what leaders do.* Over time, founders and subsequent leaders in organizations respond to the organizational culture and alter their behaviors and leader styles (e.g., Lombardo, 1983; Schein, 1992; Trice and Beyer, 1984).

5 and 6. *Societal culture and organizational form, culture, and practices influence the process by which people come to share implicit theories of leadership.* Over time, CLTs are developed in each culture in response to both societal and organizational culture and practices (e.g., Lord & Maher, 1991). CLTs thus differentiate cultures.

7. *Strategic organizational contingencies affect organizational form, culture and practices.* Organizational contingencies (size, technology, environment) impose requirements that organizations must meet in order to perform effectively, compete, and survive. Organizational practices are largely directed toward meeting the requirements imposed on organizations by organizational contingencies (Burns & Stalker, 1961; Donaldson, 1993; Lawrence & Lorsch, 1967; Tushman, Newman, & Nadler, 1988).

8. *Strategic organizational contingencies affect leader attributes and behavior.* Leaders are selected and adjust their behaviors to meet the requirements of organizational contingencies.

9. *Relationships between strategic organizational contingencies and organizational form, culture, and practices will be moderated by cultural forces.* For example, in low uncertainty avoidance cultures we expect that forces toward formalization will be weaker, and therefore the relationship between such forces and organizational formalization practices will be lower. In low power distance cultures we expect that forces toward centralization of decision making will be weaker, and therefore the relationship between such forces and decentralization and delegation practices will be lower. We specify such moderating effects in detail below when we discuss Phase 2 and 3 hypotheses.

10. *Leader acceptance is a function of the interaction between CLTs and leader attributes and behaviors.* Accordingly, leader attributes and behaviors that are congruent with CLTs will be more accepted than leader attributes and behaviors that are not congruent with CLTs.

11. *Leader effectiveness is a function of the interaction between leader attributes and behaviors and organizational contingencies.* Leaders who effectively address organizational contingencies will be more effective than leaders who do not.

12. *Leader acceptance influences leader effectiveness.* Leaders who are not accepted will find it more difficult to influence subordinates than those who are accepted. Thus, leader acceptance facilitates leader effectiveness.

13. *Leader effectiveness influences leader acceptance.* Leaders who are effective will, in the long run, come to be accepted by all or most subordinates. Subordinates will either be dismissed or voluntarily leave the organization led by leaders they do not accept.

In summary, the attributes and practices that distinguish cultures from each other, as well as strategic organizational contingencies, are predictive of the leader attributes and behaviors, and organizational practices, that are most frequently perceived as acceptable, are most frequently enacted, and are most effective.

Cultural change.   Thus far, the theory does not accommodate or account for cultural change. For example, exposure to international media, cross-border commerce, international political and economic competition, or other forms of cross-cultural interaction may introduce new competitive forces and new common experiences, which may result in changes in any of the culture or leadership variables previously described.

Further, when strategic organizational contingencies change as a result of new technological developments or changes in the economic or political environment, new leader behaviors and organizational practices that violate cultural norms may be required. These new behaviors and practices, when enacted, will constitute new common experiences, which can in turn result in changes in psychological commonalties and consequently changes in any of the cultural variables previously described.

Although cultural change can be stimulated by external events and forces, the process of change is hypothesized to be governed by the set of relationships described in the preceding propositions. There will almost certainly be resistance to new leadership and organizational practices when such practices violate existing collectively shared norms and expectations for leaders (Gagliardi, 1986). Recent work by Hanges and colleagues on person perception confirms this hypothesis by demonstrating that people resist new leaders when the new leader initially behaves in a manner inconsistent with perceivers' expectations or stereotypes (Hanges et al., 1991; Hanges et al., 1997; Sipe & Hanges, 1997). These laboratory studies have shown that the resistance to acceptance of a new leader is so strong that the functional relationship between leadership perceptions and other variables is non-linear and discontinuous. Various individual difference variables (e.g., personality, stereotypical attitudes), as well as situational factors (e.g., mental workload, job-context), have been found to increase or diminish this resistance to accept new leaders (Hanges et al., 1997; Sipe & Hanges, 1997). This research suggests that newly introduced practices will often be modified to accommodate existing norms in an emic (culture specific) manner, and there may be substantial lags in the rate at which changes in the variables of the theory take place.

Substantial additional theoretical development is required to reach a better description of the forces of resistance, the likely resulting conflicts within cultural entities, the time lags and the feedback processes that will occur among the relationships, and the functional form of the relationships depicted in Figure 1. Nevertheless, we advance the theory presented here as a framework to guide investigation of the major relationships and variables relevant to cultural influences on leadership and organizational practices and effectiveness. The theory is depicted in Figure 1 in the form of a systems model. The complexity of the model, however, mitigates against its being tested in its entirety. Rather, individual linkages or subsets of linkages can be tested, and the validity of the model can be inferred from such tests. For a more detailed, fine-grained elaboration of the relationships depicted in Figure 1, see House et al. (1997).

TWO FUNDAMENTAL CROSS-CULTURAL ISSUES

Two central aspects of cultures are frequently discussed in the cross-cultural literature: etic aspects and emic aspects. For Project GLOBE, we employ multiple methodologies to assess etic and emic issues.

Etic phenomena are common to all cultures, or at least to all cultures studied to date. A phenomenon is etic if all cultures can be assessed in terms of a common metric with respect to the phenomena. Thus, cultures can be compared in terms of etic phenomena. In contrast to etic phenomena, emic phenomena are culture-specific phenomena that occur in only a subset of cultures.

Etic Issues: Cross-cultural Comparisons and Relationships

Project GLOBE employs a number of different methods to make etic comparisons among the cultures studied. The primary method will be latent constructs that measure the nine core GLOBE dimensions. These constructs are developed from questionnaire responses obtained from middle managers and unobtrusive measures of the dimensions. The industries studied are food processing, financial services, and telecommunications services. Our sampling strategy for the collection of questionnaire data controls for nation, industry, occupation broadly defined (managers), and organizational level broadly defined (middle management). The samples for Phase 2, in which hypotheses are tested, are described later on.

Sampling from middle managers permits us to generalize to the subcultures of middle managers in the countries and the three industries studied. This sampling strategy increases the internal validity of the study by ensuring that the units of analysis are well defined and internally homogeneous. We expect the findings to reflect some aspects of the national cultures of the countries represented. Strictly speaking, we are studying the cultures of middle managers in 62 cultures. Thus, we must be cautious when making generalizations about national cultures or differences among them because of the specific nature of our sample. As we show later, however, the use of latent constructs each composed of two indicators to measure the nine core GLOBE *As Is* dimensions at the societal level, increases the generalizability of our findings beyond the culture of middle managers alone. And, cross-industry analysis will enable us to assess the relative impact of strategic imperatives imposed by industry constraints as well as cultural influences.

Emic Issues: Country-specific Information

While the GLOBE quantitative data allow comparisons and contrasts among cultures, they do not allow for emic, or culture-specific, descriptions of the cultures studied. CCIs will describe selected emic attributes and entities of the national setting in which the middle management informants are embedded. The attributes and entities are those that the CCIs judge to have non-trivial influences on the interpretation and practice of leadership and organizational practices of the cultures studied.

CCIs have collected unobtrusive measures and conducted participant observations. They also collected and content-analyzed media and focus group interview transcripts. With these data CCIs are able to describe and interpret selected emic characteristics of their national cultures. Such interpretations will give cognizance to gender, ethnic, and religious diversity, generational differences, and other relevant complexities of the cultures. Thus, the complexity and variability of complex cultures with two or more subcultures will be described. These qualitative interpretive analyses will be reported as chapters of a number of anthologies resulting from the GLOBE research program. The local CCI teams will author these chapters.

CONSTRUCT DEFINITIONS

The major constructs investigated in the GLOBE research program are nine attributes of cultures, which are operationalized as quantitative dimensions: (1) Uncertainty Avoidance, (2) Power Distance, (3) Collectivism I: Societal Emphasis on Collectivism, (4) Collectivism II: Family Organizational Collectivistic Practices, (5) Gender Egalitarianism, (6) Assertiveness, (7) Future Orientation, (8) Performance Orientation, and (9) Humane Orientation. These dimensions were selected on the basis of a review of the literature relevant to the measurement of culture in previous large-sample studies and on the basis of existing cross-culture theory.

Uncertainty Avoidance is defined as the extent to which members of an organization or society strive to avoid uncertainty by reliance on social norms, rituals, and bureaucratic practices to alleviate the unpredictability of future events.

Power Distance is defined as the degree to which members of an organization or society expect and agree that power should be unequally shared.

Collectivism I reflects the degree to which organizational and societal institutional norms and practices encourage and reward collective distribution of resources and collective action.

Collectivism II reflects the degree to which individuals express pride, loyalty, and cohesiveness in their organizations or families.[5]

Gender Egalitarianism is the extent to which an organization or a society minimizes gender role differences.

Assertiveness is the degree to which individuals in organizations or societies are assertive, confrontational, and aggressive in social relationships.

Future Orientation is the degree to which individuals in organizations or societies engage in future-oriented behaviors such as planning, investing in the future, and delaying gratification.

Performance Orientation refers to the extent to which an organization or society encourages and rewards group members for performance improvement and excellence. This dimension is similar to the dimension called Confucian Dynamism by Hofstede and Bond (1988). It reflects achievement-oriented behavior described by McClelland (1980).

Finally, *Humane Orientation* is the degree to which individuals in organizations or societies encourage and reward individuals for being fair, altruistic, friendly, generous, caring, and kind to others. This dimension is similar to the dimension labeled Kind Heartedness by Hofstede and Bond (1988). It reflects affiliative-oriented behavior described by McClelland (1980). These definitions and examples of questionnaire items for each dimension are presented in Table 2.

The first six culture dimensions had their origins in the dimensions of culture identified by Hofstede (1980). The first three scales are intended to reflect the same constructs as Hofstede's dimensions labeled Uncertainty Avoidance, Power Distance, and Individualism. The Collectivism I dimension measures organizational and societal emphasis on collectivism, with low scores reflecting individualistic emphasis and high scores reflecting collectivistic emphasis by means of norms, policies, rules, procedures, laws, social programs, or institutional practices. The Collectivism II dimension measures group (family and/or organization) collectivism—pride in and loyalty to family and/or organization and family and/or organizational cohesiveness. In lieu of Hofstede's Masculinity dimension, we

Table 2. Culture Construct Definitions and Sample Questionnaire Items

Culture Construct Definitions	Specific Questionnaire Item
Power Distance: The degree to which members of a collective expect power to be distributed equally.	Followers are (should be) expected to obey their leaders without question.
Uncertainty Avoidance: The extent to which a society, organization, or group relies on social norms, rules, and procedures to alleviate unpredictability of future events.	Most people lead (should lead) highly structured lives with few unexpected events.
Humane Orientation: The degree to which a collective encourages and rewards individuals for being fair, altruistic, generous, caring, and kind to others.	People are generally (should be generally) very tolerant of mistakes.
Collectivism I: The degree to which organizational and societal institutional practices encourage and reward collective distribution of resources and collective action	Leaders encourage (should encourage) group loyalty even if individual goals suffer.
Collectivism II: The degree to which individuals express pride, loyalty, and cohesiveness in their organizations or families.	Employees feel (should feel) great loyalty toward this organization
Assertiveness: The degree to which individuals are assertive, confrontational and aggressive in their relationships with others.	People are (should be) generally dominant in their relationships with each other.
Gender Egalitarianism: The degree to which a collective minimizes gender inequality.	Boys are encouraged (should be encouraged) more than girls to attain a higher education. (Scored inversely.)
Future Orientation: The extent to which individuals engage in future-oriented behaviors such as delaying gratification, planning, and investing in the future.	More people live (should live) for the present rather than for the future. (Scored inversely.)
Performance Orientation: The degree to which a collective encourages and rewards group members for performance improvement and excellence.	Students are encouraged (should be encouraged) to strive for continuously improved performance.

developed two dimensions labeled Gender Egalitarianism and Assertiveness. Future Orientation is derived from Kluckhohn and Strodtbeck's (1961) Past, Present, Future Orientation dimension, which focuses on the temporal mode of a society. Performance Orientation was derived from McClelland's work on need for achievement. Humane Orientation has its roots in Kluckhohn and Strodtbeck's (1961) work on the Human Nature Is Good versus Human Nature Is Bad dimension, as well as Putnam's (1993) work on the Civic Society and McClelland's (1985) conceptualization of the affiliative motive.

THE FOUR PHASES OF GLOBE

Four phases of empirical research are planned as part of Project GLOBE. Phase 1 has been completed and reported in a monograph by Hanges and colleagues (1998, under review). Phase 2 questionnaire data collection has also been completed. The analysis of scale properties of the questionnaire administered to approximately 17,000 middle managers in Phase 2 is also completed. Unobtrusive measures for the nine dimensions have also been developed.

Phase 1: Scale Development and Validation

In this section, we describe Phases 1 and 2 in modest detail. Phase 1 of GLOBE concerned the development and validation of the GLOBE questionnaire scales designed to measure societal and organizational culture variables as well as CLTs. The GLOBE scales have sound psychometric properties, and findings indicate justification for the use of the scales as aggregate measures of cultural phenomena. All 54 GLOBE scales demonstrated significant and non-trivial within-culture response agreement, between-culture differences, and respectable item reliability of response consistency. Generalizability coefficients, which are joint measures of these psychometric properties, exceed .85 for all scales. These coefficients indicate that the scales can be meaningfully used to measure differences between cultures in terms of societal, organizational, and leadership phenomena. In this section, we provide a brief description of the questionnaire development process. Detailed descriptions of scale development and validation can be found in Hanges and colleagues (1998, under review).

Item Generation

The first author of this monograph accomplished item generation for the culture scales with substantial help from Paul Koopman, Henk Thierry, and Celeste Wilderom of the Netherlands. The original item pool contained 753 items, of which 382 were leadership items and 371 were societal and organizational culture items.

Table 3. Sample CLT Questionnaire Items and Response Alternatives

Definition of Leadership	Ability to influence, motivate, and enable others to contribute to success of their organization.
Sample CLT Items	Sensitive: Aware of slight changes in moods of others.
	Motivator: Mobilizes, activates followers.
	Evasive: Refrains from making negative comments to maintain good relationships and save face.
	Diplomatic: Skilled at interpersonal relations, tactful.
	Self-interested: Pursues own best interests.
Response Alternatives	Impedes or facilitates unusually effective leadership
	1. Substantially impedes
	2. Moderately impedes
	3. Slightly impedes
	4. Neither impedes nor facilitates
	5. Slightly facilitates
	6. Moderately facilitates
	7. Substantially facilitates

Note: CLT, culturally endorsed implicit leaderships theory.

In generating leadership items, our focus was on developing a comprehensive list of leader attributes and behaviors rather than on developing a priori leadership scales. The initial pool of leadership items was based on leader behaviors and attributes described in several extant leadership theories. The theories are described in House and Aditya (1997). These leadership items consisted of behavioral and attribute descriptors and their definitions. Examples of these items are presented in Table 3. Items were rated on a 7-point Likert-type scale that ranged from a low of "This behavior or characteristic greatly inhibits a person from being an outstanding leader" to a high of "This behavior or characteristic contributes greatly to a person being an outstanding leader."

Organizational and societal culture items were written for the nine core GLOBE dimensions, previously described, at both the societal and the organizational levels. We also wrote the items to reflect two culture manifestations: institutional practices reported "*As Is*" and values reported in terms of what "*Should Be*." The items were written as "quartets" having isomorphic structures across the two levels of analysis (societal and organizational) and across the two culture manifestations (*As Is* and *Should Be*). Note that the should be items reflect specific and concrete contextualized values rather than general and abstract values such as love, peace, order of freedom.

The basic structure of the items comprising quartets is identical, but the frame of reference is varied according to the particular cultural manifestation and levels of analysis being assessed. Table 4 contains an example of a quartet of parallel culture items, showing essentially the same question in four forms: Organization *As Is*; Organization *Should Be*; Society *As Is*; and Society *Should Be*. Items were derived from a review of relevant literature and interviews and focus groups held in several countries, as well as from extant organizational and culture theory. Psy-

Table 4. Example of Parallel Items for the Culture Scales

Organization *As Is*						
The pay and bonus system in this organization is designed to maximize:						
1	2	3	4	5	6	7
Individual Interests						Collective Interests

Organization *Should Be*						
In this organization, the pay and bonus system *should* be designed to maximize:						
1	2	3	4	5	6	7
Individual Interests						Collective Interests

Society *As Is*						
The economic system in this society is designed to maximize:						
1	2	3	4	5	6	7
Individual Interests						Collective Interests

Society *Should be*						
I believe that the economic system in this society should be designed to maximize:						
1	2	3	4	5	6	7
Individual Interests						Collective Interests

chometric analyses indicated justification for grouping the items into scales relevant to the nine core GLOBE dimensions of societies and organizations.

Item Screening

Societal and organizational culture questionnaire items were screened for appropriateness by use of three procedures: Q sorting, item evaluation, and translation/back-translation. Leadership items were screened by item evaluation and conceptual equivalence of the back translation. The Q sorting procedure consisted of sorting the culture items into theoretical categories represented by the a priori dimensions of culture described above, first by seven Ph.D. students in the Department of Psychology at the University of Maryland and subsequently by CCIs representing 38 countries. The sorters were not informed of the theoretical dimensions for which the items were intended. Items that were sorted by 80% of the sorters into the categories for which they were theoretically intended were retained for further analysis. There were no dimensions of societal or organizational culture for which a majority of items failed to meet this criterion. Thus, a sufficient number of items was retained for the measurement of each dimension.

The ability of the sorters to agree on the allocation of items to dimensions indicates that the sorters were sorting according to common interpretations of both the theoretical dimensions and the items that they sorted into these dimensions. This level of agreement indicates that the scales comprising the retained items were interpreted to have the same meaning in all of the cultures represented by the CCIs. This is an especially important result because it strongly suggests commonalty of meaning of the questionnaire scales across cultures.

In addition to this sorting task, CCIs provided Item Evaluation Reports, in which they noted any items containing words or phrases that were ambiguous or could not be adequately translated in the target country's native language. CCIs also identified questions that might be culturally inappropriate. Most of the items that were problematic were dropped from further consideration. In a few cases, we were able to rewrite items to eliminate potential problems but retain the intent and dimensionality of the original item.

In order to avoid any systematic bias that may be present when respondents complete a survey that is not in their native language (Brislin, 1986), CCIs were responsible for having the survey translated from English into their native language. This was done by the CCI, by some other person fluent in both languages, or by a professional translator. The translation was then independently translated again, from the native language of the culture back to English. This back-translation was then sent to the GLOBE Coordinating Team (GCT), where it was compared to the original English version of the survey to verify the veridicality of the translation. Through the process of deleting items based on sorting, item evaluation, and translation, the item pool was reduced to a total of 379 items, which were retained for further evaluation.

Pilot Studies

Two pilot studies were then conducted to assess the psychometric properties of the resulting a priori culture scales and to empirically develop leadership scales.

Pilot study 1. The CCIs in 28 countries distributed the survey of retained items to individuals in their respective countries who had full-time working experience as a white-collar employee or manager. Because the survey was lengthy, it was divided into two parallel versions, A and B. Each version contained approximately half of the leadership items and half of the organizational and societal culture items. A total of 877 individuals completed the first pilot study survey.

Several different statistical analyses were performed to assess the psychometric properties of the scales. Specifically, we conducted a series of exploratory factor analyses, reliability analyses, and aggregability analyses (r_{wg} analyses, intraclass correlations [ICC-1], one-way analyses of variance), and generalizability analyses (ICC-2) of the scales. These analyses were performed at the *ecological* level of analysis; that is, on the means of the country item responses for each scale. We refined our scales on the basis of these analyses while trying to maintain, whenever possible, the isomorphic quartet structure of the culture scales described above and illustrated in Table 4. These statistical analyses, when considered together, provide evidence of the construct validity of the culture scales.

A separate factor analysis of each of the culture scales indicated that they were all unidimensional. A first-order exploratory factor analysis of the leader attributes items yielded 16 unidimensional factors that describe *specific* leader attributes and behaviors.

The r_{wg} analyses (James, Demaree, & Wolf, 1984) demonstrated that the scales could be aggregated to either the organizational or the societal levels of analysis (average $r_{wg} = .73$, n = 54). Intraclass correlation coefficients (ICC-1) and one-way analyses of variance for each of the scales indicated statistically significant within-culture agreement and between-culture differences. The societal culture scales exhibited low to moderate correlations with each other. Thus, they provide independent and unique information about societal cultures. The leadership scales substantially differed in their relationship to one another. The absolute correlation among the first-order leadership scales ranged from a low of .00 (Status-Conscious with Calmness) to a high of .86 (Status-Conscious with Procedural). Thus, the leadership scales exhibited acceptable levels of unidimensionality and internal consistency. Overall, 20 percent of the interrelationships were statistically significant. A second-order factor analysis of the 16 leadership factors yielded four unidimensional factors that describe *classes* of leader behaviors that represent *global* leader behavior patterns.

It is interesting to note that some of the same culture dimensions were highly inversely correlated across the two *As Is* and *Should Be* scale orientations for particular dimensions of culture. The findings indicate that there are substantial differences in people's perceptions of how things *should be* as opposed to how things *are perceived to be*. This raises an interesting and very important question: Are the most meaningful indicators of the cultures of collectives' current practices reflected by *As Is* scales or values reflected by *Should Be* scales? We shall assess the relationship between (1) societal *As Is* and *Should Be* scores, and (2) organizational *As Is* scores. The findings from this analysis will indicate which of the two ways of measuring cultural variation is most strongly associated with organizational practices as measured by the organizational *As Is* scores.

We ended Pilot Study 1 with 16 first-order factorially derived leadership scales that represent specific leader behaviors, four second-order factorially derived leadership dimensions that represent global leader behavior patterns, nine organizational culture *As Is* scales, nine organizational culture *Should Be* scales. The factor analyses conducted as part of Pilot Study 1 also demonstrated that the themes in all of the scales could be meaningfully identified and labeled.

Pilot study 2.   The purpose of the second pilot study was to replicate the psychometric analyses of the scales in a different sample to assess sampling robustness. Data for this study came from 15 countries that did not participate in the previous pilot study. In general, the psychometric properties of all of the scales were confirmed by replication. We replicated the ecological analyses conducted in Pilot Study 1 at the *individual level of analysis*. We used this level of analysis because there were too few countries in the replication sample to conduct an ecological-factor analysis. A total of 1,066 individuals completed one of the two versions of the pilot study questionnaires. Using an individual-level analysis to replicate an ecological-level analysis is a conservative approach. If this analysis is found to correspond to the ecological analysis, the findings constitute strong evidence for the generality of the factor structure and evidence of *strong etic* phenomena (Leung & Bond, 1989). Pilot Study 2 confirmatory factor analyses yielded acceptable fit for the first- and second-order CLT factor structures and replicated the unidimensionality of the societal culture scales.

In summary, we developed 16 unidimensional leadership scales and 36 societal scales that exhibit acceptable levels of internal consistency. The aggregation tests indicated that we are justified in aggregating these scales to the societal level of analysis. Correlational analysis indicated that the leadership scales substantially differed in their relationship to one another. The leadership scales also exhibited acceptable levels of unidimensionality and internal consistency. We found sufficient agreement within societies and sufficient differences between societies to aggregate the scales to the society level of analysis. Further, the shared themes in all of the scales were replicated by the Pilot Study 2 factor analyses.

Phase 2: Measurement and Hypothesis Testing

Phase 2 consists of further assessment of scale properties and measurement of (1) the core societal and organizational *As Is* and *Should Be* dimensions, (2) the CLT dimensions, (3) the organizational contingencies and strategic processes of firms reported by high-level executives, and (4) respondent demographic variables. Phase 2 also consists of tests of theoretical hypotheses presented below. Data collection for these aspects of Phase 2 is complete. In addition, Phase 2 involves further development of unobtrusive measurement scales to assess the societal-level cultural dimensions. These scales are described on the following pages.

The questionnaire data collected in GLOBE Phase 2 consist of (1) responses to approximately 17,000 questionnaires relevant to societal and organizational dimensions of culture, from middle managers of approximately 825 organizations in 62 cultures, and (2) unobtrusive measures of the societal dimensions (Table 5) and responses to four different executive questionnaires administered to separate top-level executives in the organizations from which the middle management data were collected. The executive questionnaires, described in the paragraphs that follow, elicited responses relevant to organizational attributes, organization strategic processes, organizational contingencies, and performance. These responses will be used in Phase 2 to test hypotheses relevant to structural contingency theory of organizational form and effectiveness.

Questionnaire data collection for Phase 2 is complete. Table 6 provides a summary and overview of the latent constructs used to test the GLOBE hypotheses and their indicators.

Based on the pilot studies and on focus groups and interviews conducted by CCIs, which were ongoing during the pilot studies, several additional CLT items were added to the middle manager questionnaires. These new items were written to ensure that including only Western leadership behaviors did not bias the 16 leadership scales. Further, we wrote several items that described autocratic, narcissistic, manipulative, and punitive behaviors, because it was suggested in interviews and focus groups that in some societies such behaviors would enhance leader effectiveness.

Finally, we added several new items to the survey to develop a second measure of collectivist cultural orientation, because the collectivistic scale derived from the pilot studies did not include items relevant to family or organizational collectivism. The new items were adopted from Triandis's work on collectivism (Triandis, 1995) and concerned several descriptors of organizational and family practices

Table 5.   Sample Unobtrusive Measures*

Avoidance of uncertainty	High number of information processing equipment items (e.g., fax machines, cell phones) per 1,000 people, indicating high emphasis on information availability.
Power distance	Limited number of scientists per gross national product (GNP), indicating suppression of intellectual inquiry.
Societal emphasis on collectivism	Early time zone, indicating eastern and southeastern location where societal collectivism is predominant.
Family collectivism	Low divorce rates per marriage, indicating pressure for sustaining intimate relationships.
Gender egalitarianism	High proportion of females with earned income, indicating low discrimination against females and females' contribution to workforce.
Future orientation	High proportion of public education expenditure devoted to higher education, indicating public investment for future opportunities and future economic performance.
Performance orientation	Low share of government-funded research and development (R and D), indicating free market competition and low government intervention.
Humane orientation	Few retail outlets per capita, indicating low emphasis on economic amenities and high emphasis on relationship orientation.

Note: *There is no effect of GNP, per capita income, population size of country, or year of independence on the correlations between the unobtrusive measures and their isomorphic questionnaire based measures, for the total sample of 54 cultures. However, selected subsamples such as more or less wealthy countries, indicated differences in correlations suggesting boundary conditions for some of the unobtrusive measures. These boundary conditions are being further investigated.

usually associated with collectivistic cultures: organizational and family pride, loyalty and cohesiveness. We confirmed the two Collectivism scales by factor analytically deriving two dimensions of Collectivism: Societal Emphasis on Collective Behavior and Organizational and Family Collectivism (see note 5). Thus, there were 18 scales to measure the nine culture *As Is* and nine *Should Be* culture dimensions—one scale for each of the dimensions except Collectivism, which had two scales.

Measurement of Organizational Attributes

The executive questionnaires to which we previously referred were designed to measure several attributes and processes of the organizations from which middle manager data were collected. The questionnaires included scales to measure attributes of strategies, perceived organizational effectiveness, and three organizational strategic contingency variables: size in terms of number of employees; the dominant technology of each organization in terms of the degree to which the work is repetitive, well understood, and controllable; and environments in terms of competitiveness, hostility, and predictability/uncertainty. Organizational strategy was assessed in terms of strong versus weak customer orientation, incremental versus comprehensiveness of strategic decision making, consensus versus individual formulation, formality versus informality, and adaptability versus rigidity and

Table 6. Latent Constructs and Manifest and Qualitative Indicators

Latent Constructs	Manifest Indicators	Qualitative Indicators
Societal cultural norms: nine core dimensions (Phase 2)	Questionnaires Unobtrusive measures	Interviews Media analysis Focus groups CCI participant observation
Organizational practices: nine core dimensions (Phase 2)	Questionnaires by middle managers	
Organizational contingencies: technology, environment, size (Phase 2)	Questionnaires by top executives	
Societal culturally endorsed implicit leadership theories (CLTs)	Middle manager questionnaire ratings	Interviews and media analysis Focus groups CCI participant observation
Leader behavior (Phase 3)	Questionnaires	Interviews Media analysis
Leader acceptance (Phase 3)	Questionnaires	CCI participant observation Interviews, media, and analysis
Leader effectiveness (Phase 4)	Lab/field experiments	Interviews with subjects

Note: Country Co-Investigator (CCI).

entrepreneurial/risk orientation. The strategic contingency scales were adapted from questionnaires used in several previous studies in which their construct validity was established (Khandwalla, 1977; Lumpkin & Dess, 1996). The executives reported the level of their firms' performance, relative to major competitors, during the previous 3 years with respect to sales and pretax profit. The executives also provided information relevant to the general market and economic conditions of the firms, frequency of organizational changes, degree of government regulation of firm's activities, and demographic variables relevant to the firm and to themselves. The psychometric properties of these scales and the impact of the strategic contingency variables on organizational practices and effectiveness is currently being assessed as part of the Phase 2 research.

Phase 2 Hypotheses

The results of Pilot Studies 1 and 2 set the stage for Phase 2 by providing the necessary questionnaire scales to test hypotheses. Hypotheses will be tested, concerning (1) relationships between societal culture dimensions, organizational culture dimensions, and CLTs; (2) relationships specified by structural contingency theory of organizational form and effectiveness; and (3) the moderating effects of societal culture dimensions on relationships specified by structural contingency theory. Tests of the first two GLOBE hypotheses are reported below. Although we do not report tests of the remaining GLOBE hypotheses, we present these hypotheses here.

Hypotheses concerning relationships between societal culture dimensions, organizational culture dimensions, and CLTs.

Hypothesis 1.   The global CLT dimension charismatic/value-based leadership will be universally endorsed.

The component subscales that constitute the global (second-order factor) charismatic/value-based leadership dimension are visionary, inspirational, self-sacrifice, integrity, decisive, and performance orientation. We expect charismatic/ value-based leader behavior to be universally endorsed because the visions articulated by, and the integrity enacted by, value-based leaders stress values that have universal appeal (House et al., 1997). Charismatic/value-based leaders articulate and emphasize end-values. Examples of end-values are dignity, peace, order, beauty, and freedom. End-values are values that are intrinsically motivating, self-sufficient, and need not be linked to other values. Also, end-values are not exchangeable for other values and have universal appeal (Rokeach, 1973). Thus, the values stressed by charismatic/value-based leaders are more likely to be universally accepted and endorsed. Consequently the visions of charismatic/value-based leaders usually stress end-values that are congruent with the values stressed in the culture (House & Aditya, 1997). Similarly, we expect leader integrity to be universally endorsed because integrity is an end-value that is also universally held in all cultures (Rokeach, 1973).

We recognize that Hypothesis 1 is controversial. Bass (1997) argues that transformational leadership, a form of charismatic/value-based leadership, is universally acceptable and effective. In contrast, it may be argued that some cultures may more highly value leaders who can find pragmatic accommodations with all influential parties. In such cultures, value-based leadership may be far less important than ability to achieve pragmatic effects, regardless of the means by which such effects are attained.

Regardless of whether it is supported or not, the test of Hypothesis 1 is of both theoretical and practical interest. Failure to support this hypothesis would result in identification of the specific cultures in which value-based leadership is and is not endorsed. The issue of universal endorsement of leadership dimensions, of necessity, needs to be answered on the basis of empirical evidence. The test of Hypothesis 1 is intended to contribute to clarification of that issue. The discovery of both universally endorsed and culture-specific leadership dimensions is of major importance to the development of cross-cultural leadership theory and of practical importance to individuals whose work involves cross-cultural interaction.

Hypothesis 2.   There will be positive correlations between societal dimensions and isomorphic CLT dimensions.

The rationale for this hypothesis is that the dimensions of societal culture will influence the legitimacy and acceptance of leader behaviors. More specifically, societal culture will influence the kind of attributes and behaviors that are reported to be expected, acceptable, and effective. Correlations between these dimensions constitute a test of the *cultural influence proposition* (Hofstede, 1980; Kluckhohn & Strodtbeck, 1961; Triandis, 1995), which asserts that societal culture has a pervasive influence on the values, expectations, and behavior of its members. Therefore, societal culture is expected to influence organizational values (*Should Be* measures) and practices (*As Is* measures), as well as expectations for leader behaviors that are expressed as CLTs in the form of questionnaire item responses.

Hypothesis 3.   There will be positive correlations between organizational culture dimensions and isomorphic CLTs.

Dimensions of organizational culture are also expected to influence the legitimacy and acceptance of leader attributes and behaviors.

The rationale for this hypothesis is that shared organizational values and practices will influence the legitimacy and acceptance of leader attributes and behaviors.

Hypothesis 4.   The magnitude of relationships between organizational cultural dimensions and isomorphic CLT dimensions will be greater than the magnitude of relationships between societal culture dimensions and isomorphic CLT dimensions.

The rationale for this hypothesis is that organizational variables are more salient, more proximate, and more relevant to the tasks and behaviors of managers than societal cultural variables. Therefore, organizational cultural variables will have a stronger influence on CLTs than societal cultural variables. Correlations between organizational culture dimensions and CLT dimensions constitute a test of the *organizational influence proposition.*

› The *cultural influence proposition* asserts that societal culture has a pervasive influence on values, expectations, and behavior and will therefore influence CLTs. Correlations between societal culture dimensions and CLT dimensions constitute a test of the *cultural influence proposition.* Thus, comparisons of the regression coefficients of the relationships between societal culture dimensions and CLTs with the regression coefficients of the relationships between organizational culture dimensions and CLTs constitute competitive tests of the cultural influence and the organizational influence propositions.

Hypothesis 5.   Relative to organizations in the food-processing industry, organizations in the financial-services industry will have higher scores on the organizational cultural dimensions of gender egalitarianism, humanism, and future orientation, and lower scores on power distance practices.[6]

The rationale for this hypothesis is that financial institutions need to be employee- and customer-service–oriented, future-oriented, and flexible in order to compete. Customer satisfaction depends on the degree to which financial institutions treat customers individually, design their services to meet customer preferences, and make investments that protect or enhance the future value of client and organizational assets. Financial institutions also need to adopt a more humane orientation toward their employees, more future orientation toward their clients, and less centralization of decision making in comparison with the food processing organizations. Such practices require employees with relatively high levels of education. Thus, financial institutions need to (1) minimize employee turnover to retain well-educated employees who would be costly to replace, and (2) maintain stability with clients.

Hypotheses Concerning Relationships Specified by Structural Contingency Theory and the Moderating Effects of Societal Cultural Dimensions

In addition to the research described in the preceding paragraphs, we will also conduct tests of structural contingency theory of organizational form and effectiveness (Donaldson, 1993; Hickson et al., 1974), and tests relevant to the effects of culture on relationships between organizational contingencies, organizational practices, strategy formulation processes (Hauser, House, & Puranam, 1999), and effectiveness.

> **Hypothesis 6.** Organizational contingency variables will be associated with relevant organizational practices as specified by Structural Contingency Theory (Hickson et al., 1974). However, societal dimensions of culture that are isomorphic with the organizational practices will moderate these correlations.

The rationale for this hypothesis is that organizations are expected to have a tendency to align their practices with both strategic contingency variables and the cultural forces of the society in which they function. More specifically, structural contingency theory asserts that organizations become more formalized with size. This theory also asserts that under conditions of technological and environmental uncertainty organizations will engage in less formalization in order to maintain flexibility and thus adaptability to uncertain environmental demands.

The GLOBE data set includes a measure of organizational uncertainty avoidance practices. Organizational uncertainty avoidance practices take the form of formalization of rules, procedures, and policies. The GLOBE data set also includes a measure of the degree to which the strategy planning process is formalized. Using these measures we will test the following hypotheses which are operationalizations of this proposition.

> **Hypothesis 6a.** Organizational size will be positively correlated with formalization of strategic planning processes.

> **Hypothesis 6b.** Organizational size will be positively correlated with degree of uncertainty avoidance practices.

We expect managers in high uncertainty avoidance cultures to be more receptive to organizational uncertainty avoidance practices and formalization of strategic planning processes. Therefore,

> **Hypothesis 6c.** The relationships specified in hypotheses 6a and 6b will be more strongly supported in high uncertainty avoidance cultures.

> **Hypothesis 6d.** Technological uncertainty will be negatively correlated with organizational uncertainty avoidance practices.

> **Hypothesis 6e.** Environmental uncertainty will be negatively correlated organizational uncertainty avoidance practices.

We expect managers in low uncertainty avoidance cultures to be less receptive to organizational uncertainty avoidance practices. Therefore,

Hypothesis 7.   The relationships specified in hypotheses 6c and 6d will be more strongly supported in low uncertainty cultures.

Under conditions of environmental hostility, high-level managers are expected to be under substantial stress. We expect managers in high stress enviornments to increase control over organizational operations and therefore to centralize and closely control decision making (Aldrich, 1979; Staw, Sandelands, & Dutton, 1981). Consequently centralization and control are expected to be manifested in increased power distance practice. Therefore,

Hypothesis 8.   Environmental hostility will be positively correlated with degree of organizational uncertainty avoidance and power distance practices and degree of formalization of strategic planning processes.

Hypothesis 9.   The relationships specified in hypothesis 8 will be stronger for organizations in high power distance and high uncertainty avoidance cultures.

In addition to the above hypotheses we will also test hypotheses relevant to strategic alignment of strategic and structural organizational practices, CLT dimensions, and societal cultural forces. Specifically we will test the following hypotheses:

Hypothesis 10.   Future-oriented organizational strategies will be positively correlated with future orientation of organizational cultures and the future-oriented CLT dimension.

Hypothesis 10a.   Hypothesis 10 will be more strongly supported in future-oriented societies.

Hypothesis 11.   Entrepreneurial orientation of organizational strategies will be positively correlated with the assertiveness and performance orientation dimensions of organizational cultures and the performance-oriented CLT dimension.

Hypothesis 11a.   Hypothesis 11 will be more strongly supported in assertive and performance-oriented societies.

Hypothesis 12.   Consensually based strategy formulation practices will be positively correlated with middle manager endorsement of participative leadership and negatively correlated with organizational power distance practices.

Hypothesis 12a. Hypothesis 12 will be more strongly supported in low power distance societies.

Hypothesis 13. Flexible strategy formulation practices will be associated with organic organizational cultures.

Organic organizational cultures are manifested by low organizational power distance and low uncertainly avoidance practices (Dickson, 1997).

Hypothesis 13a. Hypothesis 13 will be more strongly supported in low power distance and low uncertainty avoidance societies.

Hypothesis 14. The higher the correspondence between structural contingencies, societal culture dimensions, organizational culture dimensions, and CLTs specified in Hypotheses 6 through 13a, the higher the economic performance of the organizations studied.

The rationale for this hypothesis is that organizations that have strong alignment of CLTs, strategic processes, organizational practices, with societal culture will be most effective. However, we caution that some societal culture dimensions might be detrimental to the competitive and technological environment of business organizations. For example, in societies with a low future and performance orientation, low assertiveness and high uncertainty avoidance and humane orientation, an organizational misfit with societal practices is likely positively correlated with economic performance of organizations. This proposition will also be tested as part of Phase 2.

Samples

National borders may not be an adequate way to demarcate cultural boundaries, since many countries have large subcultures. It is impossible to obtain representative samples of such multicultural nations as China, India, or the United States. Nonetheless, the samples drawn from such countries need to be comparable with respect to the dominant forces that shape cultures, such as ecological factors, history, language, and religion. The country samples also need to be relatively homogeneous within cultures. For multicultural countries, whenever possible we sampled the subculture in which there is the greatest amount of commercial activity. When possible we also sampled more than one subculture (indigenous and Caucasian subcultures in South Africa, French and German subcultures in Switzerland, and East and West subcultures in Germany).

The units of analysis for the GLOBE project consisted of cultural level aggregated responses of samples of typical middle managers in three industries: food processing, financial services, and telecommunications services. The food-processing industry is a relatively stable industry. The telecommunications and financial industries may be stable or unstable, depending on country and economic conditions. By including these industries, we have obtained a fair number of dynamic industries and high-technology industries in the overall sample. Cultures in at least three countries in each of the following geographical regions are represented in the GLOBE sample: Africa, Asia, Europe (eastern, central, and northern), Latin America, North America, North Africa, Middle East, and the Pacific Rim, as indicated in Table 1.

Middle managers in these industries were asked to use a 7-point scale to describe leader attributes and behaviors that they perceive to enhance or impede outstanding leadership. They were also asked to give their perceptions of the practices and values (in the form of *As Is* and *Should Be* responses, respectively) in the society in which they live, and of the organizations in which they are employed, using 7-point scales as illustrated in Table 4. Independent samples of middle managers completed one of two questionnaires. Half of the respondents in each culture completed the societal culture questionnaire (Sample 1), and the other half completed the organizational culture questionnaire (Sample 2). All respondents completed the Leadership Attributes Questionnaire. Thus, the societal culture and the organizational culture questionnaires were completed by independent samples of respondents.

In addition, CCIs collected qualitative information about their societies and organizations in the industries they studied with respect to etic and emic dimensions of their cultures. Middle managers participated in interviews and focus groups and completed questionnaires. CCIs have also recorded archival information and participant observations, and collected unobtrusive measures to be used to describe and interpret the cultures studied. CCIs also conducted content analyses of the dominant general and business media in their cultures. In this capacity, they provided both etic and emic information concerning the study dimensions previously described.

Our design strategy consisted of obtaining responses of middle managers in two of the three target industries in each country studied.[7] This yielded samples from approximately 40 countries in each of the target industries. As stated earlier, data relevant to 54 countries were available at the time this chapter was written.

The sample design also permitted us to relate the within-culture mean dimension responses to the societal and organizational questionnaires to the within-culture mean dimension responses to the Leader Attribute Questionnaire. The means of the leadership item responses of Sample 1 and Sample 2 within each country were not significantly different. Thus, the individual leadership scale scores for the two samples were averaged to produce means on the leadership scales for all cultures. As a result of the independent assessment of the organizational and societal variables, and because the mean CLT responses in each sample in each culture were not different, the responses are free of common source response bias.

Unobtrusive Measures[8]

All instruments are subject to potential unknown biases. One procedure for minimizing response bias contamination is to use multiple methodologies to measure the same constructs. Measuring a construct with multiple methodologies permits verification of the measurement of cultures on the latent construct of interest by triangulation. Latent construct measurement based on two or more manifest indicators allows one to reduce, if not eliminate, potential response bias associated with questionnaire responses. The latent constructs used to measure societal level responses consist of questionnaire responses and unobtrusive measures. As previously noted, examples of unobtrusive measures are shown in Table 5.

The intercorrelations of the unobtrusive measures and the core *As Is* questionnaire scale scores for each dimension are all above .5 (all significant, p < .05). These intercorrelations indicate validity of the GLOBE societal *As Is* questionnaire measures. They also indicate that the middle manager responses to the societal questionnaire reflect the broader society in which the managers are embedded and not a more narrowly defined culture of middle managers.

Questionnaire Response Bias

Triandis (1995) has noted that the various cultures have different response patterns when responding to questionnaires. The presence of these different response patterns can bias cross-cultural comparisons. Thus several different statistical techniques have been developed to eliminate the contamination of survey responses. Following Triandis's (1995) suggestion, individual responses to all questions were standardized before aggregation to the societal and organizational levels of analysis. This procedure minimizes the effects of individual response bias. Using latent constructs composed of aggregated within-person standardized questionnaire response scores and unobtrusive measurement scales further lessens the effects of questionnaire response bias on the between-country comparisons.

Phase 2 CLT Scales

One of the objectives of GLOBE is to determine whether there are dimensions of CLTs that are universally endorsed and dimensions that are differentially endorsed across cultures. Recall that CLTs are culturally endorsed profiles of perceived effective or ineffective leader attributes or behaviors about which members within each culture agree. Profiles of CLT dimensions reflect what is commonly referred to as "leadership styles" in the leadership literature.

Shaw (1990) suggests that much of the cross-national literature indicating differences in managerial beliefs, values, and styles can be interpreted as showing culturally influenced differences in leader prototypes, which are analogous to

CLTs as conceptualized for Project GLOBE. A study by O'Connell, Lord, and O'Connell (1990) supports the argument that culture plays a strong role in influencing the content of leader attributes and behaviors perceived as desirable and effective. Their study specifically examined the similarities and differences between Japanese and American CLTs. For the Japanese, the traits of being fair, flexible, a good listener, outgoing, and responsible were highly rated in many domains, such as business, media, and education. For Americans, traits of intelligence, honesty, understanding, verbal skills, and determination were strongly endorsed as facilitating leader effectiveness in numerous domains. A study by Gerstner and Day (1994) also provides additional evidence that ratings of leadership attributes and behaviors vary across cultures. These investigators identified three dimensions relevant to distinct CLTs as expressed by university students from eight nations. These dimensions had rank order correlations with Hofstede's (1980) measures of power distance, uncertainty avoidance, and individualism of .81, 1.00, and .70, respectively and thus can be interpreted to measure these constructs. The GLOBE research project follows in the tradition of these studies. Following is a brief description of the development of the final Leader Attribute Questionnaire to identify CLTs.

Using the means of Phase 2 Leader Attribute Questionnaire subscales from 54 countries, we performed multilevel confirmatory factor analysis to confirm the 16-dimension factor structure of the leadership scales developed in the two pilot studies. This factor structure was confirmed. However, Phase 2 research included several additional items not included in the pilot study questionnaires that reflected the findings from ongoing interview and focus group research. We conducted a maximum likelihood exploratory factor analysis with a varimax rotation of these CLT items. This analysis resulted in five additional CLT subscales which exhibited sound psychometric properties. Thus, we have a total of 21 leadership subscales for Phase 2 analysis. These subscales and sample items are presented in Table 7.

As with the pilot data, our analysis revealed significant interrelationships among the factors, hence the need to create a second-order factor structure. A second-order factor analysis produced four factors: (1) Charismatic/Value-Based Leadership that is Team-Oriented, (2) Autonomous Leadership, (3) Humane Leadership, and (4) Non-Participative Self-Protective Leadership. Guided by prevailing theory, we divided Factor 1 into Charismatic/Value-Based Leadership and Team-Oriented Leadership to create two dimensions. We also divided Factor 4 into two dimensions: Self-Protective Leadership and Participative Leadership (the scores of the non-participative subscales were reversed to reflect participative leadership). These divisions of the empirically derived second-order factors were made to preserve conceptual clarity and to have dimensions that can be related to prevailing leadership theory and previous empirical studies.

The 21 subscales are grouped into six higher order leader behavior/attribute dimensions, which are presented in Table 8. As previously stated, we refer to the higher order dimensions as *global* CLT dimensions because they represent *classes*

Table 7. Leadership Prototype Scales: First-order Factors and Leader Attribute Items

- **Administratively Competent**
  - orderly
  - administratively skilled
  - organized
  - good administrator
- **Autocratic**
  - autocratic
  - dictatorial
  - bossy
  - elitist
- **Autonomous**
  - individualistic
  - independent
  - autonomous
  - unique
- **Charismatic I: Visionary**
  - foresight
  - prepared
  - anticipatory
  - plans ahead
- **Charismatic II: Inspirational**
  - enthusiastic
  - positive
  - morale booster
  - motive arouser
- **Charismatic III: Self-sacrificial**
  - risk taker
  - self-sacrificial
  - convincing
- **Conflict Inducer**
  - normative
  - secretive
  - intra-group competitor

- **Decisive**
  - willful
  - decisive
  - logical
  - intuitive
- **Diplomatic**
  - diplomatic
  - worldly
  - win/win problem solver
  - effective bargainer
- **Face Saver**
  - indirect
  - avoids negatives
  - evasive
- **Humane Orientation**
  - generous
  - compassionate
- **Integrity**
  - honest
  - sincere
  - just
  - trustworthy
- **Malevolent**
  - hostile
  - dishonest
  - vindictive
  - irritable
  - noncooperative
  - intelligent (reverse scored)
- **Modesty**
  - modest
  - self-effacing
  - patient

- **Non-participative**
  - non-delegator
  - micro-manager
  - non-egalitarian
  - individually oriented
- **Performance Oriented**
  - improvement oriented
  - excellence oriented
  - performance oriented
- **Procedural**
  - ritualistic
  - formal
  - habitual
  - procedural
- **Self-protective**
  - self-centered
  - non-participative
  - loner
  - asocial
- **Status Consciousness**
  - status-conscious
  - class conscious
- **Team 1: Collaborative Team Orientation**
  - group oriented
  - collaborative
  - loyal
  - consultative
- **Team II: Team Integrator**
  - communicative
  - team-builder
  - informed
  - integrator

Table 8. Global Culturally Endorsed Implicit
Leadership Theory (CLT) Dimensions

1. *Charismatic/Value Based*, 4.5–6.5	2. *Team Oriented*, 4.7–6.2
*Charismatic 1: Visionary	*Team 1: Collaborative Team Orientation
*Charismatic 2: Inspirational	*Team 2: Team Integrator
*Charismatic 3: Self-sacrifice	*Diplomatic
*Integrity	*Malevolent (reverse scored)
*Decisive	*Administratively competent
*Performance oriented	
3. *Self-Protective*, 2.5–4.6	4. *Participative*, 4.5–6.1
*Self-centered	*Autocratic (reverse scored)
*Status conscious	*Non-participative (reverse scored)
*Conflict inducer	*Delegator[a]
*Face saver	
*Procedural	
5. *Humane*, 3.8–5.6	6. *Autonomous*, 2.3–4.7
*Modesty	*Individualistic
*Humane orientation	*Independent
	*Autonomous
	*Unique

Note: The numbered, italicized topics are Global CLT Dimensions. They are composed of CLT subscales. The only exception is Topic 6 (Autonomous) which is composed of questionnaire items, not subscales, and the item delegator ([a]) which is included in the participative dimension since it had a .81 correlation with the sum of the two subscales: autocratic and non-participative (scores revised). Numbers represent worldwide mean values on a 7-point scale ranging from 1 (substantially impedes) to 7 (substantially facilitates) effective leadership.

of leader behavior rather than specific leader behaviors. We refer to the 21 first-order factors as CLT subscales. These subscales measure more specific leader attributes and behaviors. Composite profiles of the six CLT dimensions represent what is generally referred to as leadership styles.

Universally Endorsed Leader Attributes

Hypothesis 1 states that charismatic/value-based leadership and integrity attributes will be universally endorsed as contributors to outstanding leadership. From Table 8, it can be seen that the global CLT charismatic/value-based leadership dimension had culture scores ranging from 4.5 to 6.5 on the 7-point response scale, thus indicating positive endorsement by all cultures.

To test Hypothesis 1 more rigorously, we established the following criteria for Leader Attribute Questionnaire items to be considered universally endorsed as contributors to outstanding leadership: (1) 95 percent of country scores had to exceed a mean of 6 on a 7-point scale for that attribute, and (2) the worldwide grand mean score for all countries had to exceed 6 for the attribute. The results of

Table 9. Universal Positive Leader Attributes

Questionnaire Items	Corresponding Leadership Scale (First-order Factors)
Trustworthy	Integrity
Just	Integrity
Honest	Integrity
Foresight	Charisma 1: visionary
Plans ahead	Charisma 1: visionary
Encouraging	Charisma 2: inspirational
Positive	Charisma 2: inspirational
Dynamic	Charisma 2: inspirational
Motive arouser	Charisma 2: inspirational
Confidence builder	Charisma 2: inspirational
Motivational	Charisma 2: inspirational
Dependable*	
Intelligent	Malevolent (reverse score)
Decisive	Decisiveness
Effective bargainer	Diplomatic
Win-win problem solver	Diplomatic
Administratively skilled	Administratively competent
Communicative	Team 2: team integrator
Informed	Team 2: team integrator
Coordinator	Team 2: team integrator
Team builder	Team 2: team integrator
Excellence oriented	Performance oriented

Note: *This item did not load on any factor.

this analysis are presented in Table 9. Three of the positively endorsed items concern aspects of integrity. Note that most of the other universal positively endorsed items are components of the first-order Charismatic/Value-Based Leadership and Team-Oriented dimensions. The portrait of a leader who is universally viewed as effective is clear: the person should exhibit the integrity and charismatic qualities listed in Table 9 and build effective teams. Thus, Hypothesis 1 is strongly supported.

Table 10. Universal Negative Leader Attributes

Questionnaire Attributes	Corresponding Leadership Scale (First-order Factors)
Loner	Self-protective
Asocial	Self-protective
Noncooperative	Malevolent
Irritable	Malevolent
Nonexplicit	Face saver
Egocentric	*
Ruthless	*
Dictatorial	Autocratic

Note: *These items did not load on any factor.

Universal Impediments to Leadership Effectiveness

The criteria for specific attributes, measured at the item level, to be considered universally viewed as impediments to effective leadership required that (1) an item grand mean for all countries be less than 3, and (2) 95 percent of country scores on the item be less than 3. These combined criteria indicate that the attribute was universally perceived as inhibiting outstanding leadership. Results are presented in Table 10.

Culturally Contingent Endorsement of Leader Attributes

Most interesting, from a cross-cultural viewpoint, are the attributes that in some countries were considered to enhance outstanding leadership and in other countries were considered to impede outstanding leadership. We present in Table 11 those attributes (items) that yielded scores above and below the scale midpoint of 4, contingent on country-specific responses. For instance, while the attribute Individualistic had a grand country mean of 3.11 (slightly inhibits outstanding leadership), individual country scores ranged from a low of 1.67 (moderately impedes) to a high of 5.10 (moderately contributes). Similarly, the item Status Conscious ranged in value from a low of 1.92 (moderately impedes) to a high of 5.77 (moderately contributes). Even more striking was the Risk Take item, which is a com-

Table 11. Culturally Contingent CLT Items

Anticipatory (3.84–6.51)	Intuitive (3.72–6.47)
Ambitious (2.85–6.73)*	Logical (3.89–6.58)
Autonomous (1.63–5.17)	Micro-manager (1.60–5.00)*
Cautious (2.17–5.78)*	Orderly (3.81–6.34)*
Class conscious (2.53–6.09)	Procedural (3.03–6.10)
Compassionate (2.69–5.56)	Provocateur (1.38–6.00)*
Cunning (1.26–6.38)*	Risk taker (2.14–5.96)
Domineering (1.60–5.14)*	Ruler (1.66–5.20)*
Elitist (1.61–5.00)*	Self-effacing (1.85–5.23)*
Enthusiastic (3.72–6.44)	Self-sacrificial (3.00–5.96)
Evasive (1.52–5.67)	Sensitive (1.96–6.35)*
Formal (2.12–5.43)	Sincere (3.99–6.55)*
Habitual (1.93–5.38)	Status-conscious (1.92–5.77)
Independent (1.67–5.32)	Subdued (1.32–6.18)*
Indirect (2.16–4.86)	Unique (3.47–6.06)
Individualistic (1.67–5.10)	Willful (3.06–6.48)
Intra-group competitor (3.00–6.49)*	Worldly (3.48–6.18)*
Intra-group conflict avoider (1.84–5.69)*	

Notes: CLT, culturally endorsed implicit leadership theory.
    Numbers represent worldwide minimum and maximum values on a 7-point scale ranging from 1 (substantially impedes) to 7 (substantially facilitates) effective leadership.
    *These items did not load on any factor.

ponent of the Charismatic/Value-Based second-order factor. Risk Taken ranges in value from a 2.14 (moderately impedes) to a 5.96 (moderately contributes).

These findings raise several important questions. For instance, if some attributes (items) and some global CLT dimensions are differentially endorsed among nations, as indicated by our analyses thus far, are they equally compelling and influential? What psychological and sociological processes link the CLT dimensions to dominant cultural values? Are CLT dimensions more rigidly set for homogeneous societies, such as Japan, than for culturally diverse societies, such as the United States?

Test of Hypothesis 2 and 3

The sine qua non of the GLOBE project concerns the link between culture and leadership. While all of the analyses addressing this issue have not been completed, we do have positive preliminary findings. Hypotheses 2 and 3 states that there will be significant positive relationships between CLT dimensions and their isomorphic societal and organizational culture dimensions and organizational.

Table 12 shows our predictions concerning the specific cultural dimensions that should predict cross-cultural differences in the second-order global CLT dimensions. We generated these hypotheses by examining each first-order leadership

Table 12. A Priori Hypotheses Predicting Effective Leadership Style from Societal and Organizational Culture

Second-Order Leadership Factor	Predicted Culture Dimension
Charismatic/Value Based	1. Performance Orientation
	2. Future Orientation
	3. Humane Orientation
Team Oriented	1. Collectivism I
	2. Collectivism II
	3. Humane Orientation
	4. Assertiveness*
	5. Uncertainty Avoidance*
Participative	1. Assertiveness*
	2. Power Distance*
	3. Humane Orientation
Humane Orientation	1. Humane Orientation
	2. Gender Egalitarianism
Autonomous	1. Collectivism I*
	2. Collectivism II*
Self-protective	1. Humane Orientation
	2. Power Distance
	3. Uncertainty Avoidance

Note: Dimensions followed by asterisks hypothesized to be inversly related to leadership factors.

scale and identifying the societal and organizational cultural dimensions that are isomorphic with each second-order leadership dimension (e.g., perceived effectiveness of Charismatic/Value-Based leadership was expected to be associated with the societal and organizational dimensions entitled Performance, Future, and Humane Orientation). Table 12 shows these hypotheses.

Table 13.   Results for Hierarchical Linear Modeling
Analyses Predicting Leadership Dimensions from
Organizational and Societal Culture

Dependent Variable: Team-oriented Leadership	
	Coefficient
Constant	5.89**
Organizational Level	
Collectivism Should Be	.28**
Societal Level	
Humane Orientation Should Be	−.13*
Collectivism Should Be	.40**
Organizational Variance Explained:	37.4%
Societal Variance Explained:	32.7%
Total Variance Explained:	10.8%

Dependent Variable: Participative Leadership	
	Coefficient
Constant	4.79**
Organizational Level	
Power Distance Should Be	−.16**
Uncertainty Avoidance Should Be	−.13**
Societal Level	
Uncertainty Avoidance Should Be	−.46**
Power Distance Should Be	−.35**
Humane Orientation Should Be	.25*
Assertiveness Should Be	.12*
Organizational Variance Explained:	29.7%
Societal Variance Explained:	82.2%
Total Variance Explained:	26.9%

Dependent Variable: Humane Orientation	
	Coefficient
Constant	4.83**
Organizational Level	
Humane Orientation Should Be	.37**
Societal Level	
Humane Orientation Should Be	.41**
Organizational Variance Explained:	20.7%
Societal Variance Explained:	31.6%
Total Variance Explained:	7.0%

(continued)

Table 13.   (Continued)

Dependent Variable: Charisma

	Coefficient
Constant	5.88**
Organizational Level	
Performance Orientation Should Be	.22**
Societal Level	
Performance Orientation Should Be	.35**
Organizational Variance Explained:	41.6%
Societal Variance Explained:	14.2%
Total Variance Explained:	11.9%

Notes: $*p < .05; **p < .01; ***p < .0001.$
The unit of measurement for these regressions is the organization. The number of organizations is 391. The degrees of freedom are 390. All organizations existed in societies from which three or more organizations provided data.
Organizational variance explained is calculated by dividing the total variance accounted for by the organizational predictors by the total amount of variance occurring at the organizational level of analysis. Societal variance explained is calculated by dividing the total variance accounted for by the society predictors by the total amount of variance occurring at the society level of analysis.

We tested Hypotheses 2 and 3 by using hierarchical linear modeling, a procedure that allows one to identify the amount of variance in a dependent variable that is accounted for by organizations as well as the societies in which the organizations function. The total amount of variance of CLTs accounted for is thus a joint function of the societal-level variables and the organizational-level variables in the societies in which the organizations are nested. Table 13 reveals that the endorsement of CLT global leader behavior dimensions are associated only with respondent value orientation (i.e., *Should Be* responses), and not with observed practices (i.e., *As Is* responses). The statistically significant relationships between societal and organizational culture dimensions and CLT dimensions presented in Table 13 are as follows:

1.   Approximately 11 percent of the total variance in team-oriented leadership endorsement is accounted for by organizational collective value orientation and by the humane and collective value orientations of societies in which these organizations reside. It is important to realize, however, that some of the variance in team-oriented leadership is likely attributable to levels of analysis in which we are not presently interested (e.g., industry, individual levels). When only the portions of variance that are of direct interest were examined, the organizational variable accounted for 37 percent of the variance in endorsement of all team-oriented leadership that occurred at the organizational level of analysis. The two society variables accounted for 32 percent of the endorsement of team-oriented leadership variance that occurred at the society level of analysis.

2. Approximately 27 percent of the total variance in participative leadership endorsement is accounted for by organizational-level power distance and uncertainty avoidance value orientation and by four societal-level variables: uncertainty avoidance, power distance, humane orientation, and assertiveness value orientations. The two organizational-level variables accounted for approximately 30 percent, and the societal-level variables accounted for approximately 82 percent of the variance in endorsement of participative leadership that occurred at their respective levels.

3. Approximately 7 percent of the total variance in endorsement of humane-oriented leadership is accounted for by organizational-level and societal-level humane value orientation. The organizational-level variable accounted for approximately 21 percent, and the societal-level variable accounted for approximately 32 percent, respectively, of the variance in endorsement of humane-oriented leadership that occurred at their respective levels.

4. Approximately 12 percent of the total variance in endorsement of charismatic/value-based leadership is accounted for by organizational-level and societal-level value placed on performance orientation. The organizational-level variable accounted for approximately 41 percent, and the societal-level variable accounted for approximately 14 percent, of the variance in endorsement of charismatic/value-based leadership that occurred at their respective levels.

5. The variance in endorsement of self-protective and autonomous leadership accounted for by organizational-level and societal-level variables is negligible and not reported in Table 13. This finding indicates that the variance in these two types of CLT endorsement is likely attributable to industry or individual differences, or other unmeasured situational variables.

Hypotheses 2 and 3 are supported with respect to endorsement of the above four global leader dimensions. These findings show that both societal and organizational cultural variables have non-trivial influences on CLTs and explain, in part, why there is variance across cultures with respect to what is expected of leaders and the influence and privileges they are granted.

Country-Level Uses of the Middle Manager Data

A profile shall be constructed for each nation consisting of the societal, organizational, and global CLT scores. In essence, for each culture CCIs shall construct a quantitative description of the attributes perceived as facilitating or impeding outstanding leadership, the culturally endorsed values (*Should Be* responses), and the common practices (*As Is* responses) in the societies and organizations studied. The CCIs can then interpret the results and compare the data from their culture to the data relevant to all other cultures. Fourteen of these interpretations have been included as part of the culture-specific chapters of the first of several GLOBE anthologies. The content of the anthologies is described in the following paragraphs. Upon completion of Phase 2, we shall have profiles of the dominantly endorsed leader behaviors and attributes and of the societal and organizational dimensions of each culture. We shall also have substantially greater knowledge concerning cultural and organizational influences on endorsed leader attributes in the dominant cultures or subcultures of the 62 cultures studied. This information shall be based on both the quantitative and the qualitative findings, and when published, it shall have substantial practical value for leaders who practice management in the cultures studied or deal with individuals of these cultures.

In-Depth Country-specific Descriptions of Cultures

Country-specific qualitative research by the CCIs has been ongoing from the beginning of Phase 1 and will continue to the final phase of the project. Many of the CCI teams will write a qualitative description of the major cultural variables that are relevant to leadership and organizational practices in their particular culture. The in-depth description of each culture will incorporate the following topics: (1) an overall description of the culture in terms of its political and economic system and the major historical forces and leaders that have shaped that system; (2) a brief description of prevailing organizational practices in the industries and organizations studied by the CCIs in terms of the constructs that underlie the core study dimension; (3) a description of the emic (culture-specific) manifestations of the core dimensions of the study at the societal, organizational, and leader levels of analysis; (4) a description of other emic characteristics of the society, industries studied, and leadership practices within these industries that have nontrivial implications for the practice of leadership and organizations; (5) the culture-specific semantic interpretation of the concept of leadership—what it means, the role and status of leaders in the culture, leadership functions, privileges, responsibilities, and the like; (6) identification of qualitative unobtrusive indicators of the importance assigned to leadership or leaders based on CCI participant observation; (7) an interpretation of the quantitative dimensions relevant to their cultures and in relation to other cultures; (8) an interpretative discussion of the kinds of leadership behavior required for effective leadership in the industries under investigation; and (9) prescriptive implications.

In essence, the CCIs will write a qualitative analysis of major variables relevant to leadership and organizational practices in the industries studied. The qualitative description and interpretation will be based on CCI participant observation, unobtrusive measures, and content analyses of media, interviews, and focus group discussions. CCIs have been provided with a set of self-instruction guides to ensure at least a moderate level of uniformity and quality of the qualitative research.

The completed chapters will be based on the combination of the quantitative survey data and the qualitative research findings produced by CCIs. An interpretive analysis of all of the findings will then be possible. It is hoped that this interpretation will lead to the development of a cross-cultural theory of leadership and organizational practices.

Projected Phase 3: Prediction of Leader Behavior, Organizational Practices, and Their Effectiveness

Phase 3 will consist of longitudinal tests of the following hypotheses:

Hypothesis 14a. Societal culture dimensions assessed in Phase 2 will predict isomorphic organizational practices and leader behavior dimensions assessed in Phase 3.

The rationales for Hypotheses 8 and 9 are specified following Hypotheses 2 and 3, earlier.

Hypothesis 15. The stronger the alignment among strategic organizational contingencies, societal culture dimensions, and organizational culture dimensions measured in Phase 2, as specified in Hypotheses 6a through 13a, the higher the economic performance of the organizations studied. The rationale for this hypothesis is specified following Hypothesis 14, earlier.

In addition, armed with Phase 2 measures of CLTs and the nine core GLOBE societal dimensions for 62 cultures, we will be able to test the following hypotheses with regard to leadership:

Hypothesis 16. CLTs measured in Phase 2 will predict observed leader behaviors in Phase 3.

Hypothesis 17. The more congruent the individual leader behaviors are with the CLTs, (1) the more readily leadership attempts by such individuals will be accepted and effective, (2) the more the individuals will be perceived as legitimate leaders, (3) the more highly motivated will be their subordinates/followers, (4) the more committed will be their subordinates/followers, and (5) the higher will be the leaders' performance and that of their subordinates.

Hypothesis 18. For purposes of introducing substantial organizational change, charismatic/value-oriented leadership will be the most effective leader behavior.

Phase 3 Method

The data collection for Phase 3 has begun. Based on the findings of Phase 2, a Multi-Culture Leader Behavior Description Questionnaire (MCLQ) designed to capture respondents' perceptions of leaders with whom they are familiar, was developed. The samples to be investigated will be CEOs from a variety of industries in approximately 25 cultures. In countries in which it is not a violation of cultural norms, respondents will be asked to describe the leader behavior of their immediate supervisor.[9] Independent measures of the immediate supervisor's performance and work units will also be collected.

The MCLQ was developed to reflect the leader behaviors identified in Phase 2, described earlier, and listed in Table 7. For example, since leader integrity is identified as a specific leadership attribute, the MCLQ includes several items describing behaviors that reflect leader integrity. Leader integrity items of the MCLQ will take the form, "The leader is ethical, follows a moral code, practices what he or she preaches."

Respondents will also be asked to express their emotional and evaluative responses to the leaders, their willingness to support the leaders, their willingness to go above and beyond the call of duty in the interest of the leaders' vision and direction, their confidence in the leaders, and their commitment to the leaders' goals. Measures of leadership and work-unit effectiveness shall also be collected. As in Phase 2, high-level executives shall be asked to complete the organizational practices and structural contingency scales developed in Phase 1.

Search for Emic Leader Behaviors and Emic Manifestations of Etic Dimensions of Cultures

In addition to the etic research previously described, we are interested in identifying the specific behavioral manifestations and mannerisms employed in enacting CLTs. Since respondents in all countries could describe the degree to which the leader attributes included in Table 7 contribute to or impede leader effectiveness, these dimensions are etic. They represent universal continua, along which leader behavior or attributes in all countries can be scaled. As mentioned above, the second-order CLT dimensions describe global etic leader behavior *patterns*. However, some important *specific behaviors* or attitudes by which these global etic dimensions are enacted will likely vary among cultures. For example, Smith, Misumi, Tayeb, Peterson, and Bond (1989) found that American managers are more likely to provide directions to subordinates on a face-to-face basis, whereas Japanese managers are likely to use written memos. In the United States, subordinates are usually provided negative feedback directly from their supervisors in face-to-face interactions. In Japan, such feedback is usually channeled through a peer of the subordinate. Thus, Smith and colleagues (1989) concluded that the global etic behavior dimension referred to as "performance-oriented leadership" is enacted with different specific emic behaviors in Japan and the United States. These differences in behaviors reflect the U.S. individualistic norm of "brute honesty" and the Japanese collectivistic norm of "face saving."

We expect to find emic organizational practices as well as emic organizational forms in several cultures. Family-founded and -managed firms in Hong Kong, and post-Soviet entrepreneurial firms managed by the "New Russians" in Russia are examples of such emic organizational practices. For each culture, emic organizational practices as well as emic leader behaviors will be described in the country specific chapters of the GLOBE anthologies.

Summary: Projected Phase 3 Results

In summary, respondents will describe their organizational cultures and their immediate superiors. Measures of leader and work-unit effectiveness and individual emotional and cognitive evaluative responses to leader behaviors will also be obtained. These measures will be used to test Phase 3 hypotheses and to determine the performance effectiveness of the leader behaviors described by the dimensions of the CLTs identified in Phase 2. Measures of organizational culture, structural contingencies, and effectiveness of organizations will also be collected. These measures will be used to conduct longitudinal tests of structural contingency theory. Measures of emic leader behaviors and organizational practices shall also be obtained to gain culture-specific knowledge about leadership in each of the cultures studied. We shall eliminate the possibility of common source bias by collecting measures of organizational cultures and leader behavior from different subsamples within each culture studied.

Projected Phase 4: Laboratory and Field Experiments

The research through Phase 3 will allow us to determine: (1) those leader behaviors that are universally *perceived* as facilitators of or impediments to outstanding leadership; (2) whether there are any universally *practiced* leader behaviors and universal organizational practices; (3) leader behaviors and organizational practices that have positive or negative cognitive, affective, and performance consequences; (4) leader behaviors and organizational practices that are culture specific; that is, those that are practiced in only some cultures and have positive or negative effects in only some cultures; (5) the effects of culture on the frequency, acceptability, and effectiveness of organizational practices; (6) whether the associations among organizational contingencies, organizational practices, and organizational effectiveness predicted by structural contingency theory hold longitudinally; (7) the moderating effects of societal culture on the associations predicted by structural contingency theory, (8) the moderating effect of CLTs on CEO leader behavior and leader and organizational effectiveness relationships, and (9) relationships between CEO leader behaviors and the introduction of strategic organizational change.

Phase 4 of the program will be designed to determine *experimentally* the effects of the various leader behaviors by cultures and thus determine *causal* relationships among leader behaviors and outcomes. Here we describe the conceptual fundamentals of the projected Phase 4 research. An operational research design will be specified when the results of Phase 3 are available.

Phase 4 Hypotheses

Hypotheses 17 and 18 of Phase 3 concerning the moderating effect of CLTs on leader behavior-outcome relationships and charismatic/value-based leadership to stimulate organizational change will be tested experimentally as Hypotheses 19 and 20 to determine the *causal effect* of leader behaviors and CLTs on the dependent variables.

Hypothesis 19. Leader behaviors that are consistent with CLTs measured in Phase 2 will be more accepted and will have more positive cognitive, affective, behavioral, and performance effects on followers than leader behaviors that are inconsistent with CLTs measured in Phase 2.

Hypothesis 20. For purposes of introducing substantial organizational change in organizational practices, charismatic/value-based leadership will be the most effective leader behavior.

Phase 4 Method

Using the culture-specific endorsed leader profiles obtained in Phase 2 as guides, we shall conduct controlled field and laboratory experiments in at least two cultures in each major region of the world. The leader behaviors to be studied will be those that were found in Phase 3 to be most relevant to leader effectiveness, either positively or negatively, in the 62 cultures studied. The experiments will be designed so that we will be able to assess the effects of various leader behaviors on follower affective responses, behavior, and effectiveness. The cultures to be selected for the experiments will be those with well-defined and consensually agreed CLT profiles as indicated by low within-country variance of responses to Phase 2 CLT scales. The experiments will be designed so that we shall be able to assess the effects of various leader behaviors on follower affective responses, behavior, and effectiveness.

The laboratory setting in which Hypothesis 19 will be tested will be a realistic simulation of an organization. The independent variables will be three kinds of leader behaviors. Confederate leaders will enact the leader behaviors. The dependent variables will be the affective responses, behavior, and performance effectiveness of individual followers and groups of followers.

In Treatment Condition 1, the effects of the leader behaviors endorsed by each culture will be assessed. That is, the experimental treatment will consist of leader behaviors endorsed by the CLT of the country in which the experiment is conducted.

In Treatment Condition 2, the effects of those leader behaviors found in Phase 3 to have the most consistent positive effects on follower cognitions, affect, and performance across cultures will be assessed. Thus this treatment will consist of universally or near universally endorsed leader behaviors enacted by confederate leaders.

In Treatment Condition 3, confederates will enact leader behaviors that are in conflict with the CLT profiles of each culture.

The outcome of these experiments will be substantially increased knowledge concerning the following questions:

1. Are there any universally effective leader behaviors?
2. What is the effect of violating strongly held culturally endorsed preferences for selected leader behaviors?
3. Are behaviors that are consistent with culture specific preferences more effective than a select set of other behaviors that have been found in Phase 3 to be the most consistently positively endorsed leader behaviors across cultures? The answer to the latter question will tell us whether the behaviors specified in CLTs are also the behaviors that are more effective and will indicate whether leaders can make a difference by being different. More specifically, we will be able to determine whether a select set of behaviors can consistently have more positive effects than a set of culturally endorsed behaviors, even if the former behaviors are in conflict with culturally endorsed norms.

Hypotheses 19 and 20 will also be tested by using a field experimental design. As one possible example, we may ask university business school students to respond to a proposed change in the system by which they are graded in their educational program. It will be proposed that the grading system be changed to grade subjects on the basis of their relative standing and a forced curve distribution. It will be explained that this system is consistent with competitive schools, will enhance the reputation of their school, and will enhance the amount of learning achieved by students.

In the first experimental treatment, the confederate leader, acting as a representative of the school's curriculum committee or in another relevant official capacity, will introduce and advocate the proposed change by enacting the leader behaviors most strongly endorsed by the CLT of the culture.

In the second treatment, the leader will introduce and advocate the proposed change by linking it to a vision that emphasizes increased international status and competitiveness of the school and appeals to the patriotism and to the values endorsed in the culture. The leader will also express high performance standards and strong confidence in the students and appeal to country loyalty by stressing international competition among business schools. These behaviors are part of the Charismatic/Value-Based Leadership global dimension.

In sum, in Phase 4 we hope to make a substantial contribution to knowledge concerning the behavioral and performance effects of leader behaviors as well as their cognitive and affective effects. The results of Phase 4 will be reported in a monograph or book.

UNIQUE STRENGTHS OF THE GLOBE RESEARCH DESIGN

Project GLOBE differs from previous cross-cultural research in several ways. The primary strength of this research is that we have not made assumptions about how best to measure cultural phenomena. Rather, we use multiple measurement methods in order to empirically test which methods are most meaningful. This is most evident in the development of three sets of measures assessing culture: (1) those based on shared values of organizational or society members, (2) those based on current organizational and societal *practices*, and (3) unobtrusive measures. In addition, we developed measures of leader attributes that differentiate cultures in terms of perceived effectiveness, as well as leader attributes that are *universally* endorsed (or rejected) across cultures. Further, we have collected data relevant to organizational contingency variables and organizational effectiveness.

We developed new measures and collected original data for our hypotheses and research questions, rather than collecting data on only some variables and relying on measures developed at other times in other places from other samples for the other variables. Since the organizational culture, societal culture, and leadership measures employed in Phase 2 were completed by different people, we were able to eliminate the frequently encountered problem of common source bias. By use of multiple indicators of societal culture, we were able to eliminate common method variance. The psychometric properties of the GLOBE scales and tests of their validity exceed normal empirical research standards and are described in the previously mentioned monograph (Hanges et al., 1998, under review).

CONTRIBUTIONS

The GLOBE research program is directed toward filling a substantial knowledge gap concerning the cross-cultural forces relevant to effective leadership and organizational practices. The research findings will be useful for resolving several important theoretical social science issues and for a wide variety of practical purposes. In this section, we briefly describe the various contributions we expect to result from the GLOBE research.

Practical Relevance

The final product of the GLOBE research program, the books and articles in which the various cultures will be described and interpreted, will include practically useful information about the cultures studied.

It is expected that the quantitative findings resulting from the GLOBE research program will provide substantial enlightenment concerning the processes by which culture influences leadership and organizational practices. In the GLOBE anthologies consisting of culture-specific chapters, cultures will be described in terms of the nine core dimensions as well as their unique (emic) attributes. A description will be provided concerning universal and culturally contingent leader attributes and behaviors, the commonly enacted and most favored leader behavior patterns and organizational practices found in the cultures studied, and the cultural influences on the effectiveness of leader behaviors and organizational practices. In addition, leader behaviors that are culturally offensive will be identified and described. As mentioned previously, 14 chapters, which will comprise the first anthology, have been completed.

The qualitative research chapters in the GLOBE anthologies describe the most critical leader behaviors and organizational practices in each culture studied, the constraints imposed on leaders by cultural prescriptions and proscriptions, and unique norms of the cultures studied relevant to leadership and organizational practices. This information will be useful as case content for leadership training and career development programs and for the design of management and leadership education programs intended to prepare individuals who will manage and lead others in cultures other than their home cultures.

The descriptions of cultural prescriptions and proscriptions will be useful for the adjustment and effective interaction of individuals who work with others from the cultures studied. More specifically, this information will be useful to expatriates assigned to other than their native cultures, managers of diverse cultural and ethnic groups both domestic and abroad, individuals involved in the management of public and private international affairs, and those who conduct negotiations with commercial and political organizations in other cultures.

Knowledge of the culturally endorsed implicit theories of leadership in each culture, and most and least effective leader attributes and behaviors, will be useful for selecting, counseling, and training individuals who are to be assigned to, or who work with, members of the cultures studied. The resulting findings will be useful for informing potential managers of the kinds of behaviors and organizational practices that are acceptable and effective and unacceptable and ineffective in the cultures studied.

Information concerning the constraints imposed on leaders by cultural norms will be useful to decision makers who need to anticipate and respond to the actions of leaders of other cultures. Knowledge about cultural and organizational norms and practices in the cultures studied can inform the formulation of meaningful prescriptions for managing in other cultures—for strategy and policy formulation, organizational improvement interventions, human resource management practices, and the design of organization structures and incentive and control systems.

The industries studied are subjected to a wide variety of organizational contingencies. Many of the findings relevant to the effects of organizational contingencies on organizational practices and effectiveness in these industries are thus likely to be relevant to other industries and, therefore, useful to managers whose industries face similar organizational contingencies.

In sum, the findings of the study will provide a wide variety of information about 62 cultures, representing all major regions of the world, that can help managers and leaders in their adjustment, strategy and policy formulation, human resource management practices, and organizational practices.

Beneficial Social and Economic Applications

The research program is expected to have several additional beneficial social and economic applications. Within regions, countries that share similar regional resources and backgrounds can make comparisons to determine similarities and differences among themselves and share ways to improve inter-country relationships, economic productivity, and quality of life for their citizens. The research program is also expected to lead to increased intercultural communication among educators who normally would not have contact with each other, and thus it will result in greater intercultural awareness and cooperation among scholars. CCIs have been extremely active in practicing cross-cultural communications. GLOBE-related research has been presented in over 90 conference papers, chapters of books, or journal publications.

Many of the Country Co-Investigators, being indigenous to their cultures, are influence and change agents within those cultures, at least with respect to those with whom they have contact in their roles as university faculty members, social scientists, and consultants. The intra-country social influence of the CCIs will most likely be substantially enhanced by participating in the GLOBE research. These CCIs, in turn, will serve as country boundary spanners and will facilitate importation and transfer of knowledge within their countries. Forty scholarly papers based on GLOBE data have been presented at national or regional conferences thus far.

CCIs in several nations have begun to translate the products of the research (which will be several books and scholarly articles) into other languages and thus increase the dissemination of this information to a wider number of countries. The chapters of the books will make reports on each of the cultures studied available in the public domain.

Ancillary Social Science Contributions

The resulting data can be used for multiple purposes beyond the hypotheses of the study. For example, the worldwide Phase 2 data can be used to compare countries with their trading partners or their major competitors with respect to cultural, organizational, or leadership practices that are relevant to improving trade between them or with respect to practices that facilitate harmonious and productive trade. We have already witnessed over 50 research projects and papers presented at scholarly conferences in which cultural and managerial practices have been compared among subsets of the GLOBE participating nations. An entire issue of the *Polish Psychological Bulletin* has been devoted to this research (Maczynski, 1997).

Relationships between the variables under study and economic practices and outcomes can also be subjected to analysis. The societal-level data can be used in econometric or sociological models and related to firm-level practices such as forms of production systems and organization, transfer of technology, pricing, risk taking with respect to entry into new markets, investment with respect to research and development, and foreign investment practices. With the exception of four studies we were able to locate concerning economic growth, little attention is given to cultural influences on economic practices and output. The four studies to which we refer are those authored by Hofstede and Bond (1988); Franke (1997); House et al. (1977), and McClelland (1961).

The measures of culture can also be related to national levels of saving, distribution of wealth and social privileges, consumption levels and patterns, issues of economic growth and development, regulatory practices, and national productivity and efficiency. To date, cultural influences on such variables have gone largely ignored.

Indices of economic practices, adherence to norms of human rights, safety, and quality of life, by country, are either available in published form or can be collected by CCIs, other scholars, or interested government agencies or foundations. The GLOBE Phase 2 worldwide data can be analyzed in relation to these indices. Thus, it will be possible to determine concurrent or predictive relationships between the GLOBE dimensions and such indices.

The worldwide data can also be analyzed to determine relationships between the variables under study and many indices of social and physical well-being. For example, the GLOBE societal culture dimensions can be related to such outcomes as mortality rates, life expectancy rates, hygiene practices, preventive or remedial medical practices, stress levels, suicide rates, frequency of ethnic and border conflicts, indicators of social unrest, and violations of human rights. Following are some examples of expected relationships between GLOBE societal dimensions and socially and practically relevant variables:

- Cultural tendencies toward power stratification and assertiveness are likely positively related to tendencies toward intra-country conflict among labor and management and possibly even to tendencies of nations to enter into aggressive ethnic border conflicts and military actions.
- Humane orientation is likely inversely related to the frequency and severity of hostile actions within cultures. Humane orientation is also likely positively related to such practices as the establishment and enforcement of human rights norms and laws, and inversely related to their violations.
- Assertiveness is likely positively related to the frequency and severity of hostile actions within cultures.
- Performance and future orientation are likely positively related to national competitiveness and economic development.
- Gender equalization is likely inversely related to female abuse and positively related to female literacy, education, and labor market participation.

Following are four examples of findings that show how some of the cultural variables under study have been shown to relate to, or predict, important behavior. In *The Achieving Society,* David McClelland (1961) demonstrated rather convincingly that cultural indicators of achievement motivation were predictive of subsequent economic development in developing countries over a 25-year period. Hofstede and Bond (1988) found that a measure of cultural future orientation and delay of gratification referred to as the Confucian Dynamic was positively related to the economic growth of the Asian tigers from 1965 to 1985. Kogut and Singh (1986) have shown that the level of cultural uncertainty avoidance is inversely related to the level of risk taken by organizations when entering markets in foreign nations. Finally, one of the unobtrusive measures that correlates with the GLOBE measure of gender equalization is the United Nations index of female participation in labor markets.

OUTCOMES

The outcomes of Phases 1 and 2 of the GLOBE project will consist of several books and a series of articles. The first book will report the comparative quantitative cross-cultural results and hypothesis tests of GLOBE Phase 2 research. Another book or article will report the research findings relevant to the tests of structural contingency theory of organizational form and effectiveness as well as other findings relevant to organizational culture and practices enacted cross-culturally. The remaining books will be the anthologies described earlier, consisting of country-specific descriptions of cultures and interpretations of the Phase 2 quantitative data. Two or more methodological monographs or articles will illustrate new quantitative methods of cross-cultural research and also illustrate how recently developed sophisticated cross-level statistical procedures can be applied in cross-cultural research. One such monograph is currently under review (Hanges et al., 1998). Measurement papers will present the development and validation of questionnaires, unobtrusive measurement, and participant observation scales.

Phase 3 will test relationships found in Phase 2 longitudinally and will investigate emic as well as etic phenomena. Phase 3 results will appear in at least one additional book and several articles. Phase 4 will also result in at least one book or monograph that will report the results of the laboratory and field experiments.

CONCLUSION AND FUTURE ACTIVITIES

In summary, the GLOBE research is designed to contribute to the development of empirically based cross-cultural leadership and organizational theory by investigating the roles of societal and organizational values and institutionalized practices, organizational contingency variables, and implicit leadership theories as antecedents to cross-cultural variance in leader behavior, leader influence, leader effectiveness, and organizational practices and performance. GLOBE research is also designed to contribute to organizational theory and practice by exploring relationships between societal and organizational cultural variables and organizational effectiveness and by conducting cross-cultural tests of structural contingency theory. Based on the preliminary findings reported in this monograph, we are encouraged to believe that the GLOBE project has the potential of making a noteworthy contribution to the cross-cultural leadership and organizational literature.

ACKNOWLEDGMENT

The authors are indebted to Markus Hauser for his thoughtful comments and suggestions relevant to this monograph.

NOTES

1. The first seven authors participated in the statistical analyses and the writing of this monograph. The Senior Research Associates provided general research support to the Principal Investigator and the GLOBE Coordinating Team, assisted country representatives in translation and back-translations of instruments and in data collection, and assisted in the coordination of the GLOBE data collection. The remaining authors represented their cultures as Country Co-Investigators, made suggestions concerning the design and execution of the GLOBE program, collected the data on which this monograph is based, and provided interpretations of research findings in their respective cultures.

2. Phases I and II of the GLOBE research program were funded by the Dwight D. Eisenhower Leadership Education Program of the Department of Education of the United States.

3. While there are 62 cultures in the full Project GLOBE sample, the findings reported here are based on only 54 countries. The data for the remaining countries were not yet entered into the computer files at the time this monograph was finalized. The remaining cultures are Albania, China, Denmark, France, French-speaking Switzerland, Japan, Kazakhstan, and the United States.

4. Current members of the GCT are: Staffan Akerblom, Stockholm School of Economics, Sweden; Felix Brodbeck, University of Munich, Germany; Jagdeep S. Chhokar, Indian Institute of Management, Ahmedabad, India; Marcus W. Dickson, Wayne State University, United States; Peter W. Dorfman, New Mexico State University, United States; Paul J. Hanges, University of Maryland, United States; Robert J. House, University of Pennsylvania, United States; Mansour Javidan, University of Calgary, Canada; Enrique Ogliastri, University of Los Andes, Colombia; Antonio Ruiz-Quintanilla, Cornell University, United States; Marius van Wyk, University of South Africa, South Africa.

5. Data relevant to organizational practices were collected using the organizational level questions. Data relevant to families and societal practices were collected using the societal level questions.

6. This hypothesis was suggested by Celeste Wilderom, Tilburg University, The Netherlands.

7. CCIs were asked to collect data from organizations in only two industries per country because it was believed that CCIs would find collection of data from three industries to be excessively burdensome. In fact, approximately two-thirds of the CCI teams collected data from all three target industries.

8. Vipin Gupta identified the specific unobtrusive measures based on a literature survey of information published by the United Nations and the World Bank and other relevant published information. Gupta also conducted the statistical analyses to develop and validate the unobtrusive measures.

9. Interviews and focus groups revealed that, in several of the cultures studied, it would be a violation of cultural norms for subordinates to complete a questionnaire or answer interview questions that might be construed as evaluative with respect to individuals in positions of authority.

REFERENCES

Ajzen, L., & Fishbein, M. (1970). *Understanding attitudes and predicting social behavior.* Englewood Cliffs, NJ: Prentice-Hall.

Aldrich, H. E. (1979). *Organizations and environments.* Englewood Cliffs, NJ: Prentice-Hall.

Bass, B. M. (1985). *Leadership and performance beyond expectations.* New York: Free Press.

Bass, B. M. (1990). *Bass & Stogdill's handbook of leadership: Theory, research, and managerial applications* (3rd ed.). New York: Free Press.

Bass, B. M. (1997). Does the transactional-transformational leadership paradigm transcend organizational and national boundaries? *American Psychologist, 52*(2), 130-139.

Brislin, R. W. (1986). The wording and translation of research instruments. In W. J. Lohner & J. W. Berry (Eds.), *Field methods in cross-cultural research* (pp. 137-164). Beverly Hills, CA: Sage Publications.

Burns, T., & Stalker, G. M. (1961). *The management of innovation.* London: Tavistock Publications, Tavistock Centre.

Child, J. (1981). Culture, contingency, and capitalism in the cross-national study of organization. In L. L. Cummings (Ed.), *Research in organizational behavior* (pp. 303-356). Greenwich, CT: JAI Press.

Dickson, M. (1997). *Universality and variation in organizationally cognitive prototypes of effective leadership.* Unpublished doctoral dissertation, Department of Psychology, University of Maryland, College Park.

Donaldson, L. (1993). *Anti-management theories of organization: A critique of paradigm proliferation.* Cambridge: Cambridge University Press.

Dorfman, P. W. (1996). International and cross-cultural leadership research. In B. J. Punnett & O. Shenkar (Eds.), *Handbook for international management research* (pp. 267-349). Oxford, UK: Blackwell.

Franke, R.H. (1997). Industrial democracy and convergence in economic performance: Comparative analysis of industrial nations in the 1970s and 1980s. In R. Hodson (Ed.), *Research in the sociology of work.* Greenwich, CT: JAI Press.

Gagliardi, P. (1986). The creation and change of organizational cultures: A conceptual framework. *Organization Studies, 7*(2), 117-134.

Gerstner, C. R., & Day, D. V. (1994). Cross-cultural comparison of leadership prototypes. *Leadership Quarterly, 5*(2), 121-134.

Hanges, P. J., Braverman, E. P., & Rentsch, J. R. (1991). Changes in raters' impressions of subordinates: A catastrophe model. *Journal of Applied Psychology, 76,* 878-888.

Hanges, P. J., Lord, R. G., Day, D. V., Sipe, W. P., Smith, W. C., & Brown, D. J. (1997). Leadership and gender bias: Dynamic measures and nonlinear modeling. In R. G. Lord (Chair), *Dynamic systems, leadership perceptions, and gender effects.* Symposium presented at the Twelfth Annual Conference of the Society of Industrial and Organizational Psychology, St. Louis, MO.

Hanges, P., House, R. J., Ruiz-Quintanilla, S. A., Dickson, M. W., Dorfman, P. W., & 109 co-authors. (1998). The development and validation of scales to measure societal and organizational culture. Under review.

Hauser, M., House, R.J., & Puranman, P. (1999). *Strategy process: Cultures consequences.* Academy of Management Conference, Chicago, IL.

Hickson, D. J., Hinings, C. R., McMillan, J., & Schwitter. (1974). The culture-free context of organization structure: A tri-national comparison. *Sociology 8,* 59-80.

Hofstede, G. (1980). *Culture's consequences: International differences in work-related values.* London: Sage.

Hofstede, G., & Bond, M. H. (1988). The Confucius connection. From cultural roots to economic growth. *Organizational Dynamics, 16,* 4-21.

House, R.J. (1997). GLOBE: The Global Leadership and Organizational Behavior Effectiveness research program. *Polish Psychological Bulletin, 28*(3), 215-254.

House, R. J., & Aditya, R. N. (1997). The social scientific study of leadership: Quo vadis? *Journal of Management, 23*(3), 409-473.

House, R. J., Wright, N. S., & Aditya, R. N. (1997). Cross-cultural research on organizational leadership: A critical analysis and a proposed theory. In P. C. Earley & M. Erez (Eds.), *New perspectives in international industrial organizational psychology* (pp. 535-625). San Francisco: New Lexington.

James, L. R., Demaree, R. G., & Wolf, G. (1984). Estimating within-group interrater reliability with and without response bias. *Journal of Applied Psychology, 69*(1), 85-98.

Khandwalla, P. N. (1977). *The design of organizations.* New York: Harcourt Brace Jovanovich.

Kluckhohn, F. R., & Strodtbeck, F. L. (1961). *Variations in value orientations.* New York: HarperCollins.

Kogut, B., & Singh, H. (1988). The effect of national culture on the choice of entry mode. *Journal of Informational Business, 19,* 411-432.

Kopelman, R. E., Brief, A. P., & Guzzo, R. A. (1990). The role of climate and culture in productivity. In B. Schneider (Ed.), *Organizational climate and culture* (pp. 282-318). San Francisco: Jossey-Bass.

Lawrence, P. R., & Lorsch, J. W. (1967). *Organization and environment.* Cambridge, MA: Harvard University Press.

Leung, K., & Bond, M. H. (1989). On the empirical identification of dimensions for cross-cultural comparisons. *Journal of Cross-Cultural Psychology, 20,* 133-151.

Lombardo, M. M. (1983). I felt it as soon as I walked in. *Issues and Observations, 3*(4), 7-8.

Lord, R., & Maher, K. J. (1991). *Leadership and information processing: Linking perceptions and performance.* Boston: Unwin-Everyman.

Lumpkin, G. T., & Dess, G. G. (1996). Clarifying the entrepreneurial orientation construct and linking it to performance. *Academy of Management Review, 21* (1), 135-172.

McClelland, D. C. (1961). *The achieving society.* Princeton, NJ: Van Nostrand.

McClelland, D. C. (1985). *Human motivation.* Glenview, IL: Scott, Foresman.

McClelland, D. C., Atkinson, J. W., Clark, R. A., & Lowell, E. L. (Eds.). (1953). *The achievement motive*. New York: Appleton-Century-Crofts.

McFarland, L. J., Senen, S., & Childress, J. R. (1993). *Twenty-first-century leadership*. New York: Leadership Press.

Miller, D., & Droge, C. (1986). Psychological and traditional determinants of structure. *Administrative Science Quarterly, 31*(4), 539-560.

Misumi, J. (1985). *The behavioral science of leadership: An interdisciplinary Japanese research program*. Ann Arbor, MI: University of Michigan Press.

O'Connell, M. S., Lord, R. G., & O'Connell, M. K. (1990, August). *Differences in Japanese and American leadership prototypes: Implications for cross-cultural training*. Paper presented at the meeting of the Academy of Management, San Francisco.

Putnam, R. D. (1993). *Making democracy work*. Princeton, NJ: Princeton University Press.

Rokeach, M. (1973). *The nature of human values*. New York: Free Press.

Schein, E. H. (1992). *Organizational culture and leadership: A dynamic view* (2nd ed.). San Francisco: Jossey-Bass.

Schneider, B. (1987). The people make the place. *Personnel Psychology, 40,* 437-454.

Schneider, B., Goldstein, H. W., & Smith, D. B. (1995). The ASA Framework: An update. *Personnel Psychology, 48,* 747-783.

Shaw, J. B. (1990). A cognitive categorization model for the study of intercultural management. *Academy of Management Review, 15*(4), 626-645.

Simonton, D. K. (1994). *Greatness: Who makes history and why*. New York: Guilford Press.

Sipe, W. P., & Hanges, P. J. (1997). Reframing the glass ceiling: A catastrophe model of changes in the perception of women as leaders. In R. G. Lord (Chair), *Dynamic systems, leadership perceptions, and gender effects*. Symposium presented at the Twelfth Annual Conference of the Society of Industrial and Organizational Psychology, St. Louis, MO.

Smith, P. B., & Bond, M. H. (1993). *Social psychology across cultures: Analysis and perspectives*. London: Harvester Wheatsheaf.

Smith, P. B., Misumi, J., Tayeb, M. H., Peterson, M., & Bond, M. H. (1989). On the generality of leadership style across cultures. *Journal of Occupational Psychology, 30,* 526-537.

Staw, B. M., Sandelands, L. E., & Dutton, J. E. (1981). Threat-rigidity effects in organizational behavior: A multilevel analysis. *Administrative Science Quarterly, 26*(4), 501-524.

Thompson, K. R., & Luthans, F. (1990). Organizational culture: A behavioral perspective. In B. Schneider (Ed.), *Organizational climate and culture* (pp. 319-344). San Francisco: Jossey-Bass.

Triandis, H. C. (1993). The contingency model in cross-cultural perspective. In M. M. Chemers & R. Ayman (Eds.), *Leadership theory and research: Perspectives and directions* (pp. 167-188). San Diego: Academic Press.

Triandis, H. C. (1995). *Individualism and collectivism*. Boulder, CO: Westview Press.

Trice, H. M., & Beyer, J. M. (1984). *The cultures of work organizations*. Englewood Cliffs, NJ: Prentice-Hall.

Tushman, M. L., Newman, W. H., & Nadler, D. A. (1988). Executive leadership and organizational evolution: Managing incremental and discontinuous change. In R. H. Kilman & T. J. Covin (Eds.), *Corporate transformation: Revitalizing organizations for a competitive world* (pp. 102-130). San Francisco: Jossey-Bass.

Yukl, G. A. (1994). *Leadership in organizations* (3rd ed.). Englewood Cliffs, NJ: Prentice-Hall.

WHEN EAST MEETS WEST
LEADERSHIP "BEST PRACTICES" IN THE UNITED STATES AND THE MIDDLE EAST

Terri A. Scandura, Mary Ann Von Glinow, and
Kevin B. Lowe

ABSTRACT

A review of the literature on leadership indicates a paucity of studies that employ samples from the Middle East. Cultural aspects that may influence leadership in the Middle East suggest that task-oriented leadership will be related to employee satisfaction and leadership effectiveness. Data from two samples, the United States ($N = 144$) and the Middle East ($N = 107$), were analyzed using exploratory factor analysis to investigate the consistency of construct composition across the two samples. Following determination of a consistent factor structure, hierarchical regression analysis was employed to examine leadership and organizational outcomes in the Middle East, with the U.S. sample results providing a frame of reference. Results indicated that people-oriented leadership (Consideration) was related to job satisfaction and leadership effectiveness in the U.S. sample. In stark contrast, task-oriented leader-

Advances in Global Leadership, Volume 1, pages 235-248.
Copyright © 1999 by JAI Press Inc.
All rights of reproduction in any form reserved.
ISBN: 0-7623-0505-3

ship (Initiating Structure) was related to satisfaction and leadership effectiveness in
the Middle East. Implications and directions for future research are discussed.

From a Western Hemisphere perspective, the Middle East remains one of the most
mysterious regions in the world. Despite the recent "globalization" of research on
management, including leadership, we still know very little about this important
region. The "Middle East" includes the countries of Egypt, Sudan, Algeria,
Morocco, Tunisia, Libya, Iran, Iraq, Jordan, Palestine, Syria, Turkey, Lebanon,
and the Gulf countries of Saudia Arabia, Bahrain, Yeman, Kuwait, the United
Arab Emirates, Qatar, and Oman. Israel is geographically part of the region; however, it differs culturally in many respects, since considerable immigration to the
region commenced in the 1940s and the Arabic culture is mixed with European,
Russian, and other traditions. This has been supported by empirical research on
National Culture measures (Hofstede, 1980). Countries in this region represent
some of the oldest cultures in the world; they are predominantly Islamic, and some
are among the wealthiest countries in the world on a per capita basis, primarily due
to crude oil production (the Middle East holds an estimated 67 percent of the total
oil discovered in the world) (Mabro, 1991). The population of the region is estimated to be between 175 and 200 million (Butt, 1987). In addition to the region's
power with respect to its abundant oil reserves, recent sociopolitical events have
focused attention on this part of the world. The Gulf War of 1992, the Middle East
peace process, and continued attention to the Palestinian situation have been daily
focal points for the western news media. And yet, management and leadership literature is virtually silent on the nature and effects of leadership in Middle East
organizations.

In a review of leadership theory and research, Yukl (1998) notes that "most of
the research on leadership during the past half century has been conducted in the
United States, Canada, and Western Europe" (p. 461). Thomas, Shenkar, and
Clarke (1994) reviewed the global coverage of studies published in the *Journal of
International Business Studies (JIBS)* during the 25 years of that journal's existence. Their review resulted in analysis of 602 articles and research notes. Of these
602 studies, 15 were published using samples from Israel; however, as mentioned,
Israel is considered culturally distinct from other Mideast countries (Hofstede,
1980). Also, it is important to note that although Iran and Turkey are in the region,
they speak Farsi rather than Arabic. Iran is a Muslim country and is similar to other
Arabic countries in that respect, but Turkey is not predominantly Muslim. Hence,
caution should be exercised in interpreting studies that employ Iran and Turkey as
representative of the Mideast region. Given this caveat, Thomas and colleagues
(1994) report that 13 studies were conducted with samples from Turkey and 7
studies were conducted with samples from Iran. Eleven studies were conducted on
Egypt, which is somewhat more similar to other Arabic countries in language, religion, and culture. Apart from these 31 studies, no other Middle East studies were

published in *JIBS* during its 25-year history, which is significant since *JIBS* is arguably the premier journal in international business. This report reveals a clear gap in the research base; more research needs to be conducted on Arabic countries, including the Arabian Peninsula (e.g., Saudia Arabia). Based upon their review, Thomas and colleagues (1994) conclude that our "mental maps" of the world are parochial because of the restriction of geographical coverage in our journals. One goal of the present study is to address this gap by inclusion of a sample drawn from countries in the Middle East.

The lack of data on the Middle East is probably due more to the difficulty of conducting research in the region than to neglect on the part of international researchers. Our own experience suggests that collecting data from the Middle East is a huge challenge. In addition to geographical distance, we found that cultural distance, in terms of understanding what research is and why it is important, was a factor. It is necessary that surveys be translated into the Arabic language, typed in that language, and then back-translated to ensure cultural equivalence— skill sets that are not common in Western cultures where more empirical research is currently generated. In our research, we found that it was absolutely necessary to have Arabic nationals travel to the Middle East and personally ask respondents to complete surveys. This type of "face work" is common in other parts of the world (e.g., in Mexico), and it makes survey research a costly and highly labor-intensive process. The importance of the research project and comparisons to other countries was explained. In some instances, the respondent considered it a personal favor to the person making the request. Personal networking was the most effective, and perhaps the only, means of collecting data. Mail-out requests were not attempted, because it was expected that the response rate would be very low. We consider the face work approach of personal connections and networking to be essential in order to collect high-quality data in the Middle East. It is not enough to translate the survey and mail it abroad. Research on the Middle East requires a personal approach to the collection of data, in addition to careful translation and back-translation of survey instruments. In part, we found that research concerning Middle Eastern respondents involved an educational process regarding what the purpose of research is, why it is important, and how it will improve understandings between the West and the Middle East. When these things were explained to the respondents, most chose to cooperate with the research project.

BEYOND STEREOTYPES: RESEARCHING LEADERS IN THE MIDDLE EAST

Our "Western" knowledge of leadership in the Middle East is often garnered from television clips of various Mideast leaders such as Mu'ammar Gadhafi, Yitzak Rabin, and Yassir Arafat. In some sense, Westerners perceive the unlikely pairing of leadership with terrorism in the Middle East, thus creating biased or stereotypical views of the Middle Eastern leader. Clearly, a better understanding of leadership will help to destroy unfortunate and possibly inaccurate stereotypes as well as to augment our knowledge of typical Middle Eastern leadership styles and behaviors.

Given that there are large cultural gaps between Middle Eastern countries and the frame-of-reference country (the United States), it is quite plausible that the leadership process itself may differ greatly. Thus, we sought to investigate leadership practices using a theory of leadership that is well grounded in Western empirical studies as a useful starting point for "getting our feet wet" with respect to leadership practices in the Middle East.

One of the best-known approaches to leadership is the Ohio State model of leader Consideration and leader Initiating Structure (Bass, 1990; Stogdill, 1963; Yukl, 1998). *Consideration* is the leader behavior that indicates caring and concern for employees, and *Initiating Structure* is the leader behavior that is based upon attention to task demands. Hundreds of studies have affirmed the construct validity of these two leadership constructs in predominantly Western samples (Bass, 1990), and well-established measures of Consideration and Initiating Structure have been developed (Schriesheim & Kerr, 1974, 1977; Schriesheim & Stogdill, 1975). Given their established validity in the United States, an interesting question for leadership research is whether Consideration and Initiating Structure (a "classic" leadership approach) will hold in the Middle East. Since we know so little about leader behavior in the Middle East, the use of Consideration and Initiating Structure as constructs for beginning a research program on Arabic countries appears to be a reasonable point of departure.

LEADER BEHAVIOR IN THE MIDDLE EAST

According to Von Glinow (1993), task-oriented leadership and people-oriented leadership represent two key leadership behaviors that are not only well documented in the United States, but also intuitively appealing in developing countries. She notes that research on leadership has demonstrated that "leadership training produces behavior training in subordinates" (p. 105). It cannot be assumed, however, that leadership training developed and tested in the United States will have the same effects on subordinates in or from other cultures. For example, leadership in Sweden, Mexico, and Japan is seen as being derived from one's seniority in the organization and is also viewed as paternalistic (Von Glinow, 1993). In the United States, employees expect a leader to be a good listener and often expect the leader to share power in participative leadership modalities (Conger, 1989; Vroom & Jago, 1988). Given the research to date, it seems clear that leadership differs across cultures (Smith, Misumi, Tayeb, Peterson, & Bond, 1989), however, so very little is known about leadership in many regions of the world.

As noted by Hagan (1995), the pervasive influence of the Islamic religion is key to understanding the Arab world. A common expression from the lips of an Arab is "INSHA' ALLAH," which translates as "if God's willing." Many Arabs have a tendency to be rather fatalistic in their approach to life, and thus time orientations are predominantly past and present rather than the past, present, and future cycle characteristic of the United States (Varner & Beamer, 1995). As a high-context culture, they often have a lesser need for clarity in their business and interpersonal interactions (Hall, 1976). Hofstede (1980) found the Middle Eastern countries of Iran and Turkey to be relatively high on collectivism and power distance. Collectivist cultures use social pressure to regulate individual behavior. For example, one of the most well-known, highly collectivist cultures is Japan, in which the needs of the individual are often subordinated to the good of the group. Power distance is the degree to which workers accept the authority of those in higher level positions in the organization. Given the strong role of Islam in respect for one's elders and for hierarchical position, the task-oriented style of leadership (Initiating Structure) might be expected by employees in the Middle East. Also, given that power distance is higher in the Arabic world than in the United States, which has a more egalitarian approach to leadership, it can be expected that task-oriented leadership will be related to employee satisfaction and leadership effectiveness in the Middle East. Although this may seem counterintuitive, it is important to remember that obedience to authority is valued, and trust in the wisdom of those in senior positions is important to the family structure. Arab workers may prefer more directive leadership because they respect and admire the wisdom of those more senior in the organization. Coupled with high collectivism, task-oriented leadership in the Middle East may be seen as more effective by employees because it is the leader who knows what is best for the organization, the group, and the worker. Also, Hofstede (1980) found that respondents from Iran and Turkey had a strong need to avoid uncertainty, which is probably true of other Arabic countries as well. For example, Almeer (1992) found that collectivism and femininity still characterize Tunis, Jordan, Eqypt, and Qatar. This also suggests that task-oriented leadership would be more effective, as task directives from a supervisor might reduce ambiguity for employees. Many Arabic countries are characterized as feminine (Almeer, 1992; Hofstede, 1980), suggesting that the employee will try to maintain harmonious relationships with others at work. Given what is known about Middle Eastern cultures, we hypothesize that task-oriented leadership will be related to employee job satisfaction and leadership effectiveness:

Hypothesis 1. Leader Initiating Structure will be positively and significantly related to employee job satisfaction in the Middle East.

Hypothesis 2. Leader Initiating Structure will be positively and significantly related to leadership effectiveness in the Middle East.

In contrast to the Middle East, we expect that leader Consideration will be related to both employee satisfaction and leadership effectiveness in the United States. Showing concern for employees, having a "people orientation," and allowing their input into decisions, has been termed the "New Leadership" (Vroom & Jago, 1988) in the United States. Increasingly, organizational leaders are talking about empowering employees and providing them with the skills necessary to make their own decisions regarding their work (Conger, 1989). Consistent with research on Initiating Structure and Consideration (Schriesheim & Bird, 1979), we expect leader Consideration to be related to satisfaction, as well as leadership effectiveness (Schrieheim & Bird, 1979; Schriesheim & Kerr, 1974; Schriesheim & Stogdill, 1975). While these links are well established in the U.S. leadership literature, as a frame of reference, we wanted to include data from the United States in our analysis of leadership in the Middle East. Hence, we hypothesize that people-oriented leadership will be related to employee job satisfaction and leadership effectiveness.

Hypothesis 3.   Leader Consideration will be positively and significantly related to employee job satisfaction in the United States.

Hypothesis 4.   Leader Consideration will be positively and significantly related to leadership effectiveness in the United States.

METHOD

Samples

United States

The U.S. sample includes $N = 144$ managers. Approximately 50 percent of the sample are managers from a diverse set of organizations who participated in two executive business education programs associated with a large southwestern university. The other half of the sample are managers in a large defense corporation located in the southwestern United States. A comparison of the mean scores for this sample on the constructs of interest to a random sample of prior research investigating these constructs in U.S. organizations indicated no significant differences.

Middle East

The Middle East sample consists of $N = 107$ managers from diverse organizations ($N = 47$ from Jordan and $N = 60$ from Saudia Arabia). A special effort was made to include countries not sampled by previous research (Hofstede, 1980; Thomas et al., 1994), especially the Gulf countries. Two Arabic males who were visiting Jordan and Saudi Arabia collected the data. Personal contacts are necessary to do business in the Middle East (Hagan, 1995), and based upon our experience, they are also essential in collecting research information. Although personal contacts were used to obtain participants, the data collectors were careful to include a variety of organizational types including government, service, and manufacturing.

The Arabic-language version of the survey was translated and back-translated by the two Arabic males who collected the data. These individuals were English-Arabic bilinguals and also U.S.-Arabic biculturals. The goal of the translation process was conceptual rather than literal equivalence (Graen, Hui, Wakabayashi, & Wang, 1997), but care was taken to preserve the integrity of the research instrument.

Measures

Instrument

This study is part of a larger research program that includes a number of Human Resource Management (HRM) practices and organizational contextual factors (Von Glinow, 1993). The present study focuses on three groups of variables: leadership practices (task and people orientation), employee job satisfaction, and leadership effectiveness. Short forms of measures were employed because our experience in collecting data from different cultures indicates that shorter forms increase response rates.

Independent Variables

Leader Consideration and leader Initiating Structure were the independent variables of interest in the present study. A 10-item short-form version of the 20-item Leader Behavior Descriptive Questionnaire (LBDQ-XII) (Stogdill, 1963) was used to measure these constructs. Previous research has identified the LBDQ-XII as the soundest available measure of Consideration and Initiating Structure (Schriesheim & Bird, 1979; Schriesheim & Kerr, 1974). The reduced measure used in this study contained 5 items to measure leader Consideration and 5 items to measure leader Initiating Structure. For both constructs, the 5 items were included in this scale. For the Middle East sample, only 9 of the 10 items were included, due to difficulty in translating item 6 into Arabic ("emphasizes high standards of performance") which was seen as redundant with item 2 ("stresses high standards of performance").

Confirmatory factor analysis is preferred when the factor structure is known or can be hypothesized from theory a priori (Sharma, 1996, p. 128). However, given the potential for different respondent frames of reference in cross-cultural samples (Cox, Lobel, & McLeod, 1991; Meindl, Hunt, & Lee, 1989), and the lack of empirical research regarding these constructs in the Middle East, we conducted

Table 1. Factor Loadings: U.S. Sample

	Factor 1	Factor 2
My immediate supervisor...		
1. Sets specific goals for me to accomplish	.11	.78
2. Emphasizes high standards of performance	.21	.74
3. Stresses the importance of work goals	.14	.87
4. Is friendly and easy to approach	.82	.14
5. Is eager to recognize/reward good performance	.69	.46
6. Stresses high standards of performance	(not translated)	
7. Is willing to listen to my problems	.84	.29
8. Treats me with respect	.86	.13
9. Checks everything; independent judgment not respected	−.53	.35
10. When suggestions made, receive fair evaluation	.77	.19

Note: $N = 144$. Some item content is abbreviated.

exploratory factor analyses to determine the underlying factor structure of the measures for the samples in this study.

Exploratory factor analysis with varimax rotation yielded two factors in each sample (United States and Middle East) (Tables 1 and 2). While the pattern of factor loadings is fairly consistent across the samples, the last two items were somewhat ambiguous in the Middle East sample ("checks everything" and "when suggestions are made to top management, they receive fair evaluation"). Interestingly, the Middle East respondents did not view the "checks everything" item as being clearly task-oriented behavior. Also, it is possible that the "suggestions to top management" item might not be relevant, due to a cultural difference in expectations regarding participation and upward feedback in a high power distance region. These results clearly need replication before further item refinement is undertaken.

Table 2. Factor Loadings: Middle East Sample

	Factor 1	Factor 2
My immediate supervisor...		
1. Sets specific goals for me to accomplish	.05	.85
2. Emphasizes high standards of performance	.01	.80
3. Stresses the importance of work goals	.21	.74
4. Is friendly and easy to approach	.69	.16
5. Is eager to recognize/reward good performance	.83	−.05
6. Stresses high standards of performance	(not translated)	
7. Is willing to listen to my problems	.84	.07
8. Treats me with respect	.86	.33
9. Checks everything; independent judgment not respected	-.53	.49
10. When suggestions made, receive fair evaluation	.77	.48

Note: $N = 107$. Some item content is abbreviated.

The consistent pattern of these loadings does not confirm that these item sets were interpreted equivalently, but they do suggest that the nine leadership items capture two distinct concepts in both samples. The items were scored to create two unit-weighted scales: Consideration (five items) and Initiating Structure (four items). Inspection of the item content for the measures is consistent with LBDQ-XII item loadings for Consideration and Initiating Structure. We believe that these distinct phenomena can be usefully interpreted as leader Consideration and leader Initiating Structure, which is consistent with leadership theory. The Cronbach alpha estimates of internal consistency (reliability) for leader Consideration were .90 in the U.S. sample and .76 in the Middle East sample. For Initiating Structure, the Cronbach alphas were .64 in the U.S. sample and .74 in the Middle East sample. Thus, both constructs achieved acceptable reliability in the two samples (Nunnally, 1979). Concern about the psychometric properties of the Initiating Structure measure in the U.S. sample is reduced by the considerable evidence supporting the English-language version of this measure (Bass, 1990; Schriesheim & Bird, 1979).

Dependent Variables

Two measures of organizational outcomes were included in the present study. These included a global measure of job satisfaction (six items) and perceptions of leadership effectiveness (three items). The employee satisfaction scales queried the respondents on their satisfaction with the job, supervisor, organization, pay, promotion, and job security. The leadership effectiveness items addressed the extent to which leadership practices help the company (1) to have high-performing employees, (2) to have employees who are satisfied with their jobs, and (3) to have employees who make a positive contribution to the overall effectiveness of the organization. Responses for the job satisfaction and leadership effectiveness measures were recorded on a Likert-type scale ranging from 1 (not at all) to 5 (to a very great extent).

For the U.S. sample, Cronbach alphas were .83 for satisfaction and .95 for leadership effectiveness. For the Middle East sample, Cronbach alphas were .71 for satisfaction and .73 for leadership effectiveness.

Analysis

Hierarchical regression analyses were performed with satisfaction and leadership effectiveness as dependent variables. Leader Consideration was entered first, since previous research suggests that this construct may capture affect for the leader ("liking") in addition to capturing the impact of leader behavior (Schriesheim & Gardiner, 1993). Subsequent analysis entering Initiating Structure determined that the results as reported are not affected by the entry order of the two measures.

Table 3.   Means, Standard Deviations, and Intercorrelations for U.S. Sample

	Mean	SD	1	2	3	4
1. Consideration	3.62	.97	(.90)			
2. Initiating Structure	3.12	.75	.27***	(.64)		
3. Satisfaction	3.51	.73	.61***	.20*	(.83)	
4. Leader Effectiveness	3.15	1.02	.65***	.30***	.57***	(.95)

Notes: Reliabilities on diagonal.
      *p < .05.
      **p < .01.
      ***p < .001..

RESULTS

The means, standard deviations, and intercorrelations among variables are shown in Tables 3 and 4 for the U.S. and Middle East samples, respectively. As indicated in Tables 3 and 4, both Consideration and Initiating Structure had positive associations with job satisfaction and leadership effectiveness. The bivariate relationships between Consideration and satisfaction and leadership effectiveness appear stronger in the U.S. sample compared to the Middle East sample. Yet, the relationships between Initiating Structure and leadership effectiveness appear stronger for the Middle East. Also, given the significant correlations between job satisfaction and leadership effectiveness, separate hierarchical regression analyses were run.

Although the discovery of a consistent factor structure for both the Middle East and the United States samples is interesting, the findings of the hierarchical regression analyses are of equal if not greater interest. As shown in Table 5, in the two separate hierarchical regression analyses for the U.S. sample with Consideration entered first, only leader Consideration was a significant predictor of employee satisfaction (beta = .61, R^2 = .37), and leadership effectiveness (beta = .65, R^2 = .43). Leader Initiating Structure failed to enter in both of the regression models. In subsequent analyses, these results held when the order of independent variable entry was reversed (Initiating Structure entered first). In the two hierarchical

Table 4.   Means, Standard Deviations, and
Intercorrelations for Middle East Sample

	Mean	SD	1	2	3	4
1. Consideration	3.06	.95	(.76)			
2. Initiating Structure	2.71	.93	.47***	(.74)		
3. Satisfaction	2.74	.84	.22***	.38***	(.71)	
4. Leader Effectiveness	3.23	1.08	.25***	.34***	.31***	(.73)

Notes: Reliabilities on diagonal.
      *p < .05.
      **p < .01.
      ***p < .001.

Table 5. Hierarchical Regression Analyses on Satisfaction,
Leadership Effectiveness, and Organizational Effectiveness
for the U.S. and Middle East Samples

	Consideration beta	Initiating Structure beta	R^2	F Ratio
Job Satisfaction				
United States	.61	*	.37	79.4
Middle East	*	.38	.42	14.5
Leadership Effectiveness				
United States	.65*	.43	102.3	
Middle East	*	.33	.11	14.5

Note: *indicates that the variable did not enter the regression model.

regression analyses for the Middle East sample with leader Consideration entered first, only leader Initiating Structure was a significant predictor of employee satisfaction (beta = .38, R^2 = .14) and leadership effectiveness (beta = .33, R^2 = .11). Leader Consideration failed to enter in either regression model. These results also held when the order of entry of the independent variables was reversed (Initiating Structure entered first).

DISCUSSION

These findings across cultural groups are notable for both the contrast in findings of those leader behaviors that predict outcomes, and the consistency of these findings across more than one outcome variable (job satisfaction and leadership effectiveness). The pattern of results indicated in Table 5 seems to clearly indicate that task-oriented leadership is related to employee job satisfaction and leadership effectiveness in the Middle East, and that Consideration is not. In contrast, the data indicate that Consideration is related to employee satisfaction and leader effectiveness in the United States and task-oriented leadership is not. It is possible, based on these data, that expectations of leaders and the relationship of leadership to organizational outcomes is a culturally bound phenomena.

In Arabic, the word for "leadership" is *AL KIYADA* (pronounced Al kee'-ah-dah), which refers to officers in the military or those with high rank in the government. Historically, *KA'ID* (leader, pronounced kee'-aahd) is a great hero who leads warriors into battle. The cultures of the Middle East are rooted in traditional military concepts of leadership. It is important to bear in mind that, at the beginning of the nineteenth century, almost all of the Middle East and North Africa was still part of the Ottoman Empire which had been conquered in the fifteenth and sixteenth centuries. It was not until the end of World War I that the Ottoman Empire completely collapsed (Slugget & Farouk-Slugget, 1991). Images of war and conquest may influence the Arabic notion of leadership, whereas Western notions of participation and listening to problems are antithetical to the Arabic cultural expectations of leadership.

Although it may surprise the Western reader that task-oriented leadership is related to employee job satisfaction and leadership effectiveness, from the point of view of an Arab person, who expects the leader to be strong and decisive, it is not at all unusual. Further, the cultural expectation that the leader knows what is best, and respect for those more senior—especially those who are older—leads to trust in the leader's judgment and willingness to follow directives. People-oriented leadership might be confusing or illustrate signs of indecision and weakness on the part of the leader.

Today, in many organizations in the Middle East, leadership positions (especially in the Gulf) are assigned to non-Arabs, since persons who are properly trained for these positions are in short supply among the ranks of labor. Home-country nationals are not yet trained to assume top positions in organizations because management has not developed into a profession. Arabic managers are primarily younger and do not have the prerequisite experience to assume the leadership role. Often expatriates from other countries are coupled with junior Arabic managers who are to guide them into leadership. Yet there is an issue with this mentoring process for the junior Arabic manager, because the expatriate manager fears that the Arabic national will take the position (Almeer, 1996). As a result of this lack of information and education regarding leadership, most Arabs do not make the distinction between "manager" and "leader." This is an academic distinction that is not yet emphasized in the universities of the Gulf and other Arabic countries, which focus more on technical training. Often, managers are assigned to positions without management education, including leadership training. Learning to lead is a process of trial and error. Hence, the need for leadership education in these countries seems obvious.

Of course, the results of one study cannot be considered conclusive. We hope, however, that this study is a first step to understanding cultural differences in leadership, using a traditional leadership approach, task-oriented, and people-oriented leadership in the Middle East. As far as we can tell, this study is the first of its kind to look at leadership in the Middle East. It serves as both a reminder and a caveat that we must be careful in asserting our assumptions about the transferability of our constructs across cultures. In this instance with Middle Eastern respondents, task-oriented leadership translates very well, though people-oriented leadership might not.

Future research is clearly needed on the Middle East (Thomas et al., 1994). Research should expand beyond the examination of the Middle East as a region and focus on specific countries. Just as there are certain acute differences between France and Germany, for example, we are confident that similar differences exist within and between the various countries of the Middle East. Other leadership perspectives should also be examined such as Leader-member exchange (LMX) (Graen & Scandura, 1987) and transformational leadership (Bass, 1985). Both

LMX and transformational leadership theory discuss the importance of the role of mentoring in the leadership process (Scandura & Schriesheim, 1994). In the Middle East, the role of mentoring in the development of leadership potential appears to be an area worthy of investigation, given the results of Almeer's (1996) work on mentoring in Gulf countries. We suggest that no assumptions be made regarding the transferability of these leadership concepts. The cultural and historical context of the area under study should be carefully examined and data carefully collected to explore the cultural boundaries of leadership theory across cultures. In this regard, ethnographic approaches and qualitative research using in-depth interviews or observation, or both, may be helpful in explicating the leadership concept in the Middle East. It should also not be expected that leadership concepts relate in the same fashion to outcome measures, such as job satisfaction in the Middle East. There is much work that needs to be done.

The Middle East will remain an important region, given its resources and continued sociopolitical issues. But it need not remain a cultural enigma, relegated to stereotypes and inaccurate viewpoints. Through constant attention to our frames of reference and genuine willingness to gain an understanding of the Middle East, its culture and its people, improved relationships between the West and the Middle East alliances may be attained.

ACKNOWLEDGMENTS

The authors are indebted to Nawaf M. Shatrat and Adel Al-Grafi for their assistance with survey translations and data collection for the Middle East sample employed in this research. Nawaf M. Shatrat and Nabila Almeer provided helpful comments on an earlier version of this manuscript. This research was supported in part by a grant from Florida International University's Center for International Business Education and Research (CIBER).

REFERENCES

Almeer, N. (1992). *A study of cultural impact of nurses' ability to make decisions in the state of Qatar.* Unpublished master's thesis, University of Texas Medical Branch at Galveston.

Almeer, N. (1996). *An exploratory study to examine the experiences of Qatari women in the nursing profession.* Unpublished doctoral dissertation, University of Miami.

Bass, B. M. (1985). *Leadership and performance beyond expectations.* New York: Free Press.

Bass, B. M. (1990). *Handbook of leadership.* New York: Free Press.

Butt, G. (1987). *The Arab world.* Pacific Grove, CA: Brooks/Cole Publishing.

Conger, J. A. (1989). Leadership: The art of empowering others. *Academy of Management Executive, 3,* 17-24.

Cox, T. H., Lobel, S. A., & McLeod, P. L. (1991). Effects of ethnic group cultural differences on cooperative and competitive behavior on a group task. *Academy of Management Journal, 34,* 827-847.

Graen, G. B., Hui, C., Wakabayashi, M., Wang, Z. M. (1997). Cross-cultural research alliances in organizational research: Cross-cultural partnership making in action. In C. Earley and M. Erez

(Eds.), *New perspectives on international industrial/organizational psychology* (pp. 160-189). San Francisco: Jossey-Bass

Graen, G. B., & Scandura, T. A. (1987). Toward a theory of dyadic organizing. In B. M. Staw and L. L. Cummings (Eds.), *Research in Organizational Behavior, 9* (pp. 175-208). Greenwich, CT: JAI Press.

Hagan, C. M. (1995). *Comparative management: Africa, the Middle East, and India* (Working Paper). Florida Atlantic University, Boca Raton, FL.

Hall, E.T. (1976). *Beyond culture.* Garden City, NY: Anchor Press/Doubleday.

Hofstede, G. (1980). Motivation, leadership, and organizations: Do American theories apply abroad? *Organizational Dynamics, 9*(1), 42-63.

Mabro, R. (1991). Oil in the Middle East. In P. Slugget and M. Farouk-Slugget (Eds.), *Tuttle Guide to the Middle East.* Boston, MA: Charles E. Tuttle.

Meindl, J. R., Hunt, R. G., & Lee, W. (1989). Individual-collectivism and work values: Data from the United States, China, Taiwan, Korea, and Hong Kong. In A. Nedd, G. R. Ferris, & K. R. Rowland (Eds.), *Research in personnel and human resources management* (Suppl. 1, pp. 59-77). Greenwich, CT: JAI Press.

Nunnally, J. C. (1979). *Psychometric theory.* New York: McGraw-Hill.

Porter, M. E. (1990). *The competitive advantage of nations.* New York: Free Press.

Scandura, T. A., & Schriesheim, C. A. (1994). Leader-member exchange and supervisory career mentoring as complementary constructs in leadership research. *Academy of Management Journal, 37,* 1588-1602.

Schriesheim, C. A., & Bird, B. J. (1979). Contributions of the Ohio State Studies of the field of leadership. *Journal of Management, 5,* 135-145.

Schriesheim, C. A., & Gardiner, C. (1993). An examination of the discriminant validity of the leader-member exchange (LMX-7) measure, commonly used in organizational research. *Proceedings of the Southern Management Association,* 91-93.

Schriesheim, C. A., & Kerr, S. (1974). Psychometric properties of the Ohio State leadership scales. *Psychological Bulletin, 81,* 756-765.

Schriesheim, C. A., & Kerr, S. (1977). Theories and measures of leadership: A critical appraisal. In J. G Hunt and L. L. Larson (Eds.), *Leadership: The cutting edge* (pp. 9-45). Carbondale, IL: Southern Illinois University Press.

Schriesheim, C. A., & Stogdill, R. M. (1975). Differences in factor structure across three versions of the Ohio State leadership scales. *Personnel Psychology, 28,* 189-206.

Sharma, S. (1996). *Applied multivariate techniques.* New York: John Wiley.

Slugget, P. & Farouk-Slugget, M. (1991). *Tuttle Guide to the Middle East.* Boston, MA: Charles E. Tuttle.

Smith, P. B., Misumi, J., Tayeb, M., Peterson, M., & Bond, M. (1989). On the generality of leadership style across cultures. *Journal of Occupational Psychology, 62,* 97-107.

Stogdill, R.M. (1963). *Manual for the leader behavior descriptive questionnaire.* Columbus, OH: Ohio State University Bureau of Business Research.

Thomas, A. S., Shenkar, O., & Clarke, L. (1994). The globalization of our mental maps: Evaluating the geographic scope of JIBS coverage. *Journal of International Business Studies, 25*(4) 675-686.

Varner, I., & Beamer, L. (1995). *Intercultural communication in the global workplace.* Chicago: Irwin.

Von Glinow, M. A. (1993). Diagnosing "best practice" in human resource management practices. In A. Nedd, G.R. Ferris, & K.R. Rowland (Eds.), *Research in personnel and human resource management* (Suppl. 3, pp. 95-112). Greenwich, CT: JAI Press.

Vroom, V. H., & Jago, A. G. (1988). *The new leadership: Managing participation in the organization.* Englewood Cliffs, NJ: Prentice-Hall

Yukl, G. (1998). *Leadership in organizations* (4th ed). Upper Saddle River, NJ: Prentice-Hall.

THE MORAL COMPONENT OF EFFECTIVE LEADERSHIP

THE CHINESE CASE

C. Harry Hui and George C. Tan

ABSTRACT

Two-factor models (e.g., task-orientation versus socioemotional orientation, transactional versus transformational, performance versus maintenance, and so forth) constitute one major paradigm that researchers have been using to understand effective leadership. One of the theoretical formulations, the PM model developed by Misumi (1985), is premised on the notion that leadership is about fulfilling the Performance (P) and Maintenance (M) functions in the work group. The model proposes that the best leadership pattern is when P and M are both at work. Recently a group of Chinese researchers expanded the PM model to include a moral character dimension (C). The rationale was that the guiding communist ideology places much emphasis on a leader's "being right." The best leaders in China are thus high on C and P, as well as M. We report empirical data from two studies to argue that the C component is equally essential to Chinese leaders who are not under communist rule. Moral superiority has been a major criterion for Chinese leadership since historic times, and this belief is still prevalent in every Chinese business circle. Moreover, we contend that

Advances in Global Leadership, Volume 1, pages 249-266.
Copyright © 1999 by JAI Press Inc.
All rights of reproduction in any form reserved.
ISBN: 0-7623-0505-3

C is a primary leadership component, not just another leadership characteristic. It generates the highest employee attitude and productivity. This chapter concludes with a discussion of the various "moral character" behaviors that distinguish an effective leader from an incompetent one, in the Chinese view. They include absence of flattery, disciplining subordinates according to fair rules, giving proper credit to others, abiding by rules, allocating resources fairly and unselfishly, thrift, and concern for others.

INTRODUCTION

The search for what makes a good leader has never ceased. With the globalization of businesses and the emphasis on the competency approach in management development and selection, industrial psychologists are once again presented with the age-old question, What are the essential characteristics of a good global leader and manager? The last decade or so has seen two trends in the study of leadership.

The first is the attention paid to the moral constituents of a leader (see, e.g., Badaracco & Ellsworth, 1989; Kanungo & Mendonca, 1996). Gone are the days when we could argue that since a business or government organization is different from a religious group, a political party, or an educational institution, ethics are not a concern. To the contrary, in some corporations chief executives are expected to show their subordinates how to practice business ethically, rather than just profitably. They should be transformational (e.g., Bass & Avolio, 1994) in their influence process. Kanungo and Mendonca (1996) further argue that the central motivation of leaders should be altruistic—a desire to benefit their followers. Following along the same lines, Greenleaf considers that leaders must first be servants and desire to serve others (see, e.g., Greenleaf, Frick, & Spears, 1996).

The second trend is the awareness of cultural differences in the essential elements of effective leadership. Certain leadership practices and traits may be functional in one culture, but less so in another. For example, Gerstner and Day (1994) found with a small student sample that the French expected their leaders to be determined and open-minded, Indians expected theirs to be industrious and competitive, and Taiwanese placed priority on responsibility and intelligence. Aram and Piraino (1979) found that integrity was the preferred leadership quality in Chile.

This chapter begins with a brief review of a general behavioral approach, namely Misumi's two-factor model. We shall demonstrate how this model was expanded in Chinese society. We argue that moral character, among other components, is essential to effective leadership. Empirical data are presented to illustrate the significance of this component in Hong Kong.

MISUMI'S PERFORMANCE-MAINTENANCE (PM) MODEL OF LEADERSHIP

The theoretical root of this model lies in the structural functionalism that characterizes the "Ohio" and "Michigan" research paradigms, which view leadership behaviors and leaders' behaviors as categorizable into task-oriented ones and social-oriented ones. Misumi's model distinguishes between the performance (P) and maintenance (M) functions of a group and its leader. The performance function involves contributions toward goal accomplishment and problem solving. The maintenance function promotes group social stability.

Performance-oriented leadership behaviors comprise two elements. The first is the coordination of work-related activities. This "planning" element implies that an effective leader must possess expert knowledge in the assigned area of responsibility. Such leaders are efficient at solving work-related problems and at planning work schedules. The second element is the leader's ability to pressure subordinates to work at maximum capacity. Such leaders are strict with regard to the observance of deadlines and regulations.

Maintenance leadership behavior is oriented toward promoting and reinforcing the drive for the preservation of the group. It is directed toward dispelling excessive tensions that arise in interpersonal relations within a group, resolving conflict and strife, providing encouragement and support, inspiring personal fulfillment, and promoting an acceptance of interdependence among group members (Misumi, 1985). An M-oriented leader creates a pleasant work atmosphere and empathizes with subordinates' problems. This dimension is thus similar to the notions of "relationship orientation" and "consideration" delineated in previous research.

The P and M leadership behaviors are not viewed as opposites of a single dimension. Instead, they combine to form various kinds of leadership patterns. For empirical purposes, Misumi (1985) distinguished four basic patterns: the PM, which substantially fulfills both performance and maintenance functions; the Pm and pM, which fulfill only one of the two functions; and the pm, which fulfills neither function.

According to Misumi (1985), PM-type leadership is likely to generate in subordinates high job satisfaction and low job-related stress. Under the influence of M-type leadership, negative reactions to the "pressure" element in P-type leadership will be positively experienced as the exercise of expert guidance. Therefore, group productivity will be highest when the P-type is combined with the M-type.

Application of the PM Model in China

The Four Modernizations in China in the late 1970s and the 1980s was the Chinese government's concerted effort to strengthen the national economy through industry and trade development. At the time, the importance of effective yet non-political leadership and management became a popular topic of discussion. Senior government officials conceded that ideological purity could no longer be the only requirement of effectively managed state-owned enterprises. A group of Chinese social scientists thus adopted Misumi's PM model to guide their work.

These social scientists began a series of survey studies in various government organizations. They found that the P and M dimensions were relevant to Chinese work settings (Xu, Chen, Wong, & Xue, 1985). However, feedback from their respondents also showed that the model could not fully account for the Chinese leadership phenomenon. The responses clearly indicated that Chinese leadership constituted more than the P and M factors, as postulated in the West and in Japan. According to Ling (1989), Chinese people believe that a good leader should also rate high on the moral dimension of righteousness and self-control. This moral character, or C, dimension enhances leadership effectiveness when present with P- and M-type behaviors.

Several factors may explain why the moral dimension is paramount in analyzing leadership behavior.

First, within the Chinese political and civil system, selection and assessment of government officials have been based on the individuals' moral standing (Ling & Fang, 1995).

Second, traditional culture prior to Communist rule similarly placed emphasis on the moral integrity of leaders. Confucian teachings stress the need for a great world ruler to be a great ruler of his own nation and of his own family. To achieve this, a leader has to be in command of his own being—in other words, to be morally upright.

A third reason why the moral dimension is crucial in analyzing leadership behavior is the fact that in a society where formal rules regulating a leader's conduct either do not exist or are not well delineated, there is always a risk that power will be abused in the name of authority. Without a well-formed judicial system to define and enforce individual rights and freedoms, social order has no basis other than the morally binding relationships connecting the members in Chinese society. Under these circumstances, the leader's moral integrity becomes the last fortress to safeguard social justice. A premium has been placed "on the benevolence of enlightened leaders whose moral character enables them to lead and control with tolerance and forbearance" (Ling & Fang, 1995, p. 276) in a political system of high power distance.

In the People's Republic of China, individual morality is about not only personal attributes but also political ideology. Indeed, it is often the case that individual morality and political purity are equivalent. Leaders who possess high moral standards are those who are not selfish or petty. They do not practice bribery or corruption. They work only for the good of the Communist Party. They are honest and do not seek personal vengeance (see Mao, 1968).

Emphasis on Morality in Non-Communist Chinese Societies

In Hong Kong, Taiwan, and other Chinese communities, political purity is not viewed as an element of moral uprightness. Yet we contend that the latter is still an important characteristic of an effective leader. One rationale underlying this theoretical stance relates to the earlier assertion that Chinese society is regulated not so much by law enforcement as by role observance (Ho, Chen, & Chiu, 1991). Moral righteousness, in turn, is an assurance of the observance of proper conduct in the various role relationships.

Furthermore, people tend to scrutinize others more closely and harshly when the relationships are meaningful or important to them. Leaders, especially in employment settings, have always been viewed as influential people. They are one, if not the only, source of control of the subordinates' livelihood in terms of salary and other benefits. This is true both in traditional Chinese business settings and in modern corporations. Thus, leader morality is an important evaluative tool of Chinese leadership effectiveness. For example, Cheng and Chung (1981) extracted an "unselfishness" factor from questionnaire responses of junior military personnel in Taiwan. The questionnaire contains items extracted from the Supervisory Behavior Description Questionnaire (Fleishman, 1953), as well as items generated by their own peers on their supervisors. "Unselfishness" consists of behaviors such as not taking advantage of subordinates, not practicing favoritism, not borrowing money from subordinates, and not establishing relationships with subordinates for personal benefit.

Using a $2 \times 2 \times 2$ factorial design and manipulating levels of task-oriented behaviors, socioemotional behaviors, and personal morality, Tse and Leung (1997) presented a job candidate description to a group of MBA students and asked the respondents to indicate whether they would consider the candidate for a general management position, and to predict the effects on the company if the person were hired.

It was discovered that personal morality was related to some, but not all, ratings. For example, all three factors had an impact on whether the person would be shortlisted and granted an interview. Whether the person would be hired depended on his task-oriented and socioemotional leadership behaviors, but not his moral character. Moreover, a general manager deficient in personal morality was viewed as causing a poor public image of the company. Nevertheless, Tse and Leung (1997) found that neither the personal morality factor nor the task-oriented leadership factor had any impact on the respondents' projection of the staff's commitment and morale.

The structure of this study, a scenario that required respondents to play the role of a third party, may have masked some important effects of the personal morality factor. In the studies reported in this chapter, we attempt to demonstrate that moral character does have a direct, independent effect on subordinates' satisfaction and stress levels. When existent with the P or M dimension, the personal morality dimension may also have an additive effect.

KEY BEHAVIORAL ELEMENTS ON THE C DIMENSION

To study the significance of the C dimension we must first have a clear understanding of the construct. While moral character can be depicted in many different ways, we chose to start with Ling's list. To capture the behaviors that were frequent, familiar, and significant in the Hong Kong Chinese workforce, we asked 82 part-time business students (29 men and 53 women) to rate 10 behavioral items taken from Ling's C (Moral Character) subscale on: (1) whether the behavior was a common topic of discussion among colleagues, (2) whether the behavior described in the item would affect their evaluation of their supervisors, and (3) how positively or negatively the behavior would affect their work attitude.

On the basis of the respondents' ratings, we selected 5 behavioral items to operationalize the C dimension. Using the same method, we also identified the key behavioral elements on the P and M dimensions in Ling's CPM Questionnaire and Misumi's PM Questionnaire.

The behaviors on the C dimension are as follows:

1. Not currying favor
2. Not seeking personal vengeance under the guise of office matters
3. Not using underhanded means
4. Acknowledging subordinates' efforts accordingly
5. Not abusing authority

The behaviors on the P dimension are as follows:

1. Setting time limits for work
2. Giving useful advice
3. Designing an effective work schedule
4. Observing strict regulations
5. Planning effective remedial actions

The behaviors on the M dimension are as follows:

1. Trusting in others' abilities/efforts
2. Being understanding and accommodating
3. Treating every group member impartially
4. Not attributing blame to others
5. Not avoiding responsibility and making excuses

AN EXPERIMENTAL STUDY ON THE EFFECTS OF LEADERS' C-, P-, AND M-TYPE BEHAVIORS ON SUBORDINATES' SATISFACTION AND STRESS

To investigate the relative strengths of leaders' C-, P-, and M-type behaviors on their subordinates, we invited 80 college students to take part in an experiment. The three behavioral dimensions (C, P, and M) were manipulated in a $2 \times 2 \times 2$ factorial design. The participants were under the impression that this was a half-day pilot program on effective marketing skills. About 70 percent of the participants were female. Each participant belonged to one of eight tutorial groups, each of which was randomly assigned to one of the experimental conditions.

Operationalization of Behavioral Items

During the experiment, the participants were under the supervision of a person who enacted a list of leadership behaviors (as described earlier). Each behavior (or its opposite or absence) was portrayed through one of the following: (1) an interaction between the supervisor confederate and a secondary accomplice, (2) an interaction between the supervisor confederate and the group of students, or (3) the supervisor confederate's reactions to incidents occurring throughout the experiment.

For example, a C dimension behavioral item, "not seeking personal vengeance under the guise of office matters," was presented in a conversation scripted between the supervisor and the confederate 20 minutes into the session. The confederate was overheard by the research participants saying, "Hey, I have students from Business Studies and, boy, am I giving them a hard time now. Remember one of their lecturers, XX? He's that guy who is always giving us a bad time in administration. I am going to make sure that his students will pay for his crime." To which the supervisor would reply, "Mr. Lam, I do not like the lecturer, but it has nothing to do with the students. It is not right to punish his students for the nasty things he has done to us. I most certainly will not do it. I am here to supervise the Network Target workshop and I will just concentrate on that."

Interactions between the supervisor and the group were used extensively in the operationalization of M-type leadership behaviors. An example is "being understanding and accommodating," where the M-type supervisor confederate expressed empathy by saying, "I know this is a very boring task, but we will finish in a moment. You are probably tired, but please don't stop." An m-type leader, on the other hand, would display callousness by saying, "This is a very boring job, but you volunteered for it. It's your fault. Ha! Ha!"

The third method was used primarily for portraying behaviors attributed to the P dimension. For the behavioral item "planning remedial actions effectively," another confederate, posing as a clerical assistant for the department, entered the room 5 minutes into the second section and asked the group to leave so that another tutorial group could start its session. The P-type leader calmly proceeded to the departmental office located next door and returned 2 minutes later to organize the group to move all equipment and materials to another nearby room. In contrast, a p-type leader showed incompetence by portraying anxiety in a verbal manner and left the room in search of the confederate, Mr. Lam. After 30 seconds, the p-type leader returned, reported that he could not locate Mr. Lam, and behaved with even more anxiety. After leaving the room once more under the pretext of looking for the experimenter, the supervisor returned in 30 seconds and told the group to move.

Experimental Confederates

Two Chinese amateur actors played the supervisor's role. Two individuals were chosen to ensure that the process was not confounded by any individual-specific characteristics or skills (e.g., ability to portray moral-, performance-, or maintenance-oriented leadership behavior patterns), or by the same actor portraying a certain leadership pattern. The actors received 3 hours of orientation on the behaviors, emotional states, facial expressions, and paralinguistic cues associated with each leadership behavior pattern. Another 3 hours were allocated to rehearsing the prepared script and associated behavioral items.

In all, eight experimental sessions were presented, with the same two actors. Each played the primary supervisor in four sessions and served as a confederate in the other four. The actors were assigned the role and the leadership pattern to be enacted 5 minutes before the commencement of the experiment and remained unaware of the purpose of the study.

Task

The session consisted of two parts, each running for approximately an hour. In the first part, the participants were given a task that involved listing names, addresses, and telephone numbers of eateries situated in the district to which they had been randomly assigned. In addition, they were required to find out which bus would take them to their assigned district from their academic institution. Each participant was provided with a Chinese-language telephone directory to accomplish the task. They had to extract the information, translate it into English, and enter the details in a notebook. The group was told to select a member to enter information into the computer for "electronic networking" purposes. No further instruction was given, but aids such as additional writing materials and a Hong Kong road directory were left on the table for the participants' use.

In the second part, participants repeated what they had done in the first section, except that the target district was the one neighboring that which they had researched in the first part.

The tasks were routine and monotonous. The intention was to keep motivation in task performance low during the short experimental session, so that the effects of leadership patterns would be discernible.

Procedure

Participants were initially told that they belonged to one of the first groups in the territory to be taught Target Network, a newly developed marketing strategy that was enjoying great success in Japan. It was explained that in order for the program to run smoothly, full participation was a necessity. The participants were to assume that their fellow group members were colleagues and the supervisor was the manager of their team.

The experimenter ushered in the supervisor, described as a member of the educational research and development department at the college, and the confederate, introduced as the supervisor of another group that was to begin a similar session. After a brief conversation among the three, aimed at operationalizing one of the behavioral items, the confederate and experimenter left and the supervisor read out scripted instructions on the task the group was to carry out.

After each member had been randomly assigned a target district, the group was told that discussion among members was permitted and the whole group would use the information gathered in a subsequent marketing activity.

The first task took 1 hour, during which the supervisor had opportunities to display behaviors appropriate to the assigned experimental condition. At the conclusion of the allotted time, the supervisor collected the data that the group had compiled and left the room on the pretext of delivering the materials to the experimenter for validation.

The supervisor reappeared 5 minutes later and delivered the instructions for the second task. The participants were to repeat what they had done in the first section but were to target the neighboring district instead of their own district. Five minutes after the commencement of the second section, a person entered and asked the group to vacate the room. This was done in order for the supervisor to display certain behaviors associated with the P and M dimensions. In all experimental conditions, the group was moved into another room and recommenced their task exactly 5 minutes after the disruption. Again, 1 hour had been allotted for the activity. When time was called, the supervisor collected the data and asked the participants to complete a questionnaire "to provide initial feedback on the program." The real intent was to measure the participant's level of job satisfaction, measure of situational stress experienced, general leadership impression, and group performance norms.

After all the participants had completed the questionnaire, the group was verbally probed for suspicion and debriefed.

Results

The data collected were submitted to a $2 \times 2 \times 2$ ANOVA with the C dimension (high, low), P dimension (high, low), and M dimension (high, low) as between-group factors. The dependent variables were productivity (indicated by the number of items correctly completed), job satisfaction, self-reported stress, and leader prototypicality (i.e., general impression of the leader).

All three leadership dimensions had significant main effects on job satisfaction, stress, and leader prototypicality. However, only the C dimension demonstrated a significant influence on productivity. This result lends support to the argument that in terms of Chinese leadership components, morality is an important determinant of various attitudes, and perhaps the primary determinant of productivity.

The fact that the C dimension showed significant main effects in each of the dependent measures establishes the importance of moral conduct in Chinese leadership. Perhaps the strongest evidence may be inferred from the perceptual measure of leader prototypicality, suggesting that morality is a definitive part of the leader schema held by participants. The presence of C-type leadership influenced work satisfaction, stress, and productivity in a positive manner. In fact, as previously noted, moral conduct was the only dimension to have a direct effect on worker productivity, even though it does not possess the characteristic of the P dimension (to directly influence attainment of performance targets). Chinese employees are more willing to put forth the effort and to be productive when they believe that the task they are doing is morally correct. The best indication is the morality of their leader.

In addition, the main effects of P and M leadership were consistently weaker than the effects of C leadership. This does not, however, imply that the P and M dimensions are not valid components of Chinese leadership. Actually, the P dimension significantly influenced subordinates' perception of leader prototypicality. Supervisors who exhibited P-type behaviors elicited greater job satisfaction and lower work stress than those who did not exhibit P-type behaviors.

Although not as strong as the main effects of the C dimension, the M-type behaviors raised job satisfaction, reduced work-related stress, and enhanced perceived leader prototypicality. Moreover, M leadership elicited greater job satisfaction and less stress than P leadership did.

The centrality of the C dimension in Chinese leadership can be demonstrated by its interactional effects on job satisfaction, stress, and leader prototypicality. Post hoc Newman-Keuls analyses revealed that the leader's moral conduct moderated the effects of the performance and maintenance dimensions. That is, when low moral conduct (c-type leadership) was present, the dependent measure did not vary as a function of differing levels on the P dimension or the M dimension. Clearly, the importance of moral conduct stands not only in its independent effect, but also in its masking influence on the performance and maintenance dimensions. The pattern of effects was the same for job satisfaction, stress, and leader proto-

Table 1. Effects of Leader's Moral Character (C) and Performance (P) on Job Satisfaction*

	C (high)	c (low)
P (high)	76.5	37.1
p (low)	54.2	33.0

Note: *Range between 8 (low job satisfaction) and 120 (high job satisfaction).

typicality. For example, an analysis of job satisfaction yielded two, two-way interactions. First, the C dimension interacted with the P dimension. A post hoc analysis revealed that the CP leadership pattern was the most effective in eliciting work satisfaction, followed by a Cp pattern, and then cP and cp (Table 1). Interestingly, the job satisfaction reported did not vary significantly between the cP and cp leadership groups. In other words, this finding suggests that P-type leaders can exert influence over subordinates' job satisfaction only when they also display a high C-leadership dimension. The other interaction effect, one between the C and M dimensions, mirrored the results of the first. That is, a CM leadership pattern was most successful in eliciting job satisfaction, followed by a Cm pattern, then cM and cm, with no significant difference between the final two.

In analyzing work-related stress, again, two 2-way interactions were statistically significant. Interestingly, the pattern of the interactions was similar to that of the job satisfaction analysis, with significant interactions between C and P dimensions, and between C and M dimensions. More specifically, post hoc analyses revealed that participants experienced less stress when their confederate leader demonstrated a CP leadership pattern or a Cp pattern. Although both of these patterns decrease work-related stress, cP and cp types did not differ in the amount of stress they elicited. In other words, any effects of P-type leadership in relieving stress are negated if high moral conduct is not also present in the supervisor.

Likewise, those subordinates who were exposed to a CM leadership pattern reported less stress than those exposed to a Cm pattern, which in turn was less than for those exposed to cM and cm patterns. Again, analysis revealed that when a c-type leadership style was employed, the leader's ability to influence work-related stress was minimal, and the difference between work-related stress reported by groups with cM style leadership did not differ significantly from those with cm style leadership (Table 2).

In terms of general leadership impression, C-type behavior again had a major influence. Interaction effects with both performance and maintenance dimensions

Table 2. Effects of Leader's Moral Character (C) and Maintenance (M) on Stress

	C (high)	c (low)
M (high)	13.9	29.0
m (low)	23.7	32.3

Table 3.   Effects of Leader's Moral Character (C) and
Performance (P) on Leadership Prototypicality

	C (high)	c (low)
P (high)	27.3	9.9
p (low)	14.9	10.7

Table 4.   Effects of Leader's Moral Character (C) and
Maintenance (M) on Leadership Prototypicality

	C (high)	c (low)
M (high)	26.6	10.5
m (low)	15.6	10.1

support this assertion. A supervisor showing P-type behavior was seen to be even more prototypical when C-type leadership was also demonstrated. When the leader was low on C, however, differing levels of the P dimension did not affect leader prototypicality (Table 3). It was the same for the interaction between moral conduct and maintenance (Table 4).

The sum of these results suggests that moral character is a significant component of Chinese leadership. It is a central and moderating variable. Not only is its importance highlighted in its role in two-way interactions, but the noticeable absence of a $P \times M$ interaction, and a $C \times P \times M$ interaction suggests that its centrality might be such that it is able to compensate for leadership deficits in the P and M dimensions.

A SURVEY OF EMPLOYEES' JOB SATISFACTION AND STRESS AS A FUNCTION OF THEIR MANAGERS' C, P, AND M DIMENSIONS

While the previous study demonstrates the relative importance of the three dimensions (morality, performance, and maintenance) in Chinese leadership, the question of generalizability from a laboratory study to the working population remains. A second study, using Misumi's survey methodology, was conducted to address this issue. A questionnaire was given to working adults regarding their work attitudes and perceptions of the work environment. We formed the following hypotheses:

Hypothesis 1.   C leadership is a primary factor in Chinese leadership and will elicit the most favorable responses regarding work attitudes.

Hypothesis 2.   When C leadership interacts with either P or M leadership, more favorable responses will be generated than in a $P \times M$ interaction when dimensions operate independently.

Hypothesis 3. The most effective Chinese leadership pattern is when C-, P-, and M- type behaviors are combined.

The participants were 108 young adults employed full-time and in pursuit of a part-time degree in Business Studies. Most of them were working in the service industry. The mean age was 25 years old, and on average they had 5.3 years of work experience. The majority (72%) of the participants were female.

The questionnaire comprised two sections. The first section probed the respondents' relationship with their immediate superiors, using Tjosvold's (1984) Leader Warmthness Scale. Participants also rated their superiors on the C, P, and M dimensions.[1] Unlike the questionnaires used by Ling and Misumi, the present set included both positively and negatively worded items to control for acquiescence bias.

The second section contained 44 items excerpted and translated from the Job Descriptive Index (Smith, Kendall, & Hulin, 1969), Work-Related Stress Scale (Misumi, 1985), and General Leadership Impression Scale (Cronshaw & Lord, 1987) to measure work satisfaction, work-related stress, and leader prototypicality,[2] respectively. The 5-item Satisfaction with Company Scale (Misumi, 1985) was included to assess participants' satisfaction with their organization's management. Most of the criteria measures used in the previous study were repeated in this study. However, participants were not asked to provide information on their own productivity, as such a measure could easily be biased. Finally, the 13-item Group Atmosphere Scale (Fiedler, 1967) was included to measure participants' perception of the social relationships in their work group.

Major Findings

Regression analyses revealed that of three leadership behavior dimensions, moral conduct has the greatest impact on outcome variables measured in the study. The findings were as follows:

1. Employees' perceived work group atmosphere was related to the superiors' standing on the C dimension, and not on the other two ($r = .46, p < .001$). A supervisor high in moral character tends to create and maintain a work group that is congenial and warm in social relationships.

2. About 69 percent of the total variance of leader warmthness could be accounted for by the C dimension (beta = .85, $p < .005$), followed by the P dimension (beta = .16, $p < .05$).[3] Thus, morality is the most informative attribute when Chinese subordinates appraise their relationship with their leaders. A highly moral character facilitates the boss-subordinate relationship. If indeed, as Tjosvold (1984) and Howell and Frost (1989) suggest, a willingness to show kindliness and warmth is a consistent attribute of the

leader archetype across different corporate cultures, then it would mean that the importance of moral conduct is again reaffirmed.

3. Moreover, of the three leadership behavior dimensions, morality was the only significant predictor of workers' satisfaction with their company (beta = .73, $p < .001$). The more a leader displays his or her moral uprightness, the more likely subordinates are to feel positive about the organization and its management as a whole.

4. Among the three leadership behavior dimensions, the C dimension was the only significant predictor of subordinates' work-related stress (beta = –.38, $p < .05$).

5. The regression equation for predicting leader prototypicality included P (beta = .88, $p < .001$), M (beta = .34, $p < .05$), P × M (beta = .05, $p < .05$), and C × P (beta = –.03, $p < .05$). The joint influence of the C dimension and the P dimension on the superior's image was remarkable. When the superior is perceived as low in performance, his or her moral standing plays a critical role in determining the subordinates' opinions of his or her leadership. People who demonstrate high moral scruples are seen to possess better leadership qualities and are accepted as leaders. When the superior ranks high on the P dimension, perceived leadership remains relatively constant irrespective of the level of moral uprightness.

6. The minus sign in the beta coefficient of the C × P interaction term implies that someone regarded as a prototypical leader is high on either the C dimension or the P dimension, but not both. Indeed, while in China many great leaders are enshrined as morally unblemished, there are also very competent leaders who are morally dubious. Under those circumstances, performance, not morality, is the pivotal dimension in determining who is the best leader. When the task at hand is very difficult, and leadership is expected to be highly performance oriented, those displaying a low level of moral conduct are seen as being as prototypical as, if not more prototypical than, those with high moral standards. Although this observation may at first seem puzzling, it may reflect the fact that Chinese workers hold schemata of leadership that are consistent with the old Chinese adage of "Thick face, black heart." This saying suggests that to succeed in life (especially in one's career), one may sometimes employ a certain amount of guile and underhandedness. Thus, an effective leader will sometimes display a certain level of moral "flexibility" or expediency coupled with a high performance orientation.

Job satisfaction was a function of the C dimension (beta = .64, $p < .05$) and the P dimension (beta = .50, $p < .05$). The fact that performance once again emerged in this study as a valid predictor, accompanying morality, shows that its influence must not be ignored.

CONCLUSION

We can make several observations. First, moral character is an important attribute of leaders in all kinds of organizations, both political and business. Earlier psychological studies of Chinese leaders' essential attributes had originated in Mainland China's organizations, which at that time were all state owned. In these "state-owned enterprises" senior managers were usually members of the Chinese Communist Party, and organizational research therefore inevitably turned into a study of political leaders, not necessarily business leaders. The emphasis on political purity and orthodoxy in studies published in China is thus understandable. This chapter, however, shows that the weight placed on morality is not restricted to political leaders, but also applied to business leaders in the capitalist society of Hong Kong. There is substantial generalizability across political boundaries, although what actually constitutes moral character may be different. We can, therefore, extrapolate to organizations in Chinese societies under strong Confucian influence (such as Taiwan) that moral character is equally, if not more, important in the definition of an effective business leader. The same can be said of non-state-owned enterprises in China which have emerged in the last decade.

Second, a manager's moral character can be demonstrated through certain key behaviors. Combining our list with that of Tse and Leung (1997) results in the following characteristics, which, when displayed in a Chinese work organization, suggest the presence of strong moral fiber:

1. *Refraining from flattery.* Morally upright leaders do not curry favor from their superiors. They do not rave about their bosses in front of them in an exaggerated manner. They speak the truth and do not use flattery to move up the organizational ladder or to gain popularity.
2. *Disciplining subordinates according to fair rules.* Morally upright leaders do not pick on their subordinates to seek vengeance. Even if they do not want to forgive and forget, they do not use their position to get even in personal disputes.
3. *Giving proper credit to others.* Morally upright leaders do not treat the fruits of subordinates' labor as their own. They do not readily accept compliments due to others' efforts. Work done by their subordinates for the organization is properly acknowledged and the subordinates are shown appreciation, often in public.
4. *Playing games by the rules.* Morally upright leaders do not use sneaky and underhanded methods to enhance their position in their organization. There is no behind-the-scenes maneuvering. "Going through the back door," by acts of deception or tampering with evidence, is unacceptable.
5. *Allocating resources fairly and unselfishly.* Morally upright leaders do not abuse their authority for their own benefit. There is no misappropriation of funds or other resources. They are willing to help others out even though

they are not so required. They do not take advantage of others. They earn the trust of those who trust them. This person also knows and avoids situations where there is a potential conflict of interest.

6. *Exhibiting thriftiness.* In their private lives as well as in business, morally upright leaders do not spend money lavishly on feasts and expensive habits. They do not frequent karaoke bars.

7. *Showing concern for others.* Morally upright leaders look after their subordinates as well as their family members. They respect their parents and the elderly. They take part in community service projects and give to charity. They are not always seeking for their own benefit.

One proviso: Perhaps the preceding list is only for leaders of Chinese subordinates to heed. As Adler and Bird (1988) suggested, cultures differ in their definitions of moral character and behavior. For example, to many American executives, "bribe no one" is one of the key codes of ethical business practice. "Take responsibility for the environment" may be another. In some Asian countries, however, gifts in exchange for personal favors are not often refused; and in fact, they are at times expected. And on environmental issues, Asians are only now beginning to appreciate the importance of caring for the world's natural resources. To help managers in multinational organizations to be effective leaders, therefore, future research should examine such differences and identify behaviors that carry different moral overtones in different cultures, as well as behaviors that are universally regarded as moral.

Third, it can be seen from the aforementioned list that the behaviors characteristic of a leader of high moral standards, as identified by our informants, consist of more "don'ts" than "dos." Apparently morality becomes an issue only when certain ethical codes are transgressed. Can people immediately recognize a morally upright leader without first having to compare this person with a "baseline" of immoral leaders? Future research should address this question.

Fourth, moral character is not the sole predictor of every dependent measure taken in this study. To be able to lead a group or organization through times of abundance or turbulence, it is not enough merely to uphold high moral standards. P behavior remains an important determinant of leadership effectiveness, followed by M behavior, which plays a somewhat minor yet noticeable role in influencing work attitudes among subordinates.

Finally, while the impact of moral character on subordinates is undeniable, the direction of influence must be delineated more carefully in future research. Our studies reveal that morally upright leaders are respected and welcomed by their subordinates. Yet as Tse and Leung's (1997) results suggest, such leaders may not be the first choice of the bosses who are concerned with the bottom line in this highly competitive corporate world. Morgan (1993) also found that managers who were rated favorably on ethics by their subordinates also received high ratings on leadership. Yet they have lower salaries. Therefore, to be a leader strong in moral fiber carries a price that some managers may be unwilling to pay. Trainers need to remember this when they set out to "train" people in the ways of morality!

ACKNOWLEDGMENTS

Chris Cheung assisted in the compilation of this paper. We are also grateful to Nancy Spelman and Diana Martin for insightful comments on an earlier draft, which was presented at a symposium titled "New Perspectives on Global Leadership" at the 1997 Society for Industrial and Organizational Psychology Annual Conference. Data reported in this article were collected by the second author for his master's thesis, which was conducted under the supervision of the first author.

NOTES

1. A series of factor analyses was conducted to select 5 items from each of the 3 dimensions so that no item would have significant loadings on 2 or more dimensions. The resultant measures of the 3 leadership dimensions are, therefore, orthogonal to each other.

2. Leadership prototypicality is operationalized as whether the person is perceived to possess leadership ability, whether the person is accepted as a leader, whether the person behaves like a typical leader, whether the person conducts himself or herself in a respectable manner, and whether the person fits into the respondent's perception of an ideal leader.

3. All beta coefficients reported here are unstandardized.

REFERENCES

Adler, N. J., & Bird, F. B. (1988). International dimensions of executive integrity: Who is responsible for the world? In S. Srivastva & Associates (Eds.), *Executive integrity: The search for high human values in organizational life* (pp. 243-267). San Francisco: Jossey-Bass.

Aram, J. D., & Piraino, T. G. (1979). Leadership preference in Chile. *Revista Interamericana de Psicologia, 13,* 73-81.

Badaracco, J. L., & Ellsworth, R. R. (1989). *Leadership and the quest for integrity.* Boston: Harvard Business School Press.

Bass, B. M., & Avolio, B. J. (Eds.). (1994). *Improving organizational effectiveness through transformational leadership.* Thousand Oaks, CA: Sage.

Cheng, P.-S., & Chung, C.-J. (1981). A factorial study of the effective leader behavior of low military staffs. *Acta Psychologica Taiwanica, 23,* 97-106. [In Chinese.]

Cronshaw, S. F., & Lord, R. G. (1987). Effects of categorization, attribution, and encoding processes on leadership perceptions. *Journal of Applied Psychology, 72,* 97-106.

Fiedler, F. E. (1967). *A theory of leadership effectiveness.* New York: McGraw-Hill.

Fleishman, E. A. (1953). The description of supervisory behavior. *Journal of Applied Psychology, 37,* 1-6.

Gerstner, C. R., & Day, D. V. (1994). Cross-cultural comparison of leadership prototypes. *Leadership Quarterly, 5,* 121-134.

Greenleaf, R. K., Frick, D. M., Spears, L. C. (Eds.). (1996). *On becoming a servant-leader.* San Francisco: Jossey-Bass.

Ho, D. Y. F., Chen, S., & Chiu, C. (1991). Relational orientation: Towards a methodology of Chinese social psychology. In K. K. Hwang & K. S. Yang (Eds.), *Chinese psychology and behavior* (pp. 95-112). Taipei: Laurel. [In Chinese.]

Howell, J. M., & Frost, P. J. (1989). A laboratory study of charismatic leadership. *Organizational Behavior and Human Decision Process, 43,* 243-269.

Kanungo, R. N., & Mendonca, M. (1996). *Ethical dimensions of leadership.* Thousand Oaks, CA: Sage.

Ling, W.-Q. (1989). Pattern of leadership behavior assessment in China. *Psychologia: An International Journal of Psychology in the Orient, 32,* 129-134.

Ling, W., & Fang, L. (1995). Theories on leadership and Chinese culture: The formulation of the CPM model on leadership behavior and a Chinese "implicit" theory on leadership traits. In H. S. R. Kao, D. Sinha, & S.-H. Ng (Eds.), *Effective organizations and social values* (pp. 269-286). New Delhi, India: Sage.

Mao, Z. D. (1968). *Selected works of Mao Zedong.* Beijing: People's Publishing.

Misumi, J. (1985). *The behavioral science of leadership.* Ann Arbor: University of Michigan.

Morgan, R. B. (1993). Self- and co-worker perceptions of ethics and their relationships to leadership and salary. *Academy of Management Journal, 36,* 200-214.

Smith, P. C., Kendall, L. M., & Hulin, C. L. (1969). *The measurement of satisfaction in work and retirement.* Chicago: Rand McNally.

Tjosvold, D. (1984). Effects of leader warmth and directiveness on subordinate performance on a subsequent task. *Journal of Applied Psychology, 69,* 422-427.

Tse, D. K., & Leung, K. (1997). *Moral character of a leader: A beginning point of today's Confucianism.* (Working Paper RCCM-97-030). Hong Kong: City University of Hong Kong, Chinese Management Research Centre.

Xu, L. C., & Chen, L., Wong, D., & Xue, A. Y. (1985). The role of psychology in enterprise management. *Acta Psychologica Sinica, 17,* 339-345. [In Chinese.]

IN SEARCH OF THE EURO-MANAGER
MANAGEMENT COMPETENCIES IN FRANCE, GERMANY, ITALY, AND THE UNITED STATES

Joy Fisher Hazucha, Sarah A. Hezlett,
Sandra Bontems-Wackens, and Amy Ronnqvist

ABSTRACT

This study examined managerial competencies in light of previous research on cultural values performed by Hofstede. Using data from managers in four countries, the study addressed two questions of concern to practitioners using 360-degree feedback systems in multiple cultures: Are different competencies important in different countries? Are skill levels different in different countries? Similarities and differences among France, Italy, Germany, and the United States were evaluated using analysis of variance between means and profile correlations. Hypotheses were formulated by extending Hofstede's work on cultural values to competency importance and skill level.

As hypothesized, fewer differences were found in management competencies than in cultural values. The shapes of the profiles were quite similar to each other, and the U.S. profile was about as similar to the other countries as the European profiles were

Advances in Global Leadership, Volume 1, pages 267-290.
Copyright © 1999 by JAI Press Inc.
ISBN: 0-7623-0505-3

to each other. As expected, however, there were also consistent mean differences between countries. Also as hypothesized, there were more significant differences between countries in terms of skill level than importance ratings. In other words, stronger links were found between cultural values and skills (actual behaviors) than between cultural values and importance ratings (ideal job requirements). However, the pattern for self-ratings was in the opposite direction from what was predicted. Implications for the need for different models and different norms, and for the feasibility of transferring managers from one country to another, are discussed.

Organizations struggle with the type of selection criteria to use when choosing a manager for a position that requires work in a cross-cultural environment. On the one hand, it seems logical to choose people who have worked effectively in their home cultures. On the other hand, many such people find it difficult to function effectively in a new culture.

Beyond selection, an understanding of differences in the management competencies and practices required can help managers to work more effectively in intercultural environments. For example, managers provided with 360-degree feedback should receive input on competencies that are relevant to them and against norms that are appropriate.

In 1965, the following conclusion emerged from a meeting of International Labour Office (ILO) experts:

> One of the most important areas for research is the determination of exactly what is meant by managerial success and the identification of successful managers in different cultural settings. This would provide all those concerned with developing managers with clearer ideas of the sort of results they should aim at in attempting to provide knowledge and modify managerial attitudes and behavior. (ILO, 1966, in Hofstede, 1984, p. 185)

These important practical dilemmas illustrate a more theoretical dilemma with regard to management competencies and practices: If management competency requirements can be thought of as a "common core," similar across geographical locations, and with differences attributable to local culture, what is the relative size and nature of the common and unique portions?

With an economy that is increasingly global, and with a shift in many organizational structures from local entity to global business, the research topic proposed by the ILO three decades ago has only increased in importance. Yet, we are not much closer to a resolution. In fact, while many studies of comparative management between two countries exist, little research has investigated cross-cultural differences in management competencies. However, the results of Hofstede's (1984, 1991) research on national differences in values have implications for management competencies.

These issues prove even more pressing within Europe, with growing possibilities and pressures toward Europeanization. Viewed from the outside, people think of Europe as a unit, yet the palpable differences between countries and cultures, illustrated by Hofstede's research, found as much variability within Europe as between the United States and Japan. These differences result in questions about how well people from the Anglo-Saxon countries work with those from Latin countries. More and more, this is a business necessity.

Hofstede (1984, 1991) identified the following cultural dimensions:

1. Power Distance: the degree of inequality within a society, and how the society deals with it
2. Individualism (versus Collectivism): the degree of integration of individuals within groups
3. Masculinity: the degree to which gender roles are clearly distinct
4. Uncertainty Avoidance: the degree of tolerance for the unknown

The first and the fourth of these dimensions are the most pertinent to management competencies. Cultures with a large Power Distance have more hierarchical structures and a more autocratic style of leadership. Those with stronger Uncertainty Avoidance will attach more importance to rules, planning, and expert knowledge. More individualistic cultures will value teamwork less. More masculine cultures will attach more importance to competition.

Several factors are likely to make management competencies more alike across cultures than the corresponding general cultural values. First, they are largely a function of the work to be accomplished (at least in modern western organizations). For example, because a major task of management is to work with and through several people, whether in Germany, Italy, or the United Kingdom, communication is important. Second, people from any culture who are given management responsibility within an organization are likely to share the basic values of the organization, and to possess the competencies that the organization requires.

It is with the goal of sorting out which management competencies are common across European countries and the United States, and which are country-specific, that this program of research was initiated. The research will result in the definition of (1) a core model, and (2) country-specific models of management competencies. As the research progresses, so will identification of competency profiles for managers who are to work in a specific country or across several countries. These profiles should help improve the accuracy of selection and the effectiveness of individualized management development programs. This study is the third in a series of such studies.

OBJECTIVES OF THIS STUDY

This study focused on comparing U.S. and European managers from different countries on the competencies required in their current position, and the compe-

Table 1.   Skills Definitions

Satisfy the Customer	Accurately identifies internal and external customers; develops strong working partnerships with customers; anticipates and meets customer needs; continually searches for ways to increase customer satisfaction
Display Organizational Savvy	Initiates and develops relationships with others as a key priority; understands the agendas and perspectives of others; effectively balances the interests and needs of one's own group with those of the broader organization
Demonstrate Trust and Judgment	Demonstrates principled leadership and sound business ethics; builds trust with others through own authenticity and follow-through on commitments; demonstrates socially responsible behavior; risks doing the right thing
Utilize Diversity	Recognizes that the organization's competitive strength is based on the contributions of people from diverse backgrounds; facilitates a productive environment for people from diverse backgrounds; appreciates and supports successful performance of people different from one's own culture, organization level, background, race, age or gender
Coach and Motivate Others	Accurately assesses the strengths and development needs of others; gives specific and candid feedback; provides effective coaching; encourages and empowers others to achieve; recognizes positive performance and confronts problem performers
Promote Open Communication	Creates an atmosphere in which timely and high-quality information flows smoothly between self and others; is approachable; consistently uses active-listening skills
Manage Differences	Views conflict as necessary for productive change; brings substantive conflicts and differences into the open; strives for win-win solutions
Speak Effectively	Speaks clearly and expresses self well in groups and in one-to-one conversations
Charter Teams	Forms and supports team structures to accomplish goals; communicates the team mission; provides clear direction and priorities; provides necessary resources for team functioning
Team with Others	Fosters collaboration among team members and among teams; is both an effective team leader and team member; ensures participation and involvement of all team members; recognizes team accomplishments
Apply Personal Influence	Gains the support and commitment of others; negotiates effectively; sells ideas
Focus on Process Improvement	Focuses on key process improvement efforts; effectively uses Total Quality (TQ) tools to improve processes and promote speed; relentlessly works to reduce cycle time; facilitates appropriate benchmarking; allocates necessary human resources when necessary

(continued)

Table 1. (Continued)

Practice Personal Efficiency	Allocates own time efficiently; works effectively in uncertain and stressful situations; conveys a sense of urgency; delegates appropriate work
Guide Organizational Change	Paves the way for organizational change; effectively manages the implementation of change and includes the contribution of others in the change process; establishes an expectation of continuous improvement
Demonstrate Personal Courage	Steps forward to address difficult issues; puts self on the line to deal with important problems; takes risks in a changing environment
Encourage Creativity	Persistently generates new ideas; encourages others to take risks; practices and promotes a continuous learning environment
Think Strategically	Identifies critical, high-payoff strategies and prioritizes team efforts accordingly; recognizes the broad implications of issues; considers the implication of global competition on performance and process initiatives; balances "big picture" concerns with day-to-day activities
Commit to Organizational Performance	Aggressively looks for ways to increase business growth; sets ambitious goals; strategically applies TQ initiatives to attain results; consistently improves productivity; promotes the "one-company" concept
Make Sound Decisions	Determines to what degree the team approach is appropriate for process improvement/problem solving; drives decision making to the most appropriate level; considers alternative solutions; makes timely decisions as appropriate
Strive for Self-Improvement	Sets high personal standards of performance; actively pursues learning and self-development; seeks feedback and welcomes unsolicited feedback; modifies behavior in light of feedback

Source: Copyright © 1991 Personnel Decisions, Inc. (PDI).

tencies they currently possess. Two exploratory questions were addressed: What do managers, and their managers, view as the most important competencies for their position? What is the managers' skill level on each competency, as rated by self and co-workers?

Several hypotheses were formulated about the relationship between the values that characterized each sample and the nature of the expected differences. These hypotheses are described in the Method section.

METHOD

The Instrument

Development

The instrument used was a questionnaire designed to give managers developmental feedback on their current skills from their co-workers: their manager(s), several colleagues, and several direct reports. The prototype instrument was developed in 1991 in the United States as part of a research program on the changing nature of work and management. It was based on reviews of managerial literature and interviews with managers from more than 12 different organizations. This version of the questionnaire was customized for an organization that wanted to provide its leaders with feedback regarding the organization's values.

This version of the instrument includes 20 dimensions, each of which includes 5 to 11 items. It was adapted for the organization and then translated into several languages so the participants could receive feedback in their mother tongue. A list of the 20 competencies and their definitions is shown in Table 1.

Reliability and Validity

The data indicate that this measurement method (360-degree feedback), with several items per competency and several raters per manager, is quite reliable. Internal consistency reliabilities for skills ranged from .70 to .91, and the average reliability of a dimension rating based on data from seven raters was .74. Self and manager ratings of skill and importance are, of course, less reliable because they are based on information from a single rater.

Other research (summarized in Holt & Hazucha, 1991) has shown that such instruments are related to both concurrent and future important criteria, such as potential, promotions, salary changes, and risk of career jeopardy.

Data Collection Process

The data were collected from managers who were offered the opportunity to participate in a management development process sponsored by their organization. Several steps were taken to ensure the integrity of the data and its usefulness for development. First, the manager receiving the feedback chose the respondents. Second, the only people in the organization who received an individual's report were the person receiving feedback, and a facilitator to help interpret the data. Third, respondents were told that the purpose was development (not selection or placement), and peers and direct reports were assured that their anonymity would be preserved through a method of averaging of all responses received.

Each of the 20 competencies is described by 5 or more behaviors, and each respondent is asked to evaluate the extent to which the target manager performs each behavior. In addition, the target manager and his or her manager indicate the relative importance of the competency for the current position, with a forced-choice scale that ranges from "important" to "critically important."

Participants. The sample consisted of managers who had participated in a management development process that incorporated the instrument. All were employed by the same U.S. multinational organization, whose worldwide focus includes a strong emphasis on quality, customers, and innovation. The French group included 197 feedback recipients, the Italian group included 30, the German group 37, and the U.S. group 325.

Cultural values indices. One result of Hofstede's work was scores on the 4 key cultural values for each country he studied. These scores were computed based on self-report attitude survey data collected from employees within one large U.S. multinational organization.

Hypotheses

The first set of hypotheses is related to the expected degree and levels of similarity across countries. Given the common tasks that managers are required to accomplish, we propose a common core of competencies across countries. We predict more agreement in what people say is important, than in the actual actions they take.

1. We expect more similarity across countries in management competencies than in cultural values.
2. We expect more differences between countries in actual behavior (skills ratings) than in ideal behavior (importance ratings).
3. We expect that some of the differences between countries can be directly linked to cultural values (Hofstede, 1984).

On the basis of Hofstede's research, several specific hypotheses were proposed with regard to the nature and direction of the differences between the groups:

1. When there are differences between the groups on a dimension, it will both be rated as more important for the position, and the managers will be seen as having stronger skills in this area.
2. The groups with stronger Uncertainty Avoidance scores will obtain lower ratings on Utilize Diversity and Guide Organizational Change.
3. The groups with larger Power Distance will obtain lower ratings on Promote Open Communication, Display Organizational Savvy, and Apply Per-

sonal Influence, because they will work in more hierarchical organizations where this is less important. They will also rate Strive for Self-Improvement lower because they tend to believe that leaders are born (or selected) rather than made (or developed).

4. The groups with higher Individualism score will rate Team with Others lower.

5. The groups with higher Masculinity score will rate Coach and Motivate Others lower, and give Demonstrate Personal Courage and Commit to Organizational Performance higher ratings.

Data Analyses

To compare the relative importance of the competencies required of managers in different groups, the importance ratings were compared, as evaluated by both the self and the manager.

The current skill levels of these managers were also compared, as viewed by themselves and by averaging the responses of their manager, colleagues, and direct reports (average other). Both the self-ratings and the "average other" ratings, obtained by averaging the data from each of the three "non-self" perspectives, were examined.

An analysis of variance (ANOVA) was used to compare the data from the four samples. A Bonferroni correction was used to adjust the alpha for the number of ANOVAs performed, such that tests with a $p < .0025$ were considered significant. In addition, each profile of ratings obtained was correlated with the profiles from the other countries in order to examine the overall match of the set of ratings.

RESULTS

Cultural Values Scores

The scores of each country on the cultural values are shown in Table 2 and Figure 1. The U.S. Uncertainty Avoidance score is 46, which is considered relatively low. France's value is the highest (86), followed by Italy (75) and Germany (65).

Table 2.   Hofstede Cultural Values by Country

	Uncertainty Avoidance	Power Distance	Masculinity	Individualism
France	86	68	43	71
Italy	75	50	70	76
Germany	65	35	66	67
United States	46	40	62	91

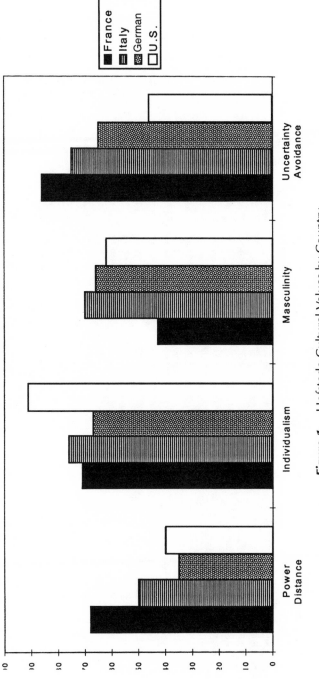

Figure 1. Hofstede Cultural Values by Country

275

Table 3. Importance Ratings (by Self)

Skill	France		Italy		Germany		United States		
	Mean	SD	Mean	SD	Mean	SD	Mean	SD	F Prob.
Satisfy the Customer	6.40	1.04	5.97	1.27	6.43	1.04	6.49	1.09	ns
Display Org. Savvy	3.96	1.75	4.53	1.66	4.33	1.60	4.03	1.70	ns
Demonstrate Trust/Judgement	5.14	1.60	4.73	1.86	5.30	1.70	5.44	1.63	ns
Utilize Diversity	3.85	1.78	3.67	1.65	4.24	1.69	3.66	1.86	ns
Coach and Motivate Others	4.81	1.79	4.57	1.57	4.68	1.97	5.22	1.60	ns
Promote Open Communication	5.17	1.58	5.17	1.58	4.70	1.71	5.31	1.44	ns
Manage Differences	3.42	1.76	2.90	1.60	4.03	1.82	3.49	1.66	ns
Speak Effectively	3.88	1.79	4.24	1.83	4.06	1.71	3.99	1.81	ns
Charter Teams	4.86	1.75	4.07	1.76	4.57	1.79	3.90	1.93	.000
Team with Others	5.52	1.51	5.03	1.50	4.69	1.76	4.41	1.77	.000
Apply Personal Influence	3.50	1.77	3.53	1.96	3.72	2.01	3.50	1.78	ns
Focus on Process Improvement	4.45	1.92	4.40	1.96	4.19	2.01	4.89	1.90	ns
Practice Personal Efficiency	4.69	1.81	4.07	1.80	4.86	1.71	3.69	1.83	.000
Guide Org. Change	4.71	1.83	4.33	1.83	3.94	1.98	4.28	2.04	ns
Demonstrate Personal Courage	4.18	1.81	3.83	2.15	4.72	1.91	4.14	1.84	ns
Encourage Creativity	3.91	1.79	4.00	1.89	4.44	1.76	4.36	1.82	ns
Think Strategically	4.80	1.98	4.13	2.03	5.00	2.06	4.31	2.10	ns
Commit to Org. Performance	5.20	1.80	5.03	1.73	5.27	1.74	4.54	2.02	.001
Make Sound Decisions	4.56	1.75	4.07	1.70	5.00	1.60	4.85	1.80	ns
Strive for Self Improvement	3.18	1.65	5.13	1.46	4.06	1.71	4.07	1.95	.000

Note: The Bonferroni Correction has been used to adjust alpha for the number of ANOVA's performed; tests with $p < .0025$ were considered significant.

Source: Copyright © 1995, Personnel Decisions, Inc., All rights reserved.

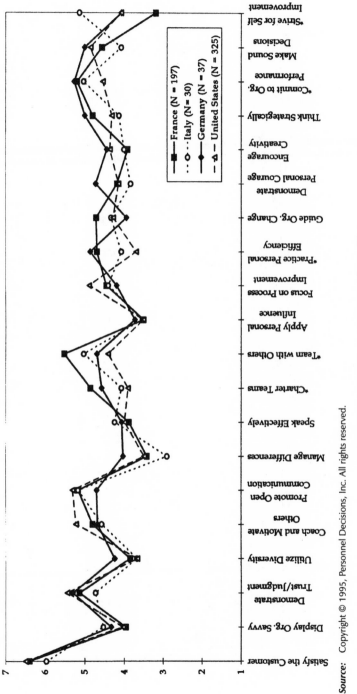

Figure 2. Importance Ratings (by Self)

277

Table 4. Importance Ratings (by Boss)

Skill	France Mean	France SD	Italy Mean	Italy SD	Germany Mean	Germany SD	United States Mean	United States SD	F Prob.
Satisfy the Customer	6.14	1.24	5.39	1.94	6.14	1.44	6.38	1.15	.001
Display Org. Savvy	3.98	1.62	4.72	1.59	4.14	1.67	3.94	1.71	ns
Demonstrate Trust/Judgement	4.92	1.53	4.15	1.73	5.17	1.42	5.33	1.56	.000
Utilize Diversity	3.36	1.68	3.28	1.98	3.91	1.69	3.37	1.60	ns
Coach and Motivate Others	4.56	1.63	4.70	1.65	4.43	1.64	5.25	1.55	.000
Promote Open Communication	4.85	1.34	5.06	1.39	4.82	1.59	5.14	1.33	ns
Manage Differences	3.39	1.51	3.61	1.79	3.84	1.69	3.78	1.63	ns
Speak Effectively	3.91	1.57	4.10	1.63	3.67	1.76	3.85	1.67	ns
Charter Teams	4.29	1.84	4.80	1.56	5.16	1.23	4.04	1.76	.002
Team with Others	5.46	1.32	4.72	1.75	5.10	1.32	4.70	1.66	.000
Apply Personal Influence	4.02	1.62	3.57	1.86	3.74	1.85	3.77	1.77	ns
Focus on Process Improvement	4.67	1.85	4.53	2.21	4.65	2.00	5.36	1.69	.000
Practice Personal Efficiency	5.03	1.51	3.94	1.38	4.35	1.68	3.70	1.65	.000
Guide Org. Change	3.97	1.73	3.90	1.78	4.04	1.79	4.22	1.94	ns
Demonstrate Personal Courage	4.05	1.65	3.73	2.03	4.69	1.36	3.84	1.44	ns
Encourage Creativity	3.83	1.68	3.90	1.81	4.76	1.84	4.40	1.65	.001
Think Strategically	4.10	1.88	3.94	2.14	5.26	1.66	4.30	1.95	ns
Commit to Org. Performance	4.92	1.74	5.02	1.73	5.27	1.70	4.76	1.87	ns
Make Sound Decisions	4.59	1.52	4.37	1.70	4.59	1.62	5.07	1.70	ns
Strive for Self Improvement	3.15	1.40	4.62	1.39	3.91	1.72	3.84	1.66	.000

Note: The Bonferroni correction has been used to adjust alpha for the number of ANOVA's performed; tests with $p < .0025$ were considered significant.

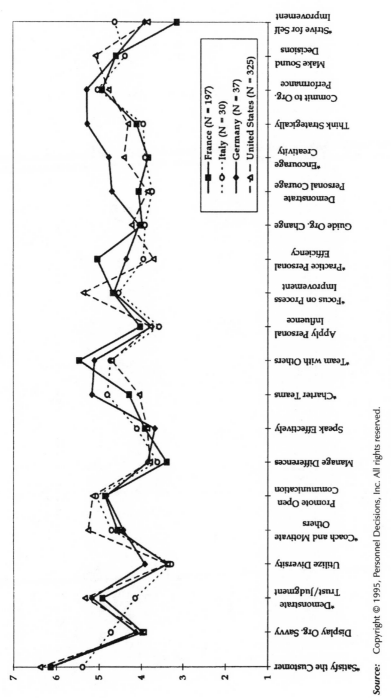

Figure 3. Importance Ratings (by Boss)

Source:

Table 5. Skills Ratings (by Self)

Skill	France		Italy		Germany		United States		
	Mean	SD	Mean	SD	Mean	SD	Mean	SD	F Prob.
Satisfy the Customer	3.66	0.47	4.01	4.41	4.17	0.61	3.85	0.48	.000
Display Org. Savvy	3.55	0.49	4.00	0.37	4.10	0.56	3.85	0.42	.000
Demonstrate Trust/Judgement	3.84	0.47	4.30	0.33	4.38	0.41	4.14	0.42	.000
Utilize Diversity	3.84	0.59	4.14	0.42	4.16	0.67	3.96	0.60	ns
Coach and Motivate Others	3.63	0.46	4.14	0.34	4.10	0.54	3.80	0.46	.000
Promote Open Communication	3.70	0.52	4.33	0.38	4.31	0.43	3.92	0.47	.000
Manage Differences	3.51	0.57	4.04	0.44	4.08	0.62	3.86	0.54	.000
Speak Effectively	3.48	0.60	4.18	0.47	3.90	0.60	3.86	0.62	.000
Charter Teams	3.62	0.44	3.93	0.36	4.00	0.64	3.67	0.50	.000
Team with Others	3.54	0.45	4.11	0.31	4.08	0.59	3.86	0.45	.000
Apply Personal Influence	3.48	0.53	3.87	0.44	3.96	0.49	3.66	0.54	.000
Focus on Process Improvement	3.53	0.52	3.99	0.39	3.97	0.63	3.70	0.49	.000
Practice Personal Efficiency	3.55	0.52	3.90	0.45	4.09	0.59	3.94	0.47	.000
Guide Org. Change	3.60	0.55	3.86	0.35	4.05	0.69	3.69	0.58	.000
Demonstrate Personal Courage	3.68	0.51	4.02	0.44	4.25	0.46	3.87	0.56	.000
Encourage Creativity	3.52	0.56	4.04	0.44	3.87	0.54	3.65	0.58	.000
Think Strategically	3.57	0.53	4.01	0.38	3.93	0.66	3.65	0.56	.000
Commit to Org. Performance	3.55	0.51	3.99	0.36	3.89	0.58	3.70	0.52	.000
Make Sound Decisions	3.53	0.50	4.13	0.36	4.07	0.60	3.91	0.48	.000
Strive for Self Improvement	3.61	0.49	4.15	0.31	4.23	0.50	3.92	0.43	.000

Note: The Bonferroni correction has been used to adjust alpha for the number of ANOVA's performed; tests with $p < .0025$ were considered significant.

Source: Copyright © 1995, Personnel Decisions, Inc., All rights reserved.

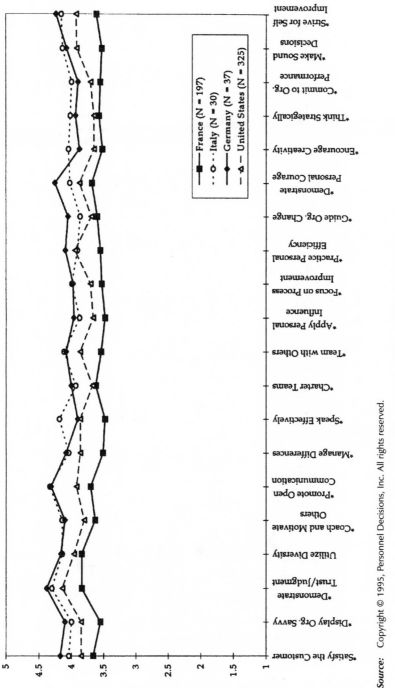

Figure 4. Skills Ratings (by Self)

Table 6. Skills Ratings (by Average Other)

Skill	France		Italy		Germany		United States		F Prob.
	Mean	SD	Mean	SD	Mean	SD	Mean	SD	
Satisfy the Customer	3.57	0.36	3.84	0.35	4.16	0.43	3.81	0.36	.000
Display Org. Savvy	3.51	0.36	3.84	0.28	4.01	0.35	3.71	0.38	.000
Demonstrate Trust/Judgement	3.70	0.33	3.93	0.32	4.30	0.32	3.92	0.34	.000
Utilize Diversity	3.60	0.35	3.84	0.35	4.16	0.34	3.76	0.41	.000
Coach and Motivate Others	3.46	0.36	3.75	0.34	4.01	0.33	3.63	0.39	.000
Promote Open Communication	3.67	0.38	4.00	0.34	4.26	0.31	3.89	0.39	.000
Manage Differences	3.42	0.40	3.82	0.30	4.01	0.38	3.68	0.42	.000
Speak Effectively	3.64	0.48	4.05	0.34	4.23	0.33	3.95	0.42	.000
Charter Teams	3.51	0.36	3.71	0.33	3.97	0.34	3.61	0.36	.000
Team with Others	3.47	0.35	3.79	0.35	4.00	0.36	3.73	0.36	.000
Apply Personal Influence	3.48	0.42	3.78	0.31	4.08	0.42	3.65	0.41	.000
Focus on Process Improvement	3.52	0.34	3.76	0.34	4.02	0.32	3.62	0.38	.000
Practice Personal Efficiency	3.53	0.38	3.65	0.32	4.12	0.36	3.78	0.34	.000
Guide Org. Change	3.48	0.35	3.69	0.36	4.00	0.35	3.58	0.39	.000
Demonstrate Personal Courage	3.49	0.38	3.69	0.32	4.13	0.38	3.66	0.39	.000
Encourage Creativity	3.45	0.39	3.67	0.34	3.86	0.43	3.54	0.38	.000
Think Strategically	3.51	0.40	3.72	0.29	4.00	0.36	3.57	0.37	.000
Commit to Org. Performance	3.49	0.36	3.73	0.31	3.93	0.32	3.62	0.35	.000
Make Sound Decisions	3.43	0.36	3.78	0.29	4.03	0.35	3.71	0.33	.000
Strive for Self Improvement	3.50	0.32	3.85	0.35	4.11	0.35	3.79	0.37	.000

Note: The Bonferroni correction has been used to adjust alpha for the number of ANOVA's performed; tests with $p < .0025$ were considered significant.

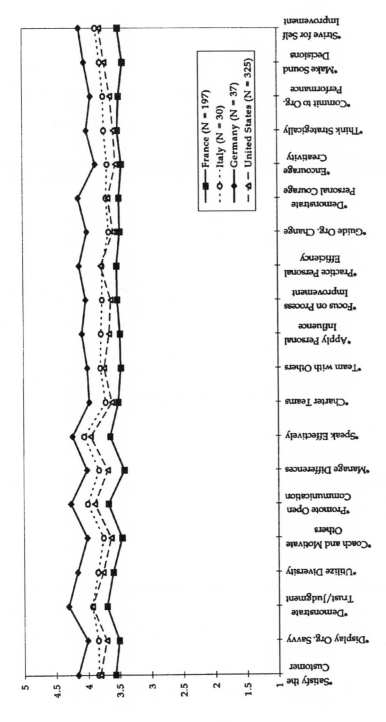

Figure 5. Skills Ratings (by Average Other)

Source: Copyright © 1995, Personnel Decisions, Inc. All rights reserved.

283

Germany had the lowest score on Power Distance (35), followed by the United States, and Italy. France was again the highest at 68.

For Masculinity, the lowest scorer was France, followed by the United States, Germany, and Italy.

For Individualism, the United States (91) scored the highest. Italy is next, followed closely by France and Germany.

We correlated the values profiles between pairs of countries as the index of cultural similarity. The correlations, which were based on four data points per country, ranged from –.17 to .98.

Importance Ratings

When asked to indicate the importance of the competencies to their own position, there were five significant mean differences between the groups, as shown in Table 3 and Figure 2. The correlations between the country profiles range from .61 to .82.

There were also nine differences in the importance that the managers' bosses attached to the competencies required in their direct reports' positions (Table 4 and Figure 3). The correlations between the profiles range from .60 to .77.

Table 7. Correlations Between Country Profiles

	France	Italy	Germany
Importance Ratings (by Boss)			
Italy	0.64		
Germany	0.76	0.61	
United States	0.77	0.69	0.72
Importance Ratings (by Boss)			
Italy	0.68		
Germany	0.82	0.61	
United States	0.76	0.76	0.76
Importance Ratings (by Boss)			
Italy	0.74		
Germany	0.84	0.78	
United States	0.78	0.91	0.89
Importance Ratings (by Boss)			
Italy	0.50		
Germany	0.75	0.57	
United States	0.59	0.68	0.80
Importance Ratings (by Boss)			
Italy	0.17		
Germany	–0.05	0.98	
United States	–0.17	0.62	0.62

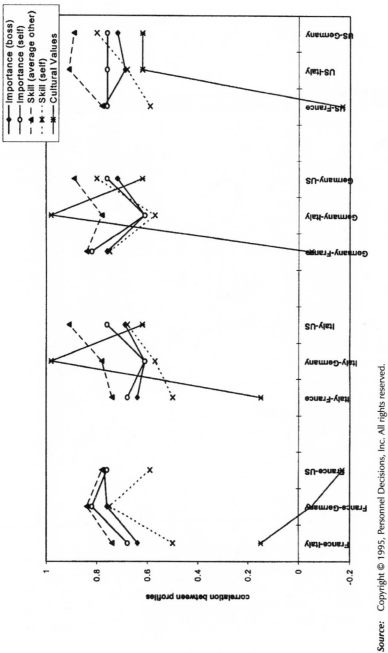

Figure 6. Similarities in Profiles across Countries

Table 8. Follow-up Tests on Differences in Importance Ratings

Study 1			Study 2				
Competency	Corr	Supported?	Competency	Corr (Boss)	Supported?	Corr (Self)	Supported?
Uncertainty Avoidance							
Establish Plans: pos	0.48	yes					
Use Tech/Func Expertise: pos	-0.47	no					
Demonstrate Adaptability: neg	0.55	no	Utilize Diversity: neg	ns F		ns F	
Champion Change: neg	0.81	yes	Guide Organizational Change: neg	ns F		ns F	
		2/4					
Power Distance							
Organizational Savvy: neg	0.27	no	Display Organizational Savvy: neg	ns F		ns F	
Develop Oneself: neg	-0.48	yes	Strive for Self-Improvement: neg	-.50	yes	-.19	yes
Foster Open Comm.: neg	-0.40	yes	Promote Open Communication: neg	ns F		ns F	
		2/3	Apply Personal Influence: neg				
Individualism							
Foster Teamwork: neg	0.36	no	Team with Others: neg	-.68	yes	-.78	yes
Show Work Commitment: pos	0.08	(yes)					
		1/2					
Maculinity							
Build Relationships: neg	-0.90	yes					
Coach and Develop: neg	-0.31	yes	Coach and Motivate Others: neg	.14	no	ns F	
Lead Courageously: pos	-0.03	no	Demonstrate Personal Courage: pos	ns F		ns F	
Drive for Results: pos	-0.00	no	Commit to Org. Performance: pos	ns F		-.58	no
		2/4					
Total	p = .50	7/13			2/3		2/3

Skills Ratings

Table 5 and Figure 4 illustrate that all 20 of the competencies showed significant mean differences across groups. The trend was for the German and Italian self-ratings to be highest, and the French self-ratings lowest. Despite these clear mean differences, the profile correlations range from .50 to .80.

The "average other" rating is based on an average of the three "other" perspectives: manager, peers, and direct reports. Again, all 20 of the tests for differences in means were significant (Table 6 and Figure 5). Again, the correlations are high: .74 to .91.

Correlations and similarities between country profiles on the importance ratings, the skills ratings, and the cultural values scale are shown in Table 7 and Figure 6.

Findings Relative to Hypotheses

Again, we expected more differences in skills than in importance ratings. This was supported by the greater number of significant differences in skills ratings than in importance ratings.

We followed up the significant F tests with a test to compare the pattern of cultural values scores across countries with the means on the scales related to these values. The results are shown in Table 8 (importance ratings), and Table 9 (skills ratings). These tables also show similar results from a previous study (Study 1), which includes multiple organizations.

Importance Ratings: Links to Hofstede

1. Neither of the two scales linked to Uncertainty Avoidance showed significant differences between countries in importance ratings, either from the self or boss perspective.

2. One of the four scales linked with Power Distance, Strive for Self-improvement, showed significant mean differences across countries. The follow-up correlations are both in the predicted direction (negative), indicating that in countries with larger Power Distance, people view self-improvement as less important.

3. Team with Others was linked to Individualism. Again, the ANOVA showed significant differences between countries, and the follow-up correlation was in the predicted direction (negative). This indicates that people in more individualistic cultures rate Team with Others as less important.

4. For Masculinity, there were significant mean differences in the boss ratings of Coach and Motivate Others, and the self-rating of Commit to Organizational Performance. However, neither follow-up correlation was in the predicted direction.

Table 9. Follow-up Tests on Differences in Skills Ratings

Cultural Values and Management Competencies: Results (Skills Ratings)

	Study 1			Study 2			
Competency	Corr (Avg Other)	Supported?	Competency	Corr (Avg Other)	Supported?	Corr (Self)	Supported?
Uncertainty Avoidance							
Establish Plans: pos	0.05	(yes)					
Use Tech/Func Expertise: pos	-0.14	no					
Demonstrate Adaptability: neg	-0.07	yes	Utilize Diversity: neg	-.29	yes	.50	no
Champion Change: neg	-0.33	yes	Guide Organizational Change: neg	-.22	yes	.51	no
		3/4			2/2		0/2
Power Distance							
Organizational Savvy: neg	-0.46	yes	Display Organizational Savvy: neg	-0.83	yes	.18	no
Develop Oneself: neg	-0.59	yes	Strive for Self-Improvement: neg	-0.90	yes	.17	no
Foster Open Comm.: neg	-0.62	yes	Promote Open Communication: neg	-0.84	yes	.15	no
			Apply Personal Influence: neg	-.84	yes	.18	no
		3/3			4/4		0/4
Individualism							
Foster Teamwork: neg	-0.51	yes	Team with Others: neg	-.17	yes	-.83	yes
Show Work Commitment: pos	-0.36	no					
		1/2			1/1		1/1
Maculinity							
Build Relationships: neg	0.19	no					
Coach and Develop: neg	-0.18	yes	Coach and Motivate Others: neg	.76	no	-.47	yes
Lead Courageously: pos	-0.24	no	Demonstrate Personal Courage: pos	.61	yes	-.49	no
Drive for Results: pos	-0.07	no	Commit to Org. Performance: pos	.76	yes	-.47	no
		1/4			2/3		1/3
Total	p = .13	9/13		p = .01	9/10	p = .98	2/10

In summary, two of the three scales that showed significant differences in boss ratings were in the expected direction, and the same success rate held for the self importance ratings. In both cases, larger Power Distance was linked to attributing less importance to Strive for Self-improvement and higher Individualism was linked to giving less importance to Team with Others.

Skills Ratings: Links to Hofstede

All of the self and average other means showed significant differences across countries. Follow-up tests supported 9 of the 10 predictions for the average other ratings, but only 2 of the 10 for the self-ratings.

Comparison in Similarities

1. It was predicted that the importance ratings profiles would be the most similar, the skills ratings profiles would follow, and the values profiles would be least similar. The pattern of correlations between countries on the various data shows that the values correlations are indeed the lowest. The greater number of mean differences in skill relative to the differences in importance also provides support for this hypothesis.
2. France is very different from the other countries in cultural values, yet close to similar in management competencies.
3. The four countries are equally similar to each other; in particular, the United States is as similar to each of the three European countries as they are to each other.

DISCUSSION

The findings of this study have several broad implications. First, the similarity in importance rating profiles across countries indicates that it is reasonable to expect similarities between what is expected in different countries, and that a fairly large common core of management competencies exists among the group of Western countries in this study. This is good news for organizations and managers who must collaborate across borders. It indicates that they can agree on what is of primary importance. It is possible that the similarity is heightened in this group because of a common organizational culture that has been emphasized and supported throughout its different countries of operation. Some of the differences that exist can be explained using Hofstede's framework.

In contrast, there are consistent differences in skills ratings, as shown by mean differences. In general, the German ratings are highest and the French ratings lowest, as seen by both self and others. This pattern is identical to that found in a previous study, yet the previous samples were drawn from a number of different organizations, and the content of the model was different. Most of the differences in ratings by others can be explained by differences in cultural values, as shown by the links with Hofstede. However, the hypotheses based on Hofstede's work were not supported as an explanation for the skill self-ratings. These mean differences imply that it is important to develop and use norms for each country, although a philosophical case can also be made for using a company-wide or European-wide norm.

This study suggests several directions for future research.

1.   Additional research should be conducted in the countries included in the present study to investigate possible reasons for the mean differences in skill ratings, including differences in how people are chosen for management positions (e.g., in Germany the trainee period is fairly long, which may turn out better-prepared managers), and in grading systems (the French grading system is very strict, which may carry over into harsher self- and other ratings).
2.   The contrast between skills ratings by others and by self also calls for further research.
3.   In order to see if there are more differences between samples that do not benefit from a common organizational culture, it would be interesting to conduct similar research with (a) a European multinational, and (b) managers from different organizations as well as different cultures.
4.   In addition to research on the content of managerial competencies, it is important to research the feedback process, what influences people's receptivity to feedback, and what they do as a result of the feedback.

REFERENCES

Hofstede, G. (1984). *Culture's consequences: International differences in work-related values.* London: Sage.

Hofstede, G. (1991). *Cultures and organizations: Software of the mind.* London: McGraw-Hill.

Holt, K., & Hazucha, J. F. (1991). *The PROFILOR technical summary.* Minneapolis, MN: Personnel Decisions, Inc.

PART III

MANAGEMENT/ACTION PERSPECTIVES

INTRODUCTION TO MANAGEMENT/ ACTION PERSPECTIVES

M. Jocelyne Gessner and Val Arnold

Our final section focuses on the practice of global leadership. The authors we hear from in this section are practitioners, coaches, consultants or, more aptly, people who work with global leaders. In working with executives and managers, they are responsible for identifying, developing, coaching, and sometimes helping to remove global leaders when they fail to meet expectations.

More than anything else, this section makes clear that the train of global leadership is not just coming down the tracks; it has been here and moved on. The number of expatriate managers and their dismal performance records (an appallingly high number "fail" in their assignments) emphasize that we must figure out ways to develop people quickly. Our first hurdle in doing so seems to be that we are not certain, or in agreement about, what it is we're developing these people to do.

What you will see in this section is a range of applications—from pointing out the difficulties in how to create joint venture leadership teams (Wang), to figuring out what skills/resources expatriate managers need (Hicks and Peterson), to figuring out how to develop executives in ways that match the realities of their responsibilities and pace (Baum and Russell). Across this broad array of approaches and

Advances in Global Leadership, Volume 1, pages 293-296.
Copyright © 1999 by JAI Press Inc.
All rights of reproduction in any form reserved.
ISBN: 0-7623-0505-3

techniques, the same confusions arise that have occurred in the previous sections. Are we developing competencies, styles, techniques, and knowledge bases?

However, there are some universals. Over and again, there are references to the need to develop communication skills, to increase access to information (as both receivers and transmitters), to focus on the increased complexity of the context in which decisions must be made, and a burgeoning emphasis on cross-cultural awareness and sensitivity. We have echoes here of the issues our theorists raised regarding the expectations and responsibilities of global leaders, and how we think they might translate into new or more polished capabilities.

In addition to the recurring themes, a few new ideas emerge. In particular, we hear a pitch for coaching in a traditional sense as a necessary developmental tool to help global leaders deal with the idiosyncratic nature of their complex roles. We also recognize a need for global leaders to master the techniques and competencies of coaching others, to help others bridge the global gap. Here, we get a profound sense of the role of the leaders as people who equip others to do their jobs. Perhaps this is the scalar difference we have been looking for in understanding the old paradigm of task orientation—the need not just to get the task done, but rather, to equip others to do the tasks. This seems to fit with some of the realities we have discussed—the challenges of managing people across time and distance.

We also learn more about the contexts that have made looking at global leadership an imperative. These authors talk knowingly of the contextual changes in the leadership landscape. They discuss a world of rapid change, with burgeoning technology, and a need to understand and harness the information overload that typifies the current age and that will only get worse. They speak of the challenges of managing people in remote locations, and of building cross-cultural teams to manage joint ventures.

In fact, there is more emphasis in this section on the realities of the global leaders' environment, the current and future challenges that characterize the brave new world. There is a much-needed emphasis on reaction. We have spent previous sections defining what the global leader is up against; in this section, we focus on what to do about it. Again, the implication for increased globalization is that more activity happens faster, further away, and with more people. The task of the global leader is to figure out how to juggle these balls and keep a bigger, more diverse audience happy.

This certainly seems to describe the realities of the global leader for our first authors in this section. Hicks and Peterson characterize the new environment as having multiple and conflicting norms, constant changes, increasing complexity, diverse workforces, intense competition, and technological revolutions. Their advice for those who are not fainthearted is to develop a key competency in coaching others. The human universal that they believe transcends national and cultural boundaries is commonalties in learning principles. An emphasis on learning and continued versatility creates a workforce more able to endure and survive the rapidly changing and diverse landscape of the future. Their coaching process also has implications for competencies that have been suggested by previous authors; in particular, the emphasis on developing relationships and deepening understandings between cultures.

The second chapter in this section has some philosophical similarities, but Otazo discusses coaching a bit differently. She refers to it as a tool for understanding the complexity in which the global leader is asked to operate. She talks of the difficulty in navigating layers of complexity in meeting work expectations, company culture expectations, and country culture expectations. In her four case studies, we see the inherent trade-off of "balancing the pressures of various allegiances and expectations to get the job done." In addition to some interesting glimpses of real-life struggles, we also expand our understanding of the shifting foci among work, organizational culture, and country culture, and begin to see why an approach from one perspective may prove to be troublesome from another. The lesson for global leaders is clear. Finding resources to help you shift perspectives (from your own worldview to someone else's) may prove to be the short-term key to survival.

In the third chapter of this section, Wang discusses a specific form of leadership that is peculiar to the changes that have accompanied increased globalization. He discusses the intricacies of leading joint ventures from the perspective of Chinese leadership, and the need for a model developing cross-cultural leadership styles. With joint ventures proliferating as a way to leverage business opportunities and resources, it becomes imperative to understand the differences in competencies between managers from different cultures. As a prime example, he points to decision making as a group of leaders in a cross-cultural setting. Wang provides us an object lesson in understanding what competencies and conditions are liable to prove effective. He gives us a mini-literature review of Chinese management literature in terms of newer international human resources trends. As a contribution to our understanding of global leadership, he provides us with a specific application—one more example of where and how we need to be broader in our skills and approaches. He adds competencies around teamwork to our list, especially in terms of team role clarification, team objective integration, and group member coordination.

In our last chapter in this section, Baum and Russell broaden our scope of practice to consider alternative methodologies in training leaders. They emphasize the need to facilitate executive learning across remote locations and in real time. Because global leaders must deal with rapid changes, Baum and Russell suggest harnessing the very technology that has largely contributed to the increased pace and scope of the brave new world. Using information technologies as an additional tool in developing leaders provides them opportunities to keep development targeted (e.g., develop/deliver courses, assessments, feedback remotely), collaborative (e.g., information sharing networks, project teams), and current or just-in-time (e.g., access to company and competitive data for decision making). Among other things, they describe a catalog of opportunities, a sampling of what is available in order to take advantage of technology for learning. They introduce another competency for global leaders: the willingness and ability to learn quickly by whatever methods are available. In their new reality, leaders must deal not just with the global, but with the technological aspects of a networked world—a global marketplace dynamically connected by the Internet. The Internet is a catalytic historical event. It is the same kind of event that Hammer discusses in the Part I of this book when she implies that leaders must adapt to situational and historical realities. Global leadership is indeed a reaction to changing realities.

LEADERS COACHING ACROSS BORDERS

Mary Dee Hicks and David B. Peterson

ABSTRACT

Leaders are increasingly relying on developmental coaching to equip their people to sustain competitive advantage and stay abreast of change. While coaching across cultural borders poses many challenges that leaders need to consider, a core of practical coaching strategies offers them the greatest leverage for change in any circumstance. These strategies, based on enduring principles of human learning, can accelerate development and can be deployed independent of culture.

Leaders who wish to establish an enduring competitive edge in business need to straddle cultures and adapt to multiple, often conflicting, norms and expectations. These demands are further confounded by a world beset with constant change and increasing complexity. Workforces are more diverse, competition is more intense, and technological revolutions are outpacing even the most progressive innovators. Against this backdrop, leaders who foster versatility and continuous growth in their people are most likely to sustain successful and resilient organizations.

To meet these challenges, many leaders are boosting their coaching skills. Unlike executive coaches, who provide personal, accelerated learning experiences

Advances in Global Leadership, Volume 1, pages 297-315.
Copyright © 1999 by JAI Press Inc.
All rights of reproduction in any form reserved.
ISBN: 0-7623-0505-3

from an objective, outside perspective (Otazo, 1999; Peterson, 1996), leader-coaches are insiders (Peterson & Hicks, 1996). Leaders in companies such as PepsiCo, Intel, Hewlett-Packard, and General Electric resolutely foster the development of the people on their teams and may even deploy people-development as a core strategy in pursuit of their business objectives (Tichy & Cohen, 1997).

This discussion outlines practical coaching strategies that are based on enduring principles of human learning—principles that are relevant in any coaching relationship. These principles draw on psychological research and practice (Highlen & Hill, 1984; Kanfer & Goldstein, 1991; Mahoney, 1991) that address the dynamics of people's motivation to change, the critical elements of a helping relationship, and the methods by which habits are broken and new skills acquired. Because the findings from this research illuminate the underlying mechanisms of how people change, coaches can use the strategies to anticipate and overcome the coaching challenges they will encounter. The strategies of coaching as presented here do not address the specifics of what people value or how they learn in a particular culture, but the strategies do capture the active ingredients in any learning venture, independent of culture. In fact, as coaches have adapted them across multiple cultural lines, the principles have proved to be quite robust.

Any discussion of this length could only begin to address the wide-ranging factors that are pertinent in working across particular cultures. Therefore, instead of offering culture-specific advice, we present a framework for understanding common coaching issues. This framework guides coaches to devise tailored approaches for any person they may coach. Coaches can customize the strategies to fit culture-specific relationship norms, learning methods, communication styles, and assumptions about leadership.[1]

WHAT IS COACHING ACROSS BORDERS?

Coaching is often defined and taught as a collection of activities—write development plans, deliver feedback, teach a skill, offer advice (Peterson, Uranowitz, & Hicks, 1996, 1998). Such a definition leads coaches to ask the wrong questions, such as, "How do I give feedback in this culture?" In contrast, we define coaching as the process of equipping people with the tools, knowledge, and opportunities they need to develop themselves and become more effective (Peterson & Hicks, 1996). The objective of coaching is to enhance people's work effectiveness and boost their ability to contribute as new challenges and opportunities arise. This definition, which focuses on the outcomes and not on the coach's activities, leads to broader questions, such as, "How can I help this person increase his or her insight?" Feedback from the coach may not provide the best vehicle to accomplish this goal.

Because coaching is a process, it extends beyond one-time events, such as preparing a development plan or conducting a performance discussion. It is integrated into people's work activities and goals. Coaching is collaborative as well. The coach helps to create the necessary conditions for learning, while the learner commits to meaningful objectives and takes responsibility for acquiring and applying new learning. Definitions of coaching and development that emphasize one player in the equation at the expense of the other, suboptimize the learning process. Coaching is not something delivered by a leader, it is a reciprocal relationship in which both parties actively participate. Further, a development philosophy that puts the onus for growth and continued employability solely on the shoulders of the individual waives the vital responsibility of leaders and organizations to provide developmental direction, resources, and accountability.

This process requires interpersonal perceptiveness, sensitivity, and a keen sense of timing. Within a single culture, these requirements place significant demands on the coach. Across cultures, the coach's challenge is magnified. Although some cross-cultural hurdles—such as language differences—are obvious, other variables—such as different values and different interpretations of common behaviors—pose subtler pitfalls.

In anticipation of these challenges, coaches should bear in mind three general guidelines.

1. *Search for hidden layers.* People from different cultures look at the world through different lenses. These lenses tint their values, assumptions, perceptions, and relationships in ways that range from strikingly dramatic to understated. Because of these differences, coaches should assume the presence of important cultural variables that they may not understand or appreciate. Coaches need to pursue these hidden layers and bring them to the surface, both in themselves and in the people they coach.

Because cultural differences can be quite distinct and vigorous, cultural norms help a coach generate hypotheses about the person being coached. Is this person likely to be better motivated by a collective goal than an individual one? Might this person prefer authoritative expertise and clear direction from a coach to a collegial, free-flowing discussion? Should the coach vault quickly into the task or spend a significant amount of time getting to know the person? Will the coach's preference for quick, linear decisions be suitable when working with this person? Testing relevant hypotheses like these can often help leaders avoid obvious pitfalls.

Leaders might generate such hypotheses by studying the culture of the person being coached and how it differs from their own culture. They can identify the cultural heroes and why they are respected (it is often intriguing to discover who is represented on the local currency, for example); who the political leaders are and how they lead; and what is reinforced in the educational system and how key lessons are taught. Coaches are also advised to review resources that discuss broad dimensions of cultural differences and the specifics of social and professional discourse in particular cultures (e.g., Cushner & Brislin, 1996; Gudykunst, Ting-Toomey, & Nishida, 1996; Hofstede, 1991; Lewis, 1996).

However, merely studying and reading about the norms of other cultures will not be adequate. Because of their own cultural blinders, coaches cannot formulate all relevant hypotheses with regard to others. They perceive and interpret information about events and people in their own culturally influenced ways. Products of their own culture, they have a ready inventory of hunches regarding what people value, how people respond to feedback or new information, how people relate to each other, and what people will expect in a learning situation. When working across cultures they need to transcend their assumptions and habits, probing further to understand both themselves and others. Then, as they uncover cultural insights, they can adjust their coaching tactics and expectations to fit the situation at hand.

Conducting research on cultural differences and anticipating unseen differences could have smoothed the way for a French leader who took on a 3-year engineering project in England. Upon commencement of the assignment, he was led to expect that few adjustments would be needed in his leadership approach. After all, his teams of French and English engineers shared a common profession and company culture. Soon after the project started, however, his team leaders began to clash. He was stunned to discover marked cultural differences with regard to the perceived role and status of engineers, and to the tactics the teams deployed to resolve problems with occupational safety. "If I had been told prior to the assignment that it would be hard," he claimed later, "I would have made fewer mistakes. Knowing it would be hard would have actually made it easier." Had he assumed the presence of unseen differences, he would have been braced for a challenge and alert to the cultural realities that he encountered.

Different presumptions about boss-subordinate roles nearly derailed an American manager's coaching with a new employee from Singapore. The manager suggested that they jointly identify development priorities and asked the employee to identify areas in which he would like to receive coaching. In some cultures this participatory approach would allow the employee precisely the kind of involvement that would optimize the chances for the coaching to succeed. In this case, however, the employee interpreted the manager's proposal as an abdication of legitimate authority. The manager's credibility was undermined. When the manager discovered this interpretation, he adjusted his approach. Instead of asking broad, open-ended questions, he began to define the process and explain, as an expert, what their roles would be and why. This modified behavior helped restore the manager in a culture-appropriate role.

2. *Personalize the approach.* Although cultural hypotheses help coaches anticipate differences, a person's perspective cannot be predicted from what might be distinctive about his or her culture. There are vast differences among people that cannot be explained by differences between national cultures. Each person is a unique configuration of a variety of influences, including personal experiences,

genetics, and subcultural forces that transcend national cultures. These factors combine to create the person's view of the world, way of thinking, and behavior.

It has also been noted that broad cultural distinctions are increasingly unreliable in the face of global communications and interactions. The expanding interconnectedness of people and the growing confluence of cultures leads to greater complexity and an erosion of traditional cultural distinctions (Hermans & Kempen, 1998).

Cultural norms are aggregates across people. They can educate coaches about potentially powerful influences on people but cannot fully capture the unique constellation of characteristics that make up a given individual.

Any one person from the United States, Germany, Brazil, or China might be methodical and punctual or impulsive and chronically late, bold, or timid. Knowledge of cultural differences with respect to time or leadership might help in understanding people from these countries in the composite, but it does not necessarily predict individual differences in behavior. When trying to understand a given individual, factors such as the person's life experiences, personality, education, age, gender, social status, and profession are often more instructive than is the national culture. While these factors and their meanings are culturally laden, they also contribute to understanding a person in ways that extend beyond culture. A coach who attends only to the cultural foundations of personal differences can miss other factors that define what is unique about a person. This is what a French engineering executive discovered, somewhat to his surprise, when he saw that his values, preferences, and style were more aligned with non-engineering British executives than with younger French engineers. His life experiences, education, status, and age contributed more to his collegial similarity than did his nationality. A coach who understood him only as a Frenchman would possibly have applied a stereotype that was at best, inaccurate and at worst, offensive.

To avoid cultural stereotypes that do not apply, a coach's ultimate objective is to understand the person as an individual and to personalize the coaching accordingly. The need to customize coaching at the individual level is supported by research from Europe and the United States, which indicates that the leading cause of people's dissatisfaction with coaching they have received is that it was impersonal (Peterson et al., 1996, 1998).

Cultural variables, while often legitimate factors for a coach to consider, can also become a cloak of avoidance. When the person being coached says, "That is not how we do things in my country" or "You don't understand me and you never will," he or she may be disguising real objections or resisting change under any terms. A leader who personalizes a coaching experience reduces the odds that people will use cultural differences as an excuse for avoiding working together or changing. Relentless listening, questioning, and curiosity are the coach's best tactics for untangling relationship or cultural issues from an underlying reluctance to change.

An Italian manager who was having trouble gaining cooperation from his team vehemently claimed that the new communication skills suggested by his American coach would never be acceptable in the Italian culture. Instead of persisting in advocating his approach, the coach probed into the manager's objections and acknowledged that the skills might in fact have a low probability of success in Italy. With few better alternatives readily apparent, and a low cost for trying the new approach, the coach suggested that the Italian manager try the new skills as an experiment. Under these terms, the Italian tried the skills and was surprised to discover that they worked smoothly. As this instance illustrates, coaches can be sensitive to cultural differences without allowing the differences to divert them from working on legitimate development issues.

3. *Orchestrate change.* Effective coaches do not try to do everything themselves. Instead, they facilitate and enable learning by orchestrating the resources and cultivating the conditions in which development can occur. In many cases, the coach is not necessarily the expert on what the person is learning and may not even prove to be the right person to help lead the learning activities. Instead, the coach orchestrates people and resources to make sure the person gets the information, opportunities, and support needed for continuous improvement. In this framework, the coach is freed from being the bearer of all feedback, advice, instruction, and expectations. Instead, the coach relies on others, including the person being coached, to ensure that change continues on course.

For cross-cultural coaching, the primary advantage of orchestrating the change process is that it affords the leader much greater flexibility. If the person being coached requires a better understanding of changing performance expectations and is not convinced by the coach's perspective, there are other sources of information, including colleagues, official organizational communications, and other leaders. If the leader is not available to provide information, advice, or instruction, other credible and respected people can be leveraged. When the person is not in the same location as the coach, the coach can ensure that people at the same site, or from the same cultural background, provide ongoing guidance and support. In cultures where direct feedback from a coach is not acceptable, indirect routes for sharing information about the person's experience can be sought.

The leader's ultimate task is to ensure that the person is learning and that his or her performance is enhanced. The question to keep in the forefront is not, "What do I need to do to coach this person?" but, "How do I help this person develop?" With this shift in objective, the coach can more easily navigate potential cultural barriers that might otherwise derail the coaching.

These three guidelines—search for hidden layers, personalize the approach, and orchestrate change—apply to all aspects of coaching. They give the leader latitude to adapt to individual and cultural differences, and to flexibly deploy the principles of how people change. These principles apply regardless of culture, and are captured in the coaching strategies that follow.

COACHING STRATEGIES

The most versatile coaches develop a repertoire of approaches and tactics that allow them to deploy general strategies in flexible ways. The five coaching strategies described here are designed around the most critical challenges in helping others develop.

Strategy 1.   Forge a Partnership—Build Trust and Understanding
                    so that People Want to Work with You

One of the most vexing problems voiced by coaches is, "How do I overcome resistance?" When trying to help someone develop, many leaders tackle this problem by first explaining what they want the person to do differently, and why. The majority of people on the receiving end of such requests question, "Why should I take you seriously? Why should I trust you? Why should I care?" The solution to this problem begins with the coach's adapting the challenge as "What can I do to make sure we want to work together?" If leaders establish mutual trust and understanding at the outset and give people reason to believe that coaching will be useful, people will want to work with them and resistance can be avoided.

Strategy 1 addresses two fundamental questions relevant to building a trusting relationship: Do the people being coached believe that the coach understands and respects their view of the world? Do they trust that the coach will take their agenda seriously and work on behalf of their best interests? When these questions can be answered affirmatively, people are much more likely to engage willingly in the development process. They are more likely to talk openly, take calculated risks to try new things, and sustain their efforts over time. Resistance, in short, becomes a non-issue. Throughout the course of development, any indication of resistance is a signal for the leader to return to the partnership strategy.

Forging a partnership is more affected by cross-cultural dynamics than any other coaching strategy. In any coaching relationship, people need to decide whether they can work constructively together. In cross-cultural settings, the potential for differences in worldviews is compounded, and the odds of failing to build sufficient trust are significantly greater. Leaders often expect affinity in expectations, style, and assumptions where little actually exists. For example, many task-oriented, outcome-driven Western leaders vault past relationship building or give it only cursory consideration (Peterson et al., 1996, 1998). When working with people from the West, leaders from Eastern cultural traditions may harbor inaccurate presumptions about the power afforded to them because of their position.

Leaders frequently fail to adapt to the relationship-building requirements of the person's culture. As a result, they lack the foundation they need to engage people in development. In some European countries, for example, the relationship is the context for any transaction between people, and thus is a prerequisite for coaching work to commence. In the United States, the relationship often follows from a constructive engagement, so moving directly into coaching with minimal relationship building might be acceptable.

Different assumptions regarding accepted processes initially blocked an American leader who was coaching a German manager. The American raised the prospect of team building as a way to enhance the manager's performance. Immediately, the manager stiffened and his face went blank. Sensing resistance, instead of trying to persuade the manager of the value of team building, the American asked, "What does 'team building' mean to you?" The manager replied with some vehemence, "You Americans do team building by starting to identify common assumptions and getting to a common understanding of the problem. Commonality is the whole goal. We start team building by putting the issue in the middle and everyone backing away and identifying our different perspectives and views. The whole principle is that we have different points of view. We don't even try to get to a common understanding." After they clarified these assumptions about the team-building process and objectives, they could work together on a process they could both accept. If they had proceeded without this clarification, the leader would have encountered persistent resistance.

Cultural stereotypes may also lure people into misconceptions about their coach. A French leader, upon moving to The Netherlands, varied his time of arrival at the office, sometimes arriving early and sometimes late. After a month, he discovered that his Dutch team was upset and assumed he was arrogant and cavalier with regard to his job. To the Dutch team, punctuality was very important, even if they did not begin work immediately upon arrival. To the leader, his attention to getting the job done was most important, not the precise hours he committed to the job. The Frenchman's inattention to the Dutch norm, and the Dutch team's presumption of arrogance in their leader, prevented them from establishing a partnership. What was potentially even more damaging to the partnership than the differences in punctuality was the lack of communication regarding the problem. One of a coach's worst invisible barriers is that the other person will stereotype or take offense, but will not communicate. In this case, the conclusion that "he's just an arrogant Frenchman" threatened to derail coaching before it began.

The goal for the coach is not "when in Rome, do as the Romans do" but rather to establish mutual cultural respect. Coaches do not exchange their view of the world for a new one. Instead, they assume "I am not Roman, but I can learn how things are done the Roman way." They initiate the building of cultural insights in themselves, and foster reciprocal understanding in the people that they coach. They are vigilant with regard to the impression they make on people from other cultures and how culture influences the impressions others form of them (Crittenden & Bae, 1994; Giacalone & Beard, 1994; Shaw, 1990). Their cultural curiosity and frustrations are shared, and they are not afraid that differences will lead to a relationship failure. With differences understood and respected, and each party relating in a way that is genuine, they can engage in constructive discussions regarding their differences.

Cultural Curiosity

Partnerships can also be intensified if the coach becomes a good student of the culture. The simple act of demonstrating interest in learning about the person's culture conveys a desire to understand. Coaches can inquire directly into how things are done in another country and can enlist other people, including those they coach, as cultural mentors. Studying the history, heroes, arts, and other aspects of the culture that reflect its soul and passion, can reveal what is valued by people and how they experience and interpret the world.

The educational system offers particular insights about how a culture conducts and values learning. Is the educational system selective or open to all? Is advanced education fairly pragmatic or highly philosophical? Is learning viewed as a life-long task or is it presumed that learning has been attained upon completion of a particular degree or certification? Does higher education typically involve significant independent questioning and initiative from students, or is it characterized by rote learning and reliance on expert teachers? The answers to these kinds of questions help the coach adjust relationship-building and learning tactics so they are more congruent with what is familiar and expected.

To coach members of his team who hailed from different cultures, an American leader varied his tactics for relationship building. When working with people from the United States, the primary basis for securing credibility was his demonstration that he had something useful to offer. As a leader for Asian managers, he first established his seniority, as coaching from someone younger and less experienced may have been difficult for the Asian manager to accept. When working with a French executive, who had an advanced degree from an elite European university, the American realized that his credibility as a source of counsel rested in part on the sophistication of his academic credentials. Not until the leader shared that he had earned a degree from the top program in his field in the United States, did the executive willingly engage in the coaching process. Without this information, the Frenchman was skeptical with regard to the leader's ability to contribute to his development.

One manager, knowing that he can never comprehend what the world is like for someone from across the border, routinely acknowledges that his views and approaches are different from those of the people he coaches. He regularly makes cultural differences a topic of discussion and asks probing questions regarding the cultural aspects of what the other person is doing, such as, "This is a chance for me to learn more about your culture. I would like to find an appropriate way to do that. What is the best way for us to talk about why you are doing things in certain ways?" One American manager working in Holland made a practice, whenever giving work to his secretary, of describing how such things are typically handled in the United States. He then asked her if the approach would work in her country or if she could suggest an alternative. Another coach routinely created opportunities for people to give him feedback about his cultural assumptions. For this coach, contrary to posing a block, the differences actually became an opportunity for building a stronger mutual understanding.

Attention to Language and Norms

Work across languages is rife with opportunities for misunderstanding. A French executive leading a team in the United Kingdom discovered, in the course of requesting a large box, that *large* means *wide* in French and *big* in English. If simple requests like this, using simple words, can be misinterpreted, the task of sustaining understanding in subtle and sometimes emotion-laden coaching situations is daunting. Even coaches who are remarkably proficient with a language other than their native tongue should not be lured by their fluency into assuming that they can correctly interpret subtleties. They need to be cautious of what one cross-cultural leader calls "unreliable friends," words that appear to be alike but have different semantic values.

Nonverbal communications also can have dramatically different meanings. As one Thai executive advised a manager who was about to move to Thailand, "There are three things to remember about how people here will react to you. When someone is smiling and nodding their head, it means they like you and agree with what you are saying. Also, when someone is smiling and nodding their head, it means they don't understand what you are saying. Finally, when someone is smiling and nodding their head, it means they disagree with you and wish you would go away."

In most cross-cultural coaching situations, the language of discourse needs to be negotiated. Often, one party is working in their native language, while the other is working in a second language. This may create a power imbalance in the relationship, because one person has to work harder to understand and be understood than does the other. Sometimes both parties may be working in second or third languages. In these situations, checking and rechecking for understanding needs to become a relentless habit. Language differences also impede the bonding that happens naturally when people can talk informally. Casual chats and discussions of common experiences are less likely to occur when communication requires extra effort.

Subtle cultural differences can even interfere with apparently obvious relationship-building tactics. One Northern European leader was advised that eating and drinking together was a prerequisite for building close relationships with his Italian team. He invited members of his team to "have a drink" after work. The team members assembled at a nearby bar, shared one drink, and went home within an hour. The leader's vision of an evening of camaraderie was shattered. Later, he discovered that for Italians, sharing a meal, not just sharing a drink, was the foundation for the relationship. He subsequently invited the team to his home for dinner. They ate and drank heartily, lingered long into the evening, and began what proved to be a very satisfying working relationship.

Sometimes, despite coaches' best efforts to build mutual trust, cultural barriers create obstacles that they cannot circumvent. A person may have strong reactions against working with a coach from a particular culture or with someone who does not speak his or her native language. Coaches who enlist the help of others who can work within the language and within the culture can avoid the inherent limitations imposed by such barriers and reactions. The ultimate goal of coaching, after all, is not that the coach provides all the answers or engages in all the coaching-related activities but that the performance of the person being coached actually improves.

Cultural variables are the most potent in the Forge a Partnership strategy. Frequently, language and culture differences are the domain where people test whether they can work productively together. If a coach can work through these differences and establish a trusting relationship, the cultural differences are often not impediments in other aspects of the coaching. Underlying any specific relationship-building tactics, the most powerful tool for forging a partnership is the desire of the coach to understand. This motive, consistently conveyed, transcends culture.

Strategy 2.   Inspire Commitment—Build Insight and Motivation so People Focus Their Energy on Goals that Matter

Once a solid working relationship is established, the next coaching challenge is, "How can I motivate someone to change?" To begin answering this question, a coach can reformulate it as, "How can I tap into and mobilize the person's natural motivation to develop?" The emphasis in this second question shifts from what the coach can do to what the coach can discover and then leverage. Building on Strat-

Table 1.   GAPS Grid: Critical Information for Development

	Where the person is	*Where the person is going*
	Abilities	**Goals and Values**
The person's view	How they see themselves.	What matters to the person.
	The person's view of his or her capabilities, style, and performance, especially in relation to important Goals and Standards.	The motivators that energize and drive the person's behavior, including interests, values, desires, work objectives, and career aspirations.
	Perceptions	**Standards**
Others' views	How others see the person.	What matters to others.
	How others perceive the person's capabilities, performance, style, motives, priorities, and values.	The success factors for the person, as defined by his or her roles and responsibilities, cultural norms, and other peoples' expectations.

egy 1, the coach's intention is to understand what is most important to the person being coached. Then, the coach discovers links between the person's desires and the needs of the organization. This connection creates a commonality of purpose that ensures that people select goals with paybacks that both they and the organization desire.

Before they choose development priorities, people need to know where they stand relative to what is expected of them. They also require clarity regarding their own values and goals. Coaches can promote people's insight into these areas by helping them to gather and discuss information in the four categories summarized in Table 1. The columns represent the most important categories of information that people need: where they are now and what matters most going forward. The rows indicate that pertinent information derives from two perspectives: what the person sees and what others see. Unless all cells are filled, critical information is missing.

Critical Information for Development: GAPS

Goals and values embody the core of that which a person cares about, including interests, desires, and values. This category refers to much more than career objectives. It designates what is important to a person and what he or she is willing to work toward. _Abilities_ encompass the person's view of what he or she can and cannot do. It includes a self-assessment of skills, capabilities, and performance. _Perceptions_ reflect others' observations and opinions about the person's capabilities, motivation, and performance. _Standards_ define expectations and criteria for a successful performance. Some standards are relatively clear, such as job descriptions and business objectives. Others are murky, such as group norms or unstated cultural values.

Identifying Important Information

To complete a GAPS grid, individuals, their leaders, and the organization need to be clear on where they stand and what is important relative to the person's performance. The discipline of analyzing and discussing these topics forces greater clarity and accuracy about development priorities. The GAPS grid is a template for seeking and sorting what is known and not known relative to the person's development. Since people and organizations are always changing, gathering GAPS information is an ongoing process. When people periodically review their GAPS, they update their assumptions about where they stand and recommit their development energies to areas that can make the greatest impact.

To complete the Perceptions cell in the grid, coaches often rely on feedback, a process that is easily tangled in cultural assumptions and expectations. In the United States, the direct sharing of behavioral observations and perceptions might be assumed to be appropriate. In Latin cultures, a more precise context for the feedback often needs to be established. Its purpose, who is delivering it, and how it is and is not helpful, all may need to be explored before a feedback conversation occurs. In some European cultures, feedback is considered not merely a description of behavior but a personal evaluation. Because of its deeper implications, the feedback conversation must begin with discussion of the person's intentions, and possibly of his or her values as well. Only within this context of personal meaning can coaches constructively discuss perceptions of behavior, its impact, and how it might change.

To help people access perceptions from others, the coach can allow the person being coached to decide how to gather the information. What information do they want? How do they want it collected? What are their preferred sources for the information? One coach also offers options for how he will provide feedback. "Some people like feedback delivered directly all at once, others like it in small doses. How do you want to discuss my observations?" He then provides ongoing openings for input on how his approach is working through comments such as, "I don't intend to offend. Let me know if I have ever done so."

Uncertainty about culturally acceptable behaviors might also prevent a coach from expressing legitimate expectations and feedback. An Italian leader observed a member of his Dutch team driving recklessly around a sprawling manufacturing plant. Unsure as to whether this behavior was appropriate in Dutch culture, he did nothing to intervene, and the problem persisted. With a clear communication strategy around cultural differences, he could have said, "If I were in Italy this behavior would be totally unacceptable. You need to explain to me if this is acceptable here or not."

Creating Positive Pull

Much coaching, and the feedback that is an important element, traditionally focuses on addressing performance problems or improving skill deficits. This framework for coaching has many drawbacks under any circumstances, but it is even more problematic in cross-cultural coaching. In some cultures, negative feedback is associated with personal failure, personal skill deficits are not readily admitted, and direct discussions of performance problems are deemed rude at best.

The prevalent emphasis on selecting weaknesses as development objectives is reinforced if the coach looks only at the Perceptions cell of the GAPS grid. Information that outlines where the person is strong and weak naturally leads to the selection of development objectives designed to shore up the weaknesses.

Weaknesses in themselves, however, are rarely the most important or motivating subjects for development. Strategy 2 shifts coaching away from fixing weaknesses and toward effectively achieving positive goals. These sources of positive pull for development are discovered through investigation of the Goals and Standards cells, which define the desired state for the person. Positively driven development helps the person obtain more of the things that they and the organization care about. Because this approach does not exclusively focus on people's problems, the potential stigma associated with coaching is reduced. Also, because this approach melds personal objectives with organizational expectations, mutual incentives and benefits are ensured.

The goal of finding positive incentives for change also makes coaching and development applicable to everyone, regardless of performance or position. In the ideal coaching environment, everyone is learning and being coached, including the top performers and the leader. Problem performance is not exclusively singled out for development attention. Instead, development becomes synonymous with continuous improvement in business performance and is a means to achieving challenging work goals.

Aligning Goals and Standards

The challenge of finding an intersection between individual aspirations and values (Goals) and organizational expectations regarding contributions and capabilities (Standards) is often accentuated in cross-cultural settings. Preferred leadership styles, for example, vary widely from one culture to another (Hofstede, 1991), creating divergent visions of the ideal leader. A Japanese worker might believe that direct challenges of a superior's opinions are disrespectful and inappropriate, whereas his American boss might believe that confident assertions from a subordinate are evidence of persuasiveness and leadership potential.

Leaders, particularly when they attempt to import their corporate culture to a new country, risk asking for culturally incompatible behaviors and attitudes from the people they coach. Faced with such expectations, an individual is compelled to choose between personal values and culturally reinforced behaviors on the one hand, and behaviors that will be rewarded and valued by the coach and organization on the other. Left unexplored, this clash of expectations can hamstring development efforts and overall performance, because the individual cannot simultaneously satisfy corporate and cultural forces that are pulling in different directions. That which one side reinforces, the other resists.

To avoid conflict or deadlock, style and values differences need to be discussed in the course of negotiating development objectives. One possible goal for such negotiations is to generate a viable hybrid objective that is compatible with different values and perspectives. Coaches and the people they coach can select aspects of the other party's expectations that are consistent with their values and priorities. The coach, for example, may relent on the expectation that a Japanese manager speak up forcefully in meetings in exchange for more candid discussions in private. The Japanese manager may agree to raise objections and propose new ideas when the boss specifically asks for input and provides a setting where open discussion feels safe. With this objective, each party's values regarding leadership and communication are accommodated, and the individual can embrace the development goal without cultural compromise.

Once the coach has accomplished the objectives of the first two strategies—establishing trust and choosing aligned objectives—the most critical cross-cultural issues have been addressed. If resistance or flagging motivation arise later in the course of the person's development, the coach returns to these two strategies to reestablish partnership and commitment. While misunderstandings and cultural sensitivities can certainly arise at any point in the coaching and development process, good communication, persistent listening, and mutual respect are the keys to resolving them. The first two strategies establish the foundation for resolving differences that derive from culture. With the need for trust and alignment met, coaches can then deploy the following strategies in nearly any situation.

Strategy 3. Grow Skills—Build New Competencies to Ensure that People Know How to Do What Is Required

Once people understand what they need to work on and are committed to doing so, this strategy helps them to acquire new capabilities. Coaches use this strategy to prevent people from stalling at their current level of proficiency or continuing to repeat old mistakes. Various familiar methods support skill acquisition, including training courses, individual instruction, reading, special assignments that stretch people in new directions, and on-the-job training. Coaches need to be aware that training methods often reflect cultural approaches to learning. Certain cultures have histories of verbal instruction and direct advice, whereas others teach by analogy, observation, and illustrative stories and parables. Hofstede (1991) points out that most structured, formal training methods have been developed in individualist countries, primarily North America and western Europe. Such methods may not readily export to other cultures.

Any learning activity will yield the greatest change if it engages the learner in meaningful challenges. Learning activities are imbued with challenge when they stretch people to the edge of their comfort zone, and they are meaningful when the skill is directly applicable to personally relevant objectives. Coaches need to explore different options to learning, recognizing that there are both cultural and individual preferences for which activities provide the most beneficial challenges.

Coaches help people discover and participate in meaningful skill-building activities through several routes, including:

- *Brokering resources.* Help people find relevant skill-building tools and link people with others who have the work-relevant expertise that they need. This might be the tactic of choice where language or distance prove significant barriers.
- *Demonstrating relevance.* Guide people to identify exactly what they need to learn. Help them pare broad objectives into accessible segments and focus their efforts on learning one lesson at a time.

- *Reflecting on experience.* Encourage people to extract the lesson from each learning experience by asking what they have learned, how it has worked, and what they intend to do similarly or differently the next time.

Coaches often must make cultural adjustments in the pace and type of skill-building experiences they create. An American coach, eager to improve decision making among Japanese managers, encountered the Japanese process *neima-washi.* Literally meaning "wrapping around the tree," this approach enlists the support of numerous people to make a decision. While the support yielded by the process is desirable, the approach is cumbersome and can dilute accountability. The coach needed to increase her patience toward the slow pace of this process and to decrease her desire for speedy, linear decisions. At the same time, she showed others how to build support without unduly jeopardizing efficiency. To accomplish this, she asked the managers to list those whom they wanted to involve in particular decisions and then coached the managers to eliminate those who were not truly necessary for the task. When someone was eliminated from the list, the managers personally explained why that person was not consulted in this instance and requested his or her help on an upcoming decision.

Strategy 4.   Promote Persistence—Build Stamina and Discipline to Ensure that Learning Lasts on the Job

While Strategy 3 tackles the acquisition of skills through a variety of means, Strategy 4 deals with the application of the new skills where they are needed. Old habits and fear of failure are the two primary obstacles to the adoption of newly acquired capabilities.

Virtually everyone can relate to the frustration of changing old habits. Even people who are deeply resolved to change can find their motivation dampened by the frenetic pace and demands of their job, or the real obstacles to trying new things. They struggle to shift from a familiar, well-rehearsed approach to a new skill that is still inefficient and requires extra effort. In addition, those who try new behaviors at work may risk failure and embarrassment if their nascent efforts are visible to others. Because cultural norms and personal styles are significant influences on the size of the risk people are willing to take, coaches must always calibrate risk from the learner's point of view. Coaches can foster new experiences at a manageable level of developmental stretch, and create opportunities for people to engage in intelligent risk-taking and experimentation at the edge of their comfort zone, wherever that edge happens to occur.

Promoting persistence is also necessary because, even though commitment to a desirable goal can be relatively quick and painless, the actual process of attaining the goal is often unpleasant and laborious. Consider the contrast between the allure of a goal to be physically fit and healthy with the sometimes painful reality of regular exercise and careful attention to diet. Similarly, a person's commitment to meet an important development goal at work is often derailed by the repetitive practice and discipline required. Unless leaders address these barriers, people's inspiration to change fades and new learning never takes hold. Leaders can sustain change efforts by helping people discover ways to embed new behaviors in daily activities so that development becomes part of the routine. They can provide attention, reminders, encouragement, and realistic expectations for the pace of change and the quality of the results yielded by early efforts to try something new. Only then will the benefits of newly learned skills be realized.

Strategy 5.   Shape the Environment—Build Organizational Support to Reward Learning and Remove Barriers

Because context is a powerful determinant of people's behavior, leaders have a vital role in fostering a climate that is conducive to learning. Even people who are highly motivated to change are dissuaded by active and passive resistance from others and perplexed by mixed messages regarding the importance of development to the organization. When leaders ignore such contextual barriers to development, they give people easy excuses to neglect or postpone their development efforts.

Leaders have three primary avenues for cultivating an environment that minimizes barriers and sets expectations for continuous learning:

1. They can be development role models. When leaders make their own learning transparent to others, they send powerful messages that no one is exempt from learning and that personal risk-taking on behalf of development is not only acceptable but also expected. Actions such as seeking feedback and coaching, sharing a learning plan, or trying a new skill in front of others can potentially contribute to an environment that heightens focus on development. Even if they are trying to change the development climate, coaches need to be careful to model behaviors that will be well suited to the culture.

2. Each leader, regardless of role or position, can influence the local learning climate. Leaders can highlight the role of development when setting and tracking group goals and can integrate discussions of development into staff meetings, performance reviews, and project debriefings. They can also foster trust and openness so that developmental information and support are readily accessible.

3. Leaders can influence organizational policies and practices. Even leaders who have no formal responsibility for development and performance initiatives can make their opinions known about how organizational tools and practices—such as competency models, performance reviews, succession management, and reward systems—can be aligned for better support of development. They can also adapt these tools and processes to the norms and needs of people from different cultures.

Cultural beliefs define the appropriate behavior for leaders, guide expectations about the potential of individuals to change, and even determine the value of individual change and improvement. As coaches discover norms and beliefs that support or impede continuous learning, their tactics for shaping the environment for learning have to adapt, sometimes dramatically. Insistence on open discussions about development would be foolhardy in a culture that values personal privacy and that traditionally employs more indirect or allegorical communications to convey personal information. In certain cultures, a coach who admits to self-development efforts could be construed as weak and ineffectual, not as a model to be emulated. In establishing an environment for development, a coach also needs to gauge the levels of developmental stretch and risk-taking that are deemed appropriate and tolerated. As with each strategy, coaches need to apply relentless vigilance and questioning to find the approaches that will work best for the circumstance.

CONCLUSION

Culture adds a layer of complexity to the necessity to cultivate the talents of others. Leaders who keep this imperative in the forefront are not deterred or intimidated by the ambiguities and unexpected barriers of cross-cultural coaching. By paying attention to three things, they remain solidly grounded and prepared for the challenges of coaching.

First, leaders know themselves and what they bring to the development process. They are willing to question and expand their own assumptions, capabilities, and methods.

Second, leaders pay attention to the process of coaching. They search for the critical ingredients that will help them connect with others to accelerate learning in meaningful ways.

Third, leaders are attuned to the person they are coaching, and respect individual goals and values in the cultural context. Even when trying to create radical change, leaders accommodate to the person's starting point and build on the person's unique identity and capabilities.

Drawing on these three sources, a leader can be vigilant, creative, and adaptable in sustaining the coaching relationship and process. Ultimately, when coaching succeeds, stronger personal and organizational performance builds self-sustaining development momentum regardless of culture.

ACKNOWLEDGMENT

The authors would like to thank their international coaching colleagues for sharing their insights and experiences: Val Arnold, Francois deBoissezon, Rosemary Getsie, Keith Halperin, Joy Hazucha, Ken Hedberg, Katherine Holt, Wing Hong Loke, Fernando Mendez, Karl-Heinz Oehler, Emma Pearson, Seymour Uranowitz, and David Walker.

NOTE

1. Despite the broad applicability of the coaching strategies, our own values and assumptions about development are reflected here, as we are admittedly products of our cultural environment. Our cultural and intellectual backgrounds include valuing personal effort and individual achievement, and the expectation of direct but respectful candor in communications at work. To the extent that the reader shares such assumptions, the suggestions in this chapter might ring even more true. In any case, a leader who wants to better enhance and build the capabilities of others should find something here to simulate thinking as well as action.

REFERENCES

Crittenden, K. S., & Bae, H. (1994). Self-effacement and social responsibility: Attribution as impression management in Asian cultures. *American Behavioral Scientist, 37*(5), 653-671.

Cushner, K., & Brislin, R. (1996). *Intercultural interactions: A practical guide* (2nd ed.). Newbury Park, CA: Sage.

Giacalone, R. A., & Beard, J. W. (1994). Impression management, diversity, and international management. *American Behavioral Scientist, 37*(5), 621-636.

Gudykunst, W., Ting-Toomey, S., & Nishida, T. (Eds.). (1996). *Communications in personal relationships across cultures.* Newbury Park, CA: Sage.

Hermans, H. J. M., & Kempen, H. G. J. (1998). Moving cultures: The perilous problems of cultural dichotomies in a globalizing society. *American Psychologist, 53*(10), 1111-1120.

Highlen, P. S., & Hill, C. E. (1984). Factors affecting client change in individual counseling: Current status and theoretical speculations. In S. D. Brown & R. W. Lent (Eds.), *Handbook of counseling psychology.* New York: Wiley.

Hofstede, G. (1991). *Cultures and organizations: Software of the mind.* London: McGraw-Hill.

Kanfer, F. H., & Goldstein, A. P. (Eds.). (1991). *Helping people change* (4th ed.). New York: Pergamon.

Lewis, R. D. (1996). *When cultures collide: Managing successfully across cultures.* London: Nicholas Brealey.

Mahoney, M. J. (1991). *Human change processes: The scientific foundations of psychotherapy.* New York: Basic Books.

Otazo, K. (1999). Global leadership: The inside story. In W. H. Mobley, M.J. Gessner & V. Arnold (Eds.), *Advances in global leadership* (vol. 1). Stamford, CT: JAI Press.

Peterson, D. B. (1996). Executive coaching at work: The art of one-on-one change. *Consulting Psychology Journal, 48*(2), 78-86.

Peterson, D. B., & Hicks, M. D. (1996). *Leader as coach: Strategies for coaching and developing others.* Minneapolis, MN: Personnel Decisions International.

Peterson, D. B., Uranowitz, S. W., & Hicks, M. D. (1996). *Management coaching at work: Current practices in Fortune 250 companies.* Paper presented at the annual conference of the American Psychological Association, Toronto.

Peterson, D. B., Uranowitz, S. W., & Hicks, M. D. (1998). *Management coaching at work II: Current practices in large European-based companies.* (Working paper). Minneapolis, MN: Personnel Decisions International.

Shaw, J. B. (1990). A cognitive categorization model for the study of intercultural management. *Academy of Management Review, 15*(4), 626-645.

Tichy, N. M., & Cohen, E. (1997). *The leadership engine.* New York: HarperBusiness.

GLOBAL LEADERSHIP
THE INSIDE STORY

Karen L. Otazo

ABSTRACT

The real-life experiences of global leaders in multinationals companies are described through the eyes of an executive coach to provide practical, usable insights that supplement theory. The five case studies portray recurring patterns of complexity that global leaders face in meeting work expectations, company-culture expectations, and country-culture expectations. The cases include Asian, American, European, and South American executives dealing with the issues. Three out of the five would be considered to be achieving differing degrees of success. Two are failures, one because he tried too hard to meet corporate expectations while ignoring his local followers, and the other because she lost her influence with the head office when she transferred overseas.

The heat is on. You're sweating bullets. You've got to make a decision. This could be one of your company's best ever markets. The right person in the job could make or break your career. Do you choose the seasoned insider who has been

Advances in Global Leadership, Volume 1, pages 317-335.

around, who knows the company and its products? He's got a solid track record and the respect of the top brass. Or do you choose the savvy local who knows the country and the market? He has good contacts with government officials and knows the customers. But is that enough? It's a tough call.

There is no easy answer. Too bad you can't have it all. Leaders aren't perfect, and companies aren't sure what constitutes the right mix of skills for global leaders.

There was a time when a leader was an "expatriate" or a "local." In our global economy, this dichotomy is dissolving. Is a Hong Kong Chinese educated in Canada and working in China considered a local, an expatriate, or something in between? Inherent in a company's definition of "expatriate" lies the tension between the parent company's culture and that of the non-central businesses. A number of authors describe this tension as navigating between two forms of allegiance—allegiance to the parent firm and to the local operations (Black & Gregersen, 1997).

There are thousands of global leaders who must serve two masters and, at the same time, get the job done. Someone who expends energy on local needs is viewed as costing too much and losing sight of the company's needs. This is detrimental to a long-term career in a company. Those who focus on leading the corporate way may be introducing systems, processes, and approaches that will be rejected in the host country as soon as the pressure is removed.

A British expatriate posed a third option in our opening dilemma: "You want someone who can represent your parent company. They should be well respected and honorable. The problem with 'homeboys' from head office is that they don't ring true locally. Local boys who maybe have worked in the head office, gone to school in the company's home country, feel about right. You've got to know that Thanksgiving is the big holiday in North America while it's Easter to the French. You've got to know when to speak up and when to keep your mouth shut."

This chapter looks at leadership's art of balancing the pressures posed by various allegiances and expectations to get the job done, an arduous role that has been called the hero's journey (Osland, 1995). The issues are complex. Therefore, our case studies use three different mental models, or lenses:

1. Work expectations—what is required to get the job done
2. Company-culture expectations—what is dictated by the company's unwritten rules
3. Country-culture expectations—what the followers in the country expect from the leaders

Leaders who do not know about, or ignore, any one of these three models, do so at their peril. They have to pay attention to all of them while simultaneously shaping expectations regarding what can be accomplished. Leaders must also place what they can realistically accomplish in the context of their career, and where they want it to go. Getting involved in global leadership with a multinational subsidiary is not necessarily a career booster.

To succeed in such a demanding role, a leader has to be willing to pay a certain price. What looks like a success in business metrics may not be so in the areas of health, relationships, family, or career.

THE INSIDE STORY: THROUGH THE EYES OF AN INTERNATIONAL EXECUTIVE COACH

The cases you will read in this chapter reveal the inside scoop on real leaders who work for multinational companies. Their stories are true; some of the details have been changed to protect the leaders and their companies. In some cases, the players represent composites to protect confidentiality and illustrate recurring patterns.

The stories come from this author's experience as an executive coach. "Executive coaching is a practical, goal-focused form of personal, one-to-one learning for busy executives. It may be used to improve performance, improve or develop executive behaviors, work through organizational issues, enhance a career or prevent derailment" (Hall, Otazo, & Hollenbeck, 1997). Although "executive coaching" may be thought of as a new approach to executive development in the 1990s, the coaching concept has been around for a long time. "World-class athletes know it. So do opera divas. Winners in nearly every profession know that without the right coach they won't perform at their peak" (Tristam, 1996). A study of subsidiaries of multinational companies found that while it is very important for all leaders to seek feedback, "it is especially true among international subsidiary leaders" (Gupta, Govindarajan, and Malhotra, 1996). Global leaders are using coaches to learn quickly and to get the feedback they need to make immediate course corrections. Coaching can be thought of as just-in-time learning for leaders to gain the perspective they need when they need it. Coaching is a powerful but costly way to learn quickly. It works best when someone is open to it because of change, transition, or crisis. With clear goals and target behaviors, a lot can be accomplished in a short time.

CASE STUDIES OF GLOBAL LEADERS

Pushing a Corporate Mandate: Leroy Jackson

Age: 52
Nationality: American
Title: Chief Operating Officer
Company: Indonesian subsidiary of an American oil company
Work locations: Headquarters in Jakarta; operations throughout offshore Indonesia

Work Expectations Issues

> Increase profits
> Improve cost-effectiveness
> Improve productivity
> Improve audit results

Company-Culture Issues

> Short-term thinking; executives judged by their quarterly results
> Multinational company with a primarily white male leadership
> Leadership image is a tough cowboy making decisions on his own

Country-Culture Issues

> The Indonesian leader is the *bapak,* the father of the village. He is expected
> to be a loving, benevolent dad who is always there to take care of his people,
> resolve conflict, and reason together with his top management.
> All leadership is personal in Indonesia. The employees care about the boss
> because he cares about them.
> Family life is of great importance to the average Indonesian.

The Situation

Leroy is a highly successful executive from Louisiana. He has always worked in the same company, starting with oil rigs in the Gulf of Mexico. He later earned a college degree at night school. The posting to Jakarta to head up the operation was the pinnacle of his career. He was looking forward to 3 to 5 years on an expatriate package, which would boost his retirement income. His marching orders were to shake things up, and get the guys to work right. He came to the job ready to make radical change and make his mark.

Even though he was advised to take it slow and get to know things before making any changes, he was determined to show corporate that he could take charge. Leroy wanted to show them who was boss. He was going "to kick ass and take names," an old oil-field expression.

When it was suggested that he go through predeparture cultural training, he could not spare the time. In fact, he moved to Indonesia so rapidly that his family did not have the time or opportunity to join him before he had to move back again.

The Problem

Leroy decided he was going to make his mark by saving money on travel expenses. The offshore rig workers, geologists, drilling engineers, and others worked 1 week on and 1 week off. They traveled to and from the rigs by helicopter, a bumpy 45-minute ride. Leroy was excited to discover that sending the workers in workboats could save millions of dollars. Without further ado, he implemented a new policy and got rid of the contract helicopter pilots. The Indonesians complained that the new method of travel took a day each way from their time off. Leroy insisted that the travel days would not count as work days.

He went on to institute a policy which stated that no American needed to learn Bahasa Indonesia because it was a U.S. company. "It's time for this company to think and act like the American company it is. If you give them an inch they'll take a mile," he said. His policies were enforced.

The workforce became hard to manage, although they were always polite and non-confrontational. What followed was a severe and universal slowdown in productivity. The cost of lifting a barrel of oil went from US$5 to US$15, and the time it took to produce the same quantity of oil tripled.

No one could tell Leroy why.

Analysis

The consensus in the parent company was that Leroy was a great guy who was able to get along with anyone. He was a real gentleman and people loved to talk with him. It seemed as if he had the makings of a good leader in any culture. However, his focus was disastrously wrong. He wanted to do things "right" rather than do the right things. Leroy wanted to look good to corporate. He lost sight of the needs of his followers and of the importance of their culture.

Indonesians are family-oriented by nature. Leroy was cutting the time they could spend with their families off the rig from 7 days to 5. They complained that since his wife had not come with him he did not understand family life, and that this was not how a leader should act in Indonesia.

To take something away from staff, especially something as significant as time off, requires good reasons. For Leroy to be successful, he needed the key leaders in the Jakarta operation on his side. Thinking he had a total mandate from corporate, he did not see why he should bother wasting time talking to lower-level managers.

Conclusion

Leroy created his own backlash. He lasted only 6 months in Jakarta before his parent company pulled him out to save the operation. Although he had coaching expertise available to him, he either did not use it or gave it only lip service. Leroy Jackson bungled his chance to make a positive first impression. He thought a corporate mandate gave him total protection. He was wrong.

Taking Command: Ed Younger

Age: 39
Nationality: Australian
Title: Chief Executive Officer
Company: Australian manufacturing, sales, and services firm with locations throughout the People's Republic of China
Work locations: China and Hong Kong

Work Expectations Issues

Lead teams of predominantly local Chinese
Maintain quality and safety
Develop a workforce dedicated to customer service

Company-Culture Issues

Empower employees to be self-directing and to work effectively in teams
Be creative and innovative
Treat employees consistently

Country-Culture Issues

The Asian leader must show that he (or she) has the power to take care of his followers—he is the father (or mother) of the work family.
Leaders should be experts who lay down the rules that must be followed; staff conflict may stem from unclear rules or roles.
Australian-style "empowerment" is often experienced as abandonment.
Men and women should not touch openly in public.

The Situation

Ed Younger, a tall, slender, sandy-haired Australian, walks down the office corridor with a ready smile, stopping to chat. All the secretaries know him as "Eddie." When he arrived on the job 2 years ago, Ed brought with him a good track record at the Australian head office and an MBA from a leading university. He works night and day and travels frequently in order to personally visit his team. Nick Larson, his predecessor and now his boss, oversees all of the Asia operations and is located on the floor above Ed's.

When Ed first took over the CEO position, his goal was to "empower" his primarily all-Chinese staff and implement the company's localization policy. Ed often told staff that they, not he, were the experts; he felt good about being well liked and that he knew how to "get along" in a different culture. He tried to be culturally sensitive, and listen to employees' many excuses and complaints about the company and its other employees. At meetings, he was considerate and let his managers speak first. He often encouraged them to be creative and brainstorm new ways of doing things along with him, but they were reluctant to do so.

The Problem

With all of his hard work, the company's results frustrate him. His employees are not increasing their productivity and quality. Numbers are, in fact, falling. Ed tells what happened: "After a period of uncertainty when I first came, the staff seemed to become more comfortable. I did have some people who were not on board yet, but after a month or two I thought I'd won them over. I spent time with each person, getting to know them and their job and always asked for their input on decisions. I treat them with respect. I empower them, but they just don't respond in the same way as my Australian employees. By the end of the third month, the staff started fighting and complaining. Things started to fall apart and I haven't been able to get them to work together since."

His staff would go around him to Nick Larson, who does not discourage this behavior. Although Ed knew that he needed to do things more like Nick, he did not know how.

Analysis

Ed would have benefitted from the much-needed perspective that an executive coaching program could have offered. He had just experienced a major transition, for which he was ill prepared. New leaders have 30 to 60 days to make a first impression, during which they must establish their power and authority. Ed's flexibility gave off the signal that he did not mean business. Ed came with an Australian model in mind and ignored (to his peril) the Asian reality.

The Solution

After he became involved in the executive coaching program, he found that one of the keys to his success would involve adopting the Chinese model of leadership, which is based on Confucian teachings. The ideal Confucian leader is a father figure. The employee, like the son, unquestioningly obeys the father. A culture's attitude toward family will be reflected in the workings of the office family. The Chinese emphasis on paternalism and hierarchy requires the business leader to foster that kind of atmosphere. The leader is expected to put in personal time by participating in karaoke, picnics, boat trips, and other company get-togethers, but he should still be the disciplinarian.

Where Ed fell down was in confusing his staff by trying to be egalitarian and open. He also wanted to demonstrate his caring for others by touching them. When he did this with his secretary, erroneous office gossip referred to them as sweethearts.

With coaching, Ed learned that he could get leadership respect from being an expert in his company's technical area. After all, he was promoted on the strength of his technical skills and knowledge of company products. He could play on those skills and show that he knew the business. Ed is the one who knows the internal politics of the head office, he should not hesitate to show off his knowledge of these things, while accepting that he needs to learn in some areas, such as in Chinese customs and language. Humility and openness have their place, if used to the right degree in areas where no one would expect him to be an expert.

The Chinese leader is not a "nice guy." This is where Ed made a crucial mistake. He learned that for his subordinates to be effective, he should not "empower" them in a Western way. It is his job to guide and instruct them in a step-by-step manner until they are ready to take on more.

The boss expects respect, which means employees should not call him by his first name. Instead they should use his title. Leadership is personal to the Chinese, who perform out of loyalty and respect for the boss and the company. It is better for a boss to be too intimidating than too nice—which leads to the issue of Ed's boss acting as the de facto leader. He had to work that out with Nick.

Conclusion

Some expectations of followers cannot be easily changed. Ed learned to adapt. His employees had to learn that they could get special favors from Ed and not just by going around Ed to Nick, his boss. Although Ed considers such favors (e.g., extra time off) to be bad policy, he is learning to give out little things that show he has the power to make things happen.

While Ed has started to run a more "Confucian" office, he made a bad first impression that could have been avoided with some guidance at the beginning of his assignment. He is proving more effective in all areas by changing his thinking about how things ought to work. For example, when he wants employees to come up with new ideas, he lets them prepare in advance, write out their ideas, and take turns in an orderly manner at meetings. The employees are currently showing increased respect for him.

Matching Cultural Values: Joaquin Jaume

Age: 45
Nationality: Colombian
Title: President
Company: Wholly owned Malaysian manufacturing complex of a Japanese high-tech firm

Work locations: Manufacturing operations in Malaysia with a representative office in Kuala Lumpur

Work Expectations Issues

Lead manufacturing facilities composed predominantly of local Malaysians, known as *bumiputera*
Maintain quality and safety
Improve productivity and work morale

Company-Culture Issues

Being on time and getting things done on time is a high value
It is difficult to surface issues at a distance
Expectations are not made clear; much has to be guessed

Country-Culture Issues

The Malaysian leader is the *bapak,* the father, of the village. He is expected to be a loving, benevolent dad who is always there to resolve conflict and reason together with other elders in the village.
Joaquin is following two other leaders, both of whom were the wrong fit for the cultural expectations.
All leadership is personal in Malaysia and in Asia. The staff would do what was needed for the job because they personally wanted to make it work for Joaquin.

The Situation

Joaquin was hired to turn around a manufacturing operation in Malaysia. While working for a Japanese company in South America, he had his own career prospects blocked by managers of approximately the same age. He knew that he had to do something to move ahead in his career. He also had to prove that he was unlike his predecessors.

A charming Colombian, Joaquin is a polite, loving, family-oriented man. He is courteous and formal, almost courtly, in his manner. It was these "soft" skills that led the company to select him when no suitable Malaysian candidate came to light.

The Problem

The Malaysian operations had suffered badly under Joaquin's two predecessors. The first, a Japanese man, had been aloof and dealt with the business through an interpreter. He was uncomfortable giving clear directions or spending time talking with the local staff. Then a Taiwanese manufacturing expert replaced him. The rationale was that he was Asian, an expert in the area, and that most of the power elite in Malaysia were Chinese anyway. The selection proved to be a big mistake.

"Before Joaquin came we were furious," said one of the company's Malaysian employees. "First we have a remote, arrogant, aristocratic, useless Japanese. Then we have a Taiwanese who doesn't speak Malay and treats us as if we were beneath contempt. He strode around the office making us feel like dirt. He actually carried a hardened bamboo stick around with him. If we made an omission or mistake, he would come by and hit us on the legs—sometimes even on the head. When we complained to his boss, he stopped hitting us, but he continued to carry it.

"We hated the Taiwanese. We slowed everything down and turned out poor products. Yes, it was sabotage. What else could we do?" the employee complained. Working for him made all the stereotypes of the Chinese seem real for the *bumiputera,* the Malaysian locals, or literally "sons of the earth." Many quit upon finding other jobs.

Analysis

The Japanese parent company realized it had made a mistake. Tanaka-san, the Administrative Director and Vice President of the company, observed, "It was ironic. If we had gone into, say, China, we'd have spent a year getting our top man ready, immersing him in the culture and language. We saw Malaysia as a small, less important operation in a small market with a compliant population. Our lack of preparation cost us."

The management consultants whom the Japanese employed drew up a list of the top 20 characteristics of the candidate who would be successful in the post. Joaquin fit the profile. His superb relationship and networking skills, which could have held him back in succeeding in other places, were what the management consultants said they needed—although they still had reservations. "We considered it a risk, since we had been wrong ourselves twice before. Everything considered, we would have preferred a Malay, but could not find one who fit the job needs."

The solution

To ensure that they did not make the same mistake again, they gave Joaquin the benefit of a coach at the time of transition. Before Joaquin took up the job, he was forewarned of the cultural issues that would affect his business effectiveness. Once in place, he spent the first 60 days just listening and doing favors. Big favors or small favors, whether for new chairs or a new system, he gave a clear indication that he was a real *bapak,* a leader of the village.

At the beginning and the end of each work day, he made himself available to talk with all levels of staff. Joaquin sat down with people and reasoned with them. He was prepared to spend days looking for consensus, whether it bore fruit in the end or not. At the same time, he gave clear directions and spelled out expectations.

Joaquin easily learned simple Malay words, like *tidak apa apa* (no problem), eventually becoming fluent enough to hold his own in meetings with government officials. The Malay language was not that different from his native Spanish; he learned it quickly.

Joaquin took care of his team and kept the Japanese head office from intruding into the operation. For example, the Japanese manager had continually chided the employees for their practice of *jam karat*—rubber time. He was familiar with a similar attitude—*mañana*, "I'll get it done tomorrow"—attitude in Colombia. When the pressure was on, Joaquin made sure the employees saw that he had to satisfy the deadlines imposed on him and that he would look bad if they did not perform. Because they did not want him to look bad, they performed.

Joaquin was able to make a good first impression, which was crucial to his eventual success. Within a short time, Joaquin's results, and the feedback from senior staff, were beyond the parent company's wildest expectations.

Conclusion

Joaquin Jaume's situation illustrates the importance of matching cultural values. It also shows the folly of thinking that a local face, in this case an Asian one, will necessarily be successful.

The Malaysian work teams began to take tremendous pride in their work and in the new corporate culture. "In a very short time, he made us feel that he was a part of our work *kampong,* our village. We had been wary of him at first, which seems strange now," explained Harith, one of the Malaysian managers. "There are three of us being groomed to take over his job. We are gratified that he is looking after our careers, but he is so wonderful that we begged him to stay on because there is no one like him. He keeps the head office from asking stupid questions. He takes care of us. We opened a kindergarten without any support from the Japanese head office; he found extra money and raised the rest with the *Imam's* [Moslem holy man's] support. He recognizes the importance of the *hadj,* the sacred journey to Mecca, and has created a system so that ten employees can go each year, without having to take vacation days."

In Joaquin, a South American, the Japanese company found a bridge for the gap between two Asian cultures. He let the Malaysians know that he valued their expertise and was truly grateful to them for making the business work, and he never let his employees look bad or allowed them to flounder. They in turn took care of him, and their loyalties were personal to him, not to the company. In the meantime, he ensured that the Japanese were kept informed of his progress and the progress of the business. The numbers showed that his methods, though seemingly unorthodox and un-Japanese, were working. He created metrics and measures that kept his bosses happy. At first he did not tell the local employees that he was using these measures of progress, because he did not want them to feel scrutinized. In the end he used them as an incentive system.

Joaquin did have weaknesses. He knew nothing about Malaysia, having been there only once before his posting. But seeking a coach at the moment of transition was a good move. While learning the culture, he also had to counteract his own tendency to let things slide for the sake of relationship building. As for the career issues and where he can go after this job, Joaquin says, "Some people call me a fool to stay here, but there isn't a day when I come in to work with a heavy heart. *Aku senang sekali disini*—I am very happy here." The entire Jaume family loves living in Malaysia.

Big Jump in Leadership Responsibilities: Josephine Yu

Age: 38
Nationality: Taiwanese
Title: Managing Director
Company: Anglo-German retail joint venture
Work locations: Taiwan, Hong Kong, and Singapore

Work Expectations Issues

Little retail experience; chosen because no one else was available
Heavy emphasis on making the numbers
Push for Josephine to focus efforts and drive results

Company-Culture Issues

British bosses expected her to be gracious and open while driving results
German bosses effected orderly stores, accounts, and planning
Emphasis on doing things in an orderly, step-by-step fashion clashes with the business's need for speed

Country-Culture Issues

Fast-moving but rule-bound Asian culture
Consumer tastes quite different from those in Europe
Start-up of retail stores in high-cost urban centers with huge cost pressures

The Situation

Josephine Yu was appointed to head up a regional retail start-up operation for an Anglo-German joint venture. Her experience base was weak at best, but she had the right profile and "the guts and determination for the dirty work of a start-up," according to her British boss, Ian Watson. She also had a reputation for getting things done quickly.

Josephine began her career after leaving secondary school. "Taiwan was a poor place in those days," she says. "My parents came from the mainland with nothing. When I finished high school I got a job as a secretary. From the outset I wanted to do more, including my boss's work. I couldn't stand the slow pace of decision making. The urge to do something else, to have a chance to lead, was strong." Looking for an area where hard work would pay off, she started selling insurance at a friend's suggestion. Within 3 years, she was managing 20 employees and exceeding all of her regional sales targets. When the firm was taken over by a British company, Josephine was viewed as a high flyer, but one without "qualifications."

"I was successful enough that they wanted me to teach others and to expand my role in the retail group. I moved into wholesale premium food products. It was a heady world of high profit and high pressure." There was also a high personal pay-off, which appealed to Josephine. "I had to deal with the French and other Europeans. I had to understand how to work globally."

Within 6 months, through hard work and sheer survival instincts, she improved sales figures to levels that other start-up operations struggled years to achieve. While the company's European and American stores could maintain sprawling suburban stores, rent in Asia compelled Josephine to separate the two and to carry less stock. In one instance, she chartered a 747 to ensure sufficient stock to open a new shop a month early.

The Problem

Despite these remarkable results, both Ian and her German boss, Andreas, considered firing her. They were very concerned about her ability to continue the dramatic growth and profits she had created in a very short time.

Ian admitted that "her lack of education and her initial insecurity did concern us. But she doesn't suffer fools gladly and won't stop until she gets a job done. I did keep expecting to have to take her out as a 'basket case.' We were surprised that she made it." Meanwhile, the British company worried that the numbers were so good that they might be fabricated; they assigned a consultant in retail sales and an audit manager to work with her.

Andreas, the representative of the German partner, complained that he had been shocked when he visited her retail facilities. The figures were wonderful, but the facilities were chaotic and dirty. The inventory system was woefully lacking; shipping was unreliable. All this was quite un-German. Like the British, Andreas started to worry about her lack of planning and follow-through. Quality controls had been sacrificed for speed. Furthermore, the German head office had been horrified by the extravagance of the 747 charter. The board wanted to get rid of her because she was seen as being "out of control."

When confronted by the British experts assigned to her, Josephine viewed their criticism as a lack of trust on the part of the British company. She reacted defensively and could not hear what they were telling her regarding what needed to be done. They thought they were being "helpful." She felt attacked. Were they trying to push her out of her job? It was at this point that she called in a coach as a desperation measure.

Analysis

Josephine was thrown into leadership waters over her head and came out a winner. In describing the hard work she put into getting to where she was, she said, "They threw me in at the deep end, and I thought I'd drown. I hired people I could trust to work hard and to support me. I just kept moving, going back later to fix what didn't work. That was the only way I knew how to be successful."

However, she did not understand what her defensive behavior projected; the coaching helped her come to terms with that aspect. By the time Andreas started suggesting ways in which she could improve, she was able to let down her defenses and listen. While she resented the systematic information gathering and planning he demanded, she adapted when she saw the utility of the systems and procedures required by the German company. She admitted, "I started to see what I didn't know in finance, logistics, and even in merchandising." This helped to build her confidence and diminish the insecurity Ian had noted in her. In this way, she could assess objectively that the expatriates assigned to her by the British company were offering her some reasonable criticisms.

The Solution

Josephine came to realize that she needed to tip the balance of power. She saw that aligning with the Germans might get the British watchdogs removed. She was due to make a tour of flagship operations in the German company's hometown. With the coach's support, she used her newfound confidence to petition the board for the help she needed. Of the 11 items in the German company's value statement, they had rated "strong trust" number one. This resonated for her, and she appealed to the Germans to find strong and capable executives she could trust to work for her to do what was needed. "It was so irregular, we said yes," said Andreas. "Her presentation to the board was unsophisticated, but she opened our eyes with her impassioned pleas for help in the areas she didn't know, like store merchandising, retail logistics, and finance." She was not the only one with a lot to learn. The German home office had not understood the realities of business in greater China. The cost of rent in Hong Kong, Taiwan, and Singapore meant that leaving the shop closed an extra month would have cost more than hiring the plane did. In 1 month, Josephine made enough to pay for the 747 five times over.

The Germans responded to her requests by finding her seasoned veterans with global experience—one from Moscow and one from Malaysia. The British reacted badly. Josephine reassured them by pointing out that the Germans were the experts in the retailing field. Finally, it became apparent that the German expatriate managers were what was needed to move the entire operation in the right direction. The British concurred, and Josephine's confidence soared as her team went to work to sort out the operation. Her growing support from the German expatriates was the masterstroke. She was now able to refer any doubts her incredible profits raised to a seasoned expatriate who spoke the financial language her bosses understood.

Lessons Josephine learned

- Timing: In this case, the coach was called in at a good time for an executive to learn fast—during a crisis.
- Staying calm and flexible: By remaining non-defensive, she alleviated concerns about her ability to learn from the experts. She had to show that she could play their game and do things the right way.
- Risk taking: Josephine took on a tremendous challenge. The change in the nature and scope of her responsibilities when she took on the managing director's job was huge. She did the best she could without mentoring. With a little bit of coaching support she was able to make an impassioned plea to the board and secure the help she needed. She never forgot, though, that "when you are visible to the gods, they may smile or they may get angry."
- Feedback was an important part of the coaching program. There was an interview with every key player in her working life: staff, supervisors, suppliers, colleagues. How did they perceive her and her position? She observed herself working with them, meeting with them, giving direction, and getting frustrated. She took on the task of ignoring her own internal constant self-criticism, which was much like hearing her father's voice in her head. Instead, she learned to observe herself without judgment and to ask others she trusted to do the same for her.
- Focus on priorities: She learned to put her energy where it would make the most difference to her bosses—respect for their business sense. She liked her new reports so much that she started hiring other seasoned expatriate talent for her new stores (to start them with the proper experience), and her bosses could not have been happier with the results. Today, when asked what one thing would make Josephine better at her job, all Andreas could think of was, "Speak German!"

Maintaining Corporate Clout: Karen Solomon

Age: 32
Nationality: American
Title: Regional Director
Company: American entertainment company with a motion picture studio in California, video sales and distribution, television programming and related businesses

Work locations: Asia Pacific region

Work Expectations Issues

Help the company become a bigger player in the entertainment business throughout the region
Get its videos and television programs into the region's television networks
Make deals for movies, programs, projects, and distribution channels
The position is being funded by seven different parts of the business, each expecting great results.

Company-Culture Issues

Deals get done when someone who has the clout gives approval
Deals are typically pitched in person
Europe has been a good, predictable market; Asia is expected to be a high-growth market, ripe for more entertainment vehicles
Capable people are the ones who can move fast and make things happen
Reputations are fickle; they can change overnight

Country-Culture Issues

Business is done with relationships built up over time. This approach is called: "family, friends, and favors."
Potential business partners are shown great "face," or respect, in Asian meetings.
After the Columbia Pictures' fiasco at Sony, Asian companies are wary of deals with entertainment companies. A U.S. company needs to establish a presence in the region and show signs of long-term commitment before deals can be made.

The Situation

Karen Solomon arrived in the region full of energy and ready to make things happen. As a single woman, she thought that the most cost-effective approach to her work was to stay in hotels and keep moving, an approach that put her on the road 100 percent of the time. She was determined to meet all the players in the region and penetrate all the markets.

"Before leaving the States I did some research about Asia and knew how important relationship building can be," Karen explains. "This was the time to use my natural friendliness and persistence. I'm considered cute and adorable. People love to talk to me. That's one of the reasons they put me out here."

One of her goals was to determine consumer tastes for each country and the tolerance for American programming. She knew the industry issues: Disney's problem with *The Little Mermaid*—having to draw in a bathing suit top for Moslem viewers; the ending of *Fatal Attraction*—Japanese audiences wanted the Glen Close character to admit her mistakes and take her own life, while Chinese audiences wanted more action and violence. Karen knew that she would have to find out more and learn about these cultures.

She also had Rosie, a great administrative support back in Hollywood. With E-mail, fax, and phone, she could get everything done from her laptop computer and keep overhead costs down. The company was already complaining about cost, since prices for meals and hotels in Asia were shocking compared to the United States.

Everyone she met in Asia was gracious and open. What was really getting in her way was the slowness of decision making. She came to realize that relationships took more time in Asia. After the first few months of getting acquainted, she focused on a joint venture with an Indian company in Thailand, with financing from wealthy Thai businessmen. It was the deal of the century, with almost no financial exposure for her parent company.

The Problem

When she brought the Thai businessmen to the California headquarters to meet the president, they were introduced instead to a junior marketing manager who listened politely and said he would get back to them. Horrified, Karen stormed into the president's office and demanded to know why her important guests had been snubbed. It turned out that research at corporate had revealed that the Thai businessman was one of Thailand's biggest chicken farmers, and the president did not want to waste his time with them. Karen pointed out that the Thais also owned one of the largest telecommunications and software companies in Thailand, but the relationship was ruined by their treatment in the L.A. office.

At that point she got some coaching help. Karen did a stakeholder analysis to determine who was doing the funding and what they expected. She strategized her next move. She worked out scenarios and developed communication strategies.

A similar incident occurred with her next big deal with a Japanese company. Over the following 8 months Karen brought in another company veteran to assist in the matter. Kevin Blair was a low-key finance colleague who spoke Japanese, understood the local culture, and could entertain the Japanese men in traditional, male-only pursuits. The Japanese loved him. When the Japanese company was ready to deal, Karen first went to talk with the top brass and was shocked to find her supporters' response lukewarm. Finally, the president confided that "Kevin Blair's support of your project is not very credible. He's not really a player. We don't see the commitment and passion that should be part of a project like this.

Frankly, with all your talk about culture, we think the two of you have gone native. You've lost your perspective."

There was also talk that she wasn't adding value to the company, that she had "lost her edge." Not only was she failing at the job, her career was at risk. When they started calling it "her" project, she knew she was in trouble.

Analysis

Karen put energy into developing long-term relationships for big deals, but she underestimated the unrealistic expectations of her company. She was also spread too thin, traveling constantly, working on too many deals for too many stakeholders, and without enough communication back home regarding her activities and their potential payoffs. With seven funding entities and 11 stakeholders, she was in a no-win situation. She had seriously overestimated her senior management's level of sophistication.

Conclusion

What Karen neglected was to educate and enroll the parent company in her vision. The support she expected evaporated with the distance, and with a 15- to 16-hour time difference, she had to get up early or stay up late to communicate with headquarters. It was too tough for them to call her. Combining that with the constant travel left her worn out and discouraged. She could see herself becoming a peripheral player in a peripheral part of the business.

After just a year and a half, she returned to the corporate head office with her reputation tarnished. Within 6 months she left the company.

SUMMARY

Within multinationals there are two kinds of global leaders: seagulls and sandpipers. Seagulls swoop in for a bird's-eye view, drop their load, and leave as quickly as they came. They may appear quarterly or for just a few days a year. They may mingle with the employees on the ground or eat their food and drink on their corporate jet (such as one high-profile CEO). They are usually carefully sheltered from the realities of the countries they visit. They stay at the best hotels, eat at the best restaurants, are chauffeured around, and have interpreters who make communication effortless. They rarely visit remote locations, and they may hardly set foot in the streets of a city.

Then there are the sandpipers, who live where they work. They experience what it is like to do business at the ground level. Corporate headquarters rarely has a sense of their day-to-day frustrations and small but crucial triumphs, like meeting with a key government official. As a human resources executive at a global communications company who had never lived abroad said, "Doesn't everybody speak English?"

Leaders inevitably make mistakes. Some learn from them and improve, as did Ed and Josephine. Some find their niche and a satisfying match for their values, like Joaquin. Some are successful in their region of the world but cannot get the support they need from the parent company, like Karen. Some fail to find their way at all and fail publicly, doing damage to their own and their company's reputations, like Leroy.

It is said that what you see depends on where you sit on the organizational chart. The same is true for global leaders. However, what you see depends on your mental model of how things work, the filter through which you interpret what appears to be reality.

ACKNOWLEDGMENTS

To my parents, whose teachings and example made me a citizen of the world. To Nina, who helps me examine my mental models. To John, who has enabled me to see through beginner's eyes.

REFERENCES

Gregersen, H. B., & Black, J. S. (1992). Antecedents to dual commitment during international assignments. *Academy of Management Journal, 35,* 65-90.

Gupta, A., Govindarajan, V., & Malhotra, A. (1996). *When do executives seek out feedback? A survey of 374 subsidiaries representing 75 multinational companies.* Paper presented at the Academy of Management meeting in Cincinnati, Ohio.

Hall, D. T., Otazo, K. L., & Hollenbeck, G. (1997). *Executive coaching: Development after downsizing* (Boston University Executive Development Roundtable). Boston: Boston University, School of Management.

Osland, J. S. (1995). *The adventure of working abroad: Hero tales from the global frontier.* San Francisco: Jossey-Bass.

Tristam, C. (1996, October-November). Wanna be a player? Get a coach! *Fast Company,* 145.

DEVELOPING JOINT VENTURE LEADERSHIP TEAMS

Zhong-Ming Wang

ABSTRACT

With the rapid economic reform and change in China, the development of effective cross-cultural leadership teams has become a major task for meeting the challenge of global leadership. This chapter discusses several aspects of the Chinese cross-cultural leadership teams. (1) *Chinese organizational context for team leadership.* Group approach as a strategy for Chinese management has been encouraged with the new emphasis not only on group cohesiveness and modeling behavior, but also on team-job fit and group task responsibility. (2) *Impact of economic reform and needs for cross-cultural leadership teams.* The major changes in management structure have facilitated the implementation of the factory director-responsibility systems and the team-building process for cross-cultural leadership. (3) *Cross-cultural work values and team leadership styles.* Task-procedural and interpersonal values and styles of managing leadership events among managers were affected by their team structures and organizational settings under different partnerships. (4) *Cross-cultural management competency.* Patterns and process of power-sharing and competence utilization among managers from state companies and joint ventures were crucial in cross-cultural organizational decision making. Expertise on functional systems,

Advances in Global Leadership, Volume 1, pages 337-353.

leadership actions, and interpersonal relations were among the key elements of the management competency. (5) *Cross-cultural team management.* Recent research on team conflict and leadership climate showed special dynamics in intra- and inter-cultural conflict resolution, Chinese team management, and leadership development. These recent investigations have provided systematic evidence about the strategies of developing effective joint venture leadership teams and global leadership. On the basis of recent leadership studies in China, a comprehensive model of cross-cultural leadership teams is highlighted.

CHINESE ORGANIZATIONAL CONTEXT FOR TEAM LEADERSHIP

Effects of Cultural Traditions and Values on Team Leadership and Organizational Behavior in China

Chinese management has its roots in ancient thinking and practices under the tradition of collective culture. Ideas of teamwork and group-oriented values were emphasized in management throughout history. The collective cultural values are the key variables in understanding cross-cultural leadership in international joint ventures in recent Chinese market-oriented business development. The focus of the Chinese team approach, however, has changed in recent years. There has been a new emphasis on team responsibility and effectiveness. There are also shifts in leadership approaches from internally oriented to externally oriented management and from relationship-oriented to task-oriented styles. The development of effective cross-cultural leadership teams has become a major task for meeting the challenge of global leadership development.

Group Approach as a Strategy for Chinese Management

Chinese society has historically emphasized collectivism and social interaction in work situations. Since 1949, team building has been popular in enterprise management. Several Chinese cultural traditions have had important effects on team leadership and the development of organizational behavior in international joint ventures in China. The group approach includes practices of group decision making, teamwork, group reward, and group cohesiveness. During the recent economic reform, the group approach has been more encouraged as an important Chinese management strategy with the new emphasis on team responsibility and team effectiveness (Wang, 1986, 1988). This approach has integrated group responsibility, authority with team interests, and enhanced work motivation and efficiency.

Current Chinese team leadership has been significantly influenced by two major nationwide movements: the Excellent Group Evaluation Campaign in the 1960s and the Optimization through Regrouping plan in the 1980s and early 1990s (Editorial Board, 1984). The first managerial movement emphasized group cohesiveness and modeling behavior through the "excellent team movement" and labor emulation. Each year, public campaigns were conducted at the national, provincial, city, and enterprise levels to evaluate and award excellent team or enterprise titles in order to improve and facilitate both team and organizational development. During the 1950s and early 1960s, this excellent team movement focused mostly upon team technical innovations and cooperation. Since China launched her recent economic reform, the emphasis has been shifted toward excellent management and productivity of team and enterprise responsibility systems. Among the excellent team/enterprise titles, the Chinese Association of Enterprise Management in 1982 established an annual national Award for Excellent Enterprise Management. Many work teams were developed through the autonomous team management of Quality Circle (QC) in nationwide quality-control activities. The excellent team/enterprise movement has greatly enhanced group and organizational commitment, cohesiveness, and performance in Chinese industries and other organizations. A related team approach in Chinese management has been labor emulation, which is mainly organized by the trade unions in coordination with management and Party organizations. The key principle of labor emulation is helping and learning for better morale, discipline, quality, efficiency, productivity, and social contributions. Labor emulation has been carried out among individual employees, between groups, departments, and even enterprises, and it has proved effective in stimulating work motivation, team cooperation, and a sense of ownership in Chinese organizations.

With the development of Chinese economic reform, it became more and more evident that the traditional way of assigning group membership by management was not effective in enhancing team cooperation and performance. Therefore, as a major step in the economic reform program, thousands of work groups have undertaken the practice of "optimization through regrouping" since 1987 (Wang, 1990a). As a solution to problems such as overstaffing, "iron rice bowl" (guaranteed jobs), lack of responsibility, and low efficiency, this second managerial movement has focused upon team-job fit and group task responsibility. Some recent studies indicated that a high degree of group involvement and a good fit between task requirements and group goals with clear member responsibility are the keys to team excellence and team goal-directed behavior (Wang, 1991). Among those studies, a field experiment was conducted to find out the effects of voluntary grouping of work teams on group cohesiveness and productivity under close supervision of the managers, who made some adjustment of the experimental groupings according to employees' abilities, skills, and attitudes (Chen, 1987). Comparisons were made between 14 experimental groups (voluntary grouping) and 14 control groups (assigned by the management). The results showed that the experimental group as a whole had significantly higher daily output and more positive attitudes toward work and the company than did the control group.

The "optimization through regrouping" reform practice has been implemented in coordination with the introduction of the labor contract system. The new system emphasizes work responsibility and allows enterprises and workers to choose each other, a significant development toward decentralization and high efficiency in management in China. These issues reflect the features of the Chinese organizational context for the development of joint venture leadership teams.

IMPACT OF ECONOMIC REFORM AND NEEDS FOR CROSS-CULTURAL LEADERSHIP TEAMS

Recent Chinese Market-Oriented Economy Development

The Chinese economic reform has called for the need to develop cross-cultural leadership teams. Recent Chinese market-oriented economic developments in reforming management systems consisted of five main stages: experimentation, formalization, systematization, transformation, and strategic reorganization.

Experimentation (1979-1983)

This stage was characterized as the exploration and evaluation of management practices, specifically including the decentralization of some management power and responsibilities to enterprises, the development of new bonus and incentive systems, and the implementation of various secondary schooling and technical training programs. These practices not only greatly motivated employees and revived the low morale and poor educational levels of employees, which resulted from the so-called 10-year Cultural Revolution (1966-1976), but they also provided experimental evidence for a more decentralized organizational structure in Chinese enterprises.

Formalization (1984-1985)

In this stage, the focus of management reform was shifted from the enterprises' employee level (e.g., motivational systems) to the leadership level. While various kinds of management responsibility systems were introduced and established in large- and medium-sized state-owned enterprises, the decision-making power was expanded to strengthen the management of the state enterprises in 10 areas, including production, sales, pricing of products, disposal of assets, organizing, selection, staffing, and monetary incentives. During this period, a major emphasis of management reform was the selection of capable managers for enterprises, and formalizing managerial decision making through more democratic and procedural systems at various levels of organization.

Systematization (1986-1989)

The formalization of management selection and decision making led to the need for management system change and adjustment. More than 90 percent of large- and medium-sized Chinese state enterprises implemented the management responsibility contract system. "Optimization through voluntary regrouping" was conducted as an action for reforming workgroups and adjusting the problem of employment redundancy.

Transformation (1990-1996)

The delegation of decision-making power in the key management areas and the structural changes at the enterprise level do not function effectively without adjustment in managerial and operational mechanisms. The mechanism-transformation stage was characterized by the implementation of socialist market economic structure. The objectives of those regulations were to delegate decision-making power and responsibilities to the state-owned enterprises in all management areas, especially in some major managerial operations and human resource practices.

Strategic Reorganization (1997-)

This new stage of development emphasizes strategic restructuring and reorganizing. Efforts will be made to convert large and medium state-owned enterprises into corporations according to the requirements of the modern enterprise system with "clearly established ownership, well-defined power and responsibility, separation of enterprise from administration, and scientific management." The main management-reform initiatives include separating management power from the ownership and reorganizing enterprises into shareholding, contracting, and grouping with transregional, inter-trade, cross-ownership, and transnational operations.

The focus of management development was then shifted to the internationalization of management practices and systems change; for example, the development of international joint ventures, the implementation of corporate strategies, and the adaptation of cross-cultural businesses (Wang, 1996). These changes have set up new requirements for developing more effective leadership teams.

Director-Responsibility Contract System as a Strategy for Leadership Team Building

A major step in the Chinese economic reform program is the nationwide transition from the unified leadership system of the state enterprise party committee to the new "director-responsibility contract system" (Child, 1988). As a result, factory directors assume overall responsibility and power to run their enterprises, and employees have more say in managing their organizations. The key principles of management-responsibility contract systems in Chinese enterprises are separating state ownership from the management of enterprises, decentralizing management power, reducing administrative interventions, linking pay (wage/bonus) directly to performance, and creating a progressive organizational environment (Wang & Fan, 1990). The implementation of director-responsibility contract systems was indeed a strategy for leadership team building: (1) Qualified directors for the management-responsibility systems were selected by search committees through competitive and public recruitment procedures. (2) Under the director-responsibility contract system, the director assumes full responsibility and power in the production, operation, and management of the enterprise in coordination with the party committee, the management functional team, and the trade union. (3) The relationship of the factory director with supervisors and employees is adjusted and enhanced. (4) An arrangement of all-member deposit for business risk links enterprise outcome with the interests of leadership teams and their subordinates, which has facilitated a positive organizational culture of shared responsibility among leadership team members in enterprises.

Rapid Development of Sino-Overseas Joint Ventures

The increasingly multinational nature of Chinese business has posed the problem of how organizational members from diverse cultural backgrounds can most effectively work together in China. By the end of October 1998, some 320,000 Sino-foreign joint venture enterprises had been established with more than 18 million employees. Among those joint ventures, more than 80 percent have begun functioning, and 75 percent of those are doing well. In a recent field study on managerial decision making and performance assessment in Sino-foreign joint ventures in China, Wang (1992) found that joint venture partners often had different motives in establishing joint ventures and that the match between the partners' motives was an important factor affecting leadership styles of the joint venture management teams. A different important factor was the compatibility of value premises in relation to factual premises in organizational decision making among leadership team members. The focus of international human resource management has shifted from traditional topics such as internal selection and rewards to concepts such as cross-cultural management skills, teamwork competence, and strategic management abilities. The adaptation of different managerial styles and skills among executives becomes a new task in international management practices. Existing studies already indicate that the recent development of international joint ventures in China has greatly enhanced the requirements of managerial competencies in cross-cultural management (Wang & Satow, 1994). Under the new demands of more-qualified managers for international joint ventures, management orientation training is becoming particularly important for overseas assignments, especially in the design of cross-cultural management competency development programs.

Wang (1992) studied the management patterns among 25 international joint ventures in China and noticed that the transformation and establishment of joint venture organizations did not automatically lead to compatibility of management styles between the partner managers. While many overseas managers adopted a kind of task-oriented "one-man" leadership style (i.e., making decisions by top executives and implementing the decisions primarily through line managers), the majority of Chinese managers were more relationship- and task procedure-oriented (concerned with how management tasks were implemented). In particular, some joint venture managers followed the same conventional Chinese managerial style and leadership behavior as in non–joint-venture companies. The kind of collective decision making requires a compatible cross-cultural leadership team. Field surveys also showed that decision-making styles among managers in international joint ventures were largely affected by the management traditions of the managers' own cultures. For instance, in a Chinese-Japanese joint venture company, a kind of hierarchical management organization with small ranks and frequent promotions was introduced to middle management, whereas in a small joint venture with the Taiwan region, a family style of decision making was adapted. The overseas partners usually had more say in making long-term decisions, while Chinese partners had stronger influence in medium- and short-term decisions. In some of the joint ventures under the "one company, two management systems (both joint-venture and state enterprise management systems)," effective leadership team interaction became a key factor for successful management.

CROSS-CULTURAL WORK VALUES AND TEAM LEADERSHIP STYLES

Task-Procedural and Interpersonal Values

Much attention has been paid to cross-cultural work values in recent years (Bond, 1996; Triandis, 1995). A number of field surveys concerning work values,

Table 1. Cross-cultural Work Values in Two Kinds of Firms

Work Values	Chinese State Firms Sample	Japanese Joint Venture Sample
Peer level		
Task-procedural value	4.95	4.08
Interpersonal value	3.91	4.45
Boss level		
Task-procedural value	5.63	5.37
Interpersonal value	4.30	2.90

Note: *N* = 343; Scale 1–7.

team leadership styles, and problem resolution approaches under different partnerships were conducted among managers who were working with overseas managers in Chinese international joint ventures. A study of cultural work values among 343 employees from 33 Chinese companies and 19 Sino-Japanese joint ventures revealed two reliable factors in both the Chinese and the Japanese samples: tasks and procedures, and interpersonal communication and coordination, respectively. As shown in Table 1, these common factors indicate a general pattern of leadership styles and organizational culture: task-procedural and interpersonal approaches.

The perception of work values across peer and boss levels was significantly different between the Chinese state company and the Sino-Japanese joint venture employees. As shown in Table 1, the task-procedural value at boss level among the state company sample is similar to that of the joint venture sample, while the interpersonal value is much higher than that of its joint venture counterpart. The interpersonal value at peer level in the state firm sample is, however, lower than that of the joint venture sample, whereas the task-procedural value at peer level in the state firm sample is higher than that of the counterpart. These results indicate that an across-level compatibility of work values would be crucial for enhancing the effectiveness of leadership teams in both Chinese state companies and Sino-Japanese joint venture firms.

Event-Management Approaches

The leadership styles of managers from different cultures are largely reflected in the way they deal with important management events. Hofstede's (1984) classic study identified overseas Chinese samples from Hong Kong, Singapore, and Taiwan as high on collectivism and power distance and low to moderate on uncertainty avoidance. Cragin (1986) used the Hofstede questions with a People's Republic of China (PRC) sample and also reported high collectivism and high power distance. In contrast to Hofstede's results for other Chinese societies, however, Cragin found high PRC scores on uncertainty avoidance. These comparative studies can be used to develop predictions regarding reliance on the different sources that managers use to handle work events. PRC managers appear likely to score high on power distance, vertical collectivism, uncertainty avoidance, and Confucian work dynamism. Overseas managers are likely to have comparatively low scores on these variables. In a field study on management approaches with partner managers in 86 Chinese-overseas joint venture hotels, Smith, Peterson, and Wang (1996) used a series of events likely to be encountered in almost any managerial role. Some events represented ordinary "day-to-day" situations, while others represented less frequently encountered, potentially more significant situations. The nine management events selected were as follows:

1.   Choosing a new subordinate to work with you
2.   Rewarding your subordinates when they do good work

Table 2. Rankings of Managers from Joint Ventures on Sources of Guidance in Management

Sources	Mainland	Hong Kong	Japan	United States	Germany	United Kingdom
Formal rules	3	2	3	3	7	6
Unwritten rules	6	4	6	7	8	7
Specialists	2	8	5	8	1	4
Subordinates	7	3	1	1	2	2
Colleges	4	7	3	6	5	3
Superior	4	1	2	2	4	5
Own experience	5	6	4	4	3	1
Widespread beliefs	1	5	4	5	6	7

3. Changing work procedures used by your subordinates
4. Dealing with your subordinates when their work is unsatisfactory
5. Improving the quality of work in your department
6. Deciding how to use raw materials more effectively
7. Improving coordination with other departments
8. Improving your department's communications with senior management
9. Improving teamwork within your department

Managers from different ownerships were asked to indicate rank orders of their leadership styles, relying upon eight sources of guidance in managing the companies. Their rank orders are presented in Table 2. As it was demonstrated, there are interesting differences between Chinese state company managers and other joint venture managers, which is crucial for developing effective joint venture leadership teams. The leadership styles among managers working with different partnerships revealed three patterns: the Chinese leadership style by state firm managers, the Asian-Pacific leadership style by managers from the Hong Kong Special Administrative Region and Japan, and the European leadership style among managers from Germany and Britain who were doing business in China.

CROSS-CULTURAL MANAGEMENT COMPETENCY

Power-Sharing and Competence Utilization

Recent studies in the areas of top management competence showed that cross-cultural management skills, teamwork skills, and decision-making skills are the most significant competence elements for executives in Chinese joint venture companies. Cross-cultural management skills involve competencies in cross-cultural awareness, communication, negotiation, and conflict management. Team-work skills consist of competencies in team role clarification, team objective integration, and group member coordination. Decision-making skills are closely related to power-influence sharing in organizations. The crucial issue is to achieve a competency-position fit at various organizational levels (Wang, 1997).

In recent years, much attention has been paid to participative decision-making and leadership styles, particularly cross-cultural management decision making (Wang, 1994). In a 6-year longitudinal study on competence utilization in decision making in 10 Chinese companies in comparison with 10 British firms, decision tasks were classified into three categories: (1) long-term decisions concerning long-term development of the organization (e.g., large investment, new product development, and major technological innovations); (2) medium-term decisions relating to actions or changes at the departmental level (e.g., departmental person-nel selection, wage and bonus systems, work study, and production procedures); (3) short-term decisions concerning daily tasks of the employees (e.g., working conditions, task assignments, etc.). The differences in managers' perception of influence-power-sharing may affect coordination between the two groups (Wang & Heller, 1993).

Power Shifts across Organizational Levels

The influence in decision making across organizational levels may significantly characterize the decision-making pattern among managers in the Chinese organi-zation. The decision-making power for short-term decisions was located more at the middle- and top-management levels. For medium-term decisions, the decision-making power held a similar pattern. For the long-term decision tasks, the level above the plant became much more powerful, and the external groups also gained power. In general, there was a shift of decision-making power from the middle- and top-management levels on short-term decisions toward the industrial bureaus (administrative offices above the companies) on medium-term decisions and toward the trade union and the external groups (e.g., banks) on long-term deci-sions. The results indicated that sharing of influence and power could increase competence utilization through a high degree of managerial transparency.

Leadership Competency Structures

The objectives of leadership competency research were twofold: (1) to change the traditional way of evaluating managers and supervisors by personal impres-sions or only political affiliations, and (2) to identify a comprehensive structure of management competency for management selection and evaluation. As reported in the previous studies, top management competencies are crucial for adapting to the rapid economic, technological, and organizational changes in the world. Although a number of relevant studies on leadership and organizational decision making have been conducted in Chinese industries, few systematic studies of management competencies have been undertaken. Although the Chinese industries are deepening their economic and structural reform, the development of top management competencies is somewhat slower than the changes in organizational systems. Therefore, an urgent need exists to investigate the structure and strategies of top management competencies in Chinese organizations through field surveys and international comparisons in order to enhance cross-cultural leadership teams.

The factorial structure of management competencies reflected some Chinese characteristics in business leadership competency:

1. *Holistic competency structure.* The structure of the Chinese management competencies is more holistic and grouped into larger reliable competence factors than what has been obtained in studies abroad.
2. *Culturally general competency factors.* There appear to be three culturally general factors: change uncertainty, independence, and work satisfaction. These competency factors are similar across several cultures.
3. *Culturally specific competency factors.* There are three additional holistic competency factors: leadership skills, communication, and feedback/people performance. These three factors follow the early findings of the three-dimensional "organizational interface model" from the Chinese enterprises (Wang, 1989); that is, the personnel expertise (skills), the systems networking (communication), and the participation (involvement). In the qualitative and comparative analysis, the Chinese state-owned enterprises were compared with international joint ventures. Table 3 illustrates that senior managers from the Chinese state-owned enterprises and their counterparts

Table 3. Different Strategies Adopted by Senior Managers from the Chinese State-owned Enterprises and International Joint Ventures

State-owned Company Managers	International Joint Venture Managers
• Internally oriented mission	• Externally oriented mission
• Specific objectives	• General objectives
• Customer- and employee-oriented marketing	• Quality- and product-oriented marketing
• Product development as a challenge	• Management development as a challenge
• Confidence and responsibility	• Confidence and competitiveness
• People and commitment oriented	• Action and efficiency oriented
• Management system as hindrance	• Managerial level as hindrance
• Market competition as a concern	• Cross-cultural management as issue
• Persistent and tolerant as key personal qualities	• Decisive and progressive as key personal qualities
• Coordination and interpersona relation management as key skills	• Motivational and public relations as key skills
• Following the majority's view	• Following developmental view

from the international joint ventures adopted different strategies and demonstrated different competency patterns.

In general, managers in state-owned enterprises showed high levels of product and systems managerial competency, whereas joint venture managers indicated high levels of business and action managerial competency. In addition, interpersonal relations proved to be a key competency for managers in both state-owned enterprises and joint ventures in China.

CROSS-CULTURAL TEAM MANAGEMENT

Team Dynamics in State Companies and Joint Ventures

In their review of Chinese leadership and organization structure, Smith and Wang (1996) noted that effective leadership behavior works within the premise of Chinese collectivist society and high power distance, although the existing studies made little reference to teamwork and little is yet known as to how leaders work together as teams. In a recent large-scale study of team conflict and leadership climate, teams from both Chinese state-owned companies and joint ventures showed special dynamics in the Chinese team management. Analysis at the individual level revealed significant differences between management teams from Chinese state-owned companies and international joint ventures in areas such as group interaction, conflict resolution, value orientation, and group belongings. At the group level, there was a significant difference between Chinese state-owned companies and international joint ventures in conflict resolution strategies, while management teams from state-owned companies showed no difference from privately owned companies. The significant difference could be attributed to the cross-cultural and international business settings. Compared with teams in state-owned companies, teams from international joint ventures tended to adopt a problem-solving approach, and used conflict avoidance more and cooperative strategies less. In the service industry, teams in joint ventures adopted more competitive strategies than those in non–joint ventures; however, in the manufacturing industry, teams from non-joint ventures used more competitive strategies than teams from joint ventures.

Conflict Management in Joint Venture Leadership Teams

Conflict management styles in cross-cultural leadership teams are different across intra- and inter-cultural settings. Differences in intra-cultural team conflict management may not generalize to inter-cultural conflict. Managers working in cross-cultural teams might be expected to use different strategies to deal with team conflict among people from a different culture and those from the same culture.

One research project focused on (1) cross-cultural differences in intra- and inter-cultural conflict management, and (2) differences between inter-cultural and intra-cultural conflict. In the study, the strategies used by either American or Chinese managers working in U.S.-Chinese joint ventures were compared in their responses of handling intra-cultural and inter-cultural conflict in the cross-cultural leadership teams. Participating in this study were 142 Chinese and 142 American managers. All of them interacted frequently with different-culture managers. The study used instances of inter-cultural and intra-cultural conflict, and the solutions to the conflict, generated from field interviews among managers in Chinese-U.S. joint ventures. One case involved a same-culture manager (intra-cultural conflict) and another involved a different-culture manager (inter-cultural conflict).

The results of the study indicated that among American managers' responses to the intra-cultural team conflicts, the behavior was vengeful versus harmonious, and a harmonious response was tactful and calm. The results also reflected a passive response versus an active response to the situation.

For the American inter-cultural conflict, the results showed an active response versus a passive response and an attempt to get along (conciliatory). The results also reflected that the response was disruptive versus accommodating. The five clusters of conflict resolution were as follows:

1. Active, direct, and cooperative response: Discussion with the colleague to address the problem
2. Passive, indirect, and uncooperative response: Ceasing to share ideas
3. Conciliatory response: Working with the colleague to be more of a team
4. Actively hostile and disruptive response: Trying to get the colleague demoted
5. Passive and accommodating response: Ignoring the colleague's behavior

For the Chinese intra-cultural conflict, the results revealed a response of direct versus indirect, and of maintaining or disrupting harmony in the workplace. The four clusters of conflict resolution behaviors were as follows:

1. Direct and harmonious responses: Discussing the problem with the colleague
2. Direct and disruptive responses: Arguing with the colleague or bringing the problem to the attention of his friends
3. Indirect and disruptive responses: Retaliation
4. Indirect and harmonious responses: Telling the boss and withdrawing from the relationship

For the Chinese inter-cultural conflict, the results reflected the response of direct versus indirect and of a constructive approach to the situation. These results provide useful information about cross-cultural differences in intra-cultural and

Table 4.   Differences and Similarities among Chinese and
American Responses to Intra- and Inter-cultural Team Conflict

American Managers	Chinese Managers
Dimensions underlying intra-cultural conflict resolution behavior	
Vengeful versus harmonious	Indirect versus direct
Passive versus active	Harmonious versus disruptive
Meanings of the demensions of intra-cultural conflict resolution behavior	
Maintaining relations	Solving problems
Willing to deal with	Avoidance
Dimensions underlying inter-cultural conflict resolution behavior	
Active versus passive	indirect versus direct
Disruptive versus accommodation	Constructive versus disruptive
Meanings of the dimensions of intra-cultural conflict resolution behavior	
Achieving a solution	Contructive action
Maintaining harmony	Intensifying conflict

inter-cultural team conflict management behavior. Table 4 shows differences and
similarities among Chinese and American responses to intra- and inter-cultural
team conflict. Even using the same responses, the meanings would be different.
For example, a "direct" response to conflict among Chinese managers would
mean "putting the problem in public or a meeting" whereas it would probably
mean "talking face-to-face" individually among American managers. Those findings will prove useful to understanding the conflict resolution styles in developing
cross-cultural leadership teams.

STRATEGIES AND MODEL FOR EFFECTIVE
JOINT VENTURE LEADERSHIP TEAMS

Strategies for Developing Effective Cross-Cultural Leadership Teams

Recent Chinese studies on leadership teams provide more-systematic evidence
for effective strategies for developing cross-cultural leadership teams. Based upon
a three-dimensional model of human-computer-organization interface, three strategies were developed, applied in the action research of organization development
in 16 Chinese enterprises, and proved to be effective (Wang, 1990b). These three
strategies could also be adopted for developing cross-cultural leadership teams:

1. *Personnel Strategy.* The personnel strategy focuses upon cross-cultural
    leadership competency development through enhanced business values,
    work motivation, cross-cultural interaction, and leadership skills so as to
    achieve compatibility in values and working styles in management. This

strategy includes special management-development programs and adaptive motivational and career development schemes.

2. *Systems Strategy.* The systems strategy aims at cross-cultural leadership networking by facilitating management structural compatibility across organizational levels. This may include interventions such as establishing effective communication/feedback networks, restructuring HRM sub-systems, and setting up new mechanisms for lateral coordination among managerial functions.

3. *Organizational Strategy.* The organizational strategy emphasizes cross-cultural leadership commitment through improving team responsibility, organizational culture, and goal-directed behavior through participative management and strategic planning. This strategy could greatly enhance business relations and lead to a high level of management skill utilization and organizational commitment.

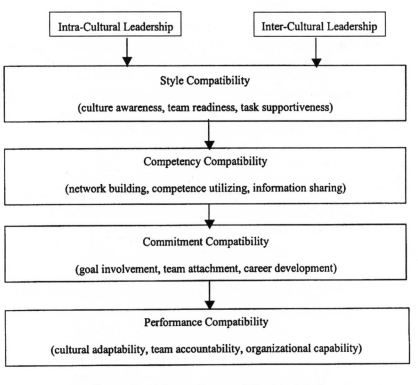

Figure 1. A Team Compatibility Model of Cross-cultural Joint Venture Leadership

In general, the above-mentioned strategies could facilitate a comprehensive development of leadership competencies for managers from both Chinese state-owned enterprises and international joint ventures in China. The key to developing cross-cultural leadership teams is to achieve a high level of team compatibility. As has been discussed, recent research on Chinese work values, leadership styles, and team management has shown that team compatibility can be differentiated into four levels. Figure 1 presents a team compatibility model of cross-cultural joint venture leadership on the basis of findings from recent Chinese organizational studies. The model is built under the framework of intra- and inter-cultural leadership and describes how team compatibility develops among cross-cultural joint venture leadership through four levels of compatibility.

1. *Style Compatibility.* Style compatibility focuses on mutually adaptive leadership styles. Specifically, it is built upon a high level of cultural awareness of the partnership, team readiness for leadership interaction, and task supportiveness for team objectives. This level of team compatibility is an interpersonal orientation in a cross-cultural management setting.
2. *Competency Compatibility.* Competency compatibility focuses on cross-cultural leadership competence. It is achieved through team network building, competence developing and utilizing, and group information sharing. This level of team compatibility is a collectivist competency orientation on the basis of style compatibility.
3. *Commitment Compatibility.* Commitment compatibility emphasizes mutual involvement in team goals and long-term organizational objectives. It is accomplished through the development of goal involvement, team attachment, and career development and is a goal orientation based upon competency compatibility.
4. *Performance Compatibility.* Performance compatibility emphasizes business performance and competitive advantage. It is achieved through cultural adaptability, team accountability, and organizational capability. This level of team compatibility is a strategy orientation based on commitment compatibility.

The team compatibility model of cross-cultural joint venture leadership provides a general framework for the development of cross-cultural leadership teams. Further research is needed to test this model thoroughly.

REFERENCES

Bond, M. H. (1996). *The handbook of Chinese psychology.* Hong Kong: Oxford University Press.
Chen, L. (1987). *Recent research on organizational psychology in China.* Proceedings of the Sixth Annual Conference of the Chinese Psychology Society, September, Hangzhou, China.

Child, J. (1988). Enterprise reform in China: Progress and problems. In M. Warner (Ed.), *Management reform in China* (pp.24-52). London: Frances Pinter Publishers.

Cragin, J. P. (1986). Management technology absorption in China. In S. R. Clegg, D. C. Dunphy, & S. G. Redding (Eds.), *The enterprise and management in East Asia*. Hong Kong: Centre of Asian Studies, University of Hong Kong.

Editorial Board. (1984). *Encyclopedia of Chinese enterprise management*. Beijing: Enterprise Management Press.

Hofstede, G. (1984). *Culture's consequences: International differences in work-related values*. London: Sage.

Smith, P. B., Peterson, M. F., & Wang, Z. M. (1996). The manager as Mediator of Alternative Meanings: A pilot study from China, the USA, and U.K. *Journal of International Business Studies, 27*(1), 115-138.

Smith, P. B., & Wang, Z. M. (1996). Chinese leadership and organizational structures. In M. H. Bond (Ed.), *Handbook of Chinese psychology*. Hong Kong: Oxford University Press.

Triandis, H. C. (1995). *Individualism and collectivism*. Boulder, CO: Westview Press.

Wang, Z. M. (1986). Worker's attribution and its effects on performance under different work responsibility systems. *Chinese Journal of Applied Psychology, 1*(2), 6-10.

Wang, Z. M. (1988). The effects of responsibility system change and group attributional training on performance: A quasi experiment in Chinese factory. *Chinese Journal of Applied Psychology, 3*(3), 7-14.

Wang, Z. M. (1989). Human-computer interface hierarchy model and strategies in systems development. *Ergonomics, 32*(11), 1391-1400.

Wang, Z. M. (1990a). Human resource management in China: Recent trends. In R. Pieper (Ed.), *Human resource management: An international comparison* (pp. 195-210). Berlin: Walter de Gruyter.

Wang, Z. M. (1990b, Spring). Action research and organization development strategies in Chinese enterprises. *Organization Development Journal*, 66-70.

Wang, Z.M. (1991). Recent developments in industrial and organizational psychology in People's Republic of China. In C. Cooper & R. T. Robertson (Eds.), *International review of industrial and organizational psychology*. London: Wiley.

Wang, Z. M. (1992). Managerial psychological strategies for Sino-foreign joint-ventures. *Journal of Managerial Psychology, 7*(3), 10-16.

Wang, Z. M. (1994). Organizational decision making and competence utilization among Chinese managers. *Journal of Managerial Psychology, 9*(7), 17-24.

Wang, Z. M. (1996). Culture, economic reform, and the role of industrial/organizational psychology in China. In M. D. Dunnette & L. M. Hough (Eds), *Handbook of industrial and organizational psychology* (2nd ed.) (pp. 689-726). Palo Alto, CA: Consulting Psychologists Press, Inc.

Wang, Z. M. (1997). Integrated personnel selection, appraisal, and decisions: A Chinese approach. In N. Anderson & P. Herriot (Eds.), *International handbook of selection and assessment*. Chichester: Wiley.

Wang, Z. M., & Fan, B. N. (1990). The task structure and information processing requirements of decision making on director responsibility systems in enterprises. *Chinese Journal of Applied Psychology, 5*(1), 13-18.

Wang, Z. M., & Heller, F. A. (1993). Patterns of power distribution in organizational decision making in Chinese and British enterprises. *International Journal of Human Resource Management, 4*(1), 113-128.

Wang, Z. M., & Satow, T. (1994). The effects of structural and organizational factors on socio-psychological orientation in joint ventures. *Journal of Managerial Psychology [Special issue]: Managing Chinese-Japanese joint ventures, 9*(4), 22-30.

TECHNOLOGY IN EXECUTIVE LEARNING

John F. Baum and Leland Russell

ABSTRACT

In this chapter, we argue that information technology has advanced to the point that executives in progressive organizations are changing the ways in which they learn. While most of these executives were trained initially in generic, expert-centered, classroom environments, they are quickly gravitating to experiential, learner-centered, on-the-job, learning environments that are not only more effective but also better tailored to the demands that are placed on them. Specifically, technology advances are enabling executives to participate in individualized, targeted development, team and peer collaboration, and just-in-time knowledge acquisition. The major unresolved question is not whether technological tools are adequate to support this fundamental change, but rather how much time and support is needed to enable executives to take full advantage of technology-based learning.

In times of great change, learners inherit the earth while the learned find themselves beautifully equipped to deal with a world that no longer exists.

—Eric Hoffer.

Advances in Global Leadership, Volume 1, pages 355-369.
Copyright © 1999 by JAI Press Inc.
All rights of reproduction in any form reserved.
ISBN: 0-7623-0505-3

More than ever before, executives in large multinational and global firms face the daunting task of learning how to cope with rapidly changing business environments and markets. In a recent review of the past 20 years of leadership development, Hollenbeck and McCall (1998) concluded that much has changed in the science, art, and practice in this important field. Although still unsure about the magnitude and staying power of the changes, they conclude that "the trend in leadership development will be toward more individualized approaches, tailored both to the growth needs of the individual executives as determined by feedback and coaching methodologies, and to the business needs of the organization" (p. 31).

In this chapter, we argue that more-individualized learning approaches are being enabled by a new generation of information technologies. Because these technologies are evolving so quickly, we also address some key questions: What is new? What is significant? What are the implications for executive learning? While we conclude that the implications are profound, we stop short of declaring that traditional learning methods oriented for the classroom or for face-to-face communication are obsolete, soon to be replaced by a computer and a pocketful of CD-ROMs, intra- and Internet addresses, and other exotic toys. We believe that technological advances in learning tools are now sufficient to enable executives to reach the lofty goal of being continuous learners in a world of constant change.

After a brief review of what we know about how modern executives learn, we explore the contributions of technology to the learning process in three organizing themes:

- *Individualized, Targeted Development*—technology to develop and deliver remotely courses, lectures, assessments, feedback, coaching, and other learning events
- *Team and Peer Collaboration*—technology to support geographically dispersed colleagues, project teams, and information-sharing networks
- *Just-in-Time Knowledge*—technology to access company and competitive data, as well as other forms of knowledge required for informed decisions

HOW EXECUTIVES LEARN

A growing body of evidence suggests that the center of gravity is shifting quickly from generic, expert-centered, classroom development to experiential, learner-centered, on-the-job learning for executives. This shift is a response to findings that show clearly that executives learn best from their job-related experiences (McCall, Lombardo, & A. Morrison, 1988; McCauley, Ruderman, Ohlott, & Morrow, 1994; R. G. Morrison & Hock, 1986; Wexley & Baldwin, 1986). Although there are individual differences in the rates of learning from experience (McCauley, 1986), executives experience strong stimuli to learn and develop while performing their jobs. In response to this realization, executive development programs are placing much more emphasis on action learning, planned rotational assignments, 360 feedback, executive coaching, mentoring, and various forms of computer-assisted learning (Hollenbeck & McCall, 1998).

With experience on the job as the foundation, it seems reasonable to expect a fundamental evolution in executive learning from more traditional methods to newer, technology-based tools and methods that are in concert with the lifestyles of executives. This evolution includes the following:

NOT ONLY	*BUT ALSO*
Preparing for Career	Continuous, Lifelong Learning
Classes, Workshops	On-the-Job, Action Learning
Fixed Times, Locales	Access Anytime, Anyplace
Physical Classrooms	Virtual, Desktop Delivery
Standard Curriculum	Customizable Curriculum
Open Enrollment	Individual Development Plans
Generic Management Skills	Business-Specific Competencies
Local, One Language	Worldwide, Multiple Languages
Narrow Focus	Knowledge Navigation

These changing learning needs can be summed up in one sentence: to be competitive in today's environment, executives need more immediate, practical, and precise approaches to learning. The current approaches alone are no longer sufficient because they fail to help executives keep pace with their rapidly evolving marketplaces and rapidly changing business scenarios. They must compete in a world that operates on much shorter cycle times, sometimes referred to as "Internet Time." This very different, dynamic business environment requires us to raise the bar for executive learning.

THE ROLE OF TECHNOLOGY

If executives learn best by doing, how can learning become a more salient and seamless part of daily activities? Although learning may be unconscious and often unacknowledged, it naturally occurs when an executive is gathering, reviewing, and reflecting on information to make decisions and solve problems. It also naturally occurs when he or she collaborates with colleagues in a team setting or with peers in knowledge-sharing networks. This line of thought leads us to a broader perspective on executive learning, one in which the role of technology can be significant. Technology provides better support for the executive's natural learning activity—decision making and collaboration. Technology also enhances targeted development methods, such as action learning, simulations, 360 feedback, and coaching. The major unknown is how fast executives can and will incorporate technology-based tools into their existing learning styles to take full advantage of the opportunity that is now available to them.

Executive interest in learning about technology is growing. Chief information officers are spending much more of their time explaining the benefits and realities of information technologies to their chief executive officers (CEOs), business unit managers, and top production people. Technology is becoming a strategic weapon, and executives want a better understanding of how it affects their lives and their business success.

There is also growing interest in technology among executive development professionals. Jim Bolt, a pioneer in executive development, has tracked trends in the field over the past decade. In his most recent study, aimed at executive development professionals, Bolt (1997) found that two important technology themes have emerged: (1) the need to help executives keep pace with technological advances, and (2) the need to use information technology to enhance executive learning. Bolt identified three factors behind these themes. First is the need for faster development of executive education programs. For example, Motorola University adopted a goal of reducing cycle time from 6 months to 6 weeks. Second is the potential to reduce learning costs, which can be considerable when senior executives are brought together for in-person workshops. Third is the possibility of faster learning and less time away from work.

Larger historical trends are driving the interests of executives in information technology. In the past few years, in addition to continuing breakthroughs in computer hardware and software, we have witnessed the mass market acceptance of the Internet. In *The Digital Economy,* Tapscott (1996) pointed out that "a new medium of human communications is emerging, one that may prove to surpass all previous revolutions—the printing press, the telephone, the television—in its impact on our economic and social life" (p. xiii). The combination of ever-increasing computing power and connectivity creates unprecedented possibilities that affect almost every executive in every industry.

TECHNOLOGY FOR TARGETED DEVELOPMENT

Information technology is being used to remotely deliver courses and lectures, as well as personal assessments, feedback, and coaching. We refer to these activities as *targeted development* because they are usually designed for a target audience with specific learning outcomes in mind. In this learning domain, technology applications include computer-based training (CBT), on-line (Internet/intranet) courses, on-line assessment and feedback, and coaching on-line or via videoconferencing, video-based or video-conferenced classes.

A number of leading corporations and university business schools are successfully using combinations of these applications in their executive development programs. One of the more innovative examples is Xerox's Leading the Enterprise program, which won the United States Distance Learning Association first-place award in 1995 (L. Henderson, personal communication, July 8, 1997). The program was initially created because Xerox was not achieving "sustainable behavioral change" with its traditional executive development programs. Although the existing programs were considered state-of-the-art and were receiving excellent participant feedback, the learning did not appear to stick (i.e., transfer back to the job). Leading the Enterprise was designed to address this shortcoming.

What is new about the Xerox program is its use of distance learning technology to support action learning among approximately 100 executives (85 percent in the United States; 15 percent in Egypt, South America, and Mexico). The executives used a private network to receive and send assignments, ask questions, get feedback, and communicate with other participants and with their facilitators. The program also included three, 2-day face-to-face meetings and one 4-day meeting. It was designed to provide managers with (1) a broader perspective of the global environment and the industry within which Xerox operates, and (2) the ability to apply strategic analysis and planning to opportunities and problems locally and across the organization.

The four program modules averaged 8 to 10 weeks each. The first module, Preparing for Self-Directed Learning, oriented the participants to the learning medium and methodology. The next three modules covered strategic leadership issues, including situation analysis, issue/opportunity framing, and preparing/presenting the business case. The modules were designed for the target audience and focused on specific skills and knowledge: developing strategic thinking skills, gaining a broader business perspective, building and presenting a strategic business case, understanding leadership and their own leadership ability, and participating fully in a community of learners.

Sun Microsystems has an unusually sophisticated intranet infrastructure that provides another example of the innovative use of technology (Milano, 1997). Sun has already delivered more than 70 modules of on-line courses. What is new here is the interactive Web-based learning environment. Java "applets" (mini-applications) are used to animate pages, track usage, and calculate test results. Learners are guided via curriculum maps and graphical pathways, customized to their needs and interests. Learners can also leave bookmarks to make it easy to pick up where they left off when they return to the site. Sun's Web-based approach is not only user-friendly, it is also efficient from an administrative standpoint. Paper catalogs were eliminated in 1995, and all courses (traditional and virtual) are now listed in a fully searchable on-line catalog. Participants register on-line and automatically receive pre- and post-course materials. Billing is also automatic. Course results are stored and can be cross-referenced with performance data.

Many university business schools are also using the Internet and other technologies to make it easier for executives to participate in their programs. For example, the Executive Development Centre at Queen's University (Kingston, Ontario) employs videoconferencing and the Internet to deliver its executive MBA program. The goal is to create a context in which executives can learn more efficiently and effectively with the support of technology. Students still attend "real" classes on Friday and Saturday every other weekend, but the majority of the learning is computer-based. For those who are not computer-literate, there is a 4-day pre-course training program to develop the basic computer skills needed to participate.

Duke University offers one of the most innovative approaches to getting the MBA on-line. Professors teach via lectures on CD-ROM and provide supplemental interactive audio and video materials via the Internet. A class of approximately 40 students at remote locations discusses the lectures on-line via E-mail, bulletin boards, and live chats. Like Xerox and Queen's University, Duke still includes in its program design some face-to-face time with the professors and other students. There are class meetings at the beginning and end of the program and on-site visits to Eastern Europe, China, and South America.

Initial reports suggest that participants find the on-line learning aspect of these programs to be successful (Bartlett, 1997). Many of the Duke students reported that they spend up to 30 hours a week on-line. A Ford executive who logs on frequently from his home in California was surprised and fascinated by what can be accomplished on-line. He went further to say that "the people who don't think this will have a big impact on the way we learn, I would liken to the makers of buggy whips" (p. 77). While empirically sound research is limited, Alavi, Yoo, and Vogel (1997) found that the use of information technology in an MBA setting significantly enriched the learning experience of students and improved faculty development.

But the future of technology in targeted development is not found exclusively in corporate and university business school settings. There are learning innovations in the commercial marketplace that are also worth noting. One example is "learning on demand" (an a la carte approach) in which learners "attend" courses or parts of courses on-line, mixing and matching as they see fit. Although not yet addressing executive-level topics, DigitalThink, a San Francisco–based firm specializing in Web-based learning, is a good benchmark for "learning on demand." Learners can "attend" all or parts of a variety of classes 24 hours a day, 7 days a week, from any Web connection worldwide. Courses feature easy-to-digest lessons, hands-on exercises, and short quizzes with immediate analysis of answers. They also include live seminars and scheduled on-line time with instructors, live and quick-turnaround curriculum support from trained tutors, live chats with fellow classmates, topic discussions, audio clips from instructors, links to related information on the Internet, and details about important off-line information. The company has exclusive agreements with several technology firms to provide professional and personal skills curricula customized for Web delivery. Their on-line instructors are widely recognized experts and many are best-selling authors. The instructors are supported by specially trained on-line tutors who are available to students—frequently in real time, as they progress through their courses.

On-line assessment and coaching is another area where innovation is occurring in the commercial marketplace. Ashridge Online, in the United Kingdom, provides a range of learning resources and expertise, via Internet or their clients' corporate intranets, including a competency-based assessment tool and on-line competency guides. Leadership Online, a service of the Jones Internet Channel, is a CD-ROM multimedia tool that combines both video and text to deliver leadership coaching right to the desktop. At one's fingertips are five top consultants speaking on a wide range of topics pertaining to leadership, as well as access to other valuable resources on leadership. These are only a few of the examples that show us the shape of the future in targeted development—a dynamic mix of electronic learning tools to enhance and in some instances replace traditional approaches to course delivery, performance assessments, and coaching.

TECHNOLOGY FOR COLLABORATION

Collaboration is the second domain for technology applications in executive learning. This includes collaborating with colleagues on project teams and with peers in knowledge-sharing networks. But why should collaboration be considered a form of learning? Malcolm Knowles has continually emphasized that discovery and curiosity are critical to the learning process (Knowles, Holton, & Swanson, 1998). When collaboration is viewed as shared creation and discovery, we see that learning and collaboration go hand in hand. As executives engage in more team-based decisions involving peers, subordinates, customers, and suppliers, the need for effective collaboration is much more obvious.

Collaborative Strategies (1996) conducted a recent benchmark study that found that many leading organizations believe collaboration is critical to future success. Many of these organizations have been exploring a wide range of collaborative technologies. What is most notable about the study is the importance of the human factors in collaboration and not the technology itself. The following points were reported about the organizations that have actually employed collaborative technology successfully:

- Most of the benchmarked companies were leaders in their industry and wanted to stay that way; most realized that they had to compete globally and that collaboration was necessary in order to achieve this goal.
- They were innovative in their approach, trying new technologies and processes to solve difficult business problems and encouraging collaboration between the company and customers or suppliers.
- Many of the benchmarked firms were experimenting with compensation and reward structures to encourage collaboration.

- The more support and use of the technologies by top executives, the more successful the project or the company was, but lower-level managers collaborate much more frequently and much better than upper-level executives.

Collaborative technology has become "mission critical" in many organizations where speed of execution is the essence of competitiveness. For example, Andy Grove, CEO at Intel, stated the case for speed by pointing out that in the future there will be two types of organizations: the quick and the dead. Technology can be a major facilitator in helping an organization to move quickly, especially if it is designed to enhance executive collaboration.

Unfortunately, the focus often tends to be on developing technology applications rather than developing collaborative relationships. Schrage (1990) clarified this point by stating, "As a general rule, too many organizations have spent too much time obsessing on the information they want their networks to carry and far too little time on the effective relationships that those networks should create and support. This is a grave strategic error" (p. 2). Having noted the importance of effective human relationships, let us look at how technology can support and enhance electronic collaboration in an organization. Given the dizzying array of choices, we find it helpful to use the organizing framework developed by the Institute for the Future (1990), in which technology is examined through the frames of "time" and "place":

- *Same Time, Same Place Collaboration.* We can make face-to-face meetings more productive by using technology to process ideas and build shared meaning. For example, an interactive meeting tool can allow 300 participants to respond to questions, conduct informed discussions, and receive instant, complete documentation of the proceedings.
- *Same Time, Different Place Collaboration.* We can move beyond the traditional conference call and collaborate in real time via videoconferencing, whiteboards, and application sharing.
- *Different Time, Different Place Collaboration.* We can share ad hoc thoughts, edited documents, and graphic images via E-mail, on-line discussions, file transfers, and shared servers. Teams can improve productivity via "groupware" programs for shared calendaring, workflow, and publishing. All of this allows us to bypass barriers like lack of physical proximity and the need to synchronize schedules.

Technologies that enable collaboration have been around for quite some time. However, trends in the marketplace today are redefining the ways that many of them are being used and are making them more valuable than ever before. *Lotus Notes,* the most mature and entrenched "groupware" product, is an application that allows users to easily create and synchronize shared databases. The practical uses run the gamut from a shared phone directory to a massive sales-tracking or inventory system. Through customization, Lotus Notes can also link to corporate databases and transport data around a network in the form of documents, video, and audio. The downside of Lotus Notes is its cost and complexity. It is also a very resource-intensive application that requires significant training time on the part of end-users. Although it is an effective product for enterprise management, especially since it is now owned by IBM, Lotus Notes has fallen short in flexibility and ease of use. Recently, however, Lotus has made Notes more user-friendly by adapting it for intranets and Web browsers.

A new generation of collaborative technologies has exploded onto the scene in the past year, and much more is on the way. This new generation is designed from the ground up to take advantage of the World Wide Web. One example is an off-the-shelf product called eRoom, currently being used by BellCore to create a learning community around particular topics. Karen Goellar (personal communication, November 10, 1997) refers to eRoom as a "wrapper" technology (mediating tool) that can be used to gather and coordinate other collaboration tools. What makes eRoom unique is that it seamlessly integrates desktop applications with the Internet and intranet. It is also been designed to be very easy to set up and manage. Since it does not require users to learn anything new, eRoom is an application that busy executives will find useful. Imagine the executive who is developing a new product that requires a business plan, capitalization, staffing of a team, and a marketing plan. Using conventional approaches, these tasks are accomplished by conducting a number of face-to-face meetings and many one-on-one and one-on-many e-mails flying around the organization. E-mails and documents are exchanged but not easily maintained in a common database (without substantial information technology [IT] support). What happens when a new person later joins the team? With a product like eRoom, ideas and documents can be easily captured and archived for future reference. eRoom brings executive work teams together in a common electronic workspace, giving them a place to share files, vote, and discuss their progress. It is ideal for the team that comes together quickly and is composed of people who are in different organizations or different geographical locations, many of whom are not necessarily tied into the same technology infrastructure. The only thing they have in common is the Internet, which they use to connect to their eRoom (via a Web browser).

NetMeeting, a Microsoft product, is another practical, easy-to-use Web-based application. Companies such as Texas Instruments (TI) use this product extensively for real-time meetings with colleagues at different locations or even at remote sites (Bruce Amendt, personal communication, September 2, 1996). They have found that it allows teams to hold shorter meetings, more frequently, while also reducing travel costs. NetMeeting is not a videoconferencing tool, which requires expensive equipment and extensive bandwidth. It is a "data-conferencing" tool. All that is needed is a PC, a telephone line, and Internet access. Some of the product features that TI ranked in the order of their usefulness are:

- *Viewing Documents:* Everyone sees the same PowerPoint slides, Excel spreadsheet, and so forth, but only one person runs the application. This works with any Windows application, including non-Microsoft ones.
- *Sharing Applications:* Meeting participants can take turns editing the same document.
- *File Transfer:* By dragging a file into the NetMeeting window, everyone in the meeting receives a copy of the file in the background.
- *Chat:* Comments can be typed for viewing real-time by others or making meeting notes that can be saved to a local file.
- *Whiteboard:* Existing screen images can be drawn, typed, or annotated.
- *Voice Communication:* Due to the bandwidth limitations of the Internet, this is practical only across the LAN/WAN network. A regular telephone call works best for the audio portion of the conference.

Council is a collaborative application designed for real-time, face-to-face meetings (Same Time, Same Place). It is useful in large-scale meetings or meetings where the stakes are high and the time is short (Lenny Lind, personal communication, July 3, 1997). Council provides a highly interactive, intuitive "thinking together" format. Participants are linked via laptops, which they use to input their ideas and prioritize themes. They tend to reach a common understanding of key issues faster and the dialogue also tends to go deeper. Council also makes "talking head" presentations more interactive. The presenter lectures for a half an hour and then gets a reading from the entire audience by asking questions using the system. "What are the high points of what you just heard?" "What are you confused about?" "What do you want to know more about?" The next portion of the presentation then focuses directly on the gaps and concerns the group raised.

The real value of Council is that it leverages learning in a dramatic way. As soon as participants start seeing their peers' ideas popping up on their laptop screen, the learning process begins. First, they learn about their peers, because they have direct access to the thoughts of the entire group. Second, they learn about where their own ideas fit in with the rest of the group. Because the input is anonymous, people tend to say what they think, emphasizing the importance of honesty and candor. Third, they learn the value of sharing deeper thoughts than are normally construed as "acceptable."

While the tools we have reviewed here are ready for executives to use now, collaborative technologies in general are still in their infancy. We are just beginning to explore their role in shaping the collaborative process. But it is almost certain that they will play an increasingly important and effective role in supporting team and peer collaboration.

TECHNOLOGY FOR JUST-IN-TIME KNOWLEDGE

The third domain for technology in executive learning is knowledge that is available when it is needed to make decisions and solve problems. This encompasses the tools and processes to access company and competitive data and other forms of knowledge required for making the best decisions possible. Before we look at the executive's perspective on just-in-time knowledge, let us put it into context. Knowledge is the fundamental fuel of every organization. It drives the quality of executive decisions, as well as the organization's potential for innovation. Knowledge is, therefore, the key to competitiveness and sustainability.

Today there is a growing interest in the art and science of acquiring, developing, and managing organizational knowledge. This challenge requires new technologies and new processes to capture the two forms of knowledge that Nonaka and Takeuchi (1995) identified in their groundbreaking work. Explicit knowledge sets the general rules; it encompasses the visible forms of knowledge that are easily captured and tend to be communicated in formal and systematic ways—for example, operating procedures, manufacturing process, and chemical formulas. Implicit (or tacit) knowledge is informal "know-how" and mental models, the less visible forms of knowledge that are often difficult to capture and tend to be communicated, if at all, in informal, ad hoc ways. "Knowledge management" has become the label du jour that spans the technology and processes to accomplish this objective. The goal of knowledge management is getting the right knowledge to the right people at the right time so they can make the best decisions.

Several progressive companies have approached this challenge by creating best-practice-sharing programs. For example, Texas Instruments has established a team of champions who advocate best-practice sharing in their own business organizations and offer guidance to the corporate Office of Best Practices. On the front line are about 150 facilitators located at plants around the world who focus on identifying and documenting best practices and brokering them among the business units. What is a best practice at TI? Cindy Johnson, Director for Collaboration and Knowledge Sharing, explained that a best practice comes from someone who has implemented it and determined that they benefitted from it. Now they want to share it with others (personal communication, July 8, 1997).

Technology played a crucial role in the success of the TI's best-practices program. A corporate intranet Web site, named Share It, provides Web browser access to a central best-practices database. It is accessible to all of the company's 25,000 Intranet users worldwide and can be searched via either full text or keywords using state-of-the-art search engines. The database is also hot-linked to another internal Web site, TI Tomorrow, that was created to catalyze and support fast-cycle innovation. TI Tomorrow contains five sections—Innovate, Explore, Connect, Learn, and Envision—designed to support innovators in real time as they explore and develop their ideas. Each section contains content modules featuring practical tools and techniques, on-line discussion groups, a menu of on-line newsletters, and key reference articles including historical and current events. In addition to these 40-plus modules, the site sections contain hotlinks to other non-TI innovation Web sites around the world.

TI Tomorrow's knowledge navigation system is designed for easy, intuitive access to all levels of the site. An executive can click on an icon to connect with colleagues on a particular project or browse through various innovation topics. For example, clicking on a "Dialogues" icon logs the user into ongoing, on-line conversations in specific subject areas. Selecting the "Stories" icon opens a database of narratives about the successful innovations of other organizations, as well as those at Texas Instruments. Clicking on the "Toolkit" icon accesses a database of practical tools and techniques. John Byers, Associate Director for Collaboration and Knowledge Sharing at TI, believes that the architecture of such Web sites is crucial. The key is to begin with an overarching view of what knowledge exists, where it needs to flow, and how it can be creatively packaged. The end goal, says Byers, is to "help TI innovators and executives to explore high-tech market opportunities, build on-line teams, perform technical research, and move through the process of turning ideas into profitable businesses as fast as possible" (John Byers, personal communication, July 2, 1997).

IBM's Global Services Group is also establishing a foundation for knowledge sharing and reuse under the label of Intellectual Capital Management. Dr. Kuan-Tsae Huang, Director of Global Intellectual Capital Management at IBM, explained that intellectual capital consists of "information, knowledge, assets, experience, wisdom, and/or ideas that are structured to enable sharing for reuse and to deliver value to customers and shareholders" (Huang, 1997, p. 3) He offers these examples of intellectual capital:

- Best practices, know-how, and heuristic rules
- Patterns, software code, business processes, and models
- Architectures, technology, and business frameworks
- Project experiences (e.g., proposals, work plans, reports, meeting agendas, presentations, designs, instructional materials, process maps)
- Tools used to implement a process (e.g., checklists, surveys, questionnaires, models, templates)

IBM is creating a knowledge-based enterprise that values and employs global collaboration and knowledge sharing. To accomplish this, the company is developing processes, leveraging technology, and building competency networks. These processes provide systematic, efficient, and effective methods of capturing and retrieving information. The key, according to Huang (1997), is ensuring "consistent standards and methodology to enable reuse by any team, any group, any where in the world" (p.7). This is no mean feat in an organization the size of IBM, and it is one of the reasons why technologies such as Lotus Notes and their intranet play such important roles in providing an electronic infrastructure that can be deployed and accessed globally.

IBM's approach is new and interesting because of the central role of competency *networks*—communities of practice that relate to a particular business issue but cut across organizational silos. IBM has 35 competency networks, with approximately 10,000 users, who access and utilize their intellectual capital, as well as provide feedback or submit potential intellectual capital for sharing. Each network has a dedicated "competency team"—subject experts who determine how the knowledge bases for their network will be published, referenced, reused, and updated. The technology enabling these networks is an intranet Web site, ICM AssetWeb. It utilizes the Lotus Domino platform and can be accessed via Lotus Notes or a Web browser. ICM AssetWeb, like Texas Instruments' TI Tomorrow, is designed for easy navigation, enhanced search capabilities, and a structured framework for issue-based discussions.

The cutting-edge efforts of companies such as Texas Instruments and IBM show us the shape of the future. It is a world of instant electronic access to practical, precise knowledge, when and where it is needed. But getting there will require focused effort because the reality of today is information anarchy. Moving from information anarchy to state-of-the-art, knowledge-based enterprises will require leadership. Senior executives must raise the bar in terms of their own expectations and their own vision about what is possible. In a world that operates on "Internet Time," they must demand that their knowledge architects tame the Internet. They should expect these architects to create intuitive pathways to access the knowledge they need to continually improve their performance.

GETTING DOWN TO ELECTRONIC BUSINESS

Tapscott (1996) pointed out that new technology and business strategies are transforming not only business processes but also the ways in which products and services are created and marketed, the structure and goals of the enterprise, the dynamics of competition, and many of the rules for business success. The bottom-line message for every executive is simple: it is time to get down to electronic business. We are now living in a networked world, a global marketplace dynamically connected by the Internet. But the journey does not end here. The Internet is a catalytic historical event, a cause set in motion. In very short order, its ripple effects will affect economics and society in many fundamental, unanticipated ways. To understand the long-range significance of the Internet, consider what happened with the automobile.

When the automobile was introduced, the first ripple of consequences related to new ways of manufacturing. Then came the second ripple of consequences with the development of highways and service stations to support the growing number of automobiles. The third ripple of consequences produced suburbs, commuting, complex traffic laws, and air pollution. What are the ripples of consequences of the Internet? How will the Internet impact the rate of change? Obviously, the tempo will continue to increase and cycle times will continue to decrease. In the early twenty-first century, we may look back and long for the leisurely pace of the late 1990s.

When change is the challenge, learning is one of the solutions. To sustain success in a rapidly changing environment, the rate of learning must equal or exceed the rate of change. Thomas Jefferson said that knowledge is power, knowledge is safety, and knowledge is happiness. This is true, with one caveat. The knowledge we possess must be relevant to our current circumstances. New circumstances require new knowledge. For executives to keep pace with rapidly evolving marketplaces and rapidly changing business scenarios and new circumstances, they need more immediate, practical, and precise approaches to learning. The current approaches alone are no longer adequate. But, as we pointed out earlier, success will require more than simply using new technologies to do the same things we are already doing. We will need to fundamentally rethink the issue of executive learning and explore what is now possible through technology.

IF WE BUILD IT, WILL THEY COME?

Despite our best efforts to make the case for the seemingly inevitable revolution in executive learning, we are left with the remaining question of what changes in the mind-sets of many executives will have to occur to enable them to take full advantage of the learning technology that is available to them. A declining segment of the executive population is still computer illiterate and thereby excluded from meaningful participation. The miniaturization of hardware and the advancements in user-friendly software provide strong incentives for this group to come on board. The long and tedious learning curve to proficient use is being reduced by the user-friendly interfaces of the newer learning tools, thereby allowing the user to concentrate on learning objectives rather than on the tools themselves. The more substantive obstacle seems to be the lingering belief among many executives that "real" learning consists of passive, expert-centered, event-oriented activities. Without discounting the importance of person-to-person interaction in the learning process, technology-based learning can be a meaningful supplement to these more traditional, and often powerful, learning methods. Our belief is that when these executives get a taste of what can be achieved through the use of tools that emphasize individualism, tailoring, and immediate business relevance, there will be no turning back. The underlying premise that experience truly is the best teacher makes us optimistic that the technology-based learning tools that can be delivered to the desktop have a bright future in the development of current and future executives.

REFERENCES

Alavi, M,. Yoo, Y., & Vogel, D. R. (1997). Using information technology to add value to management education. *Academy of Management Journal, 40,* 1310-1333.

Bartlett, T. (1997). *Business Week,* October 20, 1997, 77-80.

Bolt, J. F. (1997). *Executive development trends survey.* Unpublished study, San Diego, CA.

Collaborative Strategies. (1996). *Electronic collaboration on the Internet and intranets* [On-line]. Available: http://www.collaborate.com/publications/internet.html.

Hollenbeck, G. P., & McCall, M. W., Jr. (1998). Leadership development: Contemporary practice. Draft of a chapter to be published in A. K. Kraut (Ed.), *Changing concepts and practices for human resources management: Contributions from industrial/organizational psychology.* San Francisco: Jossey-Bass.

Huang, K. T. (1997). *Capitalizing collective knowledge for winning, execution, and teamwork.* Unpublished white paper, IBM Corporation.

Institute for the Future. (1990). *Groupware: The intersection of technology and teams.* Unpublished manuscript.

Knowles, M., Holton III, E. F., & Swanson, R. A. (1998). *The adult learner: The definitive classic in adult education and human resource development.* Houston: Gulf Publishing.

McCall, M. W., Jr., Lombardo, M., & Morrison, A. (1988). *Lessons of experience.* New York: Lexington Books.

McCauley, C. (1986). *Developmental experiences in managerial work: A literature review* (Technical Report No. 26). Greensboro, NC: Center for Creative Leadership.

McCauley, C. D., Ruderman, M. N., Ohlott, P. J., & Morrow, J. E. (1994). Assessing the developmental components of managerial jobs. *Journal of Applied Psychology, 79,* 544-560.

Milano, D. (1997). *Interactivity in action: Case studies of multimedia masterworks, innovative games, & other successful interactive products.* San Francisco, CA: Miller Freeman Books.

Morrison, R. G., & Hock, R. R. (1986). Career building: Learning from cumulative work experience. In D. T. Hall (Ed.), *Career development in organizations* (pp. 236-273). San Francisco: Jossey-Bass.

Nonaka, I., & Takeuchi, H. (1995). *The knowledge-creating company.* Oxford: Oxford University Press.

Schrage, M. (1990). *Shared minds: The new technologies of collaboration.* New York: Random House.

Tapscott, D. (1996). *The digital economy.* New York: McGraw-Hill.

Wexley, K. N., & Baldwin, T. T. (1986). Management development. *Journal of Management, 12,* 277-294.

ABOUT THE EDITORS

M. Jocelyne Gessner, Ph.D., is the General Manager of the Austin office of Personnel Decisions International (PDI). Dr. Gessner has over 15 years' consulting experience in a variety of organizations. Although her experience covers a variety of areas, including performance appraisal, individual assessment and development, assessment centers, and training, her expertise is primarily in leadership and managerial development. Dr. Gessner is especially interested in organizational effectiveness, which she sees as "the ultimate goal of any human resource process." Since joining PDI, her focus has been on using assessment, training programs, and 360-degree measurement tools to help managers and organizations use feedback more effectively in order to address both individual growth and strategic goals, as well as assisting leadership teams in the development of more effective collaboration strategies.

Dr. Gessner has consulted with a variety of industries, including computing, hospitality, banking, insurance, petrochemical, communications, and health care. Before coming to PDI, Dr. Gessner was on the faculty at the University of Houston for 6 years and is currently an Adjunct Professor. She taught courses in both applied psychology and business at the University of Baltimore and the University of Maryland.

Dr. Gessner received both her M.A. and Ph.D. in Industrial/Organizational Psychology from the University of Maryland. She received her B.A. in Psychology with a minor in Business from Vanderbilt University.

Val Arnold serves as Senior Vice President, Executive Consulting Services with Personnel Decisions International (PDI). During his 17 years at PDI, he has specialized in the assessment, development, and coaching of executives and their teams while leading the development of PDI's individual assessment and coaching businesses. His interest in the leader's character, integrity, values, and the constructive use of power shapes his succession management work with boards of directors and top executives.

Dr. Arnold's consulting experience ranges from small, family-owned businesses to Fortune 500 companies. He has extensive international consulting experience working with executives and their teams in North and South America, Europe, the Pacific Rim, and Africa. An accomplished speaker and respected authority on international executive assessment and on developing executive leadership through individual coaching, he has presented his work on these topics to a wide range of business and professional groups. He trains PDI's growing global network of consultants in assessment skills as well as presenting on the topic of assessment to human resources professionals around the world.

Before joining PDI, Dr. Arnold managed executive development at a Fortune 100 company, designing its first executive succession management program. A licensed psychologist, Dr. Arnold completed his Ph.D. in Counseling Psychology at the University of Minnesota in 1976.

William H. Mobley, Ph.D., is Vice President and General Manager of Greater China for Personnel Decisions International (PDI), and President and Managing Director of Personnel Decisions International Global Research Consortia, Ltd. (GRC). He resides in Dallas, Texas, and in Hong Kong while providing management and organizational research and consulting services for multinational firms doing business throughout Asia and the world.

Dr. Mobley is best known for his research, writing, and consulting on employee motivation, turnover, and selection, and international and strategic human resources management. His previous positions include serving as Corporate Manager of Human Resources Research and Planning for PPG Industries; Director for of the Center for Management and Organizational Research at the University of South Carolina; Dean of the College of Business Administration at Texas A & M University and, from 1988 to 1993, as President of Texas A & M University.

In addition to participating in several professional societies, Dr. Mobley currently serves on the Board of Directors of Pool Energy Services Company, Inc; Medici Medical Corporation, Inc.; and the AMMA Foundation. He has served as a member of President Bush's U.S. Commission on Minority Business Development and as U.S. Co-Chair of the Trilateral Task Force for North American Higher Education Cooperation. He currently serves on the U.S. National Committee of the Pacific Economic Cooperation Council (PECC).

Dr. Mobley earned his B.A. in psychology and economics from Denison University in Ohio in 1963 and his Ph.D. in industrial-organizational psychology from the University of Maryland, College Park in 1971. He is a Fellow of the Society for Industrial-Organizational Psychology.

ABOUT THE CONTRIBUTORS

Nancy J. Adler is currently a Professor in the Faculty of Management at McGill University in Montreal, Canada. She received her B.A. in economics, and M.B.A., and Ph.D. in management from the University of California at Los Angeles (UCLA). She Dr. Adler conducts research and consults on strategic international human resource management, global women leaders and managers, international negotiating, culturally synergistic problem solving, and global organization development. Dr. Adler has consulted with major global companies and government organizations on projects in Europe, North and South America, the Middle East, and Asia. She has taught Chinese executives in the People's Republic of China, held the Citicorp Visiting Doctoral Professorship at the University of Hong Kong, and taught executive seminars at INSEAD in France and Bocconi University in Italy. She has also authored more than 70 articles, published *Women in Management Worldwide* (1988) *Competitive Frontiers: Women Managers in a Global Economy* (1994), and *International Dimensions of Organizational Behavior* (3rd ed., 1997), and produced the film *A Portable Life*. Dr. Adler has received many distinguished awards including ASTD's International Leadership Award, SIETAR's Outstanding Senior Interculturalist Award, the YWCA's Femme de Mérite (Woman of Distinction) Award, the Sage Award for scholarly contributions to management, and McGill University's first Distinguished Teaching Award in Management (she has since received the award again).

John F. Baum is currently Professor of Management in the College of Business Administration at the University of North Texas in Denton, Texas. He is also the executive director of the North Texas Enterprise Center (NTEC), a university-based center providing consulting, training, and networking support to small and medium-sized firms in the North Texas region. Prior to this assignment, Dr. Baum was a Vice President with PDI Global Research Consortia in Irving, Texas. The majority of Dr. Baum's career was spent with Texas Instruments, where he headed up the Human Resources Development function and directed the Strategic Learning Center. After receiving his Ph.D. from the University of Wisconsin, Madison, Dr. Baum began his career teaching in the Krannert Graduate School of Management at Purdue University in West Lafayette, Indiana.

Sandra Bontems-Wackens is currently employed as an Attachee by the Commission communauteire francaise. Until 1998, she worked as a Consultant at Personnel Decisions International Brussels to develop Selection Systems and Competency Models. She has experience in the areas of job and function analysis, interview and test battery design, developmental feedback to individuals, and test validation. She also conducts individualized assessments for the selection and development of managers and runs Assessment and Development Centres. Holding a license in Industrial, Social and Organisational Psychology from the University of Brussels, Sandra gained a commendation for her thesis on the effect of employee participation on organizational culture. Prior to joining PDI, she worked in the field of global communication.

Barbara D. Clark, Ph.D., is a psychologist and consultant with Relational Leadership Systems. She is Adjunct Faculty at Texas A & M University in Psychology and Industrial/Organizational Psychology. Dr. Clark has developed an innovative theory and practice of Relational Competence based on leading-edge psychological principles. Her programs are designed to permeate both the organizational systems and the personal systems of the people with whom she works. She has over 20 years of extensive experience as a practitioner, consultant, and workshop leader in both organizational and clinical psychology.

H. Peter Dachler currently holds the chair for Organizational Psychology at the University of St. Gallen, Switzerland. He received his graduate training in industrial/organizational psychology at the University of Illinois in Champaign-Urbana, Illinois, and was subsequently professor for organizational psychology in the Department of Psychology at the University of Maryland, College Park. Mr. Dachler was a fellow at the International Institute of Management of the Science Center in Berlin for 2 years, and serves on the editorial boards of various international and American scientific journals. Currently, his primary areas of research include the theoretical and practical implications of a constructionist epistemological position for leadership, management, and organizational change, as well as the consequences of the assessment-center method for alternative selection and employee development processes. He is a fellow of the American Psychological Association and the American Psychological Society, as well as a member of the Academy of Management and various European professional associations. He is past president of the Swiss Society of Work and Organizational Psychology and president of the organizational psychology division of the International Association of Applied Psychology.

Marcus Dickson received his Ph.D. in Industrial/Organizational Psychology from the University of Maryland in 1997. He is currently a member of the graduate faculty in Psychology at Wayne State University in Detroit. He has been a Co-Principal Investigator of GLOBE since 1997, and has been involved with the project since 1992. In addition to the GLOBE project, Dr. Dickson is currently involved in research in areas including organizational decision-making effectiveness when communicating via various computer-mediated technologies, organizational differences in managers' schemas of motivation, and organizational climate-based resistence to implementation of new technologies.

Peter W. Dorfman, Ph.D., is a Professor and the Department Head of the Department of Management, New Mexico State University. Before joining the faculty at New Mexico State University, he taught at Rice University and Montana State University. Dr. Dorfman's research interest spans the human resources management, organizational behavior fields, and cross-cultural leadership and management practices. His articles on leadership and performance appraisals have appeared in many academic journals. He is currently investigating the impact of cultural influences on managerial behavior and leadership styles. In addition, he is an expert witness and consultant in employee discrimination and sexual harassment cases.

John R. Fulkerson received his Ph.D. from Baylor University. He is currently the Vice President for Education at the Young President's Organization (YPO). YPO, founded in 1950, is a worldwide, not-for-profit executive education organization of over 8,500 presidents and chief executive officers. YPO is dedicated to the development of better presidents through education and idea exchange. For the majority of his career, John was with PepsiCo and worked with all divisions (Pepsi-Cola, Frito-Lay, Pizza Hut, Taco Bell, and KFC) with the majority of his efforts focused on the development of initiatives for the international businesses. His last position with PepsiCo was as Vice President for Leadership Development. He also served as Vice President for Organization Capability & Training at Kmart during an active turnaround period with that company. In his role at Kmart, he was responsible for the design and development of initiatives driving succession planning, executive and leadership development, performance management, training and training technology, surveys, assessment, customer service, and organization development for headquarters, distribution centers, and stores. He has also been a consultant, Vice President for Human Resources, and started his career with the U.S government as a psychologist responsible for the assessment and development of high-ability intelligence officers. One of his key interests is understanding and developing executive capability across cultures.

George B. Graen received his Ph.D. from the University of Minnesota. He is the recipient of the Gene Brauns Endowed Chair Professor of International Management at the University of Southwestern Louisiana. In addition to his well-known work in leadership, role making, and Japanese studies, he and his cross-cultural research and consulting team have been engaged in projects to understand joint venture businesses in China, Hong Kong, and Taiwan and to help them build effective local "third cultures" to enhance their competitiveness.

Vipin Gupta [No copy supplied]

Tove Helland Hammer is a Professor of Organizational Behavior in the New York State School of Industrial and Labor Relations at Cornell University. She received her Ph.D. degree (1973) in industrial and organizational psychology from the University of Maryland. Her research has focused on evaluations of employee participation programs and forms of employee stock ownership, leadership effectiveness in business organizations and in trade unions, and the effects of management values on employee relations and organizational change. This research has been published in a variety of journals, including the *Journal of Applied Psychology, Organizational Behavior and Human Decision Processes, Industrial and Labor Relations Review, Academy of Management Journal,* and *Human Relations.* She is currently editor of *Industrial and Labor Relations Review.*

Paul J. Hanges is an Associate Professor of Psychology at the University of Maryland. He received his Ph.D. in industrial and organizational psychology from the University of Akron in 1986. Dr. Hange's research interests center on topics in personnel selection and individual assessment, cognition, and research methodology. In addition to his work on the GLOBE project, he is also exploring the utility of dynamic measurement and modeling for studying rater perceptual biases in assessment settings. His work has appeared in various journals such as *Journal of Applied Psychology, Psychological Bulletin,* and *Applied Psychological Measurement.* Dr. Hanges is an associate editor of the *Journal Leadership Qaurterly.*

Joy Fisher Hazucha obtained her Ph.D. in industrial and organizational psychology from the University of Minnesota, with supporting programs in counseling and measurement. She received her B.A. from Wheaton College, in Wheaton, Illinois. Dr. Hazucha has been with Personnel Decisions International Corporation (PDI) since 1983 and is currently Managing Director of PDI Europe. She is responsible for overseeing and helping grow PDI's offices in Europe, and working with both European and U.S. multinationals to extend PDI's global reach. She delivers a wide range of PDI services, including assessment, feedback, team-building, program design, workshops, and coaching to individuals and groups. She presents regularly at professional conferences, and has published several articles and a chapter in the *Handbook of Industrial and Organizational Psychology.*

Sarah A. Hezlett has served as a Consultant for Questar Data Systems and Personnel Decisions International, helping organizations implement organizational surveys and 360-degree feedback systems. She has designed instruments, consulted on survey administrations, facilitated data interpretation and developed and delivered training on feedback and action planning, and has conducted and presented numerous studies at professional conferences. Her research has focused on 360-degree feedback, management development, expatriate adjustment, and test validation, and her publications have appeared in *Personnel Psychology* and *Human Resource Management*. She has an A.B. in politics from Princeton University and is pursuing a Ph.D. in industrial-organizational psychology from the University of Minnesota.

Mary Dee Hicks, is a Senior Vice President at Personnel Decisions International and a member of the Executive Services team. She is an expert in people development, and has consulted with a range of major organizations on how to grow talent through organizational culture changes, coaching strategies, and individual development interventions. Together with her colleague David B. Peterson, she has co-authored two best-selling books on the topic of development, *Development FIRST: Strategies for Self-Development* (1995) and *Leader as Coach: Strategies for Coaching and Developing Others* (1996). She has published numerous articles on development and coaching and is a frequent presenter at business and professional forums on these topics. Dr. Hicks focuses her consulting work on building executive talent and helping senior leaders promote development in their teams. She is an executive coach and has extensive experience conducting developmental assessments. In the past, she managed PDI's multifaceted assessment services business and is a veteran at conducting selection assessments for strategic hires. Dr. Hicks earned her Ph.D. in Counseling Psychology at the University of Minnesota in 1984. Prior to joining PDI she provided career and personal counseling in business, hospital, and university settings and served as an instructor in the Department of Psychology at the University of Minnesota.

Robert J. House, Ph.D., holds the Joseph Frank Bernstein endowed Professorship of Organizational Studies at the Wharton School of the University of Pennsylvania. Dr. House received his Ph.D. in management from Ohio State University in 1960. Prior to joining Wharton, he held positions at the Ohio State University, McKinsey and Company, Inc., the Bernard M. Baruch College of the University of New York, and the University of Toronto. In addition, he has been a Visiting Professor or visiting Scholar at 11 universities in the United States, Europe, and Asia, and has lectured at universities in 28 nations. He has served as a consultant to many large U.S. firms. Dr. House's current research concerns the distribution and exercise of power in complex organizations, the nature and effects of outstanding leadership, the role of personality variables in complex organizations, and cross-cultural investigations of organizational and leadership practices. He is currently the Principal Investigator of The Global Leadership and Organizational Behavior Effectiveness Research Program (GLOBE) which involves the management of research teams in 60 nations and is funded by the U.S. Department of Education and the U.S. National Science Foundation. He is also Principle Investigator of The Cross Cultural CEO Research Program (CC CEO) in which the effects of CEO leadership on organizational performance is being investigated cross culturally. Dr. House is the author of six books and over 100 articles in management and social science journals. He has been on the editorial review boards of several management journals and is a co-founder of the Organizational Behavior Division of the Academy of Management, *Leadership Quarterly,* and MESO, an organization devoted to the integration of micro- and macro-organizational behavior theory and research.

C. Harry Hui received his doctorate training at the University of Illinois. Since returning to Hong Kong, where he was born and raised, he has been teaching and doing research in industrial and organizational psychology at the University of Hong Kong. He has also served as consultant to numerous companies in the communication, petrochemical, pharmaceutical, hospitality, transportation, and IT sectors. He specializes in the assessment of employee aptitude, attitude, and personality. Professor Hui developed items from the INDCOL Scale, which are currently used in many measures of individualism-collectivism.

Chun Hui received his Ph.D. from Indiana University. Professor Hui is currently in the Department of Management of Organizations, Hong Kong University of Science and Technology, Clear Water Bay, Kowloon. Professor Hui's research interests are in cross-cultural leadership and teamwork, organizational citizenship, and role analysis.

Mansour Javidson is a professor of strategic management at the Faculty of Management, University of Calgary in Canada. He teaches and does research in the areas of executive leadership and corporate strategy. He is currently on a part-time leave from the University and working with the CEO of a company that recently embarked on the largest merger in Canadian history.

Kevin B. Lowe is an assistant professor in the Bryan School of Business and Economics at the University of North Carolina at Greensboro. His research has appeared in a number of scholarly outlets, including the *Academy of Management Journal, The Leadership Quarterly, The Handbook of Technology Management, The Journal of Leadership Studies, Advances in International Comparative Management,* and *Public Personnel Management.* His current research focuses include the evolving role of leaders in postindustrial organizations and best practices for international human resource management. He is a member of the Academy of

Management, the Southern Management Association, and the Society for Industrial/Organizational Psychology.

Dr. Michael Matze has been in clinical and consultation practice for over 20 years in Menlo Park, California. He is co-founder of Relational Leadership Systems Consulting Group. This consulting practice has provided a forum for the development of the theory of the Relational Self and the model of Relational Competence. He is a member of the Bay Area OD Network and an Associate of the Institute for Integrative Psychotherapy, New York.

Karen L. Otazo holds a doctorate in Human Resources Development from the University of Northern Colorado and master's and bachelor's degrees in linguistics from the City University of New York. She is an internationally known consultant specializing in management assessment and coaching for individuals and groups. Her results-oriented approach to executive development, honed by more than 20 years of experience working with multinationals, has enabled her to build a blue-chip client list that includes AlliedSignal, Amgen, ARCO, Avery Dennison, Chase Bank, Digital, FMC, General Electric, GlobalOne, IBM, Jardine Matheson, Motorola, and Sprint International. She speaks Spanish, French, and Bahasa Indonesia and has lived and worked in countries where these languages are spoken. The author of numerous articles and the handbook *Coaching Winners at Work,* she is active in such international organizations as the Boston University Executive Development Roundtable and the Global Business Network.

David B. Peterson, is Senior Vice President at Personnel Decisions International (PDI). He joined PDI in 1985 and became practice leader for PDI's worldwide Coaching Services in 1990. Peterson specializes in executive coaching and consulting to help business leaders change themselves, their teams, and their organizations. He has worked with hundreds of individuals and teams in organizations such as Hewlett-Packard, America On Line, Capital One Financial Services, The Limited, Bristol Myers Squibb, Intel, Ford, ConAgra, Cargill, General Mills, Honeywell, United Healthcare, Eastman Kodak, PepsiCo, Quantum, Microsoft, MCI, and 3M. With his colleague Mary Dee Hicks, he has authored two best-selling books which provide practical advice to help people develop themselves *and* coach others: *Development FIRST: Strategies for Self-Development* (1995) and *Leader As Coach: Strategies for Coaching* and *Developing Others* (1996). He has conducted extensive research on how individuals learn, develop new skills, and change their behavior. His research demonstrates that coaching can produce significant and lasting changes—as rated by the individuals themselves *and* their bosses—at a magnitude three times greater than conventional training programs. An expert on coaching, executive development, and how organizations can create strategic advantage through learning and development, Peterson has been quoted in publications ranging from *Wall Street Journal* to *Working Woman* and *USA*

Today. He received his Ph.D. from the University of Minnesota, specializing in industrial/organizational and counseling psychology. His B.A. in linguistics and anthropology is from Bethel College in St. Paul, MN.

Richard J. Ritchie has more than 30 years' experience as an industrial/organizational psychology practitioner. His first exposure to the practice of leadership in an organization was as a graduate student intern at Exxon Company, USA in Houston, Texas. He worked at AT&T conducting leadership research, consulting both within the United States and internationally on leadership issues, and directing AT&T's leadership assessment programs. Currently, he is a Senior Consultant with Applied Research Corporation doing leadership assessment and executive coaching. Ritchie has a Ph.D. in Industrial Psychology from the University of Houston, is a Fellow of the Society for Industrial and Organizational Psychology and the American Psychological Association, and is a licensed psychologist.

Amy Ronnqvist is currently seeking a doctorate degree in sociology at the University of Minnesota. Her interests include sociology of education, cultural studies, and race relations.

S. Antonio Ruiz-Quintanilla is currently affiliated with the New York School of Industrial and Labor Relations, Cornell University, and Department of Personnel Management, Work and Organizational Psychology, University Gent, Belgium. Mr. Ruiz-Quintanilla conducts research in the areas of motivation, work values, leadership, and cross-cultural research. He has co-edited books with Wiley and Academic Press, and has published articles in *Industrial and Labor Relations Review, Human Resource Management Journal, Journal of Organizational Behavior, The Career Development Quarterly, Journal of Occupational Psychology,* and *Business Strategy and the Environment.*

Leland Russell is co-founder of *Prometheus PartnersTM* and President of *GEO Group, Inc.* He has served as a leadership and communications consultant to numerous organizations in business, health care, education, and government. His extensive credentials include: author and narrator of many widely acclaimed programs on leadership and change (his model for mastering change, *The GEO Paradigm,* has been licensed for use in leadership development programs by over 1,000 organizations in the United States and Latin America); consultant for cultural change campaigns and leadership development strategies to major organizations in both the for-profit and non-profit sectors; consultant to innovation and new product teams, including Proctor and Gamble, ETS, and Texas Instruments; executive producer of large-scale leadership conferences for the CEOs of Fortune 50 organizations (he designed and facilitated the widely acclaimed national leadership conference, *A Day In The FutureTM*, sponsored by *Fortune* magazine, GE, Motorola, and Northern Telecom); author and executive producer of cutting edge leadership workshops and learning media in a variety of platforms; designer of collaborative architectures for organizational learning and knowledge transfer (he designed *TI Tomorrow* for Texas Instruments); and collaborator on leadership and change-related research projects with educational institutions and leading professional associations.

Terri A. Scandura is a professor of management at the University of Miami, Coral Gables, Florida. She received her Ph.D. in organizational behavior from the Department of Management at the University of Cincinnati in 1988. Her fields of interest include leadership, mentorship, and management development. She has authored numerous articles and book chapters, published in the *Academy of Management Journal*, the *Journal of Applied Psychology, Industrial Relations*, the *Journal of Management*, the *Journal of Organizational Behavior, The Leadership Quarterly, The Journal of Vocational Behavior, Accounting, Organizations*, and *Society*, and others. Her research has been summarized in numerous newspapers and magazines, including the *New York Daily News*, the *Miami Herald*, the *Atlanta Constitution*, and *Forbes* magazine. She has appeared on nationally syndicated television and radio programs and is a member of the American Psychological Association (APA), the Society of Industrial and Organizational Psychology, and the Academy of Management.

George Chen Kiong Tan is an industrial/organizational psychologist who received his education at La Trobe University, Australia, and conducted postgraduate research at the University of Hong Kong. Interested in cross-cultural study and indigenous research pertaining to management issues, George has advised various corporations and published several articles in these areas.

Mary Ann Von Glinow is a professor of management and international business at Florida International University. She was previously on University of Southern California's business school faculty. She has an M.B.A., an M.P.A., and a Ph.D. in management science from Ohio State University. She was the 1994-1995 president of the Academy of Management and is a member of 11 editorial review boards. Dr. Von Glinow is consultant to a number of domestic and multinational enterprises, General Electric Company, Southern California Edison, Kaiser Permanente, First Bank of Chicago, N.Y. Life, State of Florida, and Aetna. She also serves as a Mayoral appointee to the Shanghai Institute of Human Resources in China. Dr. Von Glinow has authored numerous journal articles and six books: *The New Professionals, Managing Today's High Technology Employees* (Ballinger, 1998); *Managing Complexity in High Technology Organizations* (Oxford University Press, 1990); *United States-China Technology Transfer* (Prentice-Hall, 1992); *Technology Transfer in International Business* (Oxford University Press, 1991); *A Resource Guide for Internationalizing the Business School Curriculum* (AACSB Publication, 1991), and *International Technology Transfer and Management*

(Tainrkua University Press, 1993). She also heads an international consortium of researchers delving into "best international HRM practices."

Zhong-Ming Wang received an M.A. in applied psychology from the Gothenburg University, Sweden (1985) and a Ph.D. (1987) in industrial/organizational psychology from Hangzhou University, a joint doctoral program with Gothenburg University, Sweden. Dr. Wang is currently professor of human resource management and industrial-organizational psychology, and Dean at the School of Management, Zhejiang University, Xixi Campus (formerly Hangzhou University), in China. He is leading the Chinese national key Ph.D. program of industrial and organizational psychology, President of the Industrial Psychology Division of the Chinese Psychological Society, Director of the Center for International Joint Venture Studies and the Center for Enterprise Management, and visiting professor of the China-Europe International Business School in Shanghai. He is also Vice President for both the Chinese National Committee of Personnel Assessment and the Chinese Ergonomics Society. Professor Wang has coordinated several international projects, and his primary areas of research include personnel selection, assessment center, team process, organizational decision making, leadership, organization development, cross-cultural organizational behavior, and human resources management. In addition to publishing several books and more than 150 articles, he serves as the associate editor for the *Journal of Management Development* (UK) and on the editorial boards of several international journals.